MW00989920

THE THIN GRAY LINE

by T. A. Powell

Copyright 2009

Disclaimer

This book was inspired by actual historic events contained in public records, media archives, Covington family archives, retrieved from Covington family interviews, and/or legal documents surrounding the death of Federal Treasury Agent Charles G. Covington. Certain dialogue, events, and characters were created or combined for the purpose of dramatization and to veil the identity of those persons still living who requested to remain anonymous until the case is officially solved and/or closed. Similarly, the chronology of some events has been condensed and/or edited for the purpose of clarity.

Many of the names and places in this book, even those that have appeared within the public domain, courtroom documents, and/or print media have been altered to protect the innocent related to and/or once associated with persons of interest. The book is written from the author's personal perspective and based on her individual experience(s) while researching Mr. Covington's case, and is in no way meant to reflect and/or represent the collective experience and/or beliefs of the Covington family.

This text is written in chronological order. The paranormal events that happened to the author and her family in her home while researching and writing this book were real. Information, anecdotal and/or otherwise received from incorporeal individuals who have provided supportive information to help re-open this case have not been altered and are posted in the manuscript in italics to help distinguish them from literal conversations. Some names and locations proffered have been slightly altered to protect the integrity of any potential future evidence. Authorities have been informed as to actual names and locations. This story reflects the information received from many who wished to bring light to the inconsistencies within the original investigation of this case, the lack of integrity in forensic collection of evidence and documentation, and the blatant disregard for the professional process of discovery.

It is this collective passion for justice that allows me to ask any and/or all law enforcement to embrace all avenues of information retrieval available in regards to this case; this includes the talents of the psychic/medium detectives whose gifts have been highlighted within this story.

If you have any further information that may help in the ultimate resolution of this case, please contact the local authorities and any or all of appropriate state or federal agencies mentioned within this text before tampering or attempting to retrieve any evidence on your own.

T. A. Powell

Dedication

Jules and I had known each other casually for years. Even though we shared a few mutual interests, she had never once mentioned anything about her father's profession or his untimely demise. In fact, it wasn't until her oldest son began working at the theatre that I ever learned anything at all about her tragic past.

One night after a production, we all met downtown for pizza. During dinner we talked about our kids, our jobs, and the UGA Bulldogs; then she politely asked about the progress of my first book. Having no prior knowledge of the historic calamity at Moore's Ford Bridge, I briefly explained to Jules about the unsolved murders of four African Americans who were murdered in broad daylight during the 1946 Georgia gubernatorial race. Intrigued, she turned the conversation to why I would have been prompted to write about such a thing. Sensing an opportunity, I commented about the histrionic injustice of Southern governing and my fascination with unsolved murders. I pontificated that once folks found out about the theme of the first book, they naturally assumed it would be the same for the next. Suddenly complete strangers were beginning to contact me about investigating their murdered relatives or missing friends, and I was beginning to sense a pattern that made me uncomfortable. After all, who was I to suddenly become the social worker for the dead? She agreed it was a rather awkward epiphany, but confessed it was just the opening she had been waiting for and asked that we continue the conversation back at her house.

 While our husbands chattered about weather and sports in the kitchen, she led me to her attic. Once there, she opened a small side door and pulled out several plastic storage bins filled with old paper clippings, maps, letters, photographs, and yellowed stacks of manila folders. She told me that the summer before she had dragged it all out to the back yard with every intention of setting the lot on fire, but stopped. Confused, I asked her why and she told me until just then she hadn't known why herself.

She handed me another glass of wine to stall my retreat, popped the lid off the first bin, and whispered into the musty air, "Let me tell you a story about my daddy…." Now a little more than four years later I am finally able to respond. "No, Jules. Let me tell you a story about your daddy."

This book is dedicated to all those who have learned firsthand that divine love connects us even after death and asks that you be able to forgive someone everything…including murder.

For Charley

"A cold case murder is like a painting by Monet. Only when viewed from afar does the riotous chaos of fragmented information seem to make any sense."

T.A. Powell

CHAPTER ONE

At the age of six Jules lost her beloved father, Federal Treasury Agent Charles Gordon Covington. In that same year at the age of eight, I lost my beloved pet rat Squeaky. I know the comparison doesn't seem quite fair. Still, none of us ever gets to choose how we first experience death. Odd as it may seem, if Charley Covington hadn't lost his life in the middle of the Clyattville-Nankin Road that rainy night in 1966, he could never have come back to save mine forty-four years later. I know this to be true because in the summer of 2009, I began to write his story, and several chapters in, I stopped.

As a professional writer I have learned that if a story refuses to write itself, there are but two reasons why. Either a story is not yet ready to be told, or a story is not yet ready to be heard. In the case of Charles Gordon Covington, both reasons appeared to ring true. So I put down my pen and waited for further instructions from the cosmos as to what to do next.

Seven months later, the cosmos finally answered...

****

While working on Charley's case, I was contacted by the director of the Cold Case Investigative Research Institute (C.C.I.R.I.) in Atlanta and asked to speak to Criminal Justice students about my research methods and findings on another unsolved murder case:

the 1946 Moore's Ford Bridge Massacre. Because several of their date requests conflicted with my production schedule, I switched programs with another expert in the series. The first guest speaker was a Forensic Psychologist, Dr. Cynthia Hatfield, who dealt with criminal profiling. The second, who took over my original spot, was a psychic/medium detective, who communicated with the deceased victims. The third was an investigative author: yours truly.

Wishing to help promote my first book, *The Danburg Diary,* I decided to take an excerpt, teasing the crowd with unpublicized bits of peripheral information about the Moore's Ford Bridge Massacre not contained in the original five hundred-page FBI report. The speech went well and at the end, I asked if they might be interested in hearing me read from transcripts between me and another individual who refused to identify himself while cyber-stalking me for months during my investigation. Much to my delight they relished the idea of a modern day *"Deep Throat"* and agreed.

Since I had absorbed this individual into the actual storyline and had no legal identification until well into the editing process, I explained to the group I had arbitrarily chosen a letter from the alphabet to identify his composite character. When I got to the end of the reading, I simply signed off with the assigned signature "J" and closed the file. No sooner had I done so than the room erupted into one huge garrulous ball of chaos. Students and teachers alike cupped their hands, glaring across the room, whispering wildly among themselves. Caught off guard by the cacophony, I checked my notes, but found nothing so startling as to incite such a response and decided its origin must be from another source. I smiled graciously at the crowd, hoping to calm the mood before continuing, when suddenly a girl twelve rows back pointed in my direction and fear set in. Convinced I had somehow suffered some sort of humiliating wardrobe malfunction, I pulled the file to my chest and quickly announced a ten-minute bathroom break to be followed by a brief session of Q and A.

By the time I had counted all my buttons, checked my zippers, and felt confident the error had not been in my attire, I turned to find no less than twenty students had rushed the podium, all demanding to know if I was the mysterious "J" of the novel. I reiterated that my choice of initial was purely random and that I was not the real "J." They continued to press for more information about the character's true identity and then finally one student offered an explanation. In the last session, the expert speaker assigned had been a psychic/medium detective who had made a prediction in her final notes: *"Be aware. In 14 to 18 days, an energy identified only as the initial J in quotation marks will give you significant information pertaining to this case. Be aware--this information is significant."* And it was; thus my introduction to the Psychic/Medium Detective Spencer Reynolds.

****

On the night of October 9, 1966 after a weekend of being placed on standby, Federal Treasury Agent Charley Covington received a call from ATTD higher-ups in Atlanta, Georgia releasing him from his stay in Valdosta, Georgia. According to accounts contained in the widow's journal, several phone calls came in that day, most of them from people she didn't know. One of them was from a known felon and snitch who reminded Charley about the illegal and clandestine activities out on the Clyattville-Nankin Road every Sunday night and another from a man about a car. Having spent the better part of the weekend arguing with his wife over a rumored affair, the lure of an evening's ride away from home may have been just what the doctor ordered to clear his head. Before he left, he put his six-year-old daughter to bed, hollered a weak goodbye to his son, and agreed to a cup of conciliatory coffee with his nearly estranged wife. When Kaye confessed the pot was empty and that he would have to wait while she made a fresh one, he noted the time and promised he would be back shortly after it was finished. Without another word he pulled his fedora from the top of the fridge and left.

Two and a half hours later he was found lying dead with two bullets to the head just before the Withlacoochee River on the

Clyattville-Nankin Road outside of Valdosta. By the time his body was cold, the rumors were hot. For eighteen days federal and local agency officials danced around the purported scandal of the Federal Treasury Agent like a herd of long-tailed cats at a Southern lawn party. Eventually they closed the case, declaring his death a suicide and its taint a blight upon their shared profession. Personal empathies aside, rumors of the alleged affair still didn't seem enough of a reason for Covington to end up straddling the Clyattville-Nankin Road in a pool of blood. At least that's how I felt that spring when Jules first came to me with her father's epitaph, her mother's journal, and a series of plastic bins filled with minutiae left behind by her deceased parents.

After eleven months of rumination, I felt I knew more about the last hours of Covington's life than anyone — anyone except Covington, of course. That's why I needed Spencer. Stalled in my attempts, the slender brunette with deep brown eyes and a quick smile was my only hope to plug the holes in this case. I thought if she could make contact with the victim, there was a chance I could show Jules something more than regret. Now less than 24 hours away from the paranormal Promised Land, the narrator inside my head continued to pepper with its list of considerations. Had I written down all the questions I wanted to ask? Had I inventoried all the right papers for parley? What if the victim wouldn't come through? Anxiously I paced the floor, counting down the hours while contemplating the strength of my dossier and the validity of my intuition.

My blog, *Anatomy of a Murder,* had been up and running since before Christmas, and while advertising I was going to be working with a psychic/medium may not have been prudent, the victim had stopped communicating internally and left me little choice. I had no doubts about Spencer's abilities. I did, however, have a great many about the victim's willingness to participate, and that was beginning to rankle me. In the last year the Covington family archives had seemed to offer up everything wanted and yet nothing needed to move the case forward.

Fascinated by the recent introduction to the psychic/medium's process and self-conscious about my virginal foray into her world, I became a nervous wreck. Exceptionally gifted, she saw and heard things from the dead that defied reason. While personally riveted by her results, I was uncertain as to what to expect. Still, her instructions had been simple: "Come with an open mind and anything that might be helpful to connect with the deceased."

Of course the obvious would have been to bring the victim's daughter Jules, but what I really needed from Covington the first go around was information, not sentimental detour. Seeing as I was already two days the other side of desperate for him to speak, I hid the plastic bag of his bloodied wallet inside my purse and prayed for a miracle.

CHAPTER TWO

As fate would have it, the cold front that had crossed into the state hours before brought an endless line of storms both literally and figuratively to my personal horizons. Just after midnight, the first stab of lightning bit into the night sky. Anxious, I crawled in between the sheets and tried to calm my nerves, but my mind refused to shut down. With the second round of thunder, they shot open and a second wave of panic set in. Fingerlings of refracted rain snaked their way across the window pane and, just as in my childhood, fears began to manifest in the darkened corners of my bedroom walls.

What if it wasn't Covington who had the problem? Unconsciously I adjusted my wedding rings. Paralyzed by recent grief over the death of my parents and my connubial indecision, my life seemed to have been put on hold. Since Jules's interruption with tales of her father's surreptitious slaying, I had conveniently used him as my excuse to obliterate participation in my own life. My writing was simply the last place the cancer of abjuration reared its ugly head.

As the storm continued to batter the outside of the house, doubt continued to reign supreme inside. What if nothing happened when we met? Or, God forbid, what if it was my life that bled through my professional veneer and not Covington's? Thunder, like consequence, boomed overhead. Just how much of my existence would be open for review in this process and how much was I willing to share? I paused in my tracks and contemplated the repercussions, amazed I had never bothered to extrapolate the equation any further. What if the spirits had no problem keeping Covington's secrets from the psychic, but didn't mind broadcasting the shit out of mine? Suddenly that was all I could think about, and the marital bands around my finger began to tighten like a tourniquet, making my hand feel as numb as my heart. Unable to sleep, I crossed the floor and plucked the lid off the first of the archival bins and reached in.

What else could I bring that would, as his devoted bride Kaye had put it, "make him shit a squealing worm"? Pictures of his kids...pictures of them on their wedding day? Determined to spike a reaction, I grabbed a handful of memorabilia and then balked when I saw the pixie face of Jules. Glow from the streetlight flooded through the window, and contrails from the condensation superimposed upon her tiny cheeks made her look as though she was crying. The effect was surreal, and I nearly crumbled knowing the photo had been taken just weeks before she lost her daddy.

What if Covington really had been having an affair with the Baldwin woman? What if he really had told the tiny tot with his blue-gray eyes he was moving out that night and that her memory of searching the *Sears Roebuck Catalog* for Christmas consolation prizes had been real and not symbiotic confirmation bias?

Sympathetic, I looked at the little waif again and could not conceive of the pain that would continue to haunt her if my session garnered such a confirmation. In the end I decided that that much honesty was more than any child, whether six years old or forty-eight deserved to hear at one time. I returned the remaining prints to the container. Satisfied I could do nothing more to prepare, I crawled back in between the covers and stared at the ceiling for another hour before slumber finally descended and I dreamt.

As had been a recurring theme since my father died, I was immediately transported back to the day of his funeral — only this time I was alone. Standing in front of a stone wall which had been purchased to hold both my parents' remains on industrial-sized cookie sheets, I suddenly realized I officially qualified as an orphan. Just as before, an old man in dingy coveralls subsequently appeared and when asked, carefully removed the four stone florets that bound the granite facing to my parents' mausoleum. Waiting to pay my respects, I stiffened my upper lip and dutifully fingered the beads of my rosary while he manipulated the workings of the vault. He asked if I was ready for a final viewing and I nodded my head. Slowly the tray rolled its way out, but in the light of day we discovered the vault was empty. Since the family name plate had been removed to add the engraving of my father's, I assumed we'd simply made a collective mistake. Politely I gestured we should inspect the adjoining vaults for my parents, but they too were empty. Frustrated, I began to interrogate him.

"So where are they?"

He checked his list and shook his head.

"Are you kidding?"

He remained silent.

"Are you telling me you lost them?"

He continued to remain silent and flipped through a few more pages, but nothing seemed to register.

"This is insane. How could you have lost two people?"

While I stomped my foot like a child and muttered profanities unfit for a lady of my age, the old man shrugged his shoulders, uncertain how to console me. Not wanting to be mean, I explained that it was bad enough that my parents had been taken from me in life, but now due to some stupid computer glitch, the cemetery had managed to keep them from me in death as well. The man remained calm as he listened to my complaints and then offered to repeat the process on four more walls before confessing my parents' crypts were simply nowhere to be found.

"Well, can you at least call someone and ask where they are? It's not like you lost a pair of socks, for Christ's sake — they're my parents!"

The man apologized and advised there was no one else working that day, but he would be happy to check out one more place for me. Realizing that I would obviously have to speak to someone else with more authority, I bypassed civility and demanded the name of the person in charge and a number where the person could be reached. He apologized again for the confusion and motioned that I should follow him towards a small chapel just across the manicured lawn which housed much smaller vaults. Immediately I became concerned that the cemetery had somehow gotten their wires crossed and cremated my parents by mistake. As we traversed the open green, his boots and my heels synchronously punched holes into the dampened sod and the awkward thought that we were aerating someone's remains sent chills down my spine.

The man asked me to confirm the family name for him again and then led me to the first vault. Fully expecting to be shown a pair of matching bronze urns brandishing my parents' names, I began to list a litany of grievances I would file against the cemetery that very afternoon with my attorney — but no such action became warranted.

Instead of urns, the miniature vault revealed a small cardboard shoe box marked SEARS, size 4-1/2. Convinced there had been another mistake made, I rechecked the list myself. Having confirmed it was the right slot, he pulled out the short galvanized tray so I could better review the weathered contents and left me to decide what to do next. The soiled box listed to one side and was wrapped up with a faded pink ribbon. Why on earth anybody would have gone to all the effort to save a child's shoe box was beyond me. Confused, I held my tongue and checked the list again. There was no mistake. Carefully I pulled the box closer. It looked eerily familiar.

Once the thick ribbon was removed, one could see that the lid was festooned with what appeared to be a rotted bouquet of dandelions and the moniker of my beloved childhood pet scribbled in yellow crayon. The fifty-two-year-old orphan inside me quickly reached out to touch the faded wax mural, even as the eight-year-old child inside me froze with grief.

The old man lifted the lid and, paralyzed by emotion, I held my breath. When I was finally able to breathe, I found the box was filled with nothing more than a few additional decayed dandelions and dried dirt. Angered that I had been further compromised over what appeared to be just another cruel joke, I jammed the rosary into my pocket and with tears in my eyes began to craft a very colorful farewell.

"I suppose you accidentally lost him too? Because he didn't matter… right? After all, he was just a stupid rat," I added.

Expecting a confrontation, I was flummoxed when instead the old man patted me on my shoulder and then walked away.

"You can't just leave this open like this. Where are you going?" I yelled.

He pointed to the clouds and said, "It's starting to rain."

"What the hell does that have to do with anything?" I asked.

"I don't work in the rain," he answered, crossed through the remaining memorials, and disappeared inside an old truck.

Left alone in the drizzle, I feared whatever remained of my childhood friend would get wet. "You can't just leave him here like this," I yelled again, but to no avail. The old man had already stuffed himself into the front seat of his truck like a cannoli. With no other choice but to seal the makeshift grave myself, I snatched the ribbon from the tray and grumbled under my breath "This is insane."

Just as I was about to tie the bow, the caretaker's truck trudged up another hill and backfired. Caught off guard by the unexpected boom, I dropped the box to the ground. Without the ribbon's support and damaged by the rain, one of the walls collapsed. Horrified, I tried to shove the contents back into the cardboard casing, but it was too late. Accompanied by a few bits of sinew and a handful of straggling hairs, I barely recognized the collective imprint of the brittle mass at first. Reduced to skeletal remains, it seemed little more than sentiment clung to my childhood pet's eroded frame. Overcome by residual grief, I tearfully whispered his name in apology.

Suddenly the pitted skull turned upward and poked its way through the crusted soil. Terrified but curious, I watched as minute translucent digits began to claw away the rich Midwestern loam from his vacant sockets. Too startled to move, I listened to each fragile little vertebra as it crackled and popped into place. Astounded by what I was seeing, I whispered his name again and the child in me prayed he remembered who I was. Once atop his place of rest, disjointed cheek bones clattered as they took in huge gulps of air which whistled down through his fleshless ribs. I bent down and gathered up the damaged box. His fragmented tail vibrated beneath the darkened soil and I smiled in response. Morbid as it sounds, I felt he recognized me. He cocked his head, and just as his tiny jaws clicked open to return the favor in kind, a huge clap of thunder shook the ground beneath me and I dropped the box again. I woke sobbing, draped in a cold sweat.

In silence, I lay awake another hour trying to divine the significance of his visitation. Four decades was a long reach for any reminiscence, and though I confess to only a few photographic memories of the day my sister saved the little rodent from certain death in her high school's biology lab, I promise you I have never forgotten even the smallest details about his death.

One minute he was there, his breathing erratic and labored. And the next? My furry little friend was gone and no amount of prayer held magic enough to bring him back. Being eight, I could not conceive that the intricacies contained within a split second could define the thin gray line between life and death. Bereaved, my siblings and I gave him a proper and dignified burial, collected our tears, and then dragged ourselves off to school. When my teacher asked why I was so sad, I told her in between sniffles about the passing of my darling pet. With craggy countenance, she smiled at my compassion and naiveté. Comforted for the moment, I put on a brave face and assured her that I would eventually be ok for two reasons. First, because I knew Squeaky would never forget me and secondly, because I knew he would be safe and happy with God in heaven.

No sooner had the words left my lips than her smile faded. Incensed by my youthful disregard for church doctrine, she rattled a rosary inside her arthritic fist and informed me that a rat, beloved or not, was one of the lowliest creatures created by God and that he would most assuredly *not* be going to heaven and that even at such a tender age, I as a Roman Catholic should know that!

"A rat..." she drooled from between her starched black and white cardboard headdress, "does not possess a soul! Therefore, your Mr. Squeaky as you so lovingly called him will not be enjoying the raptures of heaven. Nor will he be allowed to remember you anymore than would he be allowed to remember the taste of the good Midwestern dirt in which he now lies!" Appalled, my aspirations for eternal consolation for my furred friend collapsed and with that, an antiquated nun in bitter repose defined my first experience with death.

Until that moment, I had never thought much about God or His part in the process of death. But for certain I had never thought of God as someone who parsed His blessings and denied entrance to His heavenly kingdom based on some religious loophole only antediluvian nuns seemed to know about or on the amount of fur one retained. Nor had I ever considered the fact that once on the other side, all memory of this life became depleted. It made no sense to me that an omnipotent being would so vehemently encourage us to forget in death what it had so desperately tried to teach us to love in life. And so at a very young age, I began to view my religion and its heaven quite differently than the religion that baptized me. In fact it wasn't until the deaths of my parents that I felt any compulsion to revisit such philosophies and once more found little in church dogma to salve my wounds.

Now four decades later, God was sending another woman of the Catholic persuasion to unhinge my world, but this time I promised myself to be ready. Lightning struck another tree outside, just as the grandfather clock in the downstairs hall chimed the approaching dawn. Soon Covington would be confronted again. It gave me comfort knowing that while he may not "shit a squealing worm" as his dearly departed wife had implored, he would most certainly squirm like one at the end of the psychic's baited hook!

CHAPTER THREE

"Call to me and I will answer you and tell you great and unsearchable things you do not know."   *Jeremiah 3:33*

Two days and two blogs earlier, I had openly begged for Charley to talk to me. Now that fate had finally led me to someone who might be able to speak for him, I hoped what the psychic detective had to tell me would be enough to fill the metaphorical coffee cup from my working title.

If you saw Spencer in a grocery store, you would immediately assume she spent her days on treadmills and dining on humus and bean sprouts. Twenty years my junior, Spencer had the kind of soulful beauty that slowly reveals itself the longer you look at her. Her manner was as casual as her appearance. High cheek bones lengthened her face, but were counterbalanced by her wide, toffee-colored eyes and inviting smile. Slender and agile, she threw her long walnut hair about her shoulders like a shawl and spoke with a calm grace that belied her age.

Once small talk and instructions had ended, the session began in earnest. Without fanfare or warning, she told me a man had come to visit her two days prior. As she reached for a menu, a streak of faded highlights sprang from a frustrated cowlick at the peak of her forehead and fell across her face. I listened intently as she told me about her first introduction to the victim. Spencer told me she had been sitting in her car at a red light when she looked up and saw him walking towards her. She made a mental note at the time that she felt he might have something to do with me.

The recollection and description she gave me was as follows:

A man came towards me, looking as though he had been sitting in a mossy mess for quite some time. He appeared damp, wet,

19

moldy...He came to visit two days ago. He was murky looking, as through water. His clothing... how to put this? Best description: zombie-ish. He was not a zombie, but appeared zombie-ish. He wanted to find out about his skin. Obsessed and very confused about his skin. He was showing me wounds, lacerations...fixating on his arms. He was rancorous.

I did not know who this person was, but felt that he must have had something to do with the author, T. A., whom I was about to meet. He appeared and left without word.

She asked me what I had done two days earlier. My gut became pinched with bile. Two days earlier I had indeed done something, something I had never done before in my entire life: I stopped writing. Frustrated with the lack of progress on the manuscript, I explained my decision to close the file until I could find his voice. She asked if there was anything more, and there was. Two days earlier I had also begged the victim to make contact. Now two days later I was desperate to master the shorthand of the dead and keep up with the conversation.

The waiter came back and asked for our order. In the wake of his departure, I acknowledged my lack of recording devices and asked if I might run out to my car and trade my computer backpack in for my writing pad. She agreed. Upon my return, she told me the man with the moldy skin had escorted me back in. I pulled off my coat, sank into my chair, and opened my notebook. In silence, I positioned my pen above a blank page of paper and began recording the remainder of what you will now see here... all the while bearing in mind I was in the presence of an entity I came to believe was Charles Gordon Covington, A/K/A Charley, Jules's deceased father.

She began again...

He is showing me a letter G. It is a name. A unisex name; it can be either male or female. Do you understand this?

I nod. She continues.

The G is perpetrator, suspected. G. He shows me an injury. He shows me his heartbroken heart. Injuries endured from this person — both emotional/physical. The reaction seems more current than it should be. He has not had enough time to process.

He is showing me a red car... or a red truck.

He is showing me a tire... an impact. A domestic dispute that happened before this event. G has to do with abdominal impact. Perhaps emotional or physical. A shock, something unexpected. Something others would have known about. He keeps referring to G as someone who moves from hurting an animal without conscience to hurting a human without the same.

He continues to show me a tire. Showing me the impact. A shock, an unexpected blow. His body moving back and forth from the tire.

At this point she asks to see something personal of his. An article of his... I hand her the plastic baggie holding the bloodied wallet. She removes it carefully and runs it over in her hands and then opens it and asks, "Was it wet?" I nod confirmation.

She tells me he breaks in to ask about his daughter. She asks if I understand. I nod.

Does he have a daughter?

I nod confirmation. She says he keeps repeating;

My little girl. My little girl...

He is showing her a location. It is woodsy... there is water... swampy.

She asks if I understand. I nod in confirmation.

She asks me to tell her where this might be. I give her the information I have about the Clyattville-Nankin Road where his body was found. She asks if there is water. I nod confirmation. There is a river (Withlacoochee River) that acts as border between

Brooks County and Lowndes County, Georgia. His body was found approximately 1000 feet from the river.

She asks if the area is swampy. I nod confirmation.

He is showing me things. He is showing me injuries he has suffered from this person before, leading up to... He is showing me an object. I will try to describe using something I recognize. It is a tool. A tool you might find in your garage.

May I borrow your pen?

I hand her my pen and she begins to draw what appears to be a small saw.

Do you understand?

The tool is like this. The handle is like this and the other areas are jagged edges, like a saw blade. Do you recognize such a tool? I nod confirmation.

"May I tell you something?" I ask. She nods. "He built houses on the side. I am uncertain, but believe this to possibly be a coping saw. It is a fine saw used for delicate carpentry work: angles on chair rails, quarter rounds for baseboards." She thanks me and admits it is outside her scope.

He is very definite about this tool. He shows me lacerations from this tool. He concentrates on his arms again.

He is showing me about G. He is showing me, G equals that bitch. She advises me they do not judge on the other side, but he is showing me so that I might understand what he felt about G.

He is showing me another object.

May I borrow your pen again? He is showing me a mallet or a gavel type object. It has a handle like this and a T shaped top. I asked if the T portion at the top was elongated or cropped.

She responds *cropped, like a judge's gavel. But not to say it was a judge's gavel.*

He is showing me an older man with a lot of money. He shows me the letters, L and T. Again he shows me G and shows "that bitch."

There is an association, a connection between G and the older man LT.

He then shows me the tire and a secondary injury/second to an initial impact. Something impacted first at abdomen. I am uncertain if this is physical or emotional.

Next, he is showing me the area on the back of his head. There is energy from the side. This is the first definite physical impact.

He is showing me a second energy on the left side of his head — a second impact. First impact a blow, then the second to the left area of the head. Great energy there. Do you understand? Do you know what this is?

I nod confirmation and ask if I may tell her something. She nods.

I tell her there were bruises found to the back of his head and that the fatal shot was behind and just above his right ear and that it traveled through the cranial vault and lodged in the upper left temporal area of the skull. I do not mention the other wound to the chin as I am assuming that will be demonstrated next.

She acknowledges and he shows her great energy to the left side of his head.

I want to ask about the second wound, but hold my tongue as she is trying to redirect.

He is showing me G. He is showing me black widow, calculated, evil. Do you understand what this means? Do you know who this is?

At this point I ask her if I can tell her who this is. She nods confirmation and says yes.

I tell her G is Gerri (Gerrilyn) Baldwin, the younger woman whom they say he was leaving his wife for. The reason he committed suicide.

At this point she is visibly affected and pulls her sleeves up to show me her arms. She tells me they will often give a physical response when something affects them strongly. The physical response is strong every time we speak her name.

I tell her the story is that he and Kaye [Charley's wife] fought that day over his affair with Gerri, that they discussed divorce and that Gerri had supposedly threatened to dump him if he didn't tell his wife he was leaving her that weekend. Rumor had it that he saw her (G) later that day on her front porch talking with her ex-husband and supposedly became distraught over what he thought was her getting back together wither husband*, and so he drove out of town and committed suicide.

 (Note: *G does remarry her husband just three weeks after Charley is buried.)

She tells me he did not commit suicide. She tells me they present suicide if indeed that is what happened. She tells me she can assure me Charley did not commit suicide.

She tells me he has become nostalgic and shows her his heart. He shows her his children, that he would never have abandoned them.

She tries to redirect.

He continues he would never have abandoned them.

She asks him to show her the car and what happened at the tire.

She asks to borrow my pen again and makes a rudimentary drawing of a car: a rectangle with four circles to symbolize tires and two smaller circles with lines coming out of them to symbolize headlights, so that I might get the locations of information I am seeking. She shows me an X at the front right tire and tells me he shows her this is his location.

He continues to refer to a red truck.

She redirects.

He shows her the tire is for the first impact... a shock. I ask her to clarify.

She redirects.

A shock, an unexpected blow. A moment of recognition when you know everything has changed. An "oh shit moment."

Do you understand?

I say yes. A kind of "What the fu…?" moment. She confirms. I ask her if I can ask him to show her, so that she may show me.

Body tingling, she responds with confirmation. I ask if G is there. Body tingling, she responds with confirmation. There are two entities there at the crime scene. The other is a younger man... a law enforcement individual.

She tells me again he came to her days ago.

She asks to redirect and he shows her he has a personal message for me.

He is showing her, he is thanking me for helping Jules.

He is showing her (J's) 2 children. Two grandbabies.

She asks if I understand. I nod confirmation. Jules has two boys.

She tells me he is having a nostalgic moment. He is showing her emptiness... void... his loss at not being able to participate. He offers support and guidance. He is a part of their lives, though he cannot participate. His sadness is overwhelming. She tells me this is very moving for her. He shows her grief, emotional pain. Emptiness...

He shows her he would never have abandoned them. He repeats this over and over.

She tries to redirect.

He shows her his connection to Kaye [wife]. That he is a good person. He shows a sense of being torn between the two, G and Kaye. He has a connection to Kaye, a respect, a love, a partnership. No description of either romantic or otherwise. A connection, strong bond. A love, great affection.

He is immediately drawn back to G.

G he equates to man eater.

G is double dipping with LT.

He shows G with an older man. Wealthy, socio-economic differences. Influential, higher up. Many years her senior. Shows her having a bond with this older man and a younger male in law enforcement.

She asks me to write down the first names that come to my mind in regards to Charley.

I write the following in this fashion and in this order:

Jeb Finch

Bill Hardy

Sal Wheaton

Beau Colbert

CW Brantley

Warren Wesley

Gerrilyn Baldwin

Colquitt Cross

Hank Sloan

Kaye

She asks for my pen and then interrupts.

He is showing me 1439 blue oak. Three times she repeats: 1439 blue oak, 1439 blue oak, 1439 blue oak.

Do you understand?

I say I think so and ask if I can have clarification. Does "oak" stand for "Oak Street"?

She closes her eyes, and then nods confirmation.

1439 Oak Street, blue house. Do you understand? Does this mean anything to you?

I respond "I think so."

In my mind I try to recall pages from Kaye's diary about that morning when she was baking a chocolate cake and had to run out for milk. In the hearing between Kaye and the American Casualty Life Insurance Company, Gerrilyn Baldwin stated that Kaye had driven by her house. Kaye swore she never went on Oak Street as it would have been out of her way. I confirm that the street name sounds significant, but cannot verify at that moment as I may have that impression confused with another. But I am almost certain that was where the Baldwins lived. I will confirm when I can get back to diary and/or city directory for Valdosta from 1966.

She redirects.

He is showing her a small red truck. A period truck – style of the day.

She redirects and places her hand above the names written and asks again for my pen, explaining names have energy. She circles three names she says are elevated off the page and appear in red.*

They are as follows:

Jeb Finch

Bill Hardy

Sal Wheaton

Beau Colbert*

Colquitt Cross

Warren Wesley

Gerrilyn Baldwin*

Hank Sloan*

Kaye

(* These three circled):

*Beau Colbert

*Gerrilyn Baldwin

*Hank Sloan

He has a definite reaction to these three names. They are connected somehow. All three names remain elevated and in red.

She redirects.

She asks for a photo of Charley.

I give her the one I have been talking to all along. It is tinted in the old fashioned way they used to do.

She smiles. She says she is happy to see who he was and not who he is now. She tells me he was a good man. He has very high energy, a good, good man.

She continues. He is showing me a woman. She is attractive; she has dark brown hair, or maybe black hair.

She asks me if I understand — if I know who this person is.

At first when he says "dark brown hair" I am uncertain. I have never seen a picture of Gerrilyn (Gerri) Baldwin at this point and do not wish to identify someone I have never seen. Then she commits to black hair and I recognize that immediately as Kaye. She was noted for her painted jet black hair, her Jackie-O look.

I tell her Kaye, his wife. She smiles. I show her photos from the bin. She recognizes the woman from the photo and I confirm her as Kaye. She looks at other photos: photos of moonshine busts, car boots filled with whiskey... scenes outside in wooded areas with stills and barrels of fermented mash.

She asks if I know if any of the men in the photos are Charley.

I cannot confirm.

She redirects.

He is showing her G.

G is a man eater. There is an association between G and Hank Sloan. She has difficulty getting clear description of connection. Strong bond, but unclear.

I ask if I can get clarification on LT. I ask if LT stands for someone's name or could it be an abbreviation for lieutenant/second in command.

She cannot confirm either way, only that he shows LT as an older man with money and a tight bond with G. She asks that I let her try to explain what he is showing her happened that night.

She tells me he shows her G did not pull the trigger. Another male, a younger male, was involved. He pulled the trigger for the fatal shot to the right side of his head. G manipulated. G ordered the hit, so to speak and had others carry it out. It was between G, the older man LT, and the younger man.

He is showing her the younger man was easily manipulated by G. That G was involved with several men at a time...that the younger man was in law enforcement.

At this point I ask to redirect so that I might get some things out of my system. Too many of the people involved in the investigation had motives or perceived motives to want Charley dead, and I am anxious to know if I am on the right path or if I need to redirect my research.

I ask what Charley presents when I say the name Sal Wheaton.

She closes her eyes for a moment and I am caught off guard by her immediate response, especially since according to the diary Kaye felt certain Sal was the one who pulled the trigger that night.

She tells me he shows camaraderie — arm around shoulders, a tight bond —nothing negative — a closeness.

Confused by the sheer swiftness and declaration of innocence by nature of the answer, I asked her to clarify.

She tells me he shows closeness like that of a brother. She asks if I know who this is.

I tell her yes... it was his partner.

I ask her then to redirect. "What does he present when I say the name Jeb Finch?" (Local Sheriff- Lowndes County)

She closes her eyes.

I am certain now I will get the nod I am looking for.

She says he tells her crooked, underhanded, good ole boy, untrustworthy.

I ask if he was part of the people who hurt him that night.

He shows her insignificant reaction — a void. Does not configure into what he suffered that night.

I pause for a moment. I ask for clarification.

Charley shows her that Finch was crooked and by all means a good ole boy — but shows nothing when it comes to the circumstance presented him that night.

I was dumbfounded by the banality of the response, but showed no reaction.

She continued. Three men, tight bond. Two to be law enforcement.

I wait with bated breath for the names, but he gives only initials.

He shows me three men who were in collusion:

Jeb Finch

K (initial only)

J (initial only)

I ask for clarification. She has none further to give. I ask about the Fraternal Order of Eagles.

She tells me he refers to those three men.

Jeb Finch

K (initial only)

J (initial only)

I am no further ahead. I ask her to redirect.

She tells me all three names/initials come up, elevate, and glow red.

I know now that Finch may only be peripherally involved somehow and that I have several more angles and individuals to investigate. I ask her to redirect.

"What does he present when I say the name Cabbot Jr.?"

She tells me he responds "moonshine situation handler."

"What does he present when I say the name Cabbot Sr.?"

She tells me he responds "puppet master."

Then she asks for my pen and draws a line from the name Jeb Finch on top of the page down to Cabbot Sr. at the ¾ mark of the page and says a bond, an association, they are together.

I mentally recall the Indictment appeals 514 F.2d 64 that shows from 514 F .2d 759 that the following were indicted and convicted for charges of illegal gambling through the Fraternal Order of Eagles and the Valdosta Entertainment Company/ Finch for obstruction of justice. April 8, 1975. This event is 9 years after Charley's death and there was no way Charley could have known of these events. Any association then would have had to have been established well before his death in '66.

I drink slowly from my cup of hot chocolate and try to keep my brain from exploding.

I asked to redirect. She nodded and said yes.

"Can he show and/or present to you whether what happened to him was over business or domestic issues?"

She tells me he shows her both, through G = death. Again, he goes back to the older man LT and the younger law enforcement officer. He shows her the younger male got pleasure from pulling the trigger, took pleasure in the beating and the killing. He shows her at least three who volunteered to take him out, several people who would have volunteered to do it. He is in their way, causing a problem. He motions with his hands. He pulls it all towards that woman.

He shows her the black widow — she has manipulated the situation.

G = 's black widow.

At this point I ask her to redirect.

"Can he show you anything about the two wedding rings G supposedly placed in the casket unknown to Kaye till after the burial?"

She asks me to explain, but before I can she says he is shaking his head, snickering. "Not rings — two pennies." He shows her he is laughing, asks how she (G) could go out and buy 2 rings. He didn't do it and she didn't have the money! He shows her, she (G) covers her tracks with pennies. Claims they were something, when they weren't just in case someone asked. Two pennies — a cover up.

I ask her to redirect.

I ask her if he can show her anything about the tapes, the missing tapes, adult porn tapes from California purported to belong to Charley.

She tells me he shows a link to the younger law enforcement individual. He has something to do with missing house keys and tapes.

He shows her, the younger man taking personal satisfaction in what he has done. Pulling trigger, cursing, kicking him.

Again I ask about Jeb Finch, as he was listed as investigator for that night along with Deputy Sheriff Colbert.

Assigned officers listed, Deputy Sheriff Beau Colbert and FBI Ken Wilson, according to GBI forms CL1 and CL2, #76917 dated 10/10/1966.

He shows her no reaction to Jeb Finch, but shows energy for younger male. He shows her Beau and Gerri are the key. She explains, G possibly juggling a triad. The younger male, Charley, and the older man LT.

I ask her to redirect.

"Was the rural/secluded location on Clyattville-Nankin Road a setup?"

She tells me he confirms; yes.

He shows me compassion, forgiveness for the younger male. He knows he was manipulated by G in the same way he was. He shows sympathy. She then tells me he forgives them all.

I ask her to redirect.

"Was Henders (the snitch) part of the setup?"

He confirms. She says she sees the side of a truck with a sign. Henders, yes, a local business.

I confirm he was busted for moonshine, supposedly went straight and then turned snitch. Even though Charley suspected most of the things he gave him were unreliable.

At this point I ask her to redirect and ask a question about Kaye's diary.

She responds black wood, roll top, work office, deep drawer and/or cabinet. In between stacks of single papers, in the middle.

I ask to redirect again and finally put forth my question about the gunshot wound to the chin.

He shows her he does not recognize. He is already dead. No pain. Not by him.

He shows her younger male kicking/screaming. He shows younger kicking and shooting him in the head.

He revisits scene. He shows her series of events.

I record them, as he shows her and she sees them:

Squatting at right front tire

Impact to chest/gut — a shock or a blow. Not certain if physical and/or emotional.

Blow to back of head

Kicking and cursing

Gunshot to right side of head

No energy, dead

Sitting on his bottom

Lifted, dragged then dropped back down

No recognition of additional wound while alive. (He shows he is already dead at this point.)

Second wound inflicted.

Person in his face despises him, but does not really even know him. He is law enforcement.

I ask to redirect and ask how he got from the tire area to the road in front of the car.

He shows her no movement of energy. Not by him. He shows he is dead at this point.

I ask to redirect. I ask how he moved from tire to road.

He shows energy of younger male.

I ask to redirect and ask about the windshield wipers.

He is emphatic in response. NO WIPERS.

He shows her NO RAIN when he is killed.

RAIN when he is dead.

Dead, wet — not alive. He shows her this several times. NO RAIN when shot. RAIN when he is dead and placed in front of car.

I ask to redirect.

*She asks what else I have in the bin that might be of help.

*At this point she bends over the bin with me, ruffles through papers, and picks out a yellowed Western Union Telegram. Looks, and then discards. No comment.

I hand her the memorial book from the Camden McLane Funeral Home and some photos.

She opens slowly. Reads first few pages, and then turns to the page that begins to register visitors. She moves her hand across the top of the first page of names. She tells me to get my pen and record what she says. The names that elevate and glow from the page are as follows:

*Allen Hillard

*Patrice Guymon

Mr/Mrs Dick Wallburg

Mr/Mrs L. R. Gunterman

Wyce Holland

Mr/Mrs Leroy Voggels

Mr/Mrs George Bidders

* Mr/Mrs W. L. Bolands*

Josephine Gerrards

She explains that this does not mean these people have anything to do with that night. She simply is chronicling any name that pulls energy and explains it could be a good friend, a neighbor, or someone whom Charley had a bond with.

This later makes sense to me as the two of the names he was so active over and had her circle get no response from him. They are completely overlooked. How curious: G, Gerrilyn Baldwin, has recorded her name in the book 4 times. Beau F. Colbert, Deputy Sheriff, Lowndes County once. Claude F. Kirby once, ATTD agent. Jordan W. Baldwin/G's ex-husband once. Mrs. Bill Hardy and then separately on another page William Hardy; ATTD Special Investigator once. Sal Wheaton, ATTD agent once. G.W. Brantley, GBI agent once. Mr./Mrs. Charles Stiller, either related to and/or the pathologist once. Colquitt Cross, Lowndes County Coroner and wife once. Several other county sheriffs and agencies signed and/or sent flowers that were recorded with names. Other ATTD officers and agents signed and/or sent flowers. Notably absent among them all were the signatures of Jeb Finch, Damon Cummings, and Hank Sloan. They do not appear recorded on any page for visitation and/or floral gift.

My question then at this point is...why? Why would they not attend the funeral of a fellow law officer? Even if only out of respect for the office and especially if they had been so integral to the investigation? I decide to clean up any suspicions tainted by Kaye's diary.

I ask to redirect.

I ask about Bill Hardy, the Special Investigator that came down from Moultrie to investigate Charley's death. He was Charley's supervisor.

She tells me he shows her crooked, shady, under the table dealings. He shows her the red truck again.

I ask for clarification; she redirects.

I ask what color Charley's 1966 Ford was, the one he drove that night to Clyattville-Nankin Road.

He shows her blue. This is confirmed by family members later.

I ask her to redirect back to crime scene.

She asks to borrow my pen and draws out the scene and goes through sequence of events with him/me. She displays motions of head and body as he directs, so that I might understand movements and directions.

It is chilling to watch and listen to. I drink from my cup, but the hot chocolate is now cold and thick with a filmy layer on top. My stomach hurts from churning, but I drink it just the same. It will be a long ride home with nothing but questions and bile to dwell on.

I watch as she draws the same familiar rectangle with four circle tires and two circle headlights — only this time she draws in a windshield for reference and lines of light the distance it will have to travel to shine at just the right strength on Charley's body.

He goes through the events, and as he does, she acts them out for my benefit.

She shows me he is at the right front tire when he feels the first blow, physical and/or emotional. She could not decipher. Motions of being sucker-punched in the gut. As he leans into the front right tire of the car, he is hit again from the side.

Then the perpetrator strikes a blow to the back of his head with the mallet-shaped object she has drawn for me earlier. He reels back and forth at tire wheel (front to back) and then is shot by the young male law enforcement officer behind and above the right ear. He shows motion of head reeling from right to left several times.

He slumps onto his bottom there while the young male continues to kick and screams at him.

I ask Spencer to ask Charley to show which hind pocket he carried his wallet in.

This is for me to act as confirmation from the right side of the head entry wound blood trail into wallet.

She tells me he shows her the indent in his pants; she confirms right hind pocket.

He is then picked up and relocated approximately four to six feet away from the right front tire of the car and propped up against something of another texture. Possibly concrete or stone of some sort.

He is left there for several minutes while the younger male continues to curse at him and throws things about the car.

The blood from the fatal wound continues to run down his back into the jutted portion of his rear right pocket. It becomes trapped inside the plastic photo protectors as the young male works about the car, staging.

At this point he shows there is no rain. Several minutes have now gone by as Charley sits propped up.

At this point second wound through the underside of his chin takes place. He shows no recognition/no pain. He shows younger male.

*At this point I ask about how the second wound was made. He shows no recognition. He shows he is already dead. He shows younger male. He shoots with Charley's hand. This is where the positive test results on traces of nitrate on the right hand come from.

*The wallet located in the right hind pocket is now soaked in blood. Several minutes after that, it begins to rain. When the young law enforcement officer hears the approach of another vehicle, he panics and relocates Charley's body back to the front right tire, then runs and hides in the woods.**

* This is substantiated by an unnamed woman/witness in *The Valdosta Review* who tells local law/ATTD agents and GBI/FBI investigators she saw a man run cross the road and into the woods some minutes just before Yarrows makes his drive by. (Article on file.)

This is the position of the body/man that witness #1, Curtis Yarrows, reports seeing as he is on his way to work. In his testimony he reports that he saw a man in a sitting or squatting position at the right front tire. He waits in the rain to see if the individual requires help. He waits several minutes and no motion is made by the individual, so he goes around the car and drives on. At this point we are told it is approximately 10:30 pm and the dead body of Charley is stationed at the front right tire. Once the car of witness #1 is clear of the area, the young male drags the body [Charley] 12-15 feet in front of the vehicle.

He places the gun under his body and makes certain there is just enough light from the headlights to make him out.

At this point, she takes the pen and marks the page with an elongated circle to show placement of the body. She then gets up from the table and attempts to display the distance from her chair to where the light becomes the correct level of dimness Charley is instructing her to show me. I am both horrified and fascinated that she is being instructed by an unseen entity, as to when to stop.

She moves in increments of about 1½' to 2' at a time and then finally stops at about 13' 8" from where I am sitting and announces it was just about this much light. He is showing this is right: this is the distance necessary to produce the right effect of light on his body from the headlights of his car. He shows her this is how he looked when he saw the two boys drive past him.

Everything is very surreal for me as she does this. I watch as she moves and waits for instructions and/or confirmation either way after each movement. The fact that he can see them and himself dimly lit in retrospect to their passing flogs my mind.

He shows her this is where he is deposited by the young male.

This is where the young male hears another vehicle approach from the opposite direction and hides beside the car as the next set of witnesses, the two boys from Florida, see the body as they drive by. The young male who staged the body is hiding roughly in between the front and rear tires on the right side of the car, though more to the rear portion of the second door as they pass from the opposite direction. This is several minutes after the first witness has purportedly passed the two boys some miles further down the road from where he saw Charley's car on the road.

They (two boys from Florida) rush several miles ahead to get to a phone and notify the Brooks County Sheriff's Department of a man shot in the middle of the road. When they give the location as on the other side of the river/bridge, they are instructed that it is in Lowndes County's jurisdiction and a phone call is placed to Lowndes County Sheriff's office.

They say the heavy rain has washed everything away, except the blood trapped in between the photos. Ironically they do not report that, but state the wallet still had $27.00 left in it, so they were able to rule out robbery.

He continues to show her:

Alive- NO RAIN

Dead- RAIN

At the end we discuss some of the details again and then just before we prepared to leave we discuss things of a more personal nature for me: my parents. It was the most amazing and mind-numbing of all the experiences of the day. I am convinced that based upon my research and these materials available only to me at this point that what I experienced and what I have been given the honor to be privy to is an actual account of that evening's events as given by Charles Gordon Covington, who was brutally murdered on October 9, 1966.

CHAPTER FOUR

I walked out of the café numb from the neck up, having trouble wrapping my head around the reality of what had just occurred. Had I truly been given the blow-by-blow depiction of this man's murder? Covington had been dead for over forty years and even though I had begged for such an encounter since my youth, what this entity had shared was far from the lovely pink and glowing apparitions of the Blessed Virgins described to me by the bug-eyed Ms. Rouse in the fourth grade. I had no idea what I was supposed to do next. Since my mother had died, I had prayed for a sign from the heavens that we could somehow reach across the great divide and still be close to the ones we loved, but this was insane.

A man I had never met had virtually vomited for over two and a half hours everything he could remember about his last few hours on earth and the woman who had betrayed him. It wasn't pretty and it wasn't happy and there wasn't anything "blessed" about what he had described. It was violent and vile, sad and angry, hopeless and wasteful all at the same time. There was no possible way for me at such an innocent stage to process that kind of information correctly without better understanding the shorthand of the dead.

Eager as I might have started out that morning, my brief exposure to the postmortem limitations of a pet rat and Spencer's process would provide little in the way of tutelage as to how to move forward. Still, I was willing to do whatever it took to learn — including solving this guy's murder if it meant I could talk to my parents through her just one more time. Emotionally exhausted, I loaded the bins in my car with nothing but the bizarre images of this man's assassination, the confusion over my role in his death, and the incessant tapping of the rain to keep me company.

By the time I got out of Atlanta proper, the precipitation had slowed to a steady drool. Everything seemed to ache. Even my brain felt swollen from fatigue and sheer expansion, but tired as I felt physically, psychologically I was firing on all eight cylinders. I wanted to pull over and read through my notes, but with another 53 miles of drizzle and traffic ahead of me, I decided just to let my mind deal with what part of the spray pattern regurgitation it could remember.

Spencer had explained that because Charley's death had been so brutal and unexpected, he had not been able to process it, thus the displays of his desperate need to show and tell everything all at once. In the case of my parents who had lived well and died timely according to heavenly law, their afterlife approach had been more congenial and they wanted only to share memories and play games. The dichotomy between the two readings was unreal and threw me off my spiritual axis. And so while the violence of Charley's death and the depression over the separation from my parents had taken up most of my attention that day, I found something that would save both Charley and me from the deep abyss of being eternally lost: my faith.

****

I spent the next few days in mental dry dock trying to process. Even though I had not been a practicing participant for years, everything I had known as a Catholic had been turned on its ear. Even more amazing was the fact that it was my parents and a 44-year-old dead ATTD agent who had done it! Ironic as the cultural whiplash must have been for them on the other side of the veil, I comforted myself with the fact that Spencer was Catholic too and had somehow come to find peace with what that religion preached and what she did. I told her how much I admired her, and we had a good laugh over the fact we were both apparently going to go to hell for what we were doing.

Beyond the gore of what Charley had described or the bliss of my parents' nostalgia in those first few readings, it was the constant air of uncertainty sprinkled throughout our relationship that had kept me teetering on the brink of madness. I had always thought of myself as open and adventurous, but this kind of divine and karmic synchronicity was way out of my league. And even though I had always known I was placed here for a special reason — not in the prosaic or pseudo evangelical sense — I just knew that my purpose and my path would be different too. But to feel something in your gut and have it splayed before you with an undeniable recognition is daunting.

When Jules first gave me the plastic containers of her family's collective angst, I thought it might make an interesting backdrop for a fictitious storyline, nothing more. After all, the subplot was trite at best: boy meets girl, they fall in love, get married, and have kids; after 19 years boy finds another girl and then ends up dead. It was Hollywood silage at best, but not real journalism. I had even toyed with trying to solve the mystery behind her father's death. But what this man had shared about his murder was too real. I was not equipped for what remedy Charley needed. Still, the cosmos had brought my parents along for the ride and I could not let that part of the equation go no matter the danger or the insult to ego. After all, Jules would be no less an orphan for my efforts if I failed, and I would be no closer to my parents if I didn't try. In the end, it was a guilty conscience and the fact that the dogs and my husband had taken offense to the extra clutter on the floor that gave me no choice.

Tentatively I began to sift through decades of archival debris. At first, I went through all the legal papers, but realized they would make much more sense with a healthy dose of hindsight on the side, so I filed them all in one tub and began on the other stack of more personal papers. It was a daunting task as Kaye had saved everything, but it made for a much better system to identify names and associations for later timelines. For the bulk of my afternoons, I read only cards or letters, one right after the other. When I finished them, I started to read Kaye's journal and got hooked.

It was full of innuendos and seemingly wild accusations, not to mention major contradictions between what she wanted to tell as a wife and what she needed to keep quiet as a mother. Each time I sat down to read something, I thought about Jules and the fact she had been only six when her father was killed. Everything she had been told and everything that I had read in the yellowed print stuffed inside those containers said Charley had committed suicide over an extramarital affair gone badly. But what he had presented in the session with Spencer was not suicide: it was murder, a murder that obviously included a massive cover up involving several agencies, the size and magnitude of which I could have not have possibly guessed at that point. Who was I to then retell the same lie she had heard over four decades before?

Eager for professional guidance, my husband made a call to an old family friend, a retired FBI agent. After we told him all about Charley, he pretty much had the same reaction as my brother, but at least he was polite enough to laugh less and listen longer. At the end of the conversation, he was encouraging but realistic.

"If they've gotten away with murder this long...you might as well forget it. There won't be anything left to dig up. It will all have been swept under the rug, files destroyed, and evidence erased. You were right the first time. This will have to be written as historical fiction because you'll have nothing concrete to go on!"

I sighed into my end of the phone. "But then why did he come to me? What am I supposed to do with all this information?"

Candler simply ignored my questions and continued with his own thoughts. "Just use it to write a cute little mystery and be done with it. No harm, no foul."

"But..."

"Hey, listen up, Rookie. You're a nice kid, but what makes you think you can crack some good 'ole boy club 44 years after the fact?" he asked. "You know they're not gonna tell you anything." I could hear the ice in his highball glass clink in the background.

"Maybe not the live ones," I mustered, "but I have a friend who talks to the dead and I'm pretty sure they might be willing to talk to her," I answered, naïve and smug in my resolve.

His laughter echoed through the cell's speaker. "Oh yeah, I forgot. You let me know how that works out for ya, kid. I'll be interested to hear all about it! Psychic detectives — what a bunch of hokey-pokey!" But before I could rally with some of Spencer's past projects, he cut me off.

"Good luck, Rookie... good luck! You crack this case and I'll fly you to Washington for a brandy and a cigar!" And with that he signed off, still chuckling into the receiver.

Encouraged by the first couple of sessions, I plowed ahead. Candler had been right. I was a rookie, but I was a determined rookie too stupid to know I shouldn't be able to accomplish much. Still, working on the likes of a racial injustice piece like Moore's Ford Bridge which had five hundred pages of FBI intelligence behind it and my stuffing its ragged edges into another fictitious storyline like a cannoli was one thing. Seriously investigating a clandestine murder like Charley's, which suffered from evidential negation and negligence, was quite another.

Determined not to be the brunt of anyone's joke, I rearranged my office to work more efficiently and broke the transcript down into sections. Next, I recorded all the names that had been listed and highlighted. From there, I set about divining who was dead and who was still alive and which of them had been involved with law enforcement of any kind and which had not. Then I looked at when any of them had been employed by an agency that might have come in contact with Charley. Once that list had been generated, I began to narrow down the names to only those who had been linked to the scene that night. And that's when things got tougher, because the next category broke the names down to who would talk. When I was finished, the list was shorter than I expected. Out of the 30-some odd names I started with in the beginning, I was shortly down to little more than a handful of people who might consent to speak. A few phone calls later, that list got even shorter. Candler had tried to warn me. Determined or not, I was abruptly running out of viable resources. Being stalled this early in the process, I would have panicked if I had been smart enough, but I wasn't.

My first call was to Alcohol, Tobacco, Firearms and Explosives (ATFE) Headquarters in Atlanta. The public relations officer assigned to me was most gracious and gave me several leads to lists and newsletters generated for retired members as well as an introduction to the ATF National Archivist to see if any peripheral information concerning Charley could be garnered. It was a short line from some to none, and I think collectively we were all surprised by the deficiencies in all accounts. Most agencies had little beyond Covington's birth, date of hire, and date of death, so the better part of that month was spent reading and reviewing the session notes. Mindful of Spencer's caveat that victims tend to throw out the most important information first for fear they may not get another chance, I read it over and over to see what else might be hidden in between the lines. Having no background input other than Kaye's files, I needed the shelter and ambiguity of my writing to wade through impression after impression of what had been shared.

What started as a dare from my husband after watching the movie *Julie and Julia* turned out to be my saving grace: my blog, *Anatomy of a Murder*. I will share some of it with you in this book, but you can read its entirety at the website listed as *www.brownstoneliteraryworks.com*

Because so much of the information given through Spencer had been cryptic in nature, it buffered us both from the immediate truth. Once the calm of acceptance had begun to settle in, I began to see what had been hidden at first blush.

It was clear that fellow law enforcement individuals had taken him out, but why? Fraternal protection was sacred, so why then would it have been so flagrantly violated? What did Charley know that was so damning that these people felt Charley dead was better for them than Charley alive? According to the rumor mill and private family accounts, Charley may have gotten as far as asking Kaye for a divorce. Print media and investigators carried it that much further and stated that Charley was given an ultimatum by G the week before. A "Tell her you want out or it's over between us" kind of thing. I believe that day Charley told Kaye it was over, told the kids he was moving out. Rumor speculated that when he saw G on the front porch of her home that night speaking to her ex, he assumed she was getting back together with him. Emotionally devastated and ashamed, he then allegedly drove himself out to the Clyattville-Nankin Road and committed suicide. For a rural agent with a history of having a very even temperament, it just didn't add up.

Kaye's account had mentioned Charley telling Jules that night that he was not going to be living with them anymore, and even though she had sworn the eldest to secrecy, he admitted to Jules that his parents had spent the better part of the day yelling at one another. In her journal she writes

I sat down at the table and started to work on my Social Security report. I had worked on it off and on all Sunday. He came upstairs to where I was and asked if Jules needed a bath before going to bed. I said no, I had given her a bath before she went to Shoney's. He took her upstairs to put her to bed. She had gotten a new book, Witches' Hills, *and he was going to read it to her. I heard him read the book several times. It was a Halloween book. After fifteen or twenty minutes, Jules started crying. I finally went up to see if she was afraid for him to leave out; she is real scary about him leaving sometimes. He was sitting on the side of the bed by her. I asked her what was wrong and she said, "Dad says he is not going to live with us anymore." She was just six years old. I told her dad was just teasing her and got her a couple of aspirins. She got quiet and went on to sleep.*

Before he went upstairs with Jules, he called someone. I thought it was Sal. He said, "Bob Callenwald called and said we could get out for a while if we wanted to, that the truck had stopped in Athens, Georgia and had pulled in between two buildings. It looks like it will be there overnight. We are to stay in touch and check in

every two hours." At this point I never had the chance to talk to
him about what Jules said. (Entry dated 10/9/1966)

Later on the same page she writes that after the ATTD stand-by
was lifted, Charley was amenable to sitting and sharing a cup of
coffee with her. A phone call from his mother interrupted their
opportunity for a meaningful exchange about his statement to Jules,
and with the clock ticking Kaye was left without recourse other
than to wait. When his call ended, he noted the time and
commented about needing to check out an alleged moonshine deal
called in by a snitch. In fact, Kaye noted in her diary the
following:

*It must have been about twenty minutes to nine when he came
downstairs and told me he was going to go ride out the road — he
called it the Redland Road and Roland section. Right after that he
told me he was going and I started to tell him to let's drink some
coffee first. His mother called. He talked to her. She had just had
some surgery on her foot and could not walk on it when we were
there the weekend before. He asked about her foot, how his daddy
was — just general conversation. I think he told her we had been
stuck at home all weekend. He did not appear to be upset, just as
calm.*

*After he finished talking to her, I said to let's us have a cup of
coffee. He said ok, took his hat off and laid it on the top of the
refrigerator. I got up to wash the pot and he said, "I thought it was
already made. You go on and put it on and I will be back shortly
after it is made."*

*Our son was in the basement watching TV and he yelled down at
him, "I will see you in a little while, old man!" Our son asked him
if he would be back in time to put him to bed and he told him yes.
He walked out to the street, got in his car, and that is the last time I
heard from him until Sal came and told me he was dead. It was five
till nine when Charley left...*

If Charley could brave such words to his child, it may not be
inconceivable that he had broached the same kind of candor earlier

with his wife. Obviously G was a real heart tug for the revenuer as during the first session he presented his heartache first, then his physical demise after. They say "Hell hath no fury like a woman scorned," but apparently it hath no comfort for the broken heart of a man either. I read and re-read Kaye's journal, trying to read between the lines, but there were so many different private agendas within the ink-stained pages that I needed the clarity of the dead to sort them out.

CHAPTER FIVE

By the time February was exhausting its hold on the calendar, I knew more publicized details of Charley's death than his life and so decided to slow the process down.

Aggravated with the lack of quantifiable information actually contained in the *Freedom of Information Act*, I reached out directly to every living agent and agency that appeared on any official or unofficial document contained therein: ATTD-ATF, Lowndes County Sheriff's Department, the Valdosta Police Department, even the law firm of Donlin, Bartholomew, Coles, Eller & Black (who had represented Kaye), FBI, and GBI. Even though it felt as if every law enforcement agency had its fingers in this pie somewhere along the line, not one of them had anything enlightening to share with me that explained what Charley had been doing out there that night or why he had died. Frustrated with the lack of progress, I decided to take another approach while waiting on my next major session with Spencer.

Eager for my background material, I Googled information on the ATTD and found a professor in California who had written a wonderful book about its history and evolution. He referred me to several retired ATF agents still alive who knew or knew of Charley before his death. They in turn led me to another man who began the aerial surveillance for ATTD/ATF back in the 70's; he is the author Charles Weems, who has become both dear friend and mentor. Contacts were made with several Valdosta individuals from my original list that were there that night when Charley was killed, who gave me information I could use as a guard rail in my research. I spoke with everyone still alive from 1966 I could get a lead on.

But every inroad found eventually became a dead end, and I began to empathize with Kaye's plight. Even her son would not talk to me at the time because of his religious aversion to my association with a psychic medium and his desire to keep his private life private. Since Jules had only been six, I was at a standstill. I couldn't keep asking the same people the same questions over and over. It wasn't long before I began to rely more and more on my relationship with Spencer and the voice inside my head that spoke whenever I looked at Charley's 8 x 10.

No matter what people had said about the Baldwin woman and him having an affair, the emotional stakes did not seem high enough to warrant suicide. I kept going back to the first session and his mournful pleas, *"My little girl... my little girl. Tell them I would not have abandoned them. I would not have left my children."* That was not the voice of a man who had dumped his family for a spring fling — that was the voice of a man who found himself in deep shit and then died. When I read the part in Kaye's journal where it talked about how Jules had cried herself to sleep that night, it became apparent that I had been so focused on her father's death that I had forgotten about her limited exposure to his life. I had so many questions I wanted to ask.... so many questions I needed to ask. Problem was, Kaye was already dead and the children had their own biases. My heart wanted to reach out to Jules's brother as he was somewhat old enough at the time to calibrate the loss, but held little patience for his consternation over my use of the psychic/medium. In the end I kept my distance but kept thinking if it had been my father, I would have talked to the devil himself to get whatever information he would grant me to solve my father's murder.

Each time I mentioned my work on this project, people seemed highly resentful of what I was doing. Because there was so little psychical evidence, everyone cautioned I was an idiot to think I could get anywhere. Privately I agreed and publicly continued to do everything by the book to keep safe of criticism. Secretly, however, the more I began to trust my intuition, the more the truth of what happened that night began to emerge.

Going for the obvious, I tried to contact Charley's partner Sal Wheaton. Folks who answered his contact number said he was either in Florida for the winter or North Carolina for the summer. Even though I left messages on both ends, my timing was always somehow just a few days off. Hank Sloan was another character that begged for attention. From what I was told, he had apparently worn both VPD and Lowndes County Sheriff office badges at various times throughout his law enforcement career. Several interviewees had painted him as a womanizer, a hothead, and according to a female resource rather well endowed. Folks said he drank heavily and had a thing for playing Russian roulette with himself, his wife, or anybody who refused to give him what he wanted. There was even a mention about him in a letter to Kaye from someone who talked about Finch and about how Hank Sloan's "attempted suicide" sounded an awful lot like Charley's supposed "suicide" (letter on file). This information placed him as a larger blimp on my radar, but he too had passed and so a direct confrontation became a moot point.

The list of characters from that night that had passed became longer by the day. There was Jeb Finch, Lowndes County Sheriff (who had died in prison); Colquitt Cross-County Coroner, Claude Kirby ATF, Warren Wesley, Darwin Devonshire, Parker Jade, Gerrilyn Baldwin, Beau Colbert, LC Deputy Sheriff. All of these were dead and most of the other names on my list eventually registered as either deceased or disinterested. I even called the snitch Wiley Henders who had recently been released from prison, but when I mentioned Charley's name, he swore he'd never heard of Charley Covington. That, of course, I knew was a bald-faced lie. Even though I had expected such from a convicted felon, it was the retired law that remained determined to obfuscate things even more.

Take, for instance, the former GBI agent (and retired Sheriff of Cook County in Adel, GA) Cutter Brantley, who said he vaguely remembered the Covington name, but not much more. Really? Covington's alleged clandestine romance and subsequent suicide was the largest scandal of that year, yet Brantley claimed he had no memory of it. I was dumbfounded that folks who could recite the exact measurements and ingredients of their great greatgrandma's corn pudding recipe suddenly grew shorter brain stems the minute I mentioned Covington's name. The list of those who remembered and those who suddenly "could not recall" grew and shrank on a daily basis until there was no one left to ask.

Ah, but then there was Damon Cummings, the retired State Trooper who continued to make up for every lost name on the list. He had an odd aura about him that made the hairs on my neck refuse to lie down in his presence. Unlike the rest, he always seemed to be available to talk. Taking into account the fact that most people's memories occasionally faltered at that age and that most men like to play the hero in their own lives… something about him still didn't sit right with me. He asked questions that he should have been able to answer and he refused to answer questions he knew I shouldn't be able to ask. When he spoke, he made me feel that even as I was tempted to think he was telling me a lie he was telling me a truth and counting on the fact I might be too dimwitted to realize it.

In one interview he had described one critical clue of the crime scene exactly the same as Spencer in the first session, which was incongruent with all reported information. No one else had done that. Because of that, he became a major person of interest for me. In the end it became more about how he made me feel than what I could immediately prove. He also advised me that he was recording my every word, every phone call, every email, and every face-to-face interview. It was an awkward statement considering I was the one doing the investigation. After all, you only record what it is you wish to remember — or are afraid to forget. No matter...Jules's son was recording his every word as well. When we played the recording back, we discovered he had more to worry about than me!

Like his accusations, my notes throughout his several interviews read like a rollercoaster ride at Wild Adventures Theme Park. But I exempted some of the smaller deviations because some conversations had been over the phone and if distracted on my end, it may have been my error in the recording of information, not his in the dispensing. Still, his presentation felt grossly inconsistent with the claim he had been first on the scene and that set up a slow-burning ulcer in the pit of my stomach.

During his interview he told me that a week before Charley died, he was at the Courthouse one night about 11:00 covering the desk for someone who had gone home early sick. He said that Charley had dropped by, all excited and when asked why he was out so late, Charley told him he was meeting somebody from Lake Park, Georgia to get some information. That he was working on something big, "Something so big it would blow the whole county wide open." When Damon asked if Charley was taking his partner Sal with him, Charley told him, no, that he was going alone. Then Damon said he warned Charley to let someone know where he was going just in case he got into trouble. Said he didn't want Charley to get hurt.

On the surface, it sounds plausible, even gallant, but let's take a closer look. First of all, no Courthouse would be open at 11:00 at night. Second of all, he was State Patrol and they had offices outside the Courthouse in another area of the county — close to the actual murder site. And thirdly, why would a veteran ATTD agent twenty some-odd years Damon's senior tell a snot-nosed rookie State Patrol officer about anything? Especially about a deal that was so big it would "blow the whole county wide open"? It's not only laughable, it's completely unbelievable. Charley claimed through Spencer that he never even told Sal about what he was doing that night, and Sal was his partner.

So what reason would Damon have to try and paint himself into the picture, or tell me that he sensed something was going down ahead of time? Even more insane, why would he insist that he was the first one there on scene, even though his name and/or likeness appeared nowhere in any print media or personal reverie I had been privy to? Why does he habitually tell me how incredibly honest he is, yet when I ask about the inconsistencies of his testimonies against the building backdrop of others, he pegs everyone else as a liar? Still with all his detours, that little something he told me that matched Spencer's description made me anxious. It was as though his head was telling him to keep his yap shut, but his ego couldn't wait to take credit for something I had yet to discover.

CHAPTER SIX

Today I write with heavy heart. A very dear friend of mine told me when I began this to be careful. That once I opened Pandora's Box, I would not be able to put the lid back on it. They were right.

Throughout the first phase of discovery, I tried to keep an open mind. In between interviews, I badgered Spencer with a million questions, and she was marvelous at fielding whatever I threw at her. Some days the world outside my office seemed less real than the man in Charley's photo, and I began to pull away and cloister myself within the confines of my room. Every morning I wished him well and every night before I turned off my writing lamp, I bid him a peaceful sleep. In between my life and his death I searched his face for answers I could not even begin to form yet. His eyes followed my every move; his ears heard my every prayer for guidance. Soon small signs of his approval began to appear in my daily life. It was an odd relationship. Almost ten years his senior at the time of his death, I had been where he had been and knew what weighty decisions were on his emotional scale when he died. Had he come into my life ten years earlier, I could not have held any empathy for him. But over 50 and contemplating similar issues, it felt more like he had come to save me from myself than to rectify his death.

In between my job and the kids, I buried myself in his tragedy. Occasionally solitude has its merits. By the end of that month I had digested every inch of print not blackened out by marker on the GBI Crime Lab report. Systematically, I deciphered the signatures and decoded the implications of the information it held. Unfortunately, too much remained hidden to my layman's eye. With no one else to turn to, I did what I did best… I directed. With empathy, I employed and exploited the good intentions of others. Phone calls were made, interviews recorded, internet research sites established. Still, with all my efforts, the information refused to lead definitively back to proverbial Rome.

Convinced I had reached the saturation point of my effectiveness with what little documentation could be found, I scheduled another face-to-face appointment with Spencer. Desperate to connect more of the dots, I reviewed peripheral documents to prepare for our meeting. Intrigued about the trial transcripts to secure Charley's government benefits, I hopped on the internet and Googled the law firm that had handled Kaye's case. To my surprise, I found her attorney still very much alive and quasi-practicing. I made a call, a secretary answered, and two hours later I received a return call.

I introduced myself and then informed him of my desires for transcripts of archival information about Charley's death, Kaye's numerous lawsuits, and any or all of the testimonial court transcripts to reclaim both dignity and dividends. I even offered to pay all copy and postal fees, plus a small stipend to his secretary for doing so.

Immediate irritation set up in his gullet, and like a wild turkey full of Southern gravel, his voice grated across my finely tuned Midwestern ears. "Miss Howell? Yes, I remember the Covington case. No, there are no more files on that particular case currently available as we purge all unchallenged legal archives every 20 years. And so you, my dear, are already two cycles too late. The case was settled and the appeals by the insurance company denied. I told that to Mrs. Covington's son...what was his name?"

"Martin. Martin Covington," I interjected, waiting to correct his mispronunciation of my name, but he cut me off and kept talking.

"Yes...Charley's boy Martin. Smart kid... genius or something...went to college early. Anyway, I told him that same thing when he was asking questions a couple years back now. And I will advise you the same. Ya'll need to go on and just leave this thing alone. There isn't anything in our files anymore and most likely nowhere else. But if you're hell-bent, you might try the American Life Insurance Company or the Federal Government's

Department of Employee Compensation. But I doubt they would have any records left on file either this far out. Like I said, it was all settled out years ago."

I asked if he could refer me to anyone else on my abbreviated list that might still have a file copy or a name I might use to contact to get another copy of the trial transcripts. I heard the rustling of paper and what sounded like a door closing.

"Mr. Eller?" There was a pregnant pause the size of Africa on the other end of the line, and then without apology, he began to bulldoze right through me.

"Who are you?"

I started to answer, but before I could get my name out again he barked into the phone like a junkyard dog. "Why is it you people can't leave this thing alone? What do you want? Who put you up to this?" he bellowed, and I could almost hear the metaphorical links in his chain grinding against one another in his charge. I reiterated that I was a friend of Jules's and that "I was doing some research on her father's death and things just didn't add up for me. Also..."

And that was it! Territory threatened, his metaphorical chain snapped and he came straight for me and cleared away any doubt for me that I was on the right track. "Alright, now you listen here... Ms. Howell, was it?" I was both happy and irritated that he had gotten my name wrong again, but this time thought better than to correct him.

"You tell your client...she needs to just let this sleeping dog lie. You just need to back off and leave this thing alone. Ya, hear? Back off this instant and quit while you're ahead. Digging around in people's past is never a good idea, nor is it gonna bring her daddy back. Bad things happened, but innocent people might get hurt if you do. People's children and grandchildren who had nothing to do with this will suffer for it."

I was flogged. All I had asked for was a referral and the guy had gone postal on me. "How much more innocent do you get than being six years old? " I flung back in his ear. "Jules was six when her father was killed. Six! And I never said she was my client." I restated my position as just a friend, stalling to prepare for the next round of directives.

Suddenly the gravel settled in his throat and I realized the chain of consequence was pinching his throat. His voice lowered, and in a low growl he continued and spoke each syllable with exaggerated measure. "You tell your client she needs to back off and go out and buy one of those T-shirts that reads 'This is the first day of the rest of my life' and move on. There's no point in ruining other people's lives at this point." And I could hear his breath run up and down his windpipe, hissing in between the sentences. "It's done... it is over. Most of the people involved are dead now anyways. Let this thing go!"

My job dropped. This guy knew more than he was telling. "And you would know that how?" I baited back. "She has a right to know what happened to her father and why." I said as clearly and as slowly as I could, refusing to be so summarily dismissed.

"I'm gonna tell you something, off the record...ya, hear?" he slimed.

"I never said I was an attorney," I said, but it was as if I had never spoken.

He gathered his breath and continued, "Seven or eight years after it happened, two detectives came to me with evidence proving that it was not a suicide. They showed me things... told me about the gun, top and bottom shells being spent, information that fit the circumstantial and physical evidence and backed up their story, that there had been a fight... a struggle over the gun, that it wouldn't have looked good for Charley, and that they had shot Charley in self-defense."

I thought about the fact that one bullet had been shot from just above and behind the right ear, lodging in the upper left hand side of his skull; the other had been shot through the bottom of his chin, plowing through his upper palette and ending up wedged in the frontal lobe above the nasal cavity. "How the hell was that self-defense?" I wanted to ask, but I needed to let him to keep talking while I looked for a recorder. And even though he had said it was off the record, I needed him to know it was definitely going on mine!

"And they told me other things. It wouldn't have shown Charley in a very good light. Your client doesn't know everything about her mamma and her daddy, and she should be glad for that."

My head was reeling. I couldn't find my recorder, but the screen was still up on my laptop, so I continued to read his bio, trying to keep him on the phone while I checked his stats. "So what year was this? 1974...'75? Was this when you were an attorney or after you became a Superior State Court Judge that they came to you?" I asked, scrolling and trying to check the dates to confirm his status at the time.

"You just tell your client to quit digging. Ya hear me?" He grunted. "It's over..."

"How could it be over if there was someone still alive who knew the truth?" I wanted to yell, but I kept my cool. "So, let me get this straight, just for my edification. Seven or eight years, as you suggested, after Charley was killed, two law enforcement officers, detectives you said, presumably from the Valdosta Police Department then, came to see you and showed you evidence that proved Charley's death was not a suicide. And you did nothing with that information?" I continued to speak slowly and clearly, trying to catch my breath, ease my palpitations, and be certain I would be able to confirm what he had just told me verbatim.

"You just tell your client about that T-shirt now, ya hear? Now I've got a meeting I need to attend and..." his voice garbled something about a time and I headed him off.

"Wait... do you remember the name of who the detectives were?"

"Seems one of them was... let me think," he balked and I could almost hear the wheels turning in his geriatric head. In the silence between his thoughts I scrolled down through his personal biography and scanned each paragraph for the date of his promotion: "graduated with a law degree in 1957... Admitted into the practice in 1958... Became a Superior State Court Judge in 1975... BINGO! I had him.

"Seems Billy Burgess was one of them, and the other one, well, it's not important," he rallied. "Most of them are dead now, but you give her that message for me just the same and have a nice..." Now it was my turn to jerk his dog chain.

"So you were a about to become a Superior State Court Judge at the time that they told you, and you decided that the information you received even seven or eight years after Charley was killed wasn't important enough to share with the authorities, the widow, or the courts?" I was fuming and pacing the floor like a caged animal, unable to believe this guy was handing me information on a silver platter — all because I had challenged his ego and not out of remorse or moral obligation.

"Now see here..." he stammered.

"There is no statute of limitations on murder, correct? So how could you have made such a decision yourself, either as attorney or anointed judge? You said some of them were dead, but that doesn't mean all of them were. Kaye wasn't! Why didn't you tell her?"

He ignored my questions and kept going with his excuses. "What good would it have done? Her husband was dead and nobody else needed to be hurt by what had happened."

"But that was not your decision to make! It was the right of the victim to make that decision. You should have told Kaye and let her decide what was or was not the right thing to do," I hammered.

He cut back quickly with biting anger. "It was my decision to make. There wasn't anything to be done about it, but cause further heartbreak so I kept it to myself! I made that decision and it was the right one to make. Now you just let this thing go. I'm warning you! Quit digging!" He paused to catch his breath, and then with all the charm of a snake, his tone eased as his Southern drawl crawled in and out of both sides of his mouth. "You tell your client to back off and remember what I said about that T-shirt, now... 'ya hear? Good day, Ms. Howell," and the phone went dead.

For the next five minutes I panicked, wandering in a circle, muttering the words "Oh my God... oh my God... oh my God!" over and over as I tried to plan my next move. I wasn't an attorney; I wasn't a cop. I was just a theatre director. What the hell was I supposed to do now? This time I was smart enough to panic and I did. I would have hyperventilated, but suddenly all the air had been sucked out of the room into my lungs and I thought I would burst. When I spun around and saw his face bobbing up and down on my laptop screen, I screamed something I cannot put into print. The chaos of anxiety toyed with my body. Too much oxygen made me heady; too little sent me spiraling. Grasping for air and equilibrium, I reached out to my husband and left a message on his cell phone to document the date and time.

"Shit. Ok.... calm down, calm down. Catch your breath. Ok. Do not erase this, ok? OK..." and I took a deep breath to try and pace myself.

"I made a call today to Gavin Eller. The date is 3/26/10. A representative of the court has just confessed he had seen evidence proving Charley's death not to be a suicide and he had chosen to do nothing with it! A retired attorney — Kaye's attorney, no less, who then became a Superior State Court Judge later, held intimate knowledge of his client's husband's murder had made a personal decision to obstruct the law."

My heart raced, and I could not get the image out of my head of this poor woman with painted jet black hair, a Jackie-O smile, weighing less than a hundred pounds due to PTS, sucking on cigarette after cigarette, begging and pleading for the local courts to re-open the case and clear his name. Eller's picture scrolled up before me again and I wanted to vomit. There he sat, puffy cheeks, ruddy nose in his tufted leather chair like a fat bullfrog, croaking about his virtue at the expense of a heartbroken family, defending strangers who knew nothing of their plight. I was horrified. Anger now consumed both lungs and limbs as I stomped across the floor of my office testing the parameters of my confusion. Why had he told me this? Did he know what he was saying? Did he realize that as an investigative reporter I would have no recourse but to use this against him? Did he really think I was an attorney and that his limp ploy for professional guard rail would buy my silence?

My dogs, hearing the thumping, set up a ruckus themselves, thinking it was time to play. Together we thumped the length of my bedroom, yelping half in hysteria and half for joy. While Eller's confession had appalled me, it had finally given me the traction I needed to move forward. I was unsure at first where to go with it, but there was no turning back no matter the personal indecision. Knowing something of this magnitude and not sharing it with proper authorities would have made me just as complicit as he.

But who would I tell? The ATF? The FBI? The GBI? How about the Lowndes County Sheriff's Department who had been part of the problem over 44 years ago? Or even better, the Valdosta Police Department whose detectives had gone to a judge and left it in his incapable hands? Not wanting the latent ego of any agency to protect itself and not the law it defends, I held my breath and thought of who might be best to hold this information till I could establish proper protocol and pecking order.

The dogs and I yelped for a few more minutes till my heart rate lowered and my hands stopped shaking. Who was gonna believe this? My computer screen blinked at me, so I rubbed the pad and brought Eller's face back into view. I had heard rumors about how he had tried to double bill Kaye and how at one point he had the local Deputy Sheriff padlock her house and car doors as levy against her skipping town before he could collect. He claimed she owed him over $9,000.00 in legal fees, but the Feds backed her claims of excessive fees and sent him packing.

As I rolled my fingers over the pad, I wondered if his silence about the detectives back then wasn't in some small way his $9,000.00 payback for the Feds' slap on the wrist he had received for his poor manners. His face scrolled past me again and in that instant I knew exactly what I had to do. I deleted Eller's face, but not the echo of his ego. Then I wrote down everything from our conversation. When I finished with that, I crafted an email to my public relations contact at the ATF and sent it on its way. Next, I copied Spencer, my husband, and another agent's email address for backup and then stared long and hard at the 8 x 10 on my desk and smiled.

"We're on our way, Charley. Thank you, thank you," I whispered into the afternoon sun. Nobody had listened to me before...but with the information I had just received, I had a funny feeling they would now. Rookie indeed!

CHAPTER SEVEN

The subsequent face-to-face meeting with Spencer proved to be even more impressive than the last in the fact that once engaged, Charley began to help solving his murder rather than obsessing over it. March had come in like a lamb and I was happy for it, as Gavin Eller had roared enough at the end February to last me a lifetime. When the day of the meeting arrived, Jules invited herself along and, though I had reservations that her presence might slow the process, I could not have denied her access to her father any more than I would have wished someone to deny me access to mine.

Jules as a woman was an older version of the pixie-faced photo Charley had held within his wallet 46 years earlier. Cropped medium brown hair in the latest fashion sat atop her mother's solid but proportionate framing. Her face proved to be a generous mixture of her parents. Charley's blue-gray eyes and aquiline nose separated generous cheeks and a smile that was all her mother's. Curious, she bit at her lower lip as I briefly explained what I had been able to garner thus far.

In preparation I'd made a list of questions I wanted to find answers for and gave Spencer a copy when we arrived. This time we had selected a Starbuck's closer to her house that had a separate conference room. Introductions made, Spencer made Jules comfortable with the process and then went to the questions first and tried to get a response. Charley answered a good many of them, but not all of them and not all in order.

An hour in, Spencer sensed that it would be better just to let whatever Charley needed to say come through, but the questions he did answer were these:

#1. Was Henders the person from Lake Park who was feeding you information? *Yes.*

Was this information on the illegal gambling ring involving Finch and Crutches? *No.*

#2. Was it Beau Colbert and Hank Sloan there that night with Gerri Baldwin? *Hank Sloan is the focus of this.*

#3. Was the domestic dispute you spoke of in the last session with Kaye or with Gerri that night? *Gerri.*

#4. Was Beau Colbert romantically involved with Gerri? *Yes, Beau Colbert was in love with Gerri.*

#5. Was she pregnant? Would it have been with your child? Was there a miscarriage? *Yes, 2 miscarriages.*

#6. Was the trigger man that night Beau Colbert? *Charley smacked the gun away — thought it was a bluff, a joke. Not going to go through with it. A bait and switch, one lures, one pulls the trigger. The younger one, the trigger puller.*

Charley refused to redirect and answer to #5, #6, and #7 which asked about a pregnancy and who the actual trigger man was: Beau Colbert or Hank Sloan.

#8. They say they shot you with your own gun in self-defense. Is this true? *Absolutely not! Unequivocally not!*

#9. Was Jeb Finch in on the murder? *No, more about the relationships, but not tied to this night directly.*

#10. Were you face down or face up when first responders show up at the crime scene? *Sitting up and lying down.*

#11. Were you 10' to 15' in front of your car or behind it? *In front of the car, white light, not red light.*

#12. Did Damon Cummings wipe your face with a piece of toilet paper from his car? *He used his shirt sleeve to wipe face.* (She makes a motion like a swipe with her forearm.) *Wiped with his sleeve, like this...*

#13. Did Gavin Eller know about the murder arrangement at the time? *No.*

#14. What direction did Beau Colbert come from when he arrived at the scene the second time that night? *From towards the front.* (She draws a diagram of the car with the headlights facing the river. Colbert is shown as coming from the Brooks County line across the river.)

#15. Did you know about the clubhouse? There was a clubhouse for the Lowndes County Sheriff's Department in that area. *We all knew about the clubhouse; assumptive.*

#16. Was that where Beau came from that night? *No.*

#17. Was that where Beau went back to that night? *Best description; tied very close to there, but not that night.* (Spencer asks... Does that make sense?)

#18. Who owns the red truck? *Beau's girlfriend.*

#19. Did you see them when you arrived? Or did they ambush you? *Not them, him. Not ambush. Only him, caught off guard, but not ambushed.*

#20. Was Colbert drunk when you were fighting? *Not drunk.*

#21. What do the initials LT have to do with your murder? *LT, shoving a badge in his face.* (Spencer adds "Did someone make lieutenant later?" Check history.)

Charley skipped answering several more questions.

#33. Did you plan to marry Gerri? How many other girlfriends did you have? *NO...none.*

#34. Did Gerri's ex-husband have anything to do with your murder? *No, just the wife.*

#35. Did the big project you were working on have anything to do with the illegal gambling Finch was involved in? *No. Damon Cummings, not gambling. Had to do with the porn.*

#36. Did Charley have anything to do with the clubhouse? *Not his buddies. Not tied to the clubhouse. The clubhouse, the porn, the cover up.*

Spencer continued to redirect and Charley became nostalgic.

To Jules: *Do you understand cooking the rabbit? Not in an icky way, but to cook and eat rabbit?* Jules did not recognize. *He is showing me an atomizer, a perfume bottle.* He was showing an heirloom, showing Spencer objects.

Jules did not recognize.

Do you understand clap and drawing a heart in the air? Non-verbal… a sign across the dining table… a clap and a heart? This is a nostalgic memory for him. When you were young, he used to clap to get your attention and then draw the sign of the heart for you.

Jules said she was too young to remember.

Do you understand, why didn't you go to graduate school? Like… ha ha, why didn't you do it? Jules has no response.

You have two boys? Ages?

Jules responded: *Yes, two: 15 and 20.*

I asked if Charley could answer any more questions and Spencer tried to redirect, but Charley continued to move forward. Spencer then decided not to push, but to just let whatever could come through, come through.

To me: *Do you understand the man with red hair?*

No.

Do you understand he talks about the man with the red hair — a cover up? Everyone will know who he is. Man with the red hair. He's the go-to guy. He does the cover up. Hypothetically it feels like... "I'll take care of it. Go home. Keep quiet. Don't talk to anyone!" There is a bond between Colbert and the red-headed man.

Spencer asked Jules what she remembered. Jules told her about the separate conversations they had with them that night. Each one [parent] talked to them separately about the potential divorce. Kaye told Jules she will buy her new dresses the next day. She [Kaye] made her son swear he would not tell a soul about what they have discussed. It is a promise he will keep until after his mother dies.

Spencer to Jules: *Your father keeps coming through with the question "Do you forgive me?"*

Jules responded: "Yes. I lived with my mother. She was just all about me, very devoted to me and my brother. Mother never looked at another man." Jules wondered if he would have really taken them (the children) away from Kaye.

Spencer said: *He's laughing. "Not on your life. She would have killed me first!"*

Do you understand canning? Pickled pears or peaches? He's showing these. Do you remember a time when something was thrown across the room at a wall? A warning? A sign that the marriage was falling apart? He is showing me a clear jar. Did she buy them? She always bought these? It was a sign, a red flag for divorce.

Jules reiterated that she was much too young to remember.

Spencer redirected Charley and even though Spencer asked question #22 again, Charley skipped ahead and answered the very next two questions.

#23. Does LT stand for Lieutenant, as in the Lt. Governor of Georgia?

#24. Was he involved with Gerri? *Yes, involved with G — the energy LT.*

(Charley skipped #25 and moved on to another question.)

#26. What is 1439? House numbers? Badge numbers? *Badge numbers. (Charley then jumps ahead to questions about the clubhouse and the pawn shop and the porn.)*

#38. Who else knew where you were going that night besides Kaye and Henders? *No one.*

#40. Did you tell Sal where you were headed? *No.*

#41. Did he go with you? *No, solo.*

(Charley skips #42)

#43. Did you always carry your gun? *No.*

(Charley skipped to #47)

#47. Did they shoot you in self-defense? *No, it doesn't fit. Not self-defense.*

Spencer moved away from the questions and let Charley come through: *G and Beau. He was her boy-toy, at her beck and call...did her bidding. Do you understand? Think: why would they have wanted Charley dead? What's the relationship there?*

New information: *Dog there too. Dog belongs to trigger puller. Loyal dog, went everywhere. The dog's feet are getting muddy. Dog feet, prints in the mud. Two things coming through; younger man discloses to the older man, a confession. Dog linked to shooter, lived with him all the time.*

(Charley gave three more personal messages to Jules and continued.)

Financial situation of G at the murder. G manipulator, tied to porn. G presents with a lot of cash, illegal, counting extra cash, spending more, dressing nicer. Look to her cash flow after the murder.

Henders equals cash. G has money flowing from two directions. Older man LT she is sleeping with. He is older, tied to law enforcement somehow, but not necessarily in law enforcement. G is the middle man, the money courier. Hypothetically, the courier gets it from A to B on the fly. Works occasionally as the go-between.

Spencer redirected: *This is interesting. They are presenting — a sign. A tennis association between the trigger puller and the confessor. They played this sport together: ball, two rackets, in a bigger space, a nice space like a country club.*

Then Charley moved on. Jules asked if they would have really gotten a divorce.

He talks about 3 years earlier, something they could never recover from. He shows a page. In my word that means they were on the same page. Both unhappy in the marriage for over 3 years. Alcohol possibly tied to the event three years before.

Then to Jules: *Do you understand mattress flipping? Yes, I do it when I get frustrated. I clean! Did you have a dream about bats? Something about bats recently? Yes, her school was infested and she caught one!*

Spencer allowed the redirect so I could ask questions:

What about Colquitt Cross? *A drunk, sloppy associations, no work ethic, coroner.*

Gavin Eller? *They show me, slithers like a snake, in and out. Connection between Gavin and Beau Colbert.*

Spencer asked: Do you feel safe going forward? *I do until you tell me not to.*

We took a bathroom break. Then Spencer redirected and Charley began again to direct information to me:

Do you understand 1510? You will find the answer: 1510-1510-1510. Look for document 1510 in between a pile of papers, 1510. You will find the answer. You will find the answer. MOT: the trail will lead to MOT. (He repeats this 3x's)

Spencer had a direct question for me from Charley: "*Do you understand the Phoenix? Does this mean anything to you?" He's showing me something I can relate to." Do you understand the Phoenix, the rising bird"? (I explain I have been toying with the idea of going back to school online.) He says "Follow this, follow your idea."*

I asked if they wanted me to continue: *They say yes, be safe... be at peace.*

Just before we got ready to leave, Spencer looked at a ring that Jules said belonged to her father. As Spencer held the ring in her hands, I asked about an event from the journal where Kaye had taken the kids to the store and returned to find the kitchen full of coffee grounds strewn everywhere.

Spencer related: *Coffee grounds, strong female energy. A "fu... you" message — a sort of spitting on your grave kind of message. She is in and out of the house very quickly, looks through 1 or 2 cabinets and grabs the coffee. Female energy has red fingernails. Same red fingernails used on the backs of men during sex, in the throes of sexual passion. She knows the house. Looks in 1 or 2 places and dumps coffee grounds all over the floor. Again, this is a "fu... you" kind of message.*

I asked about another anomaly that had me perplexed: the wet footprints that were found in the hall outside Charley's office the night he was killed. ATF said they were left by Charley. They [ATF agents] claim he went to his office to clear out some things and get his gun before he drove out to Clyattville-Nankin Road to kill himself. But it wasn't raining until after he was dead and they were not found until 2:30 am.

Wet footprints in the hall outside Charley's office. Not Charley's. Someone from the crime scene, someone who went there to go through his things searching for something. Not Charley's prints. They belong to the man who went to look for "it." They do not present what "it" is at this point, only that the prints are not Charley's, someone from the crime scene that night.

I wrote as fast as I could to keep up with the rate of information that came flowing through. On the way home Jules and I discussed what Spencer had shared. As she grappled with what she had seen and heard, I pondered the comment Charley had made about my thoughts on going back to school. Traffic in Atlanta sucked, and twenty minutes after we had started our trip home, we slowed to a crawl and three minutes later to a stop. Even though we had more than an hour back to where she lived, we decide that a stiff drink would not be out of line.

I knew the experience had affected her more than she was willing to show, and as we passed a truck that read Phoenix Produce on it, I thought her eyes would pop out of her head. "My brother would never believe this shit," she whispered, barely believing it herself.

"No, probably not." The smile left her face, so I tried to lighten the mood. "Hey...maybe I misinterpreted your father's confirmation. Maybe it had nothing to do with school. Maybe he was trying to tell me something else."

She looked at me quizzically. "What? To be a truck driver instead?" she smirked.

"Noooo," I stalled. "Maybe I'm supposed to be selling bananas!" Tension lowered, we laughed until the semi next to us moved forward and the building behind it came in to view.

It read: PHOENIX UNIVERSITY, with a banner underneath that said "ENROLL NOW!" Two exits later we pulled off and ordered a bottle of wine.

CHAPTER EIGHT

After the last session with Spencer, Jules and I decided a trip to Valdosta would be a good idea. Even though March had come in like a lamb, it roared out like a lion. As a writer, I needed to be able see where she had grown up, needed to see the house that Charley had left and not returned to. I wanted to ride out to the road where he had breathed his last breath and listen for the echo of his final heartbeat. Jules decided to bring along her teenage son Cole, and since Don was still on the mend, I was grateful to have another man in the mix. Schedules synchronized, we decided spring break would be best week for all concerned.

We headed down on March 26th, 2010, and if it was any indication of how the rest of the weekend would be, then there would not be enough coffee to get me through it. The drive down was crammed with both relaxing and anxious moments. I filled in most of the bald patches of scenery with conversation and quiet reverie, reviewing interviews in my head and mulling over tidbits of information received which had yet to be clearly understood. I concentrated on the holes of that night. There were still too many inconsistencies between several sources that needed to be laid out upon the proverbial table and vetted before I felt I could move forward with any confidence. Some gave a different view of the body and placement than what had been recorded in print. Some had no idea at all, while others stood defiant that theirs was the empirical true representation. Was this a case of overactive ego — misguided intentions, misinformation, and/or blatant deception? That many years out, it was hard to conjecture why there had become so many variations on the theme. I kept the private score to myself and tallied the number of times I revisited each of the descriptions that made no sense.

Mile markers clicked their way past my peripheral vision as I made another mental invitation for Charley to step up to the plate and guide where and when he willed. When we left at 8:00 that morning with coffee in hand, the day was pleasant with a touch of cloudiness that lifted the longer I drove. By the time we hit Tifton, the sun was bright, and I had received my first of many mysterious phone calls. Someone was overheard chatting up a storm at the local barber shop about somebody in the deceased's family wanting the case reopened and somebody else thought that I should know about it. This individual was reported as saying he didn't know why no one had bothered to contact him in the first place, as he had information — firsthand information about that night.

Cautious, I decided not to immediately alert Jules and took down the information to consider my options. I had been warned, not once, but twice already to back off and leave this thing alone. As the miles melted away, I wondered just how serious the consequences of the warning might be. According to my caller, this person had information that I had been unsuccessful in garnering elsewhere. In fact, if what I had been told was true, he might just be holding the only remaining file on this case in existence. I thought about the caller who had initiated the warnings. Well intentioned or not, a warning had been made, but I was willing to risk whatever consequence to retrieve what this man had. How ironic, I thought. The one person I wanted to approach, but had been told to avoid turned out to be the one person I should have been searching for all along. I asked my informer to hold on, took a deep breath, and motioned to my husband I needed my notebook and a pen.

As the man on the other end talked, I found a break in the traffic to pull over into a parking lot of a Burger King and took the remaining information from my source. Still in park, I took another deep breath and made the first of two phone calls. The first number I dialed volunteered no response. With no voice mail attached, I hung up and moved onto the second number. Heart pounding, palms sweating, I punched the numbers in while eyeing the buildup of traffic from the side of the road. The number rang several times before an answering machine kicked in. Disappointed but somewhat relieved, I could now compose myself better. I left a brief message and asked for a return call if interested. Seven exits later, my contact returned the call.

Just as I pulled off the ramp to head into downtown Valdosta, a deep voice reverberated through the phone with hesitant, but certain compliance. Yes, there was a file on Charley. Yes, there were photos of the crime scene that night. Yes, there was further information he could share with me, and yes, he would show it all to me if the family wanted. While he spoke about other cases of local renown, I forced myself to breathe and stay in the lane. The last place I thought I would find the missing links in this investigation turned out to be the first place I should have looked: the files of the Deputy Sheriff of Lowndes County from 1966.

By the time I pulled into the hotel parking lot, I had secured the opportunity to meet with him the following day. The rest of the afternoon was for another important meeting with men whose entire lives had revolved in and around the law and who shared two common threads: they were all still alive and they had all known Charley.

I was still reeling from the phone call when we got to the hotel and poured ourselves into two rooms that reminded me of spring breaks of yesteryear. With a husband still on the mend from recent shoulder surgery and a family crisis partially under my belt, I was ready to unpack and gather my breath. It felt surreal in the way things continued to unfold. Like the Fibonacci scale, the pattern repeated itself over and over: one clue, one confirmation at a time. I couldn't help but notice how numerology played a rather prominent role in all of this.

Note that Charley's murder was committed in 1966. His daughter was only six in 1966. The fourth horseman of Revelation 6 is Death. Charley and Kaye were married 19 years. Kaye lived for 19 years after his death. Charley was 44 when he died. It has been 44 years since his death. If one were patient and knowledgeable enough to do an in-depth numerical study of this, I imagine the other resulting patterns might stagger the mind. What's more, master numbers continued to figure into the reception of clues and confirmations. I had much to learn.

Warned ahead of time by Spencer that no one I would meet throughout my trip would be by chance, I kept mindful of all introductions made and hoped they would prove fruitful. Thus far, we had been in town less than two minutes and I had agreed to an interview with the caller who claimed to have the original case file, including crime scene photos. Having scheduled that, I began getting interview materials ready. The long drive hadn't left me a lot of time in between obligations. There was little more than an hour before the next meeting, so we headed with Jules and Cole into town to get our bearings and a quick lunch.

As it turned out, there was a place just a couple of blocks from the Historical Society building. It was a diner Jules had found a year ago on her last "fishing" trip. Pressed for time and a decent review, we committed to a light lunch to tide us over till later that night. As we entered, I tried to bear in mind the warning. Halfway through lunch while I was drooling over an antique typewriter they had once used to type out daily menus, my husband pointed out a photo three feet to the left of it. It was a man in uniform: a law enforcement uniform. It was too obvious, so I asked who it was. The waitress gave us a brief history of the diner. She said it was her grandfather, who had been in the police department at the time. I looked closer at the photo and asked what year it had been taken. Just then my phone received a text from Spencer.

The waitress replied he would have been a lieutenant (Lt.) then as the photo had been taken back in the 60's. My head began to swim. Tall, dark, handsome, and in his fifties, this uniformed figure glared back at me in mock defiance. Spencer had cautioned me, "If you are wracking your brain over clues, then you are not on the right track. It will be an 'aha moment.' That's how this thing works. Information will come to you when it is time. It will be as though someone had dropped it in your lap." I looked again at the photo. A lieutenant — the abbreviation is "Lt."

Could this be Charley's reference to LT from the first session? I noted the time and the direct line of vision to me from the photo across the counter and wondered if Spencer's warning had been right on the mark. This man may have been a lieutenant at the time, but then so had four or five of the others I suspected had something to do with Charley's murder that night. Suddenly I had a sinking but exhilarating feeling that nothing that weekend would be by chance — nothing. Spencer had been right. Everything that could happen to me in the next 48 hours had to be looked at with the same discerning eye.

I took a deep breath. It wasn't my lap, but it was pretty darn close. Seven feet from it, to be exact. I left most of my salad wilting away on my plate, and when the waitress asked me if something was wrong, I lied. I told her I was full and then waited patiently till we got outside before I mentioned my suspicions to Jules. It made me sad in a way. Although I relished a shot at another clue, these were really nice people who had no idea what was going through my mind. I kept a smile on my face as I studied the photo and returned a text message to Spencer.

The rest of my crew finished lunch in good humor, unaware of what had just been imparted. I made a mental note to get more information about the diner at the Historical Society. There was only 12 minutes left to make it on time, and I did not want to be late. While they took care of the bill, I used the restroom, then headed towards the door. Focused so much on the upcoming meeting, I completely missed the last photo on the wall as I walked out. Thank God my husband and Jules's son did not. It bore the name of the man in the uniform and another man by the same surname receiving some sort of an award. The boys mentioned it when they got in the car and asked if the name rang a bell for either of us. I said no, but the abbreviation for lieutenant sure did.

I explained that the man in the photo hit several of the high water marks of Charley's reference. He was older than G by approximately 20 years. He had been affiliated with law enforcement. He had position, influence, and some money. When I texted his name to Spencer, it came back *"They show me animal references. Tied to G."* I made a note in my binder, then asked if Jules still had the funeral registry book with her. Frozen in thought, she gripped the steering wheel and mentally went through her luggage.

I prompted her again about the funeral directory and she nodded, motioning towards the rear of the vehicle. Her son Cole took it from behind his seat and began to flip pages, searching for the registry. Most of the handwriting was difficult to read, but he finally found a match. Then out of the blue, Jules announced she had seen the same last name with a nickname in front of it: the nickname of "Red."

I was confused for a minute. Had the photo across from me at the counter been the photo of Charley's LT, or the red-headed man who he presented as being the *"red-headed go-to guy"*— the man who helped the shooter do the cover up of his murder? While Cole searched for more names, I thought about the photo. Even though it had been in black and white, this man could not have had red hair; the grain of ink had been too dark. The light changed, the car pulled out of its slip, and my spirits waned. How was I to decipher all this properly if every time I got close, another truckload of misinformation got dumped into the mix?

Just then my husband said, "Could it have been the other man?" The car grew silent. "What other man?" I asked.

"The second man in the photo on the way out the door, the one you and Jules missed in your haste to get back on the road." My heart jumped. Another photo? I had been chasing the identity of the man with the red hair for several weeks. Cole looked again for the name starting with "Red," but could not find it. Frustrated, I begged him to look once more. I told him to check the very back pages where they had listed the floral arrangements. Bingo! There he was in ink. *"# (77) Wreath with white mums, red bow, signed from "Red Devonshire and family."* Oddly enough it was just one page over from this entry: *"# (90) Wreath with white mums, 2 glads, red carnations, and bow signed from 'A Friend' (G)."*

We pulled into the parking lot of the Historical Society as I tried to catch my breath.

Minutes later, I composed myself and walked through heavy wooden doors into Valdostan history. Much as I would like to have wandered around and soaked in the experience, I was immediately reminded of the room in the lower level that had gentlemen already waiting. It was a beautiful old building, filled with a ripe patina of dust and charm. I made a mental note to spend an afternoon there on my next trip down. Having no idea how the afternoon would go, I let the others entire first. We took the elevator down one level. Breathing deeply, I tried to reestablish my equilibrium. By the time the elevator door opened, my mind had successfully switched gears and I was ready to calmly take in more information.

From the elevator alcove in the corner, we walked into another large room that held several displays pertaining to local history. Having brought my laptop for reference convenience, I situated myself at a table just above a floor outlet. My husband set his up there as well so that we might research in tandem if necessary any information that my files did not already contain. Unencumbered by gadgets, Jules and Cole set themselves up across from me. Furniture adjusted and additional chairs brought in, we were ready.

At this point I noticed a fellow who stood with starched shirt, necktie, and pleated pants reading a display. He was straight out of the sixties, and his G-man look made me think he had to be one of my guys. When he turned and I saw a shirt boasting a pocket protector and a face hosting black-rimmed glasses, there was just no other way to it. I smiled, shook his hand. He introduced himself as Winston Wahlberg and told me he had come along at the request of another man I had been talking to on a regular basis, Edgar Patterson. Once seated, another man joined the fray. This was my most staunch ally, a noble fellow with a booming voice: Edgar Patterson. He had brought his son, another retired agent, and his wife as well. Introductions made all around, I asked them all to take a seat.

Two men down, I turned and spied another tall man who had entered the room. He now stood alone in front of a display case. Tall, fair, and athletic in build, he kept his back to me for several minutes as he studied the wall before him. I hesitated, but Saturday afternoon perusing a storyboard about the history of cotton did not look like this guy's natural bailiwick, so I sallied forth to introduce myself. Once I identified him as the retired State Trooper Damon Cummings, I invited him to sit at the table with the others while I waited for more to arrive.

When we were certain that no one else would be making an entrance, I began the discussion by thanking them for their time and efforts. Everyone comfortable and recorders on, I introduced them to Charley's daughter, Jules. A brief silence filled the air and then suddenly a flurry of smiles and handshakes rounded the table. I covered the basics of the case first. What had been public fodder, what they knew, what I knew. What they didn't know I knew, I kept to myself. I next asked for clarification on some issues I had not been able to ferret out myself. While they conversed, I secretly texted the name of my first suspected "Red" herring to my psychic/medium detective.

The initial nickname of "Red" had been given to me by one of the men in the room, specifically the tall, athletic one who had once been a carrot top himself: Damon Cummings. I thought this prudent before I placed a larger target on a back of another new soul. It came back with a negative impression, not only from Spencer, but the rest of the group who concurred there was no relevance. No one even knew such an individual, except for the man with the athletic build who had suggested him in the first place: Damon Cummings.

Curious, I threw out my new second name, the one we had tracked from the diner photos and back pages of the funeral book. Eyes flashed with instant recognition: another "ah-ha moment." Conversation broke loose with details and fuzzy recollections. Yes, he too had red hair. Yes, he was from the other side of the river. Yes, he had a huge business, was very wealthy, had lots of power. As they bantered about one another's reveries, I sent this new name into the cosmos for my psychic to review. Minutes went by as we discussed other details of the case, and then a buzz tweaked my jeans. I begged them to continue, then sat and holding my phone under the table lip, read the reply privately.

"I am shown a hammer and a nail. Not sure. Could be hitting the nail on the head or another meaning."

I kept pace with the conversation while Jules spoke to them collectively about her father and that night. At a lull in the conversation, I texted Spencer back. Could it mean "The final nail in the coffin? Or related to construction?"

I had no idea when or what the response would be and so moved the conversation forward. As I listened and took notes, more details started to pour from lips both innocent and soon to be recognized as tainted. Both sides of the table were hedging; it was time to break loose. I motioned to Jules and she took the floor. She thanked them for their time and then spoke about her knowledge of her parents' marital problems to ease the flow of information from men who were obviously uncomfortable sharing what they believed might be gossip and hearsay. In the interest of allowing them latitude to introduce the possible motives of passion or jealousy, I inserted that I knew more than I had been sharing thus far. My reference was to the instability of Charley's marriage. But before I could add such a suffix the tall, athletic gentleman across from me leaned in smiling and said, "So do I."

It was an eerie sort of smile that felt acrid and patronizing. My phone hummed, distracting me for a second. I produced a thin smile in response, and he sat back into his haunches, glaring. To stall, I asked them to discuss collectively what they had heard about the layout of the crime scene that night. While listening with half an ear, I checked my phone for Spencer's reply to the "nail in the coffin or construction related" suggestion. It held one word: *possibly.*

I kept this to myself and redirected the conversation to the man whose crooked smile had unnerved me. In previous conversations, he had claimed to be the very first responder. Print media and hearsay contradicted one another, so I needed further documentation. Knowing that in less than 24 hours I would have my hands on crime scene photos to confirm or deny, I wanted more. I wanted eyewitness testimony to round out my theory of a cover up. If his description matched the papers but not the photos, then we had reason to believe in the staging and cover up theory.

This guy said he was first on scene and had the goods, so I let him take the floor. Unknown to the others, I also had Spencer's interpretation of the scene Charley had described in our first session for reference to bounce against. To clear up any confusion, I handed Mr. Crooked Smile my notepad and asked him to recreate the scene he walked into that night: the location of the vehicle, the distance between the body and the bridge, the exact placement of the arms, hands, and gun, etc. My caution for him to be precise was well founded. He took it with a grain of salt and began to draw the margin lines of the road.

I watched intently his placement of the car within the framing of the scene since the beginning this man's testimony didn't jive with what information was on record. As he spoke about what he had seen, a fellow participant asked him to confirm the identity of another first responder that night. The answer came swiftly. There was no other first responder other than himself and another gentleman no one recognized. When my ally insisted that he had been a neighbor of this additional man and believed him when he told him he had even inspected Charley's revolver with the odd placement of the spent shell, the man with the forced smile rather forcefully insisted that such confidences had been nothing but an act of bravado and lies. (A record of this is on tape… along with his drawing.)

With increasing angst, I texted another name to Spencer and waited for her reply. When the sketch was complete and the verbal description recorded, my phone hummed once again, and I let my attentions follow while they all discussed the differences between what they had heard and what Mr. Crooked Smile had drawn. I picked up the notepad, took a closer look, and then down at my side to see what she had written.

My phone read *"Dark.... Wow. I actually got Grim Reaper which I have never seen before."*

To the best of my knowledge Spencer had been using her psychic abilities since she was in her early teens. Now in her thirties, that meant for almost two decades she had worked hundreds of crime cases, untold personal contact cases. I myself had known of more current endeavors such as working with C.C.I.R.I. on the Boston Strangler case, the Moore's Ford Bridge Massacre case, and the notable Amber Haggerman (Amber Alert) case, and in all of that she had never seen anything this dark.

I rubbed at the screen of my phone and caught my breath. My knees began to buckle. Bile rose like a geyser in my throat, but I swallowed it down hard and tried to keep it from others in the room. Concerned, my husband tapped my thigh, and I looked up and across the table at the man who was just putting down my pen. I smiled weakly and reached to drag the sheet across the table to have a closer look. His jaundiced fingers gripped the corner of the page, and as I placed my hand at the edge, our hands made contact. His hand felt cold to the touch and his long fingers calloused. A chill ran down my spine, and I shivered in a room that probably registered at least 78 degrees.

"May I?" I asked, trying to keep my voice as even as possible as I tried to ease the paper from his grip.

"Sure," he grinned, and the yellow on his teeth made me queasy. His fingers released the page one digit at a time for effect, but I took the bait in stride.

"Thanks... I've got it now," I answered to cover my awkwardness. His drawing showed the car off the shoulder, just the way Spencer had seen it in her vision from Charley. When I brought my eyes up to meet his, something akin to recognition flashed in his eyes, and I suspected he knew I knew that he was telling the truth. I held an even expression as his smile stretched into a toothier smirk.

"This is exactly the way I found him," he said, and his eyes held mine as I waited for the other shoe to drop. Two seconds later, he pulled his fingers from the page, licked his lips, and closed the conversation effectively with…

 "And I never lie."

CHAPTER NINE

After we discussed several other issues regarding the notepad drawing, I redirected the conversation and dropped my bombshell. I told them since it was mutually agreed that Charley did not commit suicide, I wished to share something further. I then told them I had been informed by a reliable source that seven to eight years after Charley's death, a detective stepped forward (Billy Burgess) and told my source that he had seen evidence that proved that it was homicide, but that it would not look good for Charley and that he had been shot in self-defense. For the first time since we had begun, they fell silent.

The man with the black-rimmed glasses became openly agitated with me. Not certain what part of my information had inflamed him, I continued to watch his face as I told them that this individual also chose to do nothing with that information as he felt it wouldn't have done anybody any good. Charley would still be dead and countless innocent lives would be damaged. All around the table, expletives of every sort poured forth. They then began to badger me. Peppering me with the standard who, where, when…why?

At that point I did not feel the necessity to share my source and asked them only to respond to the information. Was it possible? Had they ever heard the same? What did they know about the initial messenger other than the fact that he too was now dead and gone? Would he have been a credible source? Why would it have looked bad for Charley? Who was this source? How had I gotten my information? The queries were endless, the answers finite and limiting. In an effort to let them plow their way through embroiled emotions, I let them simmer on this topic for a few minutes, watching the smiles fade from their lips.

The man with the crooked teeth then took center stage and produced another theory about moonshiners taking Charley out.

Endless threads of conjecture began to weave themselves into a tapestry of conspiracy. While I shared in many of their suspicions, the clock continued to tick towards closing time and I could not afford the detour of derailment. Blindsiding them with another blast of information was not my intent, but I had things I needed yet to discover and time was short. I broke through a reverie about the numbers game *Bolitas* and a black nightclub owner (Bugman McFallon), who figured prominently into the local scene, by introducing the topic of the hidden porn tapes and an envelope that referenced one particular film. Faces went blank and I could hear my pulse in the silence that followed. I waited for a second before commenting further about the envelope and the invoice admittedly sent to a post office box in Charley's name. They looked at one another and then asked if I had actually seen an invoice.

I nodded and tried not to feed their embarrassment. There I was in the midst of gentlemen my father's age and without pause or blush had spoken a word outside what I assumed was their common vocabulary. No one spoke for a second, and then I told them of the rumors about the parties over the pawn shop and the ones out at the clubhouse. With that, the clubhouse and its eclectic persuasions of entertainment took center stage and we were off and running again with wild tales of sex parties and illegal gambling — stories I will remember, stories I will have to investigate further at a later date.

As the clock raced past five and we moved towards closing ceremonies of hugs and photos, I thanked them profusely and then asked for one final favor. Had the last two and half hours not been enough? I asked if any of them might act as escort to the Clyattville-Nankin Road where Charley's body and car had been found. My ally with the booming voice stepped forward immediately and volunteered to act as guide. With the others set free, we made a promise to meet in the parking lot. Once our notes and equipment were gathered and we were well outside the building, I shared my Grim Reaper text with Jules, her son, and my husband. Jules began to put the car in reverse and then paused to ask if we should be afraid.

As we pulled onto the road, I sent a text to Spencer asking that very thing and then laughed saying "not until the psychic tells me we should be!" Ten minutes later we turned onto Clyattville-Nankin Road, heading towards the spot where Charley spent the final moments of his life, when my phone hummed again: *"Be aware. "Trust your gut instinct."* I checked with my gut, then placed my hands on my knees to stop them from shaking and smiled back at Jules.

"We're fine," I said. "Just fine. Keep driving."

It was the first time I felt the need to keep something from her since we had started this thing over a year ago.

CHAPTER TEN

On the drive over, my ally (retired ATF agent Edgar Patterson) had filled the minutes with personal remembrances of Charley, some local moonshine history involving the immediate area, and what he had been able to glean from others about that night. As we neared the hallowed ground, Jules instinctively slowed the car to 35 mph while we each began our personal descent into October 1966, and I feared it wouldn't be too difficult to do. Although the better part of the ride had shown rural aspects of Valdosta as more progressive, we were now in an area that seemed stilted by time. As the sun moved lower in the sky, the Georgia pines rose higher to meet it, sending their shadows to stretch long and exhausted in the road ahead of us. Emotionally, we too felt stretched and exhausted, but the day wasn't over yet.

I thought about what Spencer had sent in the last text message. The Grim Reaper meant only one thing: death. As Jules slowed to a crawl, I sent another message to Spencer and asked if the image was in direct correlation to Charley. The answer came back swiftly enough: "*Yes.*" Try as I might to remain in the moment, I could not seem to let go of the fear that in my eagerness to pursue this case I might have just placed us all in great danger, for the name I had sent was of a man still living. I did my best to keep an even demeanor. Spencer had written earlier that afternoon to trust my gut and I was trying. It was just that my gut was so tied up in knots by the time we maneuvered into the bend that I was having a hard time deciphering what it really meant to say.

When in doubt, always remain calm, I say. So I focused on what was just outside my window and concentrated on letting go of what was inside my head. Spring had just begun to tiptoe across the southern portion of the state, and while the afternoon had been hot, there was a coolness beginning to settle into the air and that suited me just fine. My mind had been filled with so much information in the last several hours that I was beginning to feel claustrophobic inside my own body.

Outside my window, the sun continued its dive into the treetops as we rounded a long curve, broken up by several small bridges in succession. As Jules searched for a place to light, I tried to imagine what the landscape might have looked like before suburbia's crush. There wasn't much traffic, but there wasn't much room to pull over either. Just past the last small bridge before the river, we drove onto a roughly poured asphalt pad some twenty feet beyond the curb. We got out one by one in silence. While my husband and Cole took off towards the river to pace off the distance between the bridge and where reports had claimed the body to be, our chaperone educated us that the path beyond the rope in front of us was most likely the same one that led into the woods where a clubhouse for the local law enforcement once existed and also a hidden body of water called Montgomery Lake. This was the clubhouse in question referred to in our earlier meeting of the day, but perhaps not the clubhouse I should have been focusing on. Jules took photos of the area while I tried to take it all in from another angle: Charley's.

With the recent drawing from my notebook, I began to search the terrain for where Charley's car might have been located. If I followed common thought, the car would have to have been in the right (westbound) lane and not half on the shoulder or even completely off the road as suggested by the man with the crooked teeth as there was no shoulder wide enough to house such a vehicle back then. I looked at the drawing again. There was no way he could have been correct. Too many pertinent elements had been omitted, yet it had certain fundamentals that mirrored Spencer's drawing from the first session. I knew then that whatever I would see in the report and crime photos the next morning would either confirm or deny what I was physically able to produce this afternoon.

In order to afford enough clearance for a 1966 Ford Sedan, I had to keep moving further eastward back to the second small bridge.

Even then, it would have been damn near impossible to pull off. The boys continued to count footage and ultimately ended up closer to the same small second bridge that had caught my attention. As they counted the last few steps, I recalled something else Spencer had said in that session. Charley had told her after the impact at the front right tire and the deadly blow to his skull, he presented as being moved four to five feet and propped up on something of another texture, perhaps a tree, a stone, or something concrete. I looked at the lip of the second small bridge where the embankment peeled away from the shoulder. The bridge had concrete parapets that supported the guardrails that followed. Could this have been what Charley had been propped up against while the blood from his fatal head wound flowed down his back into the right back pocket of his pants where his wallet lay? Remember, the interior of the wallet had blood in between the photo shields. You cannot get blood to settle into that location if the body was not upright for an extended amount of time. So at some point he had to have been upright, a fact which means the fatal blow was not committed in the same place the body was ultimately staged.

As the light began to shrink away from us, we each spent a private moment in commemoration and reverie. I could not imagine what Jules might have been feeling at this point. To know that the road beneath her feet and the pines just beyond her reach held a memory of her father she would never be privy to was almost unbearable for me to suffer. I tried to think of the scene in chaotic darkness, with the sounds of the night broken by the syncopation of rain, the rancorous screeching of Charley's mistress, and the abusive assaults as the shooter attacked and threatened to maliciously bring Charley to heel. Deeply moved, I climbed back into the car and kept silent vigil while the remainder of the trip was filled with further background information and a trip to the infamous four-way stop where Charley often met those with information and where Bugman McFallon's nightclub had once ruled the night. So far my trip had garnered more information in seven hours than I had been able to unearth in the previous six months. Spencer was right. No one I would meet that weekend would be by chance, and everything I would see was for a reason.

As the night progressed and we left the scene, nothing could have prepared us for what was about to happen next. In the twelve months prior I had done everything I could think of to track down documents about that night or the ensuing investigation, but had garnered little beyond the GBI Crime Lab report and what I already had in Kaye's files. What was about to take place was nothing shy of a miracle as far as I was concerned, and I could scarcely contain myself. Jules had made contact with an old family friend as a way of distraction, and the evening had been spent out with intermittent review of the day's events and information. Two glasses of wine later, the tension in my shoulder eased, but not for long. I had saved the texts from Spencer on my phone to record the following morning, but could not leave them alone. I held my phone below the tablecloth and shifted from *Sent* to *Receive* at least five times during the course of dinner, checking and rechecking what had been shared and revealed.

I watched Jules's son. He had been freaked out by the Grim Reaper statement earlier that afternoon, and it still showed in his face. Hell, I had been freaked out too and to this hour I still have the text on my phone, which, I might add, came through at exactly 3:33 in the afternoon. You've got to love the numerology in this thing! Dinner finished, we called it a day and headed back to the hotel.

The next morning we met with the son of the original LCSD Deputy Sheriff in the investigation in his office. The stack of six photos lay in the center of the table as our host began to verbally prepare us for what we were about to see. As his fingers touched the corner of the original print, I watched the smile fade from Jules's face. On her say, our host flipped the first of six photos. The granular esthetics of the black and white print was the first thing that hit you. Then suddenly your eye adjusted to the foreign medium and the content took central focus. Jules's face remained blank for several seconds as she gently fingered the rib of the photograph. I asked if she was ok, but she muttered something inaudible, so I waited. When she finally lowered the paper, I offered condolences. We remained hushed as our host reached for another photo, but waited to flip it as she continued to ponder the one before her.

"That's him. That's my daddy," she whispered and pointed to the broken figure in the center of the film. Enough seen, she handed it across the table under the low-hanging lamp. Just as the photo crossed directly under the exposed bulb, I caught a glimpse of Charley's body and could not imagine what was going through her head.

It felt so surreal to see the man with the moldy skin looking like a cardboard cutout for *L.A. Confidential*, but no more surreal than the image of my own father at 82, lying in state ten months earlier. I spent the next several minutes studying the monochromatic image before handing it off to my husband. It was hard to take in the enormity of the moment. The crumpled and bloodied soul in the photo no more resembled the compliant 8 x10 companion who sat atop my writing desk than did the man with the swollen hand and reconfigured jaw lying in the casket I had knelt at months earlier. Secretly I prayed that kind disparity would provide the anesthesia of disassociation necessary to save Jules from the crushing heartache I feared would settle in on her hours later.

Our host had winced at sharing them with her, but true to her mother's genetics, Jules viewed each one that followed with grace and composure. Six, five, four, three, two, one — they passed from her hands to mine, to my husband's, and then lastly to Cole, who held an expression equal to that of his mother's throughout the viewing. While making additional copies, our host continued to educate us as to his file's origin and the assigned officer's statements in regards to what we could verify before us in Kodachrome. None of it made sense if you were prone to linear thinking. Yet nothing in this case had ever added up rationally. In the light of what we had learned the day before, its lack of linear logic made perfect sense.

After the initial shock was over, it was difficult for me to continue to review them without objectively assessing them in terms of evidence. I understood it was important for Jules and Cole to be able to process them emotionally, but for me, I needed to disengage emotionally and look with an eye towards what I knew and what Charley had told me through Spencer in the first session. The man in those pictures was Charley, but he was so much more than Charley. He was my roadmap to the MOT — the *moment of truth* — and I knew deep down he would forgive me the breech of mourning etiquette.

Extricated from the collective experience, I was able to acknowledge the location of the car and its placement in the road. It didn't match our first responder's drawing or his verbal description of the crime scene. Nor did it jive with certain aspects of Spencer's interpretation. Next, I charted the location of the flashlight and his fedora in the road, two items ironically not mentioned nor drawn by either our first responder nor by Spencer in the first session. I made mental notes of the placement and direction of the body, of Charley's feet and how the tips of the shoes caught at the edge of the asphalt, his soles angled at odds for someone unless he had been dragged into that position. Scuff and scrape marks were on the outside of the heel backs in a vertical direction, suggesting the body was dragged backwards from one point over rough terrain and/or asphalt to another. His arms were equally peculiar in their assignment in respect to the hidden gun beneath his belly. Everything in the photographs spoke volumes about the absurdity of assumption, including the peripheral images which bled through the edges of the margin with equal importance.

Take the car, for instance, and how it sidled up perfectly to the center line, not to the shoulder of the road as described by our interviewee. And the shoulder itself: its lack of raking pitch, lack of muddy border, and proximity to the car and yet to nothing else, including the second smaller bridge.

And then there were the wounds...

One could not see the wound under the chin, as his arrangement precluded its discovery even though several photos tried to address this from different angles. While four obsessed about the body, only one captured the graphic display of the near exit wound on the upper left of his skull. Another chronicled the entry wound appearing at the bottom right of the skull, just below the right ear. Finally, empirical evidence that would clear up the GBI Crime Lab report which had mentioned only the area of bullet retrieval for the supposed first and then supposed "second and fatal" shot. Curiously, they had placed the wound at the temporal lobe, obviously a mistake as it appeared to originate just below that line in the right mastoid.

Even as a lay individual spending only a couple of minutes reviewing, I could see clearly that the crime scene had been vastly manipulated in haste and desperation. It was too obvious, too clumsy to have been carefully premeditated. This had indeed been a crime of passion. But whose? Perhaps this was why our first responder's description did not match a single detail before us. Either he was bold enough to be telling us the truth or naïve enough to think we would write it off to bravado. This was about ego, his and mine. There was so much in the photos for me to process and digest that I became damn near cataleptic in my examination.

It was clear now that I had misunderstood the claim by Spencer in the first session. The tremendous energy Spencer spoke of was not the entry point of the bullet, but the near exit of the bullet as it blasted its way into the skull bone and left it shattered just under the skin, but not breaking through it. Further, the entry wound on the right now confirmed correlation to the blood stains in the wallet. The blood flow could only have been direct with the body in an upright position, a fact which was now confirmed by the grains of sand and grass clippings shown along the entire backside of the victim's pants, but not his shirt. This was quantifiable proof that at some point he was propped upright and stationed on his bottom as well.

There were many other signs of contradiction between photos and testimonies given too. His belt boasted an empty holster, yet his wife said he left without carrying a weapon. No gun, no holster. Photos surrendered two major sites of pooled blood on the asphalt as appeared clearly in four of the six photos. Both blood pools were seven to ten inches apart, not only from one another, but apart and six to eighteen inches above and separated from Charley's head. How was this possible? And even more improbable, how did this improbability linger through several hours of rain?

My head wanted to explode. The blood was not even connected to the victim, and yet local law, ATF, FBI and GBI — all four law agencies signed off on suicide and wanted us to believe it plausible. I kept quiet in the presence of our host, but wanted to scream from the mountain tops "How could anyone have looked at these photos and not seen the inconsistencies that have plagued this investigation from its inception? How could you have thrown this man's carcass to the wolves and not tried to salvage his dignity and his reputation before they ripped at his flesh? I'll tell you how. There is such a thing as blind ignorance and then there's such a thing as self-preservation. It's a fairly easy guess which one we're talking about here!"

The screams bounced around inside my head with the presentation of the next three photos. I bit my lips to keep from being officious, as this man seemed so innocent of the offenses potentially caused by his father the Deputy Sheriff. His offer to share information had been so gracious that I tried not to get on my high horse about the lack of integrity in this investigation, swallowed hard, and moved onto the last photo. Our self-proclaimed first responder had sworn a blue streak the day before that a particular law officer another interviewer had lauded had not been on scene that night. Yet a fourth photo clearly showed a young State Trooper standing at the front window of Charley's government car, a Trooper that neither resembled the man with the crooked teeth who claimed he was first responder nor any other officer identified to us thus far.

At that point, I could ingest no more. I wanted to know who the mystery Trooper in the photograph was. Could he be identified and was he still alive to interview? I put the photos down. An hour later we left, Jules with a splitting headache and I with copies of everything our host had promised. And along with them, a million more questions about that night.

CHAPTER ELEVEN

There was little time to rest on our laurels, as we had one more afternoon visitation to make with a longtime citizen who had great peripheral information. Dressed in dapper attire, he answered the door and immediately told Jules how much she favored her mother. Touched by the sentiment, Jules gave him a hug. Gracious and giving, he shared his afternoon and his memories with us. While he spoke, I made notes, answered questions, and sent other names I had learned of over the weekend to Spencer for further discovery. With each response, I cataloged the corresponding comment and redirected my line of questions to our host accordingly. His stories were amazing. So much history, both fair and foul, stuffed within this town, it's a wonder the place hasn't imploded before now. That being said, we retrieved what information we could about Charley and let the man have the remainder of his day to do other things.

On the drive back, we went by way of the now infamous four-way and moved into the evening emotionally spent with one great adventure still waiting. As a writer and an artist, I am a visual creature and draw much from my surroundings. After my first session with Spencer, it became important for me to not only hear and read about how Charley died but also to see what he saw in the moments before: see the headlight beams bounce off the rain-slicked road, watch the bend in the treetops under the pressure of the encroaching storm, even to walk the asphalt dip line at the edge of the road before it burst into the saw grass shoulders that bound it. It was important — all of it, especially the bridge and the river. That way I could confidently calculate the distances that separated Charley from the three witnesses and possibly even his slayer.

Places have memories too, and they give them back if you listen long and hard enough. The last adventure for the day was perhaps even more important than being where he had died. It was being where he had lived. While the others took in the landscape in one fashion, I took it in quite another. I needed to internalize it, to make it the screensaver in my head so I could reenact the murder sequence with all the details intact for those who would come in the future to read about Charley and his last night on this earth. We left the four-way confident we had garnered as much information as possible for the day. Hours from breakfast, we looked forward to dinner and down time.

The meal was to be hosted again by Jules's friend who had opened both home and hearth to us that weekend. Guilt and personal preference bid us stop at a grocery store on the way to gather additional accoutrements for the meal. Just before the turn into Jules's old neighborhood, she instructed us about the four homes that her mother and father had built. Charley had been a contractor on the side, and while the neighborhood he began was once considered country, the lane now boasted mature architecture and magnificent oaks with flowing manes of Spanish moss that welcomed us with a gentle wave. I had seen random photos early on, but they paled in comparison. A home is a living, breathing thing. And just like my 8 x10 companion, I could not hope to learn what it remembered beneath its rafters unless I could trace its silhouette against a skyline or see out from within its windowed perspective.

As we made the turn onto Lake Drive, the sun danced atop the tree line to a cricket orchestra before she slipped into her evening gown of indigo. Charmed by the view, Jules educated us about which structures her father and mother had birthed. The four homes were all in a row, strung like stately pearls along a manicured curb. Their architecture, nostalgic and comforting, felt like a late night rerun of *Leave It to Beaver.* Seconds later we pulled into another friendly drive. Anxious to be about his world before I lost all daylight, I exited quickly from the car and skipped ahead. It was important to frame the moment in the context of what emotion I could coax from the house alone. The door, painted enamel black, was classic and echoed by scrolls of wrought iron that ran like trellises across the face of the porch. The steps were wide and inviting, making it easier to hear the whispers of phantom men waiting in hidden moonlight, quarrelling as to who would tell Kaye the tragic news when she answered the door.

A bird flew overhead, and my gaze moved vertically to the roofline. It was pleasing to the eye and sat low beneath a canopy of variegated greenery that hung heavy at the edge of the property. The house felt balanced between its length and height and hugged the sky with just the right measure of light and shadow in between. To the right, a huge oak squatted amid gnarled roots and bore the birthmark of childhood: a swing. To the left, another massive oak, and just beyond a carport, hidden behind open brickwork that cast patterns of dappled sunlight across its floor. I felt Charley there the most. There I could smell the scent of masculine home ownership: car oil, mower clippings, and sawdust, all tinged with sulfur, sweat, and salt. He was there…watching and waiting for me to set things right. I closed my eyes and breathed him in, renewing my promise to Jules.

As if Friday and Saturday's deluge hadn't been enough, Sunday proved latently to be just as productive. The morning broke with a mist that seemed to cloud the skies as much as our brains. The weekend had proven to be everything I had hoped and more. With the photos burning a hole in my bag, we set out to get copies made. It is difficult to get such copied without the questioning eyes of those who must process them. We tried two places and finally found an Office Max staff member who was willing and mindful of what we were trying to accomplish. Several sets of copies later, we met Jules and her son for breakfast. Hugs and instructions dispersed, my husband and I hit the road for a few hours and a final stop before we could head north from Atlanta.

Weeks earlier I had gotten information about a retired ATF agent who had written two books about his experiences. I ordered them and had hoped they might come in before my trip, but such is the wait for online publications. Contacts had been made before the trip. Did you know or know of Charley? What had you heard? Who might still be alive to contact? My litany became a mantra. While this agent had spent the bulk of his time in North Georgia and the Atlanta area, I had hopes that he might have heard something about this case that would be new. He was gracious in his response. Yes, he knew Charley. Yes, he had worked with him a time or two. Yes, he would talk to me, but no, he felt he had nothing more he could add to what I already knew. I took the shot just the same and asked if I could swing by on my way back from Valdosta.

The rain cooperated with moderation and made for more ambience than annoyance on the ride back up I-75. Quiet and content at the driver's seat, I heard the constant drone of the windshield wipers, which provided white noise for thinking. While my husband napped, I ran over every piece of information I could mentally retrieve from the past three days of interviews. The man with the crooked teeth still perplexed me. The confidence he showed with answers that matched nothing else baited further, but I could not afford to get sidetracked by ego, so I concentrated on what I could verify.

Three and a half hours later, I placed a call and confirmed that my appointment was still viable. Three and a half hours after that, I was back on the road with two autographed books and a wish for success. Charles Weems was an interesting fellow and his wife M.L. a gracious host. I learned more that day about the kind of man it took to do what Charley did, and in that regard I walked away rich with information, but no further ahead with clues.

On the last leg of the road trip I pondered what it really was I was supposed to have taken from that interview. The two books lay in the back of the car, and I promised myself I would try to read more than I would write in the next few weeks to see if perhaps I had overlooked something in my notes. I couldn't get my thoughts to tear away from the text about the Grim Reaper. No matter what other information came in about this individual, you couldn't trump a card like that. The Grim Reaper meant death, and Spencer had presented that it was in direct correlation to Charley, even though she could not get ultimate confirmation from him that this person had been the shooter. The process of this blows my mind, but Spencer says that sometimes they will not answer a question yes or no; there must be discovery and journey involved. I thought it boiled down to a matter of ethereal semantics and was losing my sense of humor fast.

The closer we got to home the clearer the skies, but not my brain. It was almost too much to take in at one time. Jules called to let us know that she had taken the original photos to get better copies than the copy of copies we had been forced to accept. Fortunately for her, local law paved the way so as not to violate anyone's sensibilities when the contents of the photos were seen. I thought about the endless parade of phone calls, emails, and letters I had sent to every state and federal program I could think of to get information about this investigation and how they all had nothing they could share. Then with one phone call, we had scored the motherlode.

Either Charley had a heck of a sense of humor or he was pacing me. I thought about Mr. Weems again. Charley would not have placed him in my path unless he had information to divulge to me through him. I said a small prayer for patience. Spencer had promised two things: that no one I would meet that weekend would be by chance and that information would be dropped into my lap. I bit my lip and tried to imagine what Charley had in mind. Though Mr. Weems had been a fascinating subject, I could not find the nugget of information I felt would catapult me onto a new path. I baited Charley and told him he was slacking. Two weeks later, he proved me wrong. Charles Weems had a great deal of information to share with me…he just didn't know it at the time and neither did I.

Two weeks after the trip to Valdosta, a child of mine had succumbed to violent seizures at a video shoot in Atlanta and had stopped breathing. She was admitted to an area hospital and kept in the Critical Care Unit for five days. For five days I slept in chairs, ate cold food, drank bitter coffee, and stared at machines that beeped and screamed incessantly throughout the night. Because of the unknown nature of her seizures, television was out of the question. In an effort to keep my sanity, I asked my husband to bring both of Weems's books to me. I didn't want my laptop there for fear it might be stolen in the moments when I was asked to leave the room, and the truth was I wasn't certain I could have formed a cohesive thought in ink. So instead of writing, I read… and read…and read in between her seizures, sedations, and my internal hysteria.

Divorced from normalcy and regular routine, my mind was free to concentrate on reading. I devoured page after page, hoping that somewhere in all of the hours I was trying to fill I might stumble across something of value. Chapter after chapter was filled with exciting escapades of ATF agents raiding stills and running down moonshiners through cow pastures and piney woods under moonlight. Deprived of sleep for so many days, your mind begins to wander. Random thoughts cascade and fill the crevices left in between your eyelids where sleep once used to dwell. Charles Weems was a hell of a guy. After twenty or so chapters, I noticed that there were about a million guys named Charley back then. Honestly, it seems as though you couldn't swing a dead cat around southern Georgia and not take out four or five of them at a time. Through it all, I tried to keep a keen eye towards other names and locations, hoping that something in this guy's memoirs would send up a flare. And then there on page 172 it began. By the end of page 173, I was convinced I had found the reason I was meant to meet this man. It was so subtle I almost missed it. Three days into my nightmare, I found what Charley had wanted Weems to show me. It was so obvious; I read the pages over three times. I looked at the clock. It was an obscene hour, but nonetheless I made a phone call to share my joy. I could barely breathe.

During one of my conversations in Valdosta, a person of interest told me a story about being threatened by a local sheriff. In this conversation he told me about a lawyer, a connection, and a favorable outcome. On the top of page 173, I read a story about a lawyer, a connection, and a favorable outcome — but this time for the criminal. My eyes were so tired I could scarcely keep them open. Still I read aloud in hushed tones to tell my husband what I had found. Even though the name of the attorney was different, the scenario triggered something that I remembered as significant to Charley's case, about a young State Trooper who had friends in high places who could remove things, cover things up, and help make people and problems disappear. I thought of Spencer and what she had said about no one being placed in my path by chance that weekend, that I would have an "ah-ha moment" and that information would come to me as if it were being dropped into my lap. And it had. I hugged my book. "God bless Charley," I thought. I read through to the end of 175. "God Bless Spencer and God Bless Charles Weems," I whispered into the night.

At 4:00 am they came into the room to draw more blood from my child. I held on for four more chapters after that crashed. At 6:43 she seized again, but this time I had my rosary and I was ready.

CHAPTER TWELVE

Somewhere between the hospital and the lack of discovery, I had lost my smile and my confidence to solve Charley's murder. Sensing the imbalance in my soul, I tried to be still in both heart and mind so I could listen for the calm just beyond my personal storm. But the gods had become quiet and left me alone to find my own way.

April showers produced many a sullen day that month, and the sky continued to act like an ill child, vomiting with alternating violence and then drooling with soured tongue. Some days it seemed like Charley would never speak to me again, and those were the hardest days of all to navigate. I could take his anger or his desperate pleas to reconnect with Jules, but his silence was something I could not bear. For so long I had allowed his voice to drown out the screaming of mine that I no longer recognized the timbre of my own. They say time heals all wounds, but as much as I counted on the calendar to move my personal healing forward, it began to fail me too. We had missed Easter that year, but in light of the fact I had almost lost my daughter, the lack of marshmallow pink and purpled Peeps seemed a small price to pay. Distracted for a time by the family crisis, everyone's attention focused on my daughter and I was free to wallow in my own depression. With my marriage still on the mend, it was all I could do to keep to myself and split the remaining hours of emotional solitude between work and Charley. My research continued, though I was still no closer to identifying the shooter with confidence.

Kaye's journal was beginning to read like a teenager's diary, and I was uncertain what and/or if any of the information would ever prove to be useful. There were so many threads to follow that I could have woven a tapestry of doubt and deceit large enough to block the panoramic view from my picture window. Even still, by the time April ended I had successfully narrowed down my shooter suspects to one of three men and the one woman: G. Eager for confirmation from Spencer as to my choices, I built case histories and biases like tall and stately castles. With each new wave of information, however, they would crumble as though built in sand. Humbled by circumstance, I spent more time looking backwards than forward and struggled to find any real traction. Bearing in mind the gifts from the first session with Spencer, I should have been more grateful, but every step forward came with a caveat. My child was home from the hospital, but not safe from the seizures that came upon her with random abandon. In the throes of constant vigil, I became as raw to life as the ends of my nerves.

After Piper was forced to drop out of college and stay at home, keeping her safe became my mantra. During the day I called her a hundred times and panicked when she would not answer her cell. At night I barely slept, listening for the changes in her breathing, watching for the body ticks and familiar onslaught of thrashing and screams that would accompany each grand mal seizure. The stress on the family was paramount, and the detours of Charley became my saving grace.

I wrote a hundred letters, made a thousand phone calls, and found that most of Charley's contemporaries had passed, relocated without forwarding address, or had nothing they could add. When local agency resources dried, I worked with the local ATF Public Relations officer, and he put me in touch with another agent and ATF's National Archivist, both from Washington, D.C. to check national archives. No surprise that they had little in their files. Still, both were gracious and offered to do anything they could to help. Local FBI was slow to respond, but finally agreed to award me ear time when I had more information to divulge.

Truth was I couldn't blame them — any of them. The world had become little more than a customized cable channel where everybody thought if they watched a few episodes of their favorite forensics team dig in the desert or dumpster dive "in the hood" they could solve it.

But as much as my brother the retired detective and my husband's FBI friend had every right to be so discouraging in February, they had every reason not to be by the end of May.

While the crime scene photos could not definitively prove homicide, they could definitely rule out suicide and conclusively confirm negligence and mismanagement of the crime scene. In addition, witness statements acted as guideposts to corruption of the scene. The statements had not only been written 22 days after the fact but also amazingly not one of them mentioned the rain. That seemed odd to me, considering even a speeding ticket includes the weather conditions at the time of issue. And it wasn't just the inconsistencies that pointed to corruption; it was the consistencies themselves that pointed to collusion. It was in the pieces that were left out that I found my path.

So much divine orchestration had already taken place that I could not imagine arguing with the cosmos over semantics. Intuition was a double-edged sword. The more I was able to piece things together, the more unbelievable the story became. Spencer had warned me that trust was the most important thing, and my only hope was to commit full bore. Having spent the better part of the last few days transcribing the first session with greater understanding, I must volunteer that I no longer grieve for the approval of others. People, places, names, numbers, and initials began to take on a life of their own and pressed for accreditation. I racked my brain to find more hard core evidence. The document *1510* was nowhere to be found in what papers were in my possession, so I surmised it had something to do with the trial transcripts that Gavin Eller said no longer existed. It seemed unrealistic that the infamous "they" would have asked me to pursue something unattainable, so I set it on the back burner of my mind wondering if I had either misunderstood its nature or if Eller had lied about that too.

The next clue had been repeated several times, and I knew that meant it held major significance. The words *"the trail will lead to MOT"* meant nothing to me at the time, but Charley was using them as a road map. And so I spent countless hours divining every conceivable combination of words to make sense of it. While some held great promise, I never got the "Holy Shit" gut reaction I was hoping for.

I became obsessed. At dinner I would write combinations of words on napkins. While working, I would doodle whatever came to mind. But the "ah-ha moment" I had wished for continued to elude me. Spencer reminded me if I was working at it that hard, I was not on the right path, so I switched paths.

Hoping another source might prove to have the key, I scheduled an interview with one of the boy witnesses, Stevie Waverleigh, who was now in his sixties. His interview echoed mostly what had been written in his statement, but there were small insights that ate away at my gut. For instance, he mentioned he never remembered either the fedora or the flashlight being in the road that night, yet they exist in the crime scene photos. When I asked him about a red truck, he told me it was raining so hard by the time they got back to the scene that night that he could not have distinguished between make, model, or color of a vehicle and that Colbert had arrived there the same time they did. This was important in establishing a timeline.

Next he told me **NO** photos were taken while they were there. That would have been between approximately 11:45 PM and 2:30 AM. But the most telling insight of all was his recollection of the call he and Buckley made to Brooks County Sheriff's Department to tell them about the body in the road. Waverleigh stated that they called Brooks County, but were informed Brooks County could not respond because the body was on the other side of the river and in Lowndes County jurisdiction. He said they were instructed to call the Lowndes County Sheriff's Department. They did so and overheard the dispatcher's conversation as he called Deputy Sheriff's home and were informed he was taking a bath, but that he would get dressed and drive on down as soon as possible. They were told to stay put at the little general store and not to go back to the scene until notified by the Deputy himself via phone. The call to Lowndes County was made somewhere around 11:00 PM. The call to allow them to return to the crime scene for statements and testimonies came into the store somewhere right around midnight.

I thought about my own husband and could not get past the word "bath." First of all, most men take only showers and do not take baths unless coaxed for other more sensational reasons than just personal hygiene. Second of all, Colbert was a known alcoholic and was barely seen awake and sober after sundown according to interviewees. Waverleigh had said it had rained on and off all day, but by the time they got back to the scene that night at midnight it was pouring so badly he could not recognize vehicles. They said they arrived just as Deputy Colbert was getting out of his car. So both parties arrived for the second time at approximately midnight or shortly thereafter. The crime scene photos showed no rain at the time, but Waverleigh swears the body was not moved, nor was any photo taken while he/they were present. In fact he/they said they overheard Colbert make the calls for backup, photos, etc. while they were there with him.

A question immediately came to mind: "How do you take photos and yet not take photos?"

If Colbert was not there before midnight and no photos were taken during the boys' stay until 2:30 AM and the statements read Rowan's transferred the body to the Pineview Hospital in Valdosta by 3:00 AM, then when did photos get taken? It takes at least thirty to forty-five minutes to get from the crime scene to the hospital on the other end of Valdosta proper. And if Colbert called for photos to be taken after midnight and they were taken between the boys' leaving and the ambulance loading in the pouring rain, how did the blood survive the rain to stay in the photos and why is there NO RAIN in the photos? There are no drops of rain on the camera lens, nor are any of the people in the photos wearing any sort of rain gear or garments. Not even an umbrella appears in any frame. Yet Waverleigh claimed that it rained hard the entire time they were there, and the National Weather Service Records back up his interview information. But not Colbert's.

So how many men do you know who take baths AFTER 11:00 at night? Hmmm… not many, I'll wager. Especially since Colbert's reputation leaves him suspect of being up so late and sober. Also, the statement shows that the boys agreed their statements matched all eight photos, NOT six. So, where are the other two and what was in them? Curious about the excessive number of discrepancies, I made a call to Spencer in May and asked for another session. This time I brought Jules with me.

Personal messages of constancy from Charley, embroidered with snippets of both current currency and great nostalgia from my parents, left me deeply moved and awed at the vastness of this intelligent universe. Still I felt small and unprepared for what it was Charley was asking of me. Working with a young woman from the Lowndes County Historical society, Erin Lassiter, I had been able to secure a high school graduation picture of Charley and of G, our Gerrilyn Baldwin. With dark hair and darker eyes, she had a haunting look about her. When we finally met, I gave it to Spencer to view. She ran her fingers across the grained paper and the smile slowly left her face.

"I'm getting the impression…good girl gone bad? She didn't start out this way. It feels like G was possibly a sexual abuse victim. Like a family member, a father or an uncle, maybe? Someone who forced themselves on her at a very young age? It ruined her: turned her inside out, made her use her body to get what she wanted, set up a cycle. Do you understand? She wasn't always like this; she was injured, damaged goods."

I looked at the coal black eyes in the photo and tried to feel compassion, but it was hard. If this woman had set Charley up for that kind of thoughtless slaughter he had suffered, it made it all the harder to take pity on her. Still as a victim of sexual abuse myself, I cringed inside for her. Spencer continued.

"This is odd. I'm getting the impression of the word ostrich. *It could be an actual ostrich or to be like an ostrich, like hiding your head in the sand. Charley is repeating this 5 times. Ostrich…ostrich…ostrich… ostrich…ostrich. I do not wish to*

interpret. It may be someone who works with ostriches, or it may be the nickname, or even a code for something. It is significant; be aware. This has something to do with someone in law enforcement, someone who has a drug association, domestic disputes. Be aware."

"Great! Really," I blustered. "Now I'm looking for freaking ratites?" I asked sarcastically. "The normal shit wasn't hard enough to try and figure out, so now they're sending me on a wild goose, or more aptly a wild ostrich chase?"

"It has something to do with a badge of some sort. Sorry. They just keep showing me the word ostrich*" she added.*

"So now I'm looking for somebody who wears a badge, beats women, does drugs or sells drugs, and, and likes or likes to act like large poultry poking their head in the sand? Are you kidding?" I slammed. "Does it have anything to do with that Wild Adventures place down there? Do they have an exotic petting zoo or something?" Spencer's face was blank, so I keyed in on Jules. "Do you know?" Jules shrugged her shoulder, and so I returned my attention Spencer.

"I don't know. That's for you to find out!" Spencer laughed, but had nothing else to add to the ostrich clue. "That's what they are showing me: ostrich. It's very significant. I wish I could tell you why, but I can't."

It made absolutely no sense to me at all, but that's what came through and so we moved on. "I'm beginning to hate Valdosta. Didn't these people have anything better to do in this town than mess with people's heads?" I begged.

"Let me continue," she interrupted. "They are showing the Grim Reaper is related to G. Not personal; it's business related. They show me deceit associated with his name, absolutely involved, but not the trigger man."

"Ok," I answered and recorded her answers.

"They are presenting two locations of energy: front tire, front of car. Staged witnesses... set up to see it... staged."

"What?" I blurted. "Are you telling me *both* boys were staged to find Charley looking like that? But the papers said..."

"They are showing me the farmer-staged witnesses. There is a Florida association. And cheese, a cheese connection. There is a triangle. Charley-Bob-Gerri. There is an association between the three names and something about the cheese."

My head began to reel. Something from the first session came back to me: *"the man with the moldy skin had been rancorous, obsessing about his skin, the lacerations on his arms."* I was in the middle of having one of my "holy shit" moments when Spencer reminded me of the drawing of the first session. I had made the assumption that it had been a coping saw because of Charley's sideline business in construction, but it was not at all what I thought. Spencer took my pen and drew the same sort of design as before, but now we both saw that the coping saw association, however plausible, had been dead wrong. The drawing was that of an old-fashioned cheese cutter.

"Bingo!" I muttered under my breath. "It was a cheese cutter. That's what they used on his arms."

"There is a direct association to the cheese cutter from Bob, the farmer from Florida. The cheese cutter is in his hand, tied to Gerri. There is a triangle with Charley. The farmer — the father of the Waverleigh boy — staged witnesses."

Distracted by the cheese cutter connection, I asked her to pause to get the information recorded before she moved on. There was a brief anecdote for Jules about a white unicorn and then Spencer proceeded and began to tell us about her trip to Florida.

"On our way to Clearwater, Florida, we drove through Georgia down I-75. As we drove past the exit for Tifton, I got the impression

of a sheriff and a number, 1545, kept coming through. It is significant."

I wrote as fast as I could and waited for more to come through.

"The four-way, that is the hotspot," she said and then reached for the copy of the statements I had brought to help us out. As she picked up the bundle, I scribbled "the four-way of Ousley and Redland Church Road" down to the side and then watched as she ran her hand over the surface. Without a word she flipped to page 5 and ran a finger down the length of each paragraph till she got to the fifth one and stopped at a sentence that read "Booker [Logan J. Booker] and I went to the Morgue at Pineview Hospital." Who is this?" she asked. "Pay attention to this man; he is significant."

I made a notation and asked about several other names that had been floated into the mix from my round table discussion with the retired law enforcement at the Historical Society.

"Larry Tanner; hat association. He liked to wear all kinds of hats. Showing wrought iron, hammering."

"Joseph Tanner. General store association: stores, toothpaste, food items, behind the counter."

"J"— Oak Street, check relationship — showing had sex with the same female as his brother." Secretly I wondered if the "J" stood for G, as she lived on Oak Street and often rumored to have referred to herself as either "Jerry" or "Gerri."

"Be aware...a young energy, an S name, like Sarah or another name that starts with an S will cross your path. Be aware."

I jotted own the "S" or "Sa" name and waited for the next clue.

"They keep showing the number 1545. Do not know what that is, but it is significant." I added a few more stars to the previous mention of this number next to the words "Sheriff" and "Tifton," and then the next thing that came out of her mouth blew my mind.

"Do you understand be aware of a heart attack in the bed, a male energy in his sixties, soon after Charley died? A male energy, under duress, a heart attack."

I shook my head no and held my pen in the air while she finished.

"This is significant; be aware."

"Does this have to do with Charley?" I asked, still digesting the fact that it appeared as though another death was now somehow part of the equation. Jules caught my eye, but there was no time to ruminate further, as Spencer began again without segues.

"Do you understand muddy footprints at the scene? Darwin Devonshire, where are they? Next, office prints. The footprints found in Charley's office claimed to have been seen by Claude Kirby that night at 2:30 am? Think! What is his intention? Why was he there? He is looking for something. What is it?"

I show her the pictures of Clyattville-Nankin Road that Jules took on our last trip down. She held the photos and then asked to borrow my pen again and circled an area and said, *"This is where his body was."*

I took the photo and then showed it to Jules, who ran her finger atop the glossy print and her lips tightened, but she said nothing and then handed it back to me. Spencer spoke about an association between Damon Cummings and the Speaker of the House at the time. This person is tied to high-ranking state officials. Then there was a mention of the relocation of Charley's body from the front right tire to the front of the car, Charley sensing another texture.

"Do you understand the seven of spades? A card. This is specific."

I answered no, so she continued.

"Do you understand the 'f' energy? This is a male energy, there that night, holding an umbrella in the downpour? He was there that night, watching. He was there, not talking; just making sure

things got done right, covering his ass. His energy is associated with an 'f,' perhaps an initial."

I immediately recognized this as Sheriff Jeb Finch. I told her so, but it made no sense. Finch was never depicted at the scene, either in print or film. Perhaps his image was caught on the other two missing photos. Not wanting to derail unnecessarily, I tucked that in my hat and told her about the story that Gavin Eller had told me about Billy Burgess coming to see him with evidence about that night. She listened and then immediately began to relate something else. I grabbed my pen and waited for further instructions.

"Do you understand the fence that is not normal? A carving in the middle, not regular kind of fencing. It is wood, but not normal. Something carved in it. The property is red hot." She takes my pen and draws what she sees. I try to interpret, but do not recognize the spiky nature of the drawing.

"I'm sorry. Should I know this?" I asked.

"Did you see something like this on your trip?" she asked.

"No, but we're going back soon. Should I be looking for this fence with a carving in it?"

"Yes. It is burning hot, which means it is very significant. I cannot interpret. Just be aware," she added and moved on. Then in another redirect, "There was a link between the Governor of the time and the Grim Reaper. Pay attention; this is significant."

Another thirty minutes were taken up with personal connections for Jules to make, one about a Cocker Spaniel named Blondie, a white unicorn, and something yellow in a jar spilling. Then the table turned to me.

"Charley does not understand why you are not using the blackboard."

"The what?"

"The blackboard." She drew a big square in the air. "The one with the magnets," she augmented, hoping this would help and it did. "He says you understand." And she mimed a square again. "The blackboard thing. Do you understand?"

Suddenly it hit me. Charley had died in 1966, so perhaps this was his idea of a blackboard without chalk. "OMG, does he mean the dry erase board my husband bought for me a few weeks ago? The one I'm hiding in the dining room behind a chair so he won't be reminded I haven't put it up?" I gasped.

Jules began to laugh and did a naughty-naughty finger wag. I was about to give her a different wagging finger back when Spencer broke in. "Did it come with magnets?"

"Yes. Well no, it didn't. Ok. My husband bought me this huge dry erase board like they use on *CSI* so I could track my clues, timelines, etc. and thought I might want to also attach my notes. So he bought the magnets because he thought the silver trim on this thing was metal, but it was only gray plastic so they can't stick to it. I put them on the fridge, but the board thing," and I let it hang in the air. "The board, I…" and I hesitated.

Spencer raised her eyebrows, waiting for the punch line. Jules raised hers in tandem, and together they leaned in and glared till I was forced to confess.

"Ok, ok. I hid the stupid thing in the dining room because..." And they glared. "Ok, because it looks cheesy, all right? I didn't want the damn thing in my bedroom," I volunteered. "There. I said it."

Jules made a face and began to giggle, so I tried to defend myself. "I couldn't put that thing in there with all my beautiful wooden furniture and oil paintings. It would make my desk area look stupid," I blubbered. "And clearly I don't need any more stupid in my life."

They both began to giggle. I, however, held my ground, amazed why such a thing would have caught Charley's attention. Their laughter was beginning to annoy me, so I reiterated my rationalization and then became even more amazed that I felt I had to justify my decorating choices to a dead guy who shouldn't have been hanging out in my bedroom to begin with.

"This is ridiculous! Can we just focus here already?" I cackled, trying to hide a smile.

"Uh-huh?" they echoed and then bit at their lips, but to no avail. Ten seconds later Jules couldn't contain her glee and in between thin lips snickered, "So does *Don* know why you haven't put it up yet?"

Guiltily I rallied back, "Of course not. I move it behind a different chair every couple of days so he won't see," I laughed, which set them off into peeling laughter of their own.

"Seriously, guys! C'mon...it's just not pretty!" I whined and proceeded to explain to both women and a dead man circling in the ethos above us why I felt it was beneath me to accessorize my boudoir with classroom kibosh and plastic magnets, regardless of my husband's best intentions.

They both crossed their arms and grinned from ear to ear. "Soooo... you haven't told Don yet why you hate his present this badly?"

"No!" I stammered. "What am I supposed to say? 'Thanks, it's really ugly?'" and they laughed again. "How am I gonna tell him a thing like that?" I blurted and began to giggle myself.

Jules bit at her lower lip to keep from coming unglued again. "You just say 'Thanks! It's really ugly!'" We all broke into laughter and then Spencer simpered, "Charley just wanted to know why. Guess that pretty much sums it up for him and us too!" and the two giggled a few seconds more at my discomfort.

Startled at the ridiculousness of my overreaction, I gasped and shoved my hand over my mouth. "Oh my God! I sound like an idiot, don't I? OK… Please don't answer that." Now Spencer was biting her lower lip too. "It's just that I didn't want to hurt his feelings. It wasn't cheap and he really thought he was helping, but I just couldn't do it...I couldn't!"

The two snickered under their breath, and once we all finished laughing, Spencer continued. "Ok, back to Charley." And her facial expression changed, so Jules changed hers as well and we collectively moved on.

"There is more information for you from the man who has the ladder tied to the house," Spencer announced.

"The what?" I asked.

"The ladder. It's leaning against the wall of a house or a garage. Something about a ladder and the farmer. Do you understand?"

Dry erase board dismissed, I was glad to refocus and tried to catch up. The farmer with the ladder I suspected was Robert Coleman, but I had already hit him up two times and he was cordial, but concealed. Jules asked a question or two more in the interim and then suddenly began to tell us about a confession her mother had made to one of her aunts. All ears, Spencer and I gave her enough emotional space to move from humor to heartache.

Apparently a few years after Jules's mother's death, an aunt had told Jules more about her mother's despondency in the first few weeks following her father's death. Driven crazy by people who insisted Charley had committed adultery with Gerri Baldwin and then suicide after her rejection, Kaye began to break down. With the investigation closed after just 18 days and a declaration of suicide, no money would be forthcoming from either life insurance or Federal pensions. Kaye knew there would not be enough after the construction loans were paid to keep them solvent, and soon they would become destitute.

Convinced there was no other way out, Kaye told her sister that she had wanted to commit suicide herself, but could not stand the thought of leaving her children with a double legacy. The only way was to take them out with her. So she decided to take the kids on a trip to the mountains. Deathly afraid of the steep and winding roads, she thought that would be the easiest way to go. So she waited till nightfall, dressed the kids in their winter coats, loaded them into the back seat, and drove to the top of some mountain near where they were staying.

When she got to the top, she told them she loved them, smoked a cigarette, put the car into gear, turned off the headlights, and then slammed on the gas. The car jerked forward into the night, but it wasn't long till the moon faded behind a cloud and the two front tires bit into gravel and chewed up the softened edges of a worn out shoulder and began to list to one side. Panic stricken, she rationalized the children had on thick coats, then suddenly capitulated. Thick coats might prevent them from being instantly killed, but not severely injured. Unable to commit to communal death, she smashed on the brakes and burst into tears. Her intention had been to drive off the face of a cliff, to kill them all. But somewhere into the first fifty feet of her descent she became fearful that the children might not die instantly and she did not want them to suffer. With the children unaware of her intended course of action, she jammed the shift into park and tried to catch her breath.

No one knows how long she sat there in the mountain moonlight contemplating another try before committing the shift to reverse. Everything had been taken from her: her husband, her future, her dignity, her love of life, and her will to live. Nothing remained but the children, quiet in the back seat, padded in synthetic fur, cooing to one another.

Three cigarettes later, she turned the lights back on and rolled down the hill slowly to the nearest pull off till she could stop shaking. Her children never realized what she had intended, and she made her sister swear she would never tell a living soul what she had almost done. That was apparently right around the same time Kaye had gotten down to only 98 pounds because she had stopped eating. The aunt told Jules her mother had thought about nothing other than the murder since the night it had happened and that Kaye had all but chain smoked herself into extinction.

Jules remained calm as she finished the tale, but my heart broke for Charley's widow all over again, and I mentally apologized for not empathizing more with her as a woman and a wife. The entire story was burdened with so many profound emotions, I wanted to call it quits for the day, but Charley wasn't through with us yet. Once Kaye's epiphany had been dispatched, Spencer shifted in her chair. I flipped to a new page and when everyone was ready, I began again by throwing out another name to consider.

"What do they present when I say the name Albert Fitzpatrick?"

"Hmmm...Albert Fitzpatrick. They show me a newspaper, something about looking at newspapers and an argument with a female. Like 'How did I get roped into this?' They show me rubber boots; they are muddy. He is angry, arguing with his wife. Wife told Kaye, Charley was up to no good with Gerrilynn. Albert is furious, says it is about the 'boys club,' fraternal protection, he must protect. The wife needs to just go along with it. No choice."

I recalled reading about that incident in Kaye's journal. After hearing more about Al's violent temper and his penchant for kicking and hitting, it gave an added twist to what Kaye had to say. I told Spencer what the journal had read:

I told him [Charley] that I would go and mail the letter. I never mentioned to him my conversation with Sal, Mr. Spinnaker, or Mrs. Fitzpatrick. On the way to the Post Office I decided to stop by to see Mr. Fitzpatrick to see if he had talked to Charley. He was home. I asked him if there was anything going on between Mrs. Baldwin and my husband. I told him that I had felt like she had been after him the night she had come to my house. He looked me straight in the eyes and said that he knew of nothing, that he had never tried to talk to Charley about her. I got mad about that time. I told him that I had better not find out that anything was going on. Mr. Fitzpatrick's own wife [Bobbie Lee] had told me less than an hour earlier that he had tried to talk to Charley about her. I told

Mr. Fitzpatrick that I would see for myself come Monday. I was mad when I left his house, I do not deny that.

I did not tell Mr. Fitzpatrick that his wife had told me that. When I started to leave, she went to the door with me and begged me not to say anything to Al about telling me. The whole thing seemed to be getting more confusing. She told me that he would talk to me. Then he denied it. I went on and mailed my letter...I was gone about 30 minutes.

Spencer came through with a few more images, and I scribbled everything she said and poised my pen above the paper, sensing there was more.

"Do you understand... it feels like the female energy with the red fingernails? She takes the P.O. Box key. She is asked to do it. Check his wallet; there should be an imprint from the key."

I made a notation to check the wallet when I got home. "Well, that would explain how the invoice for the porn tape got in his mail slot. It was ridiculous," and she cut me off.

"You have a copy of that?"

"Yes. It was sent to a P. O. Box #153 — his P.O. Box and postmarked November 21, 1966, from California. Charley died October 9, well over a month before. Somebody doesn't know how to count very well, do they?" I chuckled.

Spencer came back with another comment. "They present it was a ruse, a setup. A detour put in place by the male energy with the 'f' in his name."

"Finch, no doubt," I responded and looked across the table at Jules.

Spencer continued. "June 14 of this year there will be a shift in the case; be aware. They are showing me a lake, a place where kids hang out, have sex. A teenage hangout. Do you understand the lake where the kids hang out and have sex? There is a clubhouse." I recognize the pattern of questioning to be posture driven and rhetorical and waited for her to finish. "Do you understand a reported rape case tied to this lake? Who was the perpetrator? He got a slap on the wrist. He is law enforcement. Do not limit your sources. Tied to lake. This is known to the fraternity."

As I wrote, I realized the case had just splintered a thousand more times, and I was both excited and exhausted at the prospects of extensive discoveries. Now I not only had Charley's shooter to find, but also a strange man who died of a heart attack and also another victim who had been attacked by someone with a badge. The field broadened well beyond the scope of my limited skill sets, and I would have panicked but there was no time. How was I supposed to know what to do next?

"Is the clubhouse tied to law enforcement too?" I asked.

"Yes, there is an association," she managed and then mentioned something about the 4th of July. Jules thought this pertained to her, so I organized my notes while they talked about a Covington family event. Spencer redirected and my mother came through with the sunflower images again, then Charley with the number 1499 and the color red. That was followed by another image from that night: a male energy with brown hair and a brown mustache, face to face with Charley, yelling at him.

"Do you understand the antique typewriter? There is more information for you there." I acknowledged this as the typewriter at the diner, Kohle's Diner, Jules had taken me to on our first trip. I made a note to go back down in the next few weeks. Then she continued, "A female energy with brown curly hair will provide more information to this case. They are giving me a date: May 9. Be aware."

My notebook full, my brain exhausted, Jules and I bid Spencer a fond farewell and we drove the better part of our trip back to Athens in silence.

CHAPTER THIRTEEN

Even though Erin had come to my rescue a million times before, nobody at the Lowndes County Historical Society could find a print media record of a rape or attempted rape case in 1966, so once again I was left to Spencer's images. Desperate, I sent out numerous emails to some of the retired men I kept in contact with, but none seemed to recall such an event. Many emails were traded with my Mr. Pocket Protector (Winston Wahlberg), as he had been with VPD during that time. If anyone should have known something about a rape near their clubhouse, it should have been him. But because I didn't know if I could trust him, I went to Clint for information instead.

Once I had a ballpark idea of where the VPD clubhouse had been located, I began to concentrate on the lakes surrounding it where Spencer's images of a potential rape might have taken place. This was not as easy as it may have seemed. Unlike most landlocked areas in Georgia, Valdosta is littered with a hundred small lakes that dot the landscape like potholes in a country road. Looking at several maps, I saw that it became increasingly difficult to narrow it down to one lake, but finally settled on a string of small ponds known as Saddle Bag Lakes. This string of ponds crisscrossed the area of the original VPD clubhouse. With little information other than a potential location, I was forced to wait till more images came through.

In another session, Spencer had also mentioned that a high-ranking official flew from Atlanta to Valdosta either the night before or the night Charley was murdered. But why would anyone that high up appear before or give a shit about the alleged suicide of a lowly revenuer? Even more importantly, why would anyone feel the need to fly from Atlanta in the middle of the night to get to a rural litter box like Valdosta in 1966 over his death? I had been informed that the Governor and Finch were tight, and I had also been told by

Cummings that his family attorney and "his man in Atlanta" was none other than the Speaker of the House.

I kept my suspicions and those two high-ranking names close to my vest, as their histrionic caricatures would make my suspicions about why Charley was murdered even harder to sell. I knew ATF, FBI, and GBI wouldn't touch something that hot with a ten-foot pole without quantifiable evidence. I wouldn't have either if I were them. To even place their names in the same sentence with the words "murder" or "collusion" would be literary suicide. Was I really ready to put the two men who held the highest positions of power in the state of Georgia in 1966 on my list of persons of interest? The thought was paralyzing.

What could have been so incredibly alluring or damning as to warrant their potential involvement with such an inconsequential citizen as G? She held no position of power or expertise, not one once of political influence from either her or her family. So what was the big attraction for all these men to Gerrilyn Baldwin? Think! One was the Governor of the State of Georgia, the other the Speaker of the House. Suddenly I remembered something from a previous session with Spencer: *"About the energy LT. Who was it who was promoted to Lieutenant soon after?"* The Speaker of the House, that's who. He was promoted to be the Lieutenant Governor of the State of Georgia very shortly after Charley's death. So what could an estranged housewife in the sandy burg of Valdosta in 1966 possibly offer two power brokers from our state's capital that they didn't have in Atlanta? Nothing. So the big draw to Valdosta and this woman was what? What was the one thing Valdosta offered them that the booming metropolis of Atlanta could not? DISTANCE!

Valdosta's lack of proximity to Atlanta also meant it lacked proximity to wives, homes and hearths, and sacred reputations. Atlanta was a little too close to home for them, both figuratively and literally. Charley had hit the nail on the head. It was all about the porn, but it wouldn't have been just regular old porn. Nobody travels to that extent to cover up regular pornography, so it had had to have been pretty hardcore and/or even possibly participatory pornography they were involved in. Remember, Charley had helped plug some of the larger holes in this equation with his answers to the list of questions I had posed for Spencer to ask him in session two. Charley had clearly stated *"It all goes back to that woman, not the gambling, the porn. It has to do with porn, porn at the clubhouse, a cover up, porn."*

The rape Spencer mentioned had taken place near a lake too, but was it the same lake? All I could think was "How could Charley have been mixed up with a woman like that?" I stared at the photo of the "good girl gone bad" and tried to see the frightened high school girl beneath the black widow image Charley had presented. Had she been the rape victim at the lake? How did the black-eyed girl with the Peter Pan collar and tentative smile get so lost as to have found herself so loved and so hated by my man in the 8 x 10? Better yet, how did a girl like that learn to use her body as currency to power broker such alliances as Sorenson and Samuels?

I called Spencer with that question and instead of an answer to that she gave back this...

"Hmmm... How did she get mixed up with..." and the line went *silent for a minute.*

"Spencer? Are you there?" I asked.

"Hold on." She whispered as though in mid-conversation *elsewhere. "Oh, my gosh! Ok... got a pen?"*

"I can get one..." I blurted back and ran to my desk.

"Ready?" she asked. OK... oh, my gosh. Charley just showed me *he met Finch at the lake by the clubhouse and gave him an envelope. It has what looks like a tape inside it. A tape, but not the one from the P.O. Box. That feels like Finch planted the other tape as decoy, but this tape is different. This tape is...is...bad."*

"What's on the tape?" I ask, laying Gerri's photo aside. (Jules's brother reminded us the word "tape" most likely meant "reel to reel" back then as VHS had yet to be invented.)

"Feels like... porn. But not straight up porn, or women on women kind of porn. Something more sick, like men with men. Or men with children or animals, not straight up porn..." she trailed off as I gathered my jaw from the floor.

Again my vocabulary failed me. "What the…?" was all I could muster in response. I had called to get info about Gerri, but her name never even made it out of the gate before Spencer could redirect.

"This is so dark, T.A.; it's not regular porn stuff. This is sick, what's on this tape." She sighed, then redirected. "The Grim Reaper is tied to this tape. There is an association there. Do you feel safe going forward?" she asked.

I exhaled and laid Gerri Baldwin's picture next to Charley's, daring it not to spontaneously combust. Next I put my pen down. I could barely write what she had said, let alone describe it further. Sickened at the thought of someone recording such vile acts on tape, I gagged. Reading the script again, I uttered something equally vile.

"Men on children... or men on animals?" I asked, hoping I had misunderstood. "Jesus Christ! I just remembered Clint had said Fitzpatrick had been a Juvenile Officer, had an office somewhere in the basement of the Courthouse. You don't think he could have... or that they would have..." and my motor skills oozed from my brain.

"I told you. This is dark, T.A...." Her confirmation gave me emotional vertigo and bile began to build at the base of my throat.

"No wonder Fitzpatrick had blubbered something about fraternal protection to his wife. If they had been involved in.... If Baldwin, Fitzpatrick, Grim, and now God knows how many others had been

involved with that kind of pornography, then murder to keep it a secret would not have been that far out of line," I mustered.

I wanted to hang up and gag again, but Spencer was not to blame. She was just the messenger, and it would have been unfair to leave her wallowing in such images alone. Not more than five minutes earlier I had tried to feel some kind of compassion for the teenaged "good girl gone bad" inside that grainy photo. But that was before visions of grown men slathering their cigarette-stained lips upon innocents and humping God knows what animals had been introduced to my brain. There would be no compassion for her from me from this point forward, only absolute contempt.

"Rot in Hell, you sorry assed bitch," I whispered. Her black eyes burned back at me, and I suddenly wished for a bucket of Holy Water to drown her in. I had no idea how long I'd remained silent after that, but it must have been substantial.

Concerned, Spencer repeated her question. "Do you feel safe going forward?"

I bit my lip and looked at my 8 x 10 friend. "I have no choice," I said into the phone. "There's no one else but me to do this anymore."

The softness in his eyes had vanished, and there was a kind of sterility in his features I had not seen before. Suddenly it dawned on me that it had been unfair to have put them in such proximity to one another. Contrite, I pulled Gerrilyn Baldwin's photo as far away from him as possible, spat on it, and threw it to the floor. Charley was right. She was a black widow. I whispered my goodbyes to Spencer and took a deep breath, convinced it had been G that hovered above my bed corners the night my dog went crazy. "Crazy bitch, that's right. You can stay on the floor, lying on your backside. That's what you did best anyway, God damn you," I fumed.

My next call was to Jules. She barely answered when I blurted out "We need to return to Valdosta soon." When she asked why, I simply responded, "I need to metaphorically pry loose several more nails from Charley's coffin, so I can pound them into hers!" She never asked me who I was talking about; she already knew.

CHAPTER FOURTEEN

So much information flooded my notebooks each time I spoke with Spencer that it became almost impossible to filter what was worth mining immediately and what was simply peripheral and could afford to wait. By the start of May, I began to decipher the clues more easily, but was no better at assigning the common thread that would bind them all. Like a spoiled child, I continued to task him for more clarification. Like a parent, he continued to teach and not enable, disregarding my pleas. Thus we were at odds nightly with me banging my head against the screen of my computer and him banging his head against the veil of eternity that separated us.

Had I been a younger woman when this case came to me, I would not have been able to grasp the critical nuances in all the relationships presented, nor deal with the residual pain through humor. Maturity, they say, has its benefits. Still wading through the downside of menopause, a two-year-old breast reduction, and a migrating waistline, I was still trying to figure out exactly what those benefits were. But no matter; I surmised being closer to Charley's age this time might eventually prove to be a blessing in disguise. After all, we had so much in common. He was forever 44. I lied and pretended I was. He was married. I was struggling to stay that way. He had kids; I would have given him mine. He had had a maid and I freaking deserved one. As far as I was concerned, he and I were a perfectly matched set of bookends. When I was down, he metaphorically held my hand, and when he was down, I doubled my efforts to connect the dots. Often that required the help of others. Such was the case the day I got an extra pair of trained eyes to review the crime scene photos.

During another session at the local coffee shop with Spencer and Jules, a retired cop and criminology professor at C.C.I.R.I. stopped on her way through Atlanta to take a closer look. The photos spoke to her in a language foreign to me: the language of forensics. I learned that morning it was a cold and exacting language that did not allow the heart to enter. As she spoke I was reminded of another law enforcement friend of mine who once told me a murder is always committed over one of three things: 1) A woman. 2) Money. 3) And … a woman!

This woman agreed and talked about the lack of this and the absence of that in the photos, all the while using phrases like "void patterns," "placements," and "disassociation." She asked Jules in great detail about her father's personality. Was he neat, exceptionally organized, obsessive about being prepared for things, particular about his clothes, his appearance, almost anal about having everything in its proper place? Of course Jules had no idea; she'd only been six when he died.

With nothing further to go by, the retired cop picked up and studied the photos one by one and then set them back down in the exact order received before speaking. Having little information and no time to spare, she threw out the disclaimer that she was basing her preliminary judgments solely on the information contained in the photos. Having spent hours going over them myself, I was anxious to see if we agreed on certain details.

"At a glance," she began, "everything adds up and I agree with the pathologist's rendering of suicide."

Jules looked crushed. Spencer and I exchanged an awkward glance. Could we both have been so far off the mark? Our guest asked Spencer for her input. Spencer reiterated that the victims generally present "suicide" if they have committed such an act. But Charley had been very clear: he had been murdered. The retired cop shook her head.

"We usually are on the same track," she muttered and looked at Spencer. "In fact, I don't think this has ever happened before," she said. "Maybe I'm missing something." She picked up photo #4 and noted that the cuff button was missing. I motioned towards the discrepancy of the debris on the pants, but not the shirt. She made a comment on that and then noted the different positions of the sleeves, the location of the blood pools and pointed out a few other elements and then announced, "If this was all I had to go on, I'd still have to go with suicide."

I looked at Jules and gauged the monumental disappointment in her eyes.

"But what about the flashlight and his hat?" I volleyed. "Who wears a hat to kill himself or needs a flashlight to find his own face, if he's just going to blow the shi…." I saw Jules flinch and changed my choice of words. "If he's just going to you know. It doesn't make sense." I trailed off as the woman picked up the photo showing Charley's protruding wound at the top of the skull.

"Again… if this was all I had to go on. It's not odd that folks stage their deaths. The hat was clearly a thing with him, perhaps a signature piece. He may have placed it next to himself ceremoniously. The flashlight? I don't know. Remember, I don't have any other facts to go by. You've given me no other information to date. You just asked me to look at the photos, and I have," she added flatly. "Was there a note?" she added.

"No," I stated, although if there had been it was never talked about. Jules concurred and we both slumped slightly lower in our chairs.

Spencer's face remained the same cool expression she always wore. "So, in your professional opinion based on these that suicide was a definite possibility?" The cop nodded her head, and then Spencer rallied and followed it up with this: "So you don't see any other immediate option? Because he was very clear about this when he came through."

Jules and I perked to the revelry and held our breath.

The cop took notice of Jules's pained look and softened. "Look…it's circumstantial at best. I'm just saying photos don't lie."

"That's assuming they weren't staged to begin with, right?" I threw back, hoping for a lifeline back to Jules's smile.

"Ok, that's a possibility. Maybe his buddies tried to mask it, clean it up a bit. You know, fraternal protection? Like maybe they found him and then tried to make it look like he was trying to bust somebody when it went down. Spare the family. Flashlight, hat, car lights on... I'm just saying maybe they thought they were helping. Anything would be pure speculation at this point. You need other evidence to corroborate anything else you might want to put forth. Pictures alone aren't gonna cut it," she said, covering her bases.

"Fraternal protection, huh?" I asked.

"Yes…cops covering for cops. Like I said, maybe they were watching out for the family of the deceased. Suicide didn't pay benefits back then, ya know."

"Yea, I knew that," I said, but with everything we knew so far "fraternal protection" seemed even less likely in this case than suicide — unless, of course, the kind of "fraternal protection" she was talking about was *from* Charley and not *for* Charley.

The cop picked up another photo and continued to edify, while I continued to lose faith. What if I had failed? What if in my ignorance I could not decipher the messages correctly? Doubt began to seep in again and take root. She was a trained professional with years of experience behind her. I was a theatre director who took orders from a freaking photo on my desk. What if in my innocence of true evil, I could not perceive the dangers that could harm those about me? What if all I ever did was prolong the suffering of a child who never got to know her father? What if in my eagerness to finish the puzzle, I lost sight of the picture all the pieces were meant to recreate? I looked at my own life and measured my ability against Jules's need and could not find the balance necessary to do justice to us both.

"But you haven't heard about the attorney's confession yet," I advanced.

"All I'm saying is if I had to go with my gut, based solely on what I see and don't see in these photos, I'd say he killed himself and they tried to doll it up a bit and make it look like he had stopped someone to keep the suicide a secret, that's all. I have to go. I have a meeting on the other side of town. It was a pleasure to meet you," she threw at Jules and then gathered her things.

Spencer and she exchanged a few more good-natured remarks at the door and concerns about another case, and then we thanked her for her time. I decided that would it be a great time for a bathroom break, so while the others dispersed I remained with the photos of my mangled friend's body and drank my coffee. Nothing felt right. Could I have been chosen so ill advised by her father, or was there more to me than the "me" that had been shaken too hard by recent events?

One by one I repositioned the photos on the table and tried to justify the cop's declarations. I had too much heart to bear the weight of so much objectivity and so begged the cosmos for moral support. "Trust… trust… trust" I whispered to myself. "You can do this. Charley believes in you." I adjusted my weight in the seat and looked at my notebook. "She hasn't seen any of this. She doesn't know what I know. She doesn't… or she couldn't have seen you that way," I whispered to the photos. "If it were true, if you had taken your own life, I'd feel it in my heart and I don't."

I fingered the edges of the pictures and my stomach lurched. Before me, my Charley lay in a blur of black, white, and imaginary red. I no longer desired to see him that way. As I waited for the other two to return, I bolstered my courage with my most solid clue to date: the lawyer's confession. Gavin Eller may have been obnoxiously egotistical, but he had not lied about seeing that evidence and talking to those detectives. Too many other hints now pointed to homicide and collusion as well.

The waitress asked if I needed more coffee, and I declined. My stomach was already upset, and I had finished the first cup more out of habit than desire. The cop had made a good case for suicide, but inside I knew she was wrong. Still, if I couldn't convince her, how the devil was I ever going to be able to convince anybody else, especially the ATF? Charley was right: if I was ever going to be able to walk the walk, I needed to go back to school and get my degree.

Confounded, I went through each photo again, looking with a fresh eye to the aspects pointed out to me by our second expert. One cuff open and rolled, the other appearing not to be, and the one rolled shown at two different lengths from the wrist line in two different photos. Then there was the odd placement and unquantifiable reasoning for the hat and the flashlight. Neither is necessary for a suicide. No evidence of a void pattern for displaced brain tissues. Blood trails across the forehead ran in different directions from the other blood flow. Blood stains on the back of the head traveled completely independent of any natural gravitational flow. Stains on the collar, scrapes on the shoes, sand and grass clippings that clearly show he was on his bottom at one point, but not on his back completely (face up) as Damon Cummings swore he had found him.

The Lowndes County Deputy Sheriff's statements claimed that they did not roll him on to his back until after photos were taken. Yet clearly Charley had been moved sometime before the photos were taken. And what about the timelines of the photos? According to witness statements, no photos were taken in their presence, which was from approximately 11:45 PM until 2:30 in the morning, during the roughest weather of the night. Yet again, no mention was ever made of the body being covered to protect the scene, nor any photographic evidence that anyone had any raincoats or rain paraphernalia about them. The inconsistencies gnawed at my brain each time I reviewed the evidence.

Frustrated, I turned my attention back to Spencer and other information Jules and I had recently received. *There is a link between the Grim Reaper and the Governor at the time.*

Damon Cummings' (Grim) link to the Governor at the time had been the Speaker of the House, his family attorney in Atlanta that he claimed made him untouchable, untouchable even to the long reach of the Lowndes County king, Sheriff Jeb Finch, who ran South Georgia like it was his fiefdom. I kept going back to the information that it had all been about the cover up at the clubhouse: the cover up about the porn. So was the planting of a porn tape invoice from California part of the cover up for something else or part of the reasons why Charley was murdered? I scribbled the traditional motives in my notebook.

A woman. Money. And a woman!

The woman was obviously G...Gerri... Gerrilyn Baldwin...the good girl gone bad. Charley had vomited her name out a million times in that first two-hour session with Spencer, so there was no mistaking that. Moving on to number two of the equation was the money. But which money? There were enough illegal rackets going on in 1966 not only to choke a horse, but also to take it out for dinner and show after, plus buy half of Kentucky for him to be buried in when he died. There were the "Bug" tickets (*Bolitas*), illegal moonshine gains, prostitution profits, drug revenues, rumors of counterfeiting, gun trafficking. You could take your pick. Valdosta was a kaleidoscope of debauchery known as the "Vegas of the East Coast" back then and the pornography was the one major producer that Charley had said was connected to the woman. What was captured on that porn tape to prompt so many people to rush the dyke to keep the water level from going low enough to expose it?

Damon Cummings had called this a crime of passion. While I believed passion was part of it, I wanted to know exactly whose. The images on that tape must have been the real currency in this ordeal or they wouldn't have wanted to retrieve it so badly. The only thing I knew for certain was there was somebody out there still alive who knew exactly what the high price was for. Upset over the abridged declarations of suicide by the cop, I reviewed my files and dedicated every spare moment I had to following the most promising clues in an effort to prove her wrong.

Shortly after that session, my husband was told he would have to have another rotator cuff surgery. In the process of determining that, they discovered a lump on his shoulder blade just beneath his incision. Concerned, they scheduled another MRI. The morning of his appointment, I decided to bring my laptop and work on my blog while he was being x-rayed down the hall. While I was doing so, a woman to my right took note of my oversized pocketbook and my overstuffed book bag. She made a comment about my "bringing everything but the kitchen sink," nodded towards the floor, and smiled weakly. I was occupying two seats and part of the floor in front of me with all of my nonsense. Chastised, I smiled weakly back and apologized.

I explained I was such a geek about writing that any chance I got I would drag my laptop along for the ride. Ice broken, we struck up a conversation in between paragraphs. It proved to be fruitful. Both she and her husband were retired law enforcement, she from the Gwinnett County Sheriff's Department and he from the Atlanta Metropolitan Police Department. Seeing the natural segue, I suggested she might find Charley's story of interest. She seemed intrigued, so I baited further. After giving her the abridged tour of my information and my card, I told her to read the blog and if she was still interested to know more, she should contact me through the web site. It took about a week, but she did.

Sensing no reason not to trust her or her husband, I set an appointment to meet and share more materials. The funny thing was, two and a half weeks earlier Spencer had predicted I would meet with someone around May 11th or 12th, a female who would have information that would be useful to me. At the time I had been emphatic that I did not have any meetings scheduled for mid-May. And of course when I said it, I didn't. It was not two Mondays later that I had scheduled it.

Over dinner, I shared with them a brief summary of the history of the case and my findings. Over dessert, I showed them the bundle of Colbert's statements and the GBI Crime Lab Report I had collected on my first trip down to Valdosta. Two bites into my apple cobbler, the retired Deputy Sheriff looked at me and pointed to the second page of the GBI Crime Lab Report.

"Interesting, isn't it?" I asked. "This is the original set from Valdosta. This has another page to it. The Crime Lab set I ordered is here. It's missing that page."

"Of course it is," she replied matter-of-factly, wiping her face with a napkin. "That's the page that proves there were two guns."

"Exactly!" I gasped. I knew that there had been a discrepancy, but because I was still learning about ballistics, I acknowledged the error but wanted professional confirmation.

"See here? This is the other half of the ballistics report." She showed it to her partner, the retired Atlanta cop. "You see it?" she queried.

"Yep," he answered. "Right there. Six lands six grooves vs. three lands, three grooves. Two guns. No way could they lie about that now, unless of course they didn't have the second page to tell them so back then."

"But if the Deputy had it all along, why didn't the GBI have it when I ordered my copies from their archival records?"

"Looks like it conveniently never made it into the file. Your folks down there either had help higher up or they weren't altogether stupid." She picked up the crime scene photos and saw the fedora and the flashlight and recanted. "Well, forget that. I was giving them way too much credit. Who brings a flashlight to a suicide?" she mocked and raised an eyebrow as she took another sip of coffee. "Could you be any more obvious? A flashlight. Really?" and she swallowed another tepid sip. "Nah, looks like I was wrong about them having some smarts. They apparently really were that stupid," she snickered, handed the photos to her husband, and took another bite of cobbler.

That night when I got home, I sent this message to the retired cop who had first reviewed the six crime scene photos at Starbuck's with us.

FYI… (Based on the 1966 Crime Lab Report.)

Just received confirmation the bullets taken from Charley are from two different guns. One from the gun Charley held in his hand, probably the second shot fired, the one into the chin to establish nitrate on his hands and support the claim of "suicide." What I suspected is the first bullet, the one through the back of the head, will not match the gun Charley was found lying on top of at the scene! Lands and grooves are 3 on one and 6 on the other.

Now all I have to do is match the bullet grooves and landings to the correct gun. State Troopers had regulated standard-issue guns. Local law at the time could carry whatever they personally wanted. So now I have to match it to the right gun, and then we may have our shooter identified!

Gives me a whole different take on the fact that the morning before I went to meet the man who gave me the file with the crime scene photos, the Grim Reaper was not interested in my thanking him for his time the day before, but was very interested to ask if I had seen a ballistics report. I asked why and he said he was just curious if I know for certain if they had ever been able to match **both** bullets to the gun. I thought it odd at the time why he would ask such a thing, having not seen the report at the time. Now I know why. Think about it: why would you even ask that unless you knew there was the possibility more than one gun had been involved? They had the gun; they had both the bullets. It would seem a foregone conclusion, unless you knew otherwise.

CHAPTER FIFTEEN

I said I would always make myself available to accept information — no matter where it came from. But what happened next was beyond my comprehension.

After discovering the ballistics confirmation of two guns clearly stated on the mysterious missing page 2 of the GBI Crime Lab report, Don, Jules, her son Cole, and I scheduled our next trip down to the big V. Cognizant we were now dealing with a quantifiable homicide, we left for Valdosta on a Thursday night in mid-May, confident we were on the path to finding the killer. I had notified the ATF that I had found an original copy of the Crime Lab Report that showed a missing page, but had not heard back from them. Frustrated, I decided to continue my research alone and hoped that eventually they would find my evidence worthy and join in the fray.

I worked the week as usual. That Friday night Don and I finally got on the road just after 6. Somewhere around 11:00 pm we pulled into our hotel and shared a pizza with Jules and her son. Exhausted, we got to bed just after midnight. Three hours later, I received a panicked call from my youngest daughter Claire about Piper. Having just eased our way out of the hospital and her seizure-induced coma in April, I was frightened, but no more than the 19-year-old on the other end of the line who was in the process of trying to take care of her sister.

"Mom, I don't know what to do. Piper is freaking out. Karalee is with me, but we don't know what to do. I'm scared."

"Calm down. I can't understand you." I could hear Piper's voice in the background, whimpering something painful about making it stop while Claire was trying to keep her from hurting herself. "Do you need to call an ambulance? Is she seizing?" I yelled, pelting her with additional questions as I roused my husband from a dead sleep.

"No... I don't know. She's freaking out about something hiding in the corner, a dog or something. She isn't making any sense, but she scaring the shit out of me!"

"Is she having a seizure?" I demanded.

"No... I don't think so. She just keeps yelling at the thing in the corner and digging her nails into my arms. She's awake, but she's not here, like she's seeing and hearing things I can't see."

"Is the light on?"

"Yes... the one on your nightstand. But she says it's not enough. The thing won't leave her alone."

Crazed that I was four hours and 200 miles away and could not help, I had no idea what to do or where to turn. I sat up in bed and yelled at my husband to call Spencer's number on another phone as I tried to get Claire to give me more information before instructing her to call an ambulance.

"Tell Karalee to keep her phone with her in case you need to call 911, and then tell her to go downstairs to the kitchen and get the Ativan out of the med box and a glass of water." I heard no response other than Claire trying to get Piper to stop crying, so I yelled again. "Hurry! Tell Karalee now!"

"Mom...she is freaking me out!"

She told me how she and Piper had friends spend the night so Claire wouldn't be alone if Piper had a seizure episode. Sometime shortly before she called, Piper started talking in her sleep, something about tacos or taquitos from a gas station nearby. Piper often talks in her sleep, and so without looking, Claire simply told her to be quiet and that was it. A few minutes later she felt what she thought was Piper getting out of bed, but when she looked,

Piper fell to the floor and began to seize, then suddenly stopped. My youngest said she could not figure out how Piper fell out of her bed...into the air, landing four feet away and three feet closer to the bed and closer to the door. She said it was bizarre. Piper didn't so much as fall out of bed and roll away. It was more as if something had picked her up, carried her the several feet away from the bed and nightstand, and then dropped her to the floor in one big thud.

Frightened, Claire helped her up. Piper was disoriented, so they crawled back into bed together. Though confused, Claire assumed she had dreamed it. Once again, Piper rolled over and began drifting off to sleep.

According to my youngest, approximately thirty minutes later Piper bolted up in bed and began to speak as though to something in the room. She kept staring in the corner and asking Claire to make it stop growling. When Claire looked, there was nothing there. Inconsolable, Piper continued to scream about the thing in the corner and then stood straight up in bed again, slamming herself back against the headboard and begging her sister to turn on the lights and call me. She did. Piper continued to stress that the dog-like thing would not stop growling at her.

As Piper was mumbling something in the background, Claire continued to describe to me what was happening. She told me Piper said what she was seeing was the Grim Reaper — not the man with the crooked teeth, but the traditional faceless apparition of the Grim Reaper in his hooded black cloak, red eyes, and scythe. She could see him clearly: a dark image with burning eyes. She could smell him (she described it as a sour, sulfurous smell). He said that he had a message for me, that he (death) had come for me but that he would take her if he could not get to me, that it was a warning. She (meaning Piper) had a weakness — her seizures — and he would use it to get to me.

Then she was shown Charley's body and bloody head, blood pouring out of his skull and the body being dragged about. It was a warning to her from another source that I needed to finish it. I had to get it done, that I needed to finish things that I was in danger and that it would not end till I ended it. I was not to leave and come home, but to stay. It was not a garbled message. I listened to Piper for over thirty minutes telling me things they were conveying to her, while my husband frantically packed to return.

She told me the entity was showing her everything that happened to Charley that night, telling me I had to stay in Valdosta and finish it. That this was the message for me: that I had to stay and figure things out, that I was very close, that I was right there at it. Stay at it. She tried to draw what she was seeing, but I instructed my youngest to get Piper's medication and get her to take it and to keep her as calm as possible so as not to throw her into uncontrollable seizures. I kept Piper on the line and we said prayers that the entity and/or entities would leave as she continued to tell me what they were trying to show and tell her.

Claire gave her medicine, but Piper refused to shut down and continued to draw on my dry erase bulletin board with markers as though in a trance and talked about the warnings and tell Claire and me what I was to do about the Grim Reaper and Charley's murderer. I instructed Claire to take away the markers and to get Piper to move away from the board. She told me she pulled them from Piper's hand, but it didn't seem to matter. Piper remained in a trance at the board and scratched the same maneuvers with her fingertips till they almost started to bleed. Panicked, I begged my husband to hurry and to stay in touch. He gave me my second phone with Spencer's number on speed dial, left his loaded gun on the bed, and then made me bolt the hotel door from the inside. Over an hour went by with this via phone and then finally, she began to drift.

With Don well on his way, I told my youngest to take her sister downstairs and stay with everyone in the same room and sleep with all the lights on until their father got home. During the latter part of the conversation, I redialed Spencer's number like a mad woman at least another twenty times. Frightened, I kept one child on one phone and tried desperately to understand what the devil had happened and how much more my family would have to endure at the hands of the ethereal to put this thing to bed.

Spencer finally answered about 5:30 that morning. I explained to her this event had not presented as any other medical event we had ever observed with Piper. Usually Piper is completely unconscious and incoherent throughout a grand mal seizure episode and then falls into a deep sleep for hours after. The hospital in Atlanta can confirm this pattern because they did an 18-hour seizure study on her throughout her stay over Easter of that year. Still shaken, I told Spencer that I believed it to have been a paranormal possession, channeling, and/or psychic episode of some kind.

I checked in with Claire every hour, and though she was thoroughly exhausted from the experience herself, she was gracious enough to keep me posted. She said that Piper awoke hours later with no memory of the event at all. After each call I would update my husband as he raced the back roads to Athens and monitored his reactions. While Piper's memory of such had been erased, Claire and I knew we would never forget what took place in that room and on that phone. My husband arrived at 8:37 in the morning to a quiet and well lit home and called to let me know all seemed under control. As I hung up for the last time, I felt somehow responsible. That was not the only time that room had had visitors. I would have warned them, but I had no idea the oddities would be directed towards anybody other than me. When my husband informed me hours later he had taken precautions for the girls and was on the road back to me, I sighed in relief and finally confessed about the other events.

It was never my intention to hide anything from my family. I had just never been exposed to that level of paranormal activity before. My rational mind had chalked previous events up to overwhelming stress. Obliged to confess, I told him that four nights prior to our departure, the little white dog (West Highland Terrorist we call Harley) had begun to pace the corners of the bed, growling into the ceiling. For three nights before our trip, the little white dog had displayed extremely aggressive behavior, pacing back and forth to protect me from whatever it was that she saw. I assumed she had heard something from the outside, but her attention always focused on the ceiling. In order to keep myself from overreacting, I tried to make light of the situation and spoke directly into the corners of the roof.

"If this is you, Charley, office hours are now officially over. I will talk with you in the morning. If this is you, Mom and Dad," I joked, "I was never allowed in your bedroom after dark, so I will see you in the morning as well." When she continued to pace and snap at the air, I followed it up with "If that is you, G, or anything else evil, I am warning you. This house is protected by angels." Reaching into my nightstand, I pulled out my rosary, the very one I had dismissed early on in my grief-driven depression. Reverently, I made the sign of the cross and with my heart focused on my children and with my mind on the eternal loving protection of my parents, began "In the name of the Father, the Son and the Holy Spirit...."

Until the event with my daughter, I had thought that whatever evil was lurking in the ceiling above was meant only for me. Never for one instant did I think that by helping Charley I could have placed my children at risk.

It was an irresponsible assumption I would never make again.

CHAPTER SIXTEEN

Frightened that I was now dealing with paranormal energies outside of my control, I began to pray more and begged Charley to help protect my family. I had no idea what portholes had been unintentionally opened by my obsession with speaking to the dead and so kept my rosary handy. In a phone call with Spencer a week later, the following came through.

Spencer began with questions about the rape at the lake. I was still working on that story, but thought I had a pretty good lead on it through Clint. I asked if Charley could help with other details and she balked, but bargained that we should just deal with whatever came through first. She began talking about how on her way back from Clearwater through Tifton she got a weird feeling in her gut. It was hard to describe; something was not right.

"Isn't that the same place you got the word *Sheriff* and the number *1545* coming through?"

"Yes. But there's something else trying to come through with it: a female handing over Charley's gun. She hands it to two men. (Spencer tries to get them to show their faces.) One man is the 'Red,' the red-headed male energy that had been associated with painting signs, taxidermy...KKK association... also shown as shooting someone to death in an open field over an argument...."

I didn't have time for another random body, so I bypassed, asking more questions. "Ok... just keep going," I said and flipped to a clean page.

She continued without segue, "The other male energy, more boyish looking, freckles on the cheek. The 'Red' man is taller than the boyish. They are exchanging the gun near a gas station, one pump outside, general store inside. There is a round sign, feels like a Texaco, but not to say it is a Texaco sign. The sign has waves, red

148

and white, a brand of something. This sign is on the left side of the building if you are looking at it..."

I drew what I thought she was describing and listened for more instruction.

She began without segue: "They are getting into a car. It is like a police-type vehicle. Do you understand?"

"Is this a black and white police car, or blue like State Patrol, or brown like Sheriff's?" I ask, taking notes as she spoke.

"I get no color confirmation, but there are two horizontal lines. One goes, then dips down and goes straight. The one underneath just stays straight. The rear has a lot of red and silver and blue in it. There is a sticker or the license plate itself. It reads 'UST 41.' The younger energy is the driver."

"Wouldn't '*UST 41*' stand for United States Treasury?" I ask. "I should be able to track the car from this. Maybe ATTD/ATF can get it for me. They have to have those kinds of records still. At least I hope they will," I added, remembering how little existed on Charley.

Spencer continued, "They are making eye contact with the person in the store. It is like "Fu... you. Shut up and do what you are told." The store owner/manager is overweight, brown hair. He simply follows orders out of fear. There is a tall pole to the left, like a telephone pole to the left and behind the gas station. The man with the red hair tells him to keep his yap shut. There are two boys running around the place. The man nods his head and gathers them and goes back inside. It is not raining at this time."

I wrote everything down just the way she said it, broken sentences and all.

She started again. "The telephone pole is behind. They exchange the weapons. Older man does most of the talking; he is confident, comfortable, in charge. The younger is quieter, scared, just watching. He is unsure, puppeteered by several people. He does whatever he is told. He seems somewhat frightened, tense."

My head wanted to explode at the fact that for days or weeks I had been getting nothing and then without warning the flood gates had opened and it was all I could do to keep up with what was being said. Suddenly they redirected.

"Hmmm... this is interesting. They are trying to tell me what is on the tape. Feels like one person talking to the camera. A confession, like a documentary. It is a male energy. He is spilling the beans, so to speak, spilling his guts, and telling it all. It is a male dialogue..."

I recorded everything, and then she followed with a few questions. "They only recovered one gun... right?"

"What?" I asked.

"They only found one gun... right?"

I was blindsided because I had yet to share with her my recent information about the ballistics page of the GBI report, or my conversation with the two retired law enforcement officers. "Right... only one gun found, but the second page of the ballistics report confirms two guns. Can you get a clear view of the woman in the scene? Is it G?"

She got goose bumps on her arms, a sign of confirmation.

"You need to find the neighbor, the female who is being intimidated. They are laying into her like 'You better go along with this.' She lived near Kaye or on the same street or the same side of the street. There is another female; she has an injured foot. Talk to the woman with the bad foot injury, feels tied to Valdosta. She will talk...she will talk...she will talk."

Disclosing this information beforehand may help you see the tremendous weight that was carried by all those being aligned, both cosmically and terrestrially, to help me in this case. Spencer had

150

also said that the tape she alluded to in one of the earlier sessions was a major piece to this puzzle. The tape that Charley presented as handing to Sheriff Finch had incriminating information on it. It was not what you call run-of-the-mill or atypical pornography, but something more lurid. It was obvious there was something on that tape that would be devastating if seen by others or found out about, but she said that there was another rumor that needed to be pursued: another rumor, beyond Charley being involved with G, the other woman. At that time I had no idea what the other rumor was, but I imagined I'd be finding out before too long.

This mystery tape that Spencer kept referring to and the key to the P.O. Box that was removed from Charley and/or Charley's home by the female with red finger nails had something to do with one another and may have been the reason for the coffee grounds in the kitchen by female with red fingernails.

I pondered that connection and then sent out this:

"Can I get a nod on Logan J. Booker as being the younger, freckled law enforcement officer associated with Red Slidell, the cover up, go-to man that night with Gerri at the gun exchange spot? Or should I still be looking at Hank Sloan for that? Hank worked for the VPD back then, and he was one of the original names that elevated red from the first list I showed you. Can he grant me that much of a lead? And does the gun exchange spot have a Georgia or a Florida association?"

"In response to your first question, I am shown a target-like an arrow in a target, bull's eye, and more on female: long, red nails. She would have used the nails on men's backs in the throes of sexual pleasure, if you know what I mean. And a KKK association with one of the men: the red-headed man. Do you know anything about that? This is new. Was one of the mentioned men a member of KKK? Gun exchange feels Georgia."

"Georgia...right!" But it would have had to be relatively close to where they killed Charley to pull it off, *I whispered to myself.*

151

With that in mind, I made a side note to research the locations of any small general stores in the area that had a deli or meat and cheese type counter. I already knew about the one that the two boys stopped at to make the call in Nankin, and so I thought to begin there before branching out to the Clyattville, Rocky Ford areas. Again, Clint became my go-to guy for historical icons and background information.

So that you understand that not every day brought such gold mines of information, you will note the correspondences were greatly spaced as I would only tap into Spencer when hitting the proverbial brick wall. Most of the exchanges shared over the last two-and-a-half years with Spencer have come in bulk; like the balance in my checkbook, they have waxed and waned between feast or famine. That day was definitely a feast day and she continued to share the spoils.

No sooner had I caught my breath about the plausibility of a gun exchange and its location than she began to talk about a pair of dogs!

"There are two dogs, same breed, buried on that property."

"What is buried... the two dogs? I don't understand. What property?" I volleyed back.

"No. The two dogs are of the same breed. A gun, the second gun, is buried on that property. The dogs are tan, long-tailed, light honey color, short-haired, looks very hound-like in that face. The two look alike. Not certain why they keep showing me the dogs... something about their owner. This is at the time of the murder. The property.... it is an open property. To the back there are a lot of trees, a woodsy space. No fencing, not on the back of the house. House is wood, single story, white."

I ignored every grammatical rule and plowed across the page with ink. My wrist was beginning to cramp, but I forced myself to continue as she barely paused between impressions.

"If you were standing on the porch, on the backside of the house, to the right there's a hole with a cover. A circle, a circle made of concrete like a well cover or something. A male owns this house. Lives with his mother during this time. There is a mother energy there. The dogs are there, two of them, the hounds. Male energy is probably single or divorced. There is no significant female energy attached to him, no ring. He is taking care of his mother. Not in a relationship at the time. There is a lot of space on this property. There is a law enforcement connection here. This person feels dead."

With her final statement, I was exhilarated and crushed at the same time. If she was seeing the property where the second weapon was buried, I had a real shot at securing further hard evidence I would need to prove my hypothesis. Unfortunately, if Spencer was also seeing the shooter as clearly as the dump site for the weapon, it looked as though my person of interest had already passed and along with him any opportunity to interview and confirm.

As much as I wanted to throw down my pen and wallow in self-pity, she blurted out another set of clues that demanded my attention to dissect and connect. Halfway through May, my notebook was already full, and that was in addition to four other legal pads, one binder, three boxes, and two CD's of interviews and investigations. The pile was beginning to leave me too weary to contemplate any further complications. It wasn't as if I had expected everybody to still be alive, but it made no sense for Charley to want me to go through all this for someone who was already dead and could not be prosecuted. Spencer had warned me early on that while finding the shooter was important, according to Charley it was only the tip of the iceberg and I should concentrate on finding out why just as much as I was concentrating on whom.

After several inquiries with geriatric locals about gas stations and general stores, I narrowed the choice down to several locations: Sam Daily's, where the boy witnesses had called from, and another spot called Causey Manson's, which had a huge Texaco sign that boasted a similar round red-and-white-colored sign. Clint got back to me a few days later and informed me about another small general store with one pump off the Rocky Ford Road, right near the four-way stop and not too far from where Charley's body ended up if you used the dirt road that ran along the Lowndes County Sheriff Department's clubhouse. According to Clint, it had the one pump, a Coca Cola sign, an electrical pole to the back and left of the building, and the man there had two sons. It fit Spencer's description perfectly and kept everything in the same area for timeline sake. But even more, it sold cheese and was not but six miles from the Georgia-Florida border where our potential dump site was.

May was turning out to be very productive. If I had not found out another single thing that month, it would have still kept me hopping for weeks trying to put it all together. But Charley wasn't finished with me yet.

CHAPTER SEVENTEEN

So you can believe in this process, I am going to share a few of the preliminary cautions I received from Spencer **before** my trip back down to Valdosta.

Be aware the #19 is significant. Do you understand the tall brick building with flag pole? There is further information for you there. The #1545 is significant. A white blimp, not to say it is the Goodyear blimp, but like it... information from a young energy whose name begins with an S, Sarah or something like that... a message for you from a male whose name begins with the letter J... from a "J" or "Je," possibly Jeremy or Jeremiah. Do you understand the antique typewriter? There is more information for you there. She gave several more clues that seemed just as random.

Because I need for you to understand that while most of the leg work is just good old-fashioned research and observation, other sources play a vital role in helping me to continue in the right direction. One of these is fresh eyes that rekindle interest in various facets that I become too familiar with or skill sets in areas of forensics beyond my current station. In this fashion you can come to know that all information is not always hindsight, but really foresight. Whatever information can be gathered in this case is precious — no matter its origin.

The Valdosta trip also produced these results:

(This is an email to Spencer and copied to the director at C.C.I.R.I. for safety's sake, as at this point I became concerned for the safety of my family, Jules's family, and me.)

Ok... my mind is almost numb with so much info, so I will start with some of the things you collectively and separately have told/cautioned me about for this case and this last trip. Some include things you, Spencer, gave me heads up on before that finally became clear this trip. Forgive the lack of mechanics in this letter as it is more important for me simply to vomit what I have found. Jules (Charley's daughter) received a note of caution from friends in Valdosta this morning that we may be in danger. I was also cautioned by local Lowndes County Sheriff Clint Sims on Saturday that I might begin making too many people nervous after this last weekend.

Ok. White blimp clue. White blimp flying overhead a car dealership was found this weekend three times. A man by the name of Gabe Griggs worked for a local car dealership, originally called Eleanor Ford Motor Company and later on called Langdale. Perhaps still does. [* Note; Jeb Finch's brother Leroy Finch worked at this dealership as well. This is where the Sheriff's Department got their vehicles.] Not certain if he is still alive. Significance has to do with the rape case Spencer told me about and now also about another suicide committed by this man's wife in 1976 that involves her having an affair with Gavin Eller, the attorney/State Superior Court Judge that told me that he had seen evidence brought to him by two detectives in 1972 proving Charley's death was a homicide, self-defense. Brief explanation of Gabe Griggs's significance to this case.

Gabe Griggs was married with at least two daughters, an older daughter, Bobbie Lee. (I do not know the name yet of the younger one.) The older daughter (Bobbie Lee) was raped by Sheriff Jeb Finch (who was indicted in 1972 and ultimately died in prison) somewhere around '65 or '66 at the VPD clubhouse near the lake. Saddle Bag Lake is the name, I have been told. Information suggests that Gabe Griggs was the Chief Deputy Sheriff at the time and when he found out, he went into a rage and drove to Jeb Finch's house to kill him. Jeb found out he was coming and had all the other deputies surround the house and draw down on Gabe when he got out of his car. Jeb made Gabe resign right there in the yard, took his badge and his gun. To avoid public disclosure, Finch bought Griggs' silence with hush money and a job. Mr. Griggs went to work at Eleanor Ford Motors car dealership weeks later.

According to an interviewee, Finch paid a large sum of $$$ to Griggs to keep his yap shut and not prosecute. Years later, Gabe Griggs' wife had an affair with Gavin Eller. The day she planned to leave her husband, she called Gavin to confirm he was still going to leave his wife.

According to my informant (Winston Wahlberg,) Eller told her no, he could not afford the scandal as he was the Superior Court State Judge and that his wife had all the $$ in the family. Mrs. Griggs was distraught because her husband was abusive and this was her only way out. She begged Eller (another redhead who played tennis) to reconsider and when he refused, she told him he would have to live with what she was about to do, and then she shot herself in the head while on the phone with him. (Her suicide is a matter of public record; the affair is not, but was told to me by Winston Wahlberg/VPD retiree.) Rumor had it her (Mrs. Griggs') husband was an abusive man and was furious that day that she had not brought his lunch to the dealership on time as she had every day. After waiting for an hour after her usual arrival time, he went home to find out why. When he got there, he found her. Two hours later he went back to work and said, "Well... she finally went and did it. She shot herself." And that was it. That's all he ever said about it.

Gabe Griggs' house sat on Indian Ford Road, a property either owned or adjoining property of Sadie Caulfield (grandmother of Mitchell Caulfield, President of Woodsmen of the World Insurance Company on Hill Street and a WOW Lodge.) Possibly the connection between Bob Waverleigh (William Robert Waverleigh, "Bob," was the father of the staged witnesses Stevie Waverleigh II and his friend John Buckley. See Beau Colbert's file and witness statements and Charley regarding Spencer's impression of a bond between Charley's initiations into a fraternal order of some sort. Per Kaye's journal, a Bob Waverleigh called the house and asked for Charley that Sunday he was killed. Also, this may be the possible link between Charley, Gerrilyn Baldwin, and Bob Waverleigh's triangle association scenario. The number you saw on your drive to Clearwater, Spencer? Your recurring # of 1545 and the association with the Sheriff (Finch) is the lodge # for a WOW Lodge in Tifton, Georgia that now has a possible link to several other people, including the 61-year-old man Robert Weatherby Chancellor (from Tifton, Georgia) that died 10/15/1966 of a heart attack in Valdosta a week after Charley died. (This name and date confirmed through records at Valdosta's Camden McLane Funeral Home records for that week that I reviewed.)

They say Weatherby was a retired Sears Roebuck and Company employee who died of a heart attack in a bed, presumably somebody's house and/or a hotel bed as his residence was in Tifton. I will try to get Camden McLane to confirm address he was picked up from for me. Rowan would be the one to have the file on that as Rowan Funeral Home would have been the only one with ambulance service back then. Winston Wahlberg says his son-in-law who bought Rowan's has no records to show me. (Wahlberg later became the Lowndes County Coroner.) Camden McLane may have more, but may not share more as a matter of privacy though. (Spencer, did he belong to the Woodsmen of the World Lodge #1545 in Tifton and does this have a possible connection to a sexual liaison? Because why would you get a room or be somewhere if you only were thirty to forty miles from home? Could this be connected to the obscene sex tape thing? Possibly homosexual or pedophilia- type activities on the tape? Could this be connected to the flower, calligraphy, kissing, and older man presentation you received with the name Ashley Palmers?) I will explain further another significance of the Tifton connection to someone else later in this diatribe.

Woodsmen of the World possible connection. Jules said she believed Charley had a brochure of theirs in his personal papers. I also have his key pouch which shows the missing key slots for home and possibly the P.O. Box. Their (WOW) meeting place was out by the prison which was next to the target practice area. President Mitchell Caulfield also owned copious amounts of acreage, including a hunt club surrounding the Sheriff's Clubhouse on the river at/on Clyattville- Nankin Road and Rocky Ford Road where Charley's body was found.

A rape/mutilation case was solved ten years later in the early 80's I believe when they found the body of a woman (Helen Hank who had gone to the VPD begging for protection and was sloughed off as being hysterical for no reason) from a man called Kilgore Williams (who was VPD auxiliary). She was discovered when they sold the land and had it developed. Digging an area for a road culvert, they hit a snag: a box with her body inside. She had been raped and then chopped up and stuffed inside a box, buried in the property at or just before Gabe Griggs' front yard. (See case Kilgore Williams vs. State; victim's name was Helene Hanks. When he buried the body, he thought he was burying it on the opposite side of the road where his aunt owned property, thinking he would ultimately inherit the land and could clean it later without suspicion. According to statements made, the fog was thick, the hour late, and he got confused which side of the road his family's land was on.)

Ok... I got the Woodsmen of the World connection from the #19 Spencer had given for the flag and flagpole clue at the tall building. WOW Lodges often donated flagpoles and flags as part of their civic duty to support nonprofits. The engraved stone out at the bottom of the flagpole outside the Lowndes County Historical Society building read "Presented by Woodsmen of the World Lodge, 1995."

In Charley's personal letters there is a reminder of dues for a lodge of $12.00 due. This also led to the lodge/fraternal connection clue from Spencer about Bob Waverleigh and Charley and furthers the triangle formed between those two and Gerri Baldwin. Sam Daily's general store in Nankin, just a few miles the other side of the bridge (where the two boy witnesses called Brooks/Lowndes County offices from) mentioned as a connection to Charley and "G" could now also mean Sam Daily was perhaps a member of WOW. Am I still on track, Spencer?

Ok... I am hopeful that the message from a "J" or "Je," possibly Jeremy or Jeremiah came in the form of a church sign that read "Jeremiah 29:11. 'For I know the plans I have for you,' declares the LORD, 'plans to prosper you and not to harm you, plans to give you hope and a future.'"

I hope the hell so because my daughter's psychotic episode Thursday night scared the shit out of me. Spencer, I still need to talk more to you about that. Piper has no memory of what she did, but the other daughter and her friend Karalee sure do and they were frightened by what she saw and heard.

Ok...the information from a female whose name begins with "Sa" came in the form of a magazine connected to the diner that is owned by the woman with the antique typewriter, Kohle's Grill. Here's the scoop on that info. In Kaye's diary, she wrote about how Charley and a few of the others hung out at a café drinking coffee. It was called the Plaza Café. This is where Gerri and Charley used to hang out. Parker Jade was the head of the Parole Office. They worked at the courthouse on the 3rd floor. Deputy Sheriff Colbert worked out of the Sheriff's office on the first floor. That's how they met. The Plaza Café was on Hill Street, near the Woodsmen of the World Insurance Company. (How convenient?)

Rumor had it, if Parker Jade was in the café and Charley would show up for coffee, Parker would call his secretary, Gerri Baldwin, to come join them and sit next to Charley. If Gerri was there and Charley showed up, she would call Parker to come join them. Odd, huh??? Even odder is the fact that I found out this weekend that Darwin Devonshire, the prison warden (who, I was told, was fired for misappropriation of government funding) had a connection to "G" and owned the Plaza Café at the time and then sold it when the man who owned the entire building refused to sell all three floors to him. Devonshire then moved his restaurant to the other side of the street, opposite the Courthouse, and bought the corner building there and established the Kohle's Grill restaurant where we found the photos and the connection between Darwin Devonshire and Alvin Devonshire, a/k/a Red Devonshire, whose name appears in the funeral ledger.

Darwin Devonshire, prison warden, was eventually caught using prison workers to do private contract labor jobs and was fired for it. According to Kaye's journal, Parker Jade used to force parolees onto Charley once they were released. Charley built houses on the side and initially wanted to help the new parolees get a leg up. He obliged at first, but it became a problem. Kaye was getting tired of working with men she couldn't trust and had no carpentry skills for fine work, feeling like she was running a prison farm because they practically forced these parolees on them in the months preceding Charley's death. (Darwin's kin relation, Alvin Devonshire, a/k/a Red Devonshire, owned an asphalt company in Quitman, just across the river from where Charley was found dead. Is this a possible connection for fixing state bids for road work? Possible kickbacks and fixed bid scenarios? Originally my prospect for the red-headed go-to man who helped do cover up of C's murder, but he has been replaced by my new prospect: Red "George" Slidell, who did car detail paint jobs for Lowndes County Sheriff's Department vehicles and motorcycles. Rumored also that he was involved in the local KKK and did taxidermy.)

Now as for the female energy that will cross my path with the name that starts with "S" or "Sa," I have found that. When we were leaving Kohle's Grill with my info about the Plaza Café, I paid for lunch and bought a magazine at the register that was about Valdosta. It had an article in there about what teenagers used to do in the 60's for fun. The article was written by a woman named Sandra O'Connell. The curious thing about the article is that while she mentioned drive-ins and hot spots, she also mentioned that she read a lot and was very athletic. She was an avid tennis player, enough so that she began to spar with older tennis pros in the town, one of whom was a notoriously good tennis player. (Spencer, pay attention. A man with flaming red hair that painted/made signs, commonly called by his nickname ("Red") Slidell and he belonged to the Country Club! That fits your description of the red-headed go-to man that the shooter confessed to. Remember? "A man with red hair that everyone knew played this sport with the shooter at a nice place, a country club-type setting." Also an impression that held an association with signs and the KKK.)

* New info from "Sa" contact: a former Lowndes County Sheriff who was on the boys tennis team played tennis with her when she was in high school back then. He was on the tennis team his sophomore year and then suddenly was transferred to a private school that summer following. He may also have played tennis with Red Slidell as I believe his family also belonged to the country club. I will have to confirm this. His father/family owned the Valdosta Electric Company and was rather well off. Check out a man by the name of Ashley Palmers. He may have a connection to Red Slidell. (Spencer, see what Charley presents with his name.)

Does your head hurt yet? It should, but hang in there with me because there's more. Ok, so far I have figured out these clues/hints from Spencer:

White blimp = white blimp over a car dealership. Car dealership has a direct association to a man (Gabe Griggs,) whose older daughter was raped by LC Sheriff Jeb Finch. He was also the husband of Elliot's mistress who committed suicide while on the phone with Eller, according to Winston Wahlberg.

#19 = Woodsmen of the World Connection. Flag/flagpole.

#1545 = Tifton, Georgia Lodge of WOW. (Spencer, I believe you mentioned he said it five times and that there is an association between this Lodge and with Sheriff Finch. Is this five times to represent five of its members who may have been involved in Charley's murder or are in the tape?)

Red-headed man, the go-to man, the cover up man, a sign maker = George Slidell a/k/a Red Slidell or Sylvan (sp?)

The young energy "Sa" or "Sarah" female information = article in Valdosta magazine about teenage activities and hangouts in the 60's (Red Slidell and tennis association.) She also played with a former Lowndes Sheriff who was a young man in high school in approximately 1958-59 and then transferred to a private school for his junior and senior years before going to Clemson. He was back and forth a lot for a few years there until his father died and he had to return to run the family business: Ashley Palmers. (Will try to check the Valdosta High School Yearbook for exact years of attendance.)

Mid-May meeting with information = two law enforcement agents (Lana Rockbridge and Don Rockbridge) who confirmed ballistics proof of lands and grooves, implying use of two guns, not 1. Info direct from GBI/Crime Lab report on file with GBI and in Beau Colbert's file. Reported rape case at VPD lake = Jeb Finch attacked and raped the older Griggs girl (Bobbie Lee) and his payoff, hush money to the father to keep it quiet and out of the courts.

Man who died of heart attack week after Charley = Robert W. Chancellor is only one who fits timeline and demographics; he worked for Sears, lived in Tifton (?), died of a cardiac arrest in bed at 61 years of age. He was from Tifton, Georgia I think, but the transfer of his body was to Augusta. (Same hometown as the reigning governor of the state at that time. Need to figure out his/MOT's home address and why there is a Tifton association. Also, have not confirmed membership with WOW. He was from out of town either way, so it is plausible this bed he died in was in a hotel room and/or someone's home. Could there be an association and/or possible connection to sex ring/sex /tape issue?)

Antique typewriter owner = Darwin Devonshire, Prison Warden. Had ownership of the Plaza Café where Parole Office official Parker Jade's secretary and alleged lover of Charley, Gerri Baldwin, some local ATF, GBI, FBI agents often had coffee with Charley. Also confirms the use of prison dogs at the crime scene that night, muddy paw prints seen by Spencer and also confirmed by Beau Colbert's statements.

Also, found divorce records in the Courthouse concerning Gerrilyn Baldwin and her husband Bob Baldwin that prove Gerri Baldwin and husband owned a 1963 Ford pickup. (Spencer, color of red confirmed by neighbor. Spencer, this is the truck owned at the murder scene that night). Also, Baldwins owned two houses, one at 116 Moss Oak Road, their residence, and another one, a rental property at 2912 Oak Street. Confirmation of Spencer's lead from first session: "1439 blue oak" three times. (Another individual confirmed color of the Baldwin truck as red and the house as blue. Could 1499 or 1439 be the license plate #'s?) She filed for divorce in 1965, then they divorced in September of '66 and the husband had only been out of the residence for a week before Charley was murdered. Then she remarries her husband three weeks later?

Ok, here is the biggie. The word "ostrich" associated with the Grim Reaper (State Trooper/Damon Cummings). This one damn near killed me!! I spent hours trying to decipher this one. As I was driving home from Valdosta, I saw the billboard for Tifton and it just came to me. Ridiculous, huh? Because it was the picture of a hibiscus plant! Go figure. I thought I would have a heart attack, like our dear Mr. Chancellors, our 1510 document man, because I looked at the damn plant and suddenly it hit me. You were right. Ostrich is not a bird or a nickname of someone, not a farm, and not associated with any petting zoo element at Wild Adventures Theme Park or anyone who worked with the damn birds either. It was the very last thing you mentioned to me Spencer — a code name or code for something. Ready?

O. S. T. R. I. C. H. = *Officers Sex Tapes aRe In Charley's House

(*or possibly the word OFFICIALS could be used in place of the word above; OFFICERS and/or SNUFF used in place of SEX tapes.)

*This explains the initial desperate search of Charley's car that night as described by Charley to S during first session. They freaked. Sloan went crazy and took Charley out before he found out where the incriminating goods were! Then they searched the wallet, car, and his house for the P.O. Box key (P.O. Box #153), thinking it was there. That's why the continual breaches of the home were made after that first night when they could not find the tape. Why his house keys were removed from his personal key ring and why they were **never** returned. Why they prohibited his widow from leaving to go to see Charley the night it happened by blocking her driveway with their cars and why they searched the home that* *night while she made phone calls. And also why they kept her out of town for a week!*

If Kaye had left the house that night, there would have been no reason for them to remain at the house as the proper thing to do would have been for her to be escorted by both agents Sal Wheaton and Claude Kirby to the Pineview Hospital, thus killing their chance to search while she was hysterical and distracted. Plus she would have seen the lacerations on Charley's arms, the wrong shirt on his torso, and the holster of a gun on his belt since she claims he never took one. Then their cover would have been completely blown! Remember, Sal Wheaton's and Charley's government car radios were on the same frequency as the State Patrol and Sheriff's Department car radios too from what I learned this weekend.

This would be a setup for an interesting scenario. In Kaye's journal she says how agent Sal Wheaton was unreachable via phone that night and how she would have tried to call the State Patrol to see if they could reach Charley, but Charley had told her NEVER to do that because too many people would know where he was. Charley's and Sal's cars were the only two with radios. Damon Cummings, who claims to be first responder and whose interview and drawing of the crime scene have no relation to what was in photos found in Beau Colbert's file but matches one drawn by Spencer in first session, share one aspect only the murderers and Charley would have known about. Having the same radio frequency between the two would provide contact between Sal, Damon, and any State Patrol and/or Sheriff Department personnel such as Finch or Colbert in those untraceable hours in between and present a problem for Mr. Wheaton as he was required to check in every two hours with Charley since they were both on standby that night.

Charley anticipated being gone no longer than an hour. Sal should have checked in with Charley at the house, yet no phone call was ever received, nor was he reachable by phone after 11:00 that night. Why? The last time Charley spoke to Sal was before they

*went out for dinner, Charley to Shoney's with his kids and Sal
Wheaton to the Roosevelt Café. But Kaye spoke to him then, not
Charley. That was around 4:30 that evening. If he were to check in
every two hours, that might have been the suspected phone call at
6:15-6:30, just about the same time as Bob Waverleigh's call. If
not, he was well overdue and that would be inexcusable as they
were tracking a truck with raw materials from Athens that night.
Sal should have made at least two or three more phone calls to the
house before he could have been made aware that Charley was
dead. Why did he not check in again that night? And what about
that truck of supposed raw materials? Why the devil do you drive
from Atlanta to Athens if you are going to Valdosta? Not even a
moonshiner is that stupid!*

*More curious, Sal was the one to take all the guns that night. If he
and Kirby had escorted Kaye to Pineview, they could not have
searched the home in those first few hours. They not only didn't
offer to take Kaye to where Charley was, but they blocked her
Buick in the driveway/carport to prevent her from leaving the
premises and she was prevented from seeing her husband's body
until Tuesday of that week. Why? To keep her from seeing the
lacerations on the body and the inconsistency of the clothing and
the addition of a holster for the gun he wasn't carrying.*

*Meanwhile, Gerri Baldwin had free access to Charley throughout
the entire process. There's a lawsuit right there for the funeral
home if I ever saw one. Odd for both agents and funeral home to
accommodate such a breach of etiquette, don't you think? They
(Sal and Claude) removed guns from the front hall closet,
including the rifles, then searched the cabinets and closets in the
kitchen and the downstairs and the carport. (Why would you do
this if you were so certain he had committed suicide with a pistol
that you found under the body to begin with? Isn't this a gross
violation of private property? They even suggested his widow stay
in Millen at Charley's parents' house for that full week after his
burial. This would give them unfettered access to the Valdosta
house and garage without her there to protest. This situation might
also explain why ATF agent Claude Kirby's statement reflected a
"staged" misstatement that the jailer said Charley had taken the*

government truck. This makes no sense. Kirby was at the scene, and if not he, then other agents and officers who could have confirmed the government vehicle at the scene was Charley's sedan. Regardless, there was no need to go to the federal building at all, so why at 1:00 in the morning do you make the effort to go there? Why do you need to go inside the building if your concern is the truck in the parking lot? A drive-by would have sufficed, if even necessary. So why do you go inside the building and then to Charley's office?

In his statement he says he drove on, but that is inconsistent with both the time line and the fact that he is the one credited with spotting the "wet footprints" in the hall at 2:30 am in the morning. This statement, of course, further presents a problem for Kirby since he states he was at Kaye's house with Sal Wheaton at that hour. This timeline is confirmed by Kaye's journal. But is that the only way to explain your own wet footprints in the hall later as Charley's? And why would you go to the widow's house after you make a trip to the Federal Building? His first and only duty was to inform the widow, a duty grossly more important. So why not go to the widow's house first? And where was Mr. Wheaton when Mr. Kirby was at the Federal Building if they "went together to inform Mrs. Covington?"

This was Kirby's excuse to go back to the Federal Building and go through Charley's office, searching for the tapes or for a gun. This is where and when the footprints were left in the hall and then "discovered" by Kirby at 2:30 in the morning. "They" claimed the footprints must have been left by Charley, who must have gone to his office on his way out of town to clean things up. This makes no sense at all. Charley would have been dead before 10:00 or10:15 pm as the first witness sees a man at the front right tire by 10:25 pm. The second set of witnesses saw him by 10:35 pm with man in the road. The heavy rains came after 11:45 pm when the boys and the father returned to meet law enforcement at the scene according to statement timeline and witness interview with Scott Waverleigh 2010, age 64 now. It would have been impossible for Charley to have made them and gotten back to his car and committed suicide to fit their timeline.

But this testimony explains clearly why his office was gone through and why other porn tapes were missing and then one later turned up, used by Finch to taint Charley's reputation and promote his sexual appetite as fodder for an affair, a tape which was invoiced November 22, 1966 sent from Los Angeles, CA to Charley's P.O. Box address. Concern: How could Finch have used it as evidence? Who opened the P.O. Box with the key, the key that was missing? This was the same key they had Gerri go and get from Charley's house and /or off his key chain as proposed in the "female energy who is asked to get it."

It may also explain why they (Bill Hardy, Claude Kirby, and Sal Wheaton) kept interviewing her (in Millen) while she was there, including why they made her identify all of Charley's weapons. The one weapon she could not identify was the weapon they claimed Charley shot himself with. Kaye claims that Charley did not take his weapon that night and that she had never seen the specific gun they claimed he shot himself with before they showed her in Millen. When she asked where it (.38 special short barreled pistol) would have been, they told her Charley had given it to Gerri Baldwin for protection. Why would an ATF agent ever give his supposed "government-issue weapon" to a woman he was having an affair with? And why would this woman later on demand that Kaye give it back to her? Ballistics fears?

This scenario also would explain why she would come home in the weeks to follow to find that someone had been in the house and gone through cabinets and drawers. But there was no breaking and entering evidence at the doors. And this is why they (Hardy and investigators) demanded she allow them to search Charley's personal car and the home two weeks after, claiming they were missing several sticks of dynamite and wanted to recount. (This was dynamite that Charley kept out on a neighbor's farm in a shed so that he wouldn't have to worry about Kaye or the kids getting hurt, dynamite they would have had no idea how much he did or did not have to begin with anyway as each agent took care of buying and handling his own. And if they had had intimate knowledge of his dynamite use, they would have also known where he stored it.) And more importantly why his keys were never returned and no one claimed to have removed them. Where were all his personal effects and why did they refuse to give these back to Kaye for weeks? When they finally did, the keys were still missing and no one knew where they were. Then they claimed perhaps someone thought they were his office keys. Well, if Claude Kirby got into his office that night to claim Charley had been there, they had the office keys already! Inconsistency again.

This looking for the sex tape scenario and loss of house keys also satisfies why several key players in this — including Damon Cummings, Jeb Finch, Hank Sloan, and several others — were not present at Charley's funeral in Millen, Georgia. They were too busy searching for the tape in Charley's house while others were out of town at the funeral.

How am I doing so far, kids?

As for the 7 of spades clue, this may be a stretch. The word, "spades" also stands for shovel. Could we be talking about the #7 as a marker and manner of death involving a shovel? Also, I became concerned that an interviewee of mine (who showed up in the first meeting without invite and has not missed any conversations or meetings after and who tried to demand that he be given the only crime scene file and photos in existence so he could give them to the Historical Society or back to the Sheriff's Department) might be involved intimately with Charley's murder. His historical proximity to the Tifton PD and the sex scandal era of the VPD caused me great concern. I asked around to see if he was a tennis player in his earlier years. (This is one of the specifics to the shooter energy.) I was told he did not play tennis, but he was a big card player. I'm not convinced the card thing is right, so I will continue to keep my options open. It may mean something else completely.

Here is more info on Winston. Winston Wahlberg is a former VPD official who now looks as though he may have been involved at some level and/or had intimate knowledge of the crime. He worked for the Tifton PD and was fired. He then got a job at VPD and was eventually promoted to lieutenant and then captain during this time (somewhere in the '60's, possibly around '66 and on through sex scandal years into the 70's). Later he came on board with the Sheriff's Department. He lived two doors from Gerri Baldwin on Moss Oak and maybe had a thing for her too, went into great detail describing her as very pretty, tall, long legs, and black eyes. He could remember this but not the exact color of her truck or if they had a black dog for a pet. He (like Damon Cummings, the Grim Reaper, and State Patrol officer who pontificated about being first responder and description of crime scene on recorded interview and drawing of crime scene on my notepad) was greatly concerned about the existence of a file that contained crime scene photos and/or a ballistics report that could prove bullets were from two different guns. In fact, Damon Cummings' only comment the day after the interviews on CD was a question. He wanted to know if they were ever able to prove both bullets were from the same gun. Why would you ask that if they had the two bullets and the gun under Charley's body with nitrate on his right hand and it was declared a suicide?

We talked with Winston Wahlberg on Saturday morning on our second trip down, along with the local sheriff (Captain Clint Sims) who suddenly became very quiet while Winston talked. The sheriff spoke with us when Winston went to the bathroom, an activity which he did four or five times during our breakfast meeting. Clint told us he was concerned about the misinformation Winston was giving us and how convenient his memory loss of certain things was. He cautioned us to be careful of what we said to him. Winston's trips to the bathroom became increasing as I discussed new information. Could he have been making phone calls?? He (the sheriff) also pointed out a woman who came into the restaurant that Winston had had an affair with while he worked for the city. I found out also that Winston and Beau Colbert (the Deputy Sheriff who immediately replaced Gabe Griggs, father of rape victim by Jeb's son and is also Jeb's second cousin) were best buddies back then. Beau had a thing for Gerri and so did Winston apparently. Have we missed something in the mix with Winston,

Spence? Could he be the LT connection that night or is it Logan Booker??)

Anyway...

When we were leaving the parking lot of Denny's, he (Winston) pulled me aside from the group. He asked me who I thought did it and who else was involved and why he hadn't been given a copy of the file and photos. When I said I didn't have a copy with me and that there was no reason to give him a copy, he got agitated. When I said the shooter could have been one of several people, he wanted me to get specific. I said I believed Beau Colbert may have been involved on some level, but I did not know who the shooter was for sure, that the shooter may even be dead, but that there had been more than one other person there that night besides Gerri Baldwin, the shooter, and Charley. I told him several people had motive, but it was obvious the attorney/Judge Eller had seen all the evidence in 1974 and knew who the shooter must have been. He then proceeded to tell me about the suicide info on (the Griggs woman) Gavin Eller's mistress. He said I shouldn't trust any info from Gavin as he basically had enough skeletons in his closet too.

Winston was also the one on CD interview recording that had a fit when he heard that VPD detectives had gone to Gavin behind his back. He said it was impossible and demanded to know the second name. I told him Billy Burgess was the one and only name given me by Gavin Eller and that he (Burgess) was dead, and I guessed that the other person might still be alive since Gavin refused to give me that second name.

Guys... I know this is a lot to take in. But it all adds up if you think about it. The association with the Tifton Lodge of WOW has something to do with all these folks, the tape perhaps, and the dead guy in the bed of a heart attack, possibly sex-related. Or some sort of consequence from an orgy perhaps?

Then there was the blimp over the car dealership with the tie to the father of the rape victim and the suicide of his wife over Eller. A rape and a cover up by Jeb Finch. Jeb Finch's association with the #1545 WOW Lodge in Tifton. A suicide of the judge's mistress. The VPD sex scandals and the connections between the prison warden, Gerri, the parole officer, the asphalt company owner, and even more! The rape victim was Bobbie Lee Griggs, who married Al Fitzpatrick. He held several jobs, including as a U.S. Marshal that hauled prisoners for Darwin Devonshire. He also was involved in the Charley thing and had a bad reputation. He knew about the affair and lied to Kaye about it the day of Charley's death, when she confronted both him and Bobbie Lee about knowing and not telling her. He was also called to the trial to testify.

Jeb Finch's first wife (Audrey) married Marion Tanner, who is somehow connected to our "wrought iron T" clue from Spencer, maybe on his gate entrance to the property they live in Florida? Finch's second wife was a lady by the first name of Paula (last name not known at this point), who was a secretary in the Labor Department Office in Atlanta. Apparently Finch spent a great amount of time at the governor's office with Gov. Chandler Sorenson. (Spencer, remember the connection to the Grim Reaper/DC and the governor? Could he have been the driver for Finch on these visits or is there another type of connection to Chandler Sorenson between Cummings and the governor's office apart from Finch?) Finch used to go to Atlanta, spend a lot of time with Sorenson, and hang out at the Playboy Club there.

This may be the segue between the parolees used as contract labor on personal projects or the possible bid rigging for road work in the state and God knows what else. The Grim Reaper also had a connection to drugs as I recall and the code word "OSTRICH," which I firmly believe stands for "Officer Sex Tapes aRe In Charley's House." That explains why the keys were stolen from Charley's key chain and the desperate search by shooter at the scene that night in Charley's car and also the after searches made by agents and officers of local law through everything Charley owned.

Ok, Spencer... the only things I have yet to explain are the following:

The fence, not regular kind of fence. Wood. A fence with a carving in it, burning hot property.

Cannot identify the badge #1439 (possible FBI as they are the only group in the mix that had #'s that went that high in 1966).

The shift in the investigation that will occur on June 14th.

Why they refer to Damon Cummings as the Grim Reaper (if indeed he is not the shooter. Perhaps led Charley to his death as in angel of death who leads to death, but is not death itself?)

If the tie to the governor's office was bid rigging and/ or sex-porn, drug $$, or more?

Why my daughter had such descriptive hallucinations last Thursday night.

What role Winston Wahlberg plays in this and why he was so insistent from the very start with Wayne Colbert (Beau Colbert's son who found Billy's file with crime scene photos and statements and had offered them to Jules and me) that the pictures be turned back over to the Historical Society or to the Sheriff's Department immediately, but not to me?)

What and who is on that freaking tape!?!

What the WOW Tifton Lodge #1545 has to do with all this?

Were all the key players involved in this Woodsman of the World fraternal lodge?

Whether I am right or wrong about George Slidell, aka "Red" Slidell who makes signs and plays tennis as the go-to man for the shooter? Gavin Eller played tennis too and had red hair and also belonged to the country club, but no association with signs or KKK that I know of.

And last, but not least, who the hell is the shooter???

Beau Colbert fits everything but the tennis playing connection. (I do not know if Cummings played tennis yet.)

Damon Cummings, State Patrol is called Grim Reaper and is the O.S.T.R.I.C.H. connection, but did he play tennis? Did he have anything to do with the tape, as in participation? Is he the one with the shooter?

New info: Ashley Parkers, former Sheriff, was a tennis player back then. Fits young energy, fits tennis player, also fits law enforcement association. Any connections?

I'm working hard, but am about to give out! Can you help confirm anything here, Spencer? Take a couple of aspirins, girls: this is just part of what I think I know so far.

(Disclaimer for the above: The above were speculations based on information received up to that date. New and more defined information was received and confirmed after several more readings and research.)

If you go back, you will see that occasionally I post phrases or numbers that are for me to decipher. I am meant to piece this thing together like a puzzle, and very often the pieces are odd and so irregular that one might feign indifference as an antidote for complete befuddlement. While these pieces and patterns seem superficial to most, if I am clever enough to decipher, they hold microcosms of information. Such was the case many blogs ago when I wrote about the following segment of a session I had with Spencer.

You will find the answers. The number 1510 is significant and the trail will lead to MOT... two times he repeated "the trail will lead to MOT."

Charley said I would find the answers to the two of those. He predicted that the trail would lead to MOT and it did. While walking through a parking lot and passing over the word SLOW painted in yellow on wet black asphalt, I finally figured it out.

If you take the word SLOW and invert it… the first three letters mimic somewhat close to MOT — only the T is actually an L and so you only get half the effect. But because my mind works in mysterious ways, it became not a matter of an inverted "L" leaving me with half of what a T might look like; it became about why I would have made the association of the word "SLOW" to the "MOT" in the first place. That's when I took a leap of faith and knew that others were at the helm, so I went with whatever impressions entered my mind. The more I concentrated on the inverted word "SLOW," the more I began to rummage through the catalog of other more recent clues and the bells started going off in my head.

The language barrier between Charley and me finally broke free. It was remarkable how once I let go of my thought process and embraced his, it opened up my mind. The awkward association between "SLOW" and "MOT" got me thinking about letters presented perhaps in other angles. Letters became not just words, but phrases; numbers became addresses and dates. Suddenly as I pulled out of the parking lot, it hit me. The clock in my car rolled over to 11:11 am and I instantly knew without doubt what the MOT meant. Within seconds of that epiphany, the numbers I had been given earlier also made perfect sense. My "ah-ha moment" suddenly became a series of "oh shit moments" that lasted the entire afternoon and into the evening.

The minute I figured out the shorthand of the dead, everything became a roadmap to what Charley had been trying to lead me to since the very beginning: *"The trail will lead to MOT = the trail will lead to the Man On Tape!"*

With the information on a death certificate from Camden McLane Funeral Home that corroborated the dates mentioned, I ascertained that the "Man on Tape" was a man named Robert Weatherby Chancellor, who was found dead, supposedly of a heart attack, in a bed on October 15, 1966, just six days after the murder of Charles Gordon Covington.

CHAPTER EIGHTEEN

As I got closer to nailing down and confirming the true identity of the shooter, I got closer to what I perceived as the end of my relationship with Charley, and it began to weigh heavy on my heart. So much had happened between his 8 x 10 and me during all the days and nights of this case that I worried he would leave me if I finally called his killer by name.

From my first interview with Pat Guymon, who had been a friend and colleague of Kaye's, to my final interviews with retired ATTD agents, it all added up. Sloan was a ladies' man, heavy drinker, and aficionado of the deadly game Russian roulette. Local law was called repeatedly to Sloan's house to break up domestic disputes and had said the ceiling in the bedroom was riddled with bullet holes. Apparently Hank had a bad habit of threatening to take him or his wife out if she didn't give him what he wanted. And not just that. Both E.C. Patterson and Gavin Eller had mentioned about the top and bottom shell in the barrel being spent that night, and that meant but one thing. Somebody rolled the barrel, quite possibly in another game of Russian roulette.

I was also able to discover that Sloan had two hound dogs, had gotten divorced, and lived with his mother just six miles across the state line from the bridge where Charley died. This information corroborated Spencer's information about the type of house and the living arrangement noted about the killer. It all fit perfectly: the potential location of the shooter and the final dumping site of the buried weapon across a state line. I knew investigating that would require a federal search warrant and that made things more difficult.

Convinced I was right, I needed to find the exact address for the eventual investigation by the proper authorities. Once I began, I noted that portion of the state held hundreds of addresses listed under the name Sloan. Since I couldn't afford to send up any red flags, I pretended I was doing genealogy on the Sloan family from North Carolina. In the later part of May my persistence paid off. I'd finally narrowed it down to a few promising sites near the Georgia/Florida border that I'd mapped on Google Earth. While discussing them with Spencer, the infamous "they" came through with more information.

"This is weird," she said. "They show me the person with the lizard is the shooter. The lizard is not figurative; it is a real lizard, an iguana or a chameleon. A real lizard, alive and tangible in 1966. They show he is abusive, especially to the farm animals, chickens in particular. The name Belleview is mentioned. It is a tall building, urban setting. Looks like a hospital. How did your shooter suspect's father pass?"

"I don't know, but I could try to find out," I answer.

"They showed me he is bleeding through the nose, something about an ambulance."

"I can try and find something out through Clint, maybe."

"This Clint, who is he again?" she asks.

I told her he had worked as an EMT for Rowan's Funeral Home and helped Mr. Rowan get Charley onto the gurney and to the hospital morgue that night. He was just in his early twenties then, but that now he is the Captain of the Lowndes County Sheriff's Department.

"Help me understand this. Your last trip to Valdosta, someone had orange powder in his drink. This person is a good resource for you, a good person, very involved with," and she paused. "Very involved with...helping? He drank the orange drink like Tang, a breakfast drink?"

I laughed. "Yes, that was Clint. The last time I was down in Valdosta we met him and Winston Wahlberg at the Denny's for an interview. It amazed me. Winston had less than one cup of coffee the entire time he was there and kept going to use the bathroom, but Clint, Clint had three huge glasses of orange juice and never budged an inch from his seat!"

"Just so you know, they're showing me the other man wasn't using the bathroom," she broke in. "They are showing me a phone. Was he making calls? And something about another woman. I do not think this has anything to do with the case. It feels more personal, like, tied to your W person, another woman... not married to him."

"Ah, calling the kettle black! Well, that would explain quite a bit from that day," I sighed, "especially why he felt the need to rat Gavin Eller out about his illicit affair."

Spencer asked for a redirect and this came through:

"They want you to focus on the property. They're showing me the numbers 1 and 4, could be 14 or part of a larger number, 1, 4, something, something, something..."

"Could it be Hwy 146?" I ask.

"Possibly. Oh, this is interesting. Do you understand the reference The Wizard of Oz?*"*

*"*The Wizard of Oz? *Movie or stage play?" I added, offering to use my director's knowledge of both. "Because movies and plays are often not the same, the same way a book and a movie are usually altered for entertainment values. Sometimes they..."*

"Oz... like the movie." she cut in and explained.

"I know the movie well Why?" I queried. "I just don't see what one has to do with the other," I finished. You would think after all this time I wouldn't question such a random segue, but some habits die hard. "Ok, I give. What about the movie?"

"Do you understand the cellar door, where they run to get out of the storm? This house has a cellar door right in the front area of

the house, just like in the movie. Handle on the outside; you pull it up and open. A root cellar. This house still exists, still white," she added.

"Wow. Great segue! A white, one-story house with a cellar and the number 14 in it that could be anywhere in the states of Georgia or Florida. That should be easy to find, don't you think?" I mused.

Spencer laughed, but tried to comfort. "You're going to figure this thing out, T.A. These bits of information like the 1 and 4 are just bonus for direction; they are little confirmations of where you are headed." Then she asked me if I was planning to take another trip back to Valdosta soon. I told her I was hoping to, and she reminded me to just trust myself, to let things play out.

"It's unfolding just the way it should be," she said, and the religious charm of Saint Teresa on my necklace began to feel warm against my skin. "Yea, that's what she says too," I muttered to myself and touched the chain for good luck.

"Got it: just the way it is meant to be," I added and sighed. Faith can be a very fickle thing, but she was right. One week later during a family trip, Spencer was able to confirm my suspicions.

"So while I was in DC," she said, "I asked for resolution and woke up half asleep to "It's Sloan, the shooter." The gas station is the one with the telephone lines behind it and the Coke sign. What is the animation tie to Sloan? Did he draw animations, collect them, or work somewhere? And this is interesting. They are presenting that Damon destroyed the tape."

Disappointed, I hung up the phone. Once again, in the midst of my jubilation came my devastation. After finally receiving confirmation on the shooter, the victory felt hollow. Even if I could be certain about the burial location of the second gun, I could not access it and Hank was dead. The Sloan family undoubtedly would prohibit any excavations, the farmstead lay across the state lines, and only the feds would be able to grant me a warrant to search those family-owned grounds. With most of the key witnesses dead and the perpetrator himself long gone, why the hell would anyone even care?

In my mind, I knew even ATF would be less inclined to rally knowing the shooter to be dead. It all seemed so pointless now. In confirming Hank, I was about to lose Charley. And to make matters worse, the two best pieces of evidence that could have put me in front of every federal law enforcement agency in the land — the gun and the mystery tape — had been buried or destroyed some forty years before I had even known they existed. Instead of joyously celebrating the culmination of my epic efforts, I excused myself from the theatre, slumped into a heap, and wept uncontrollably beneath blooming wisteria vines that covered me, but could not comfort me.

CHAPTER NINETEEN

The next few weeks were wrought with family crisis and scheduling angst. My husband was scheduled to have shoulder surgery, we were getting down to the last weeks of wedding preparations for my oldest daughter, work was daunting, and it was all I could do to keep my head above water. In the midst of my personal chaos, I did my best to keep a healthy perspective about the paranormal event that had transpired with my daughter in our bedroom the month before and tried not to lose faith in the process. Finally able to confirm the shooter, I realized I still had a pot full of other clues that seemed to go nowhere that needed my attention. If Hank had been just the tip of the iceberg Charley had been talking about, what the crap represented the *Titanic* it was supposed to have sunk?

Spencer had assured me that finding Charley's killer, while monumental in light of all the obstacles, was only a precursor to everything else that would be discovered. She advised me to stay strong, trust, and to know in my heart that I would be led to the next thing when the time was appropriate. I knew she was right, but the ache in my gut continued to grow. At some point all would be revealed and then where would I be: Charley-less with a story I could write but not confirm? I would look like one of those idiots on a Maury Povich show or worse: Jerry Springer.

The more insane the clues, the more I began to feel the need to insulate myself and so ran to my laptop for comfort every chance I got. The problem was, it never seemed to last. As soon as I could put one suspicion to bed, forty more seemed to unearth themselves. I became overwhelmed by the lack of cohesion. Between the information and Charley, my life seemed inconsistent and disconnected. Everything I was told appeared to be so random. No matter how many times Spencer asked "Do you understand?" I had to face the fact that I might never understand most of what I was being told. It left me feeling incompetent and naïve for believing I was special enough for such a task. Night after night I would sit and read over impressions that I knew were supposed to make sense, yet I could not see heads or tails of what I was meant to garner from them.

They show me lakes around the number 472...disco lights... no, not disco...police lights- swirling lights at a lake...associated to Grim...

Do you understand the 7? Is this a deadline for you?

Do you understand a tiny bow connected to your grandmother... leaving little bows everywhere?

A fire truck. Do you understand the person who used to drive the fire truck? He knows everything and everyone... dead or alive. One truck... one driver... ask who this was...

Do you know of a story of a little girl who fell into a hole... or a ravine... under 9 years old... blonde hair? She is significant somehow. Fell into a ravine... has to do with her mother. Who is the mother? This woman is nicer than G. Check this out: the mother is significant...

They are talking about the chandelier, broken pieces falling off of it...

Possibly the same woman holding onto broken pieces of glass. She is tied to the girl... be aware.

I thought my mind would spontaneously combust if asked to divine one more thing. Once my husband's shoulder surgery was over, my job as caregiver began in earnest, and the added stress and strain placed me way beyond the scope of attainable calm. As June edged closer, I began to fray at the edges like an old Oriental rug. Every snag I hit unraveled me another inch, and suddenly the runs seemed to rush off in every direction. I was being deconstructed one thread at a time. Regardless how many times Spencer told me to have faith, I felt increasingly vulnerable. Having decided to go back school in August, hours in between making and serving meals and bathroom assistance were spent trying to find just the right degree and rationalization of out-of-state expense vs. the benefit. By the time my daughter's wedding invitation arrived, I was two seconds shy of a nervous breakdown.

God has impeccable timing, doesn't He? Still paying off her higher education, I was looking at adding to the bill of my own. Nora was a trooper, though. Her beloved's family was great with establishing plans for their off-scene reception, and we did our best to help with smaller details and her wedding trousseau. Being second string in her life stung a bit, and it was tough swallowing that they were now the chosen ones. In the end, however, it proved a huge blessing.

Days passed in a blur of chaos. In between calculating the family's extra medical bills and FAFSA forms, I couldn't help but think how badly I wanted to take what little money was left to run away and come back months later when it was all over. But there is no rest for the weary, so they say. The saying proved true. The bottom line was that Nora had helped all along the way with earning scholarships and high grades, so who could have complained? The issue was mine. Somehow I had failed to be the mother I was supposed to be, or her mother-in-law wouldn't have taken my spot in the sunlight. I felt small and bitter, wishing I had the money to do it right for her, but it was beyond the scope of possibility. I touched the parchment with my daughter's name aligned with the boy's name she had fallen in love with and thought about the little girl who had once trotted around the floor on her knees, tossing her hair behind her like a mane and smiled. We were so much alike and yet so very different from one another.

"How time flies," I whispered to myself and laid the invitation down on my desk, next to Charley's picture, wondering if it had hurt to watch Jules wed without him there.

"It feels like only yesterday when she called to tell us she was engaged. That was midnight on Halloween: Nora's favorite holiday." Charley congratulated me and smiled his usual smile, but I noticed the glint in his eye seemed to dim. How callous of me not to remember. Halloween had been Jules's favorite too. It was the last holiday in 1966 they'd gotten to share.

"Far back in the hill country is Hissing Hill. It's a bare and lonely spot,with one twisted house and a tall fir tree behind it."

This is the opening paragraph of *The Witch of Hissing Hill* by Mary Calhoun and pictures by Janet McCaffey, the Halloween book that Charley read to Jules several times the night he died. She loaned me her copy. I have it here on my desk, sitting next to my 8 x 10 companion whose heart must break in tandem at the sight of the little gold cat that wreaked havoc on the witch of *Hissing Hill*.

The binding broken by too many reveries, the pages soft to the touch like gray flannel under your fingertips, the book reminds me of childhood long ago. The parchment split with ragged edges of deep midnight blue, filled with stars that dipped at awkward angles into sweeping strokes of mossy green that ground the margins on either side. Atop the highest pinnacle of mottled vegetation sits a spired house of black with golden light from crisscrossed window panes that squint like evil eyes, eager to disarm you — and they do. For they remind me of sketchy moonlight that pierced the piney woods surrounding the spot he lay waiting for angels to wipe his face and dry his tears, to tell him that he was safe and that the nightmare was finally over.

I read it aloud one night so that he could hear. I held it close so that he could see and remember the tiny blue eyes that must have grown three sizes with every page and matched his gaze as he spoke of cats, black as pitch, hissing in the moonlight. I began soft and slow, purred and paused at all the spots a parent would. I made the sounds and growled low and guttural, making my cat the scariest cat of all. I felt the crush of phantom tiny fingers as they dug into the fleshy part of my palm in fear.

On page four when the witch appeared, I cackled like an old hen and rumpled my eyebrows, scrunching my face to exaggerate my wrinkles. And when her fellow witches arrived, I found a new octave to brand them each and moved the story forward with boney fingers that wriggled and wrangled. In between the turn of a page, I checked the photo to my left and read his eyes. They were calm with resignation. I told him I recalled such precious moments spent with my daughters when they were only six and so far away from being seven. He laughed and I cackled one more time as the power of my spell seemed to wane in the glowing eyes of the make believe yellow cat. Phantom air rushed from rosy cheeks that have held it tight while waiting for the good to come and save the day. The Charley in my photo softened at the edges, becoming Charley the father. The weight of his ethereal tears flooded my lungs and I could no longer breathe.

I reminded myself that it is not just her loss as a child, but his too as a parent that I mourn. My head bent and I cried.

"Oh, Charley, they grow up so fast. I cannot imagine the pain you felt in the tearing of the veil between the here and now and the then and forever lost. What grief you must have suffered through the years, watching and not being seen, whispering and not being heard, holding and not being held: each of you standing in front of a mirror that reflected one another's loss."

His eyes remained dry, but I knew there were tears behind them. "As you tucked her into bed and pulled the sheets to her tiny chin that night, what were your thoughts? What was it that made you think that to leave was better than to stay, that you must go and give credence to men who lie as involuntarily as would they breathe?" I thought about Gerri waiting out on the Clyattville-Nankin Road and blistered. "What made you think that someone else's hand fifteen minutes later would feel sweeter in yours than hers, or that another set of eyes held the power to beg for five more minutes of your time with more conviction than that of your little girl's?"

The tears fell from my eyes like scales, and I saw the fragility of my own family and wailed "Oh, how fickle the human heart. Oh, how fragile the eternal soul. What price you both have paid for temptation's sake. Would that I had the power to bring you back for just one second to hug the child inside the woman who has waited forty-four years to know you. Would that you could return just one more time to read this book, to wrinkle your nose and cackle like a hen, to hiss at the blackness of the night and howl at the bravery of a moon that still mounts clouded shelves of blue each night you are gone from her side. To say, 'Let me tuck you in, tiny one, and I shall tell you the story of how a little yellow cat with gold eyes conquered hate in the tiny house on *Hissing Hill*.'" The little cat on the cover of the book beckoned, but I wanted to stay in my world and not in his, so I laid the invitation down and filled out the RSVP.

Yes, I would be there. Yes, my husband and her sisters would be there. And somewhere in the air above and around me, Charley would be there too, reminding me how precious life really is. Renewed, I finished filling out the form for our selections, sealed the envelope, and then fired off a list of questions to Spencer. An hour later I received this back:

So instead of answering all of these specific questions, I am just going to open it up to Charley, see what comes through, and trust he is giving you information that will take you in the direction you need to go, so here I go.

Ostrich tied to Damon.

Feels like a female energy removed key, but also feels like she was asked to do it. Seems like there is a "J" associated with her... seems like she would have been friendly with Charley's wife and perhaps done it from inside the house. Was Beau's wife friendly with Kaye?

Find out the names of those next door neighbors.

Feels like Charley is telling me the shooter is dead.

Did you find a letter in an envelope from a female? From Tallahassee, FL? Or perhaps it's coming. Is Beau's wife still living?

Again, they reference a white blimp like the Goodyear one, but not to say that it is.

Palm trees on a decorative plate.

Your man on a tape appears to be a scapegoat for something, again a forced confession-type communication on tape.

The frantic search in office was to look for the key.

Significant person: pipe smoker but very specific pipe smoker. Used a certain mint-flavored tobacco and bought it locally. Store owners knew it was his favorite; it was the only type he EVER bought. Mustache and would have been involved with law enforcement, possibly even parks and recreation-type work. He is the ringleader for this tape situation.

Mention of what feels like female energy, nickname Rox.

Can your man on tape be linked to Gerri? Might be a connection there.

Keep on trucking reference from Charley.

Mention of September 29th. It is significant.

Possibly body in the lake where tape was exchanged.

Then in a postscript:

Hope you can put the pieces together. Stay positive! Also, congrats on your daughter's upcoming wedding!

I picked up the wedding invitation with my RSVP inside and smiled. Charley had not been able to make it to his daughter's wedding, but we were lucky. Don would be there for his.

Wouldn't he?

CHAPTER TWENTY

In the third week of June 2010, I was blindsided by a series of trials in my personal life that kept me from researching this case.

On Monday of that week my husband's partner called to say he had something important he wanted to discuss with him the following day. Tuesday, however, my husband was still on the road, so he didn't make it back into the office on time. The conversation was postponed. Come that Wednesday morning, bright and early, he walked into his partner's office, the Executive Vice President of the company he had helped to build and maintain for over seventeen years. Minutes later he walked out of the office defrocked of his title and benefits. Forced into early retirement, he was told it was because the company was in financial downfall. What we came to understand shortly after was that his partner had decided he could buy loyalty cheaper from younger and less experienced help.

That Wednesday night after a long drive home, I watched my husband and the walls of structure that supported his world crumble. His partner had been his best friend at one time, the godparents to our children and the brother he had always wanted. But no longer. By Thursday my husband was an emotional wreck. But by Friday, well respected and resourceful, he tucked his ego in his back pocket, pulled up his boot straps, and secured another job to begin the following Monday.

Unfortunately, it was a job he never got to start.

CHAPTER TWENTY-ONE

As they wheeled him down the hall, IV's swinging and monitors beeping, I mindlessly picked at the mud caked on the bottom of my shoes and wiped at my face. How the hell had this happened? The silver doors closed slowly behind a blur of white lab coats and blue scrubs, and I was left alone to erase my tears as fast as they fell. When the doors finally came to a rest and sealed, I tried to exhale but had forgotten how to breathe.

Two Saturdays prior I had received my royalty check for rentals of my plays. Since it was near Father's Day, I splurged on the 16'canoe and accoutrements we had been drooling over for the past three years. That, of course, was followed by the several tumultuous days surrounding his forced retirement and the overwhelming stress that embroidered every hour after its announcement.

Losing steady income was one thing, but all of our retirement was tied up in that company too. Having lost our collective ass on the last two real estate transactions and suffering under an endless supply of medical bills, we were not in a comfortable position to take such a blow. With our daughter's wedding just weeks away and not wanting to dwell on negatives, we packed a picnic lunch and tried to enjoy the new canoe and what was left of the week.

Getting up early, we ate a light breakfast and drove forty-five minutes north of Athens to the drop-off site at the Broad River Outpost. Once there, we were given the choice of three routes. The shortest route was three miles long, the next six, and the longest one ten. We opted for the ten-mile run. Two miles in, we hit our first small spurt of small rapids. Having navigated them with absolute aplomb, I declared myself Pocahontas. Another quarter mile in, he started to complain he did not feel well, so we stopped and ate some fruit. Another two miles in, he began to complain of chest pain. At first we assigned it to the incredibly stressful week and considered it an anxiety attack. Less than twenty-five minutes later, I knew it was not. Without warning, he slumped in the rear of the canoe. His face ashen and contorted with pain, he was sweating profusely and his breathing was labored.

Having received several calls while tied up to a tree and eating lunch, I felt certain I could get help. With his chest in a vice grip and his arm twisted in pain, I dialed 911 and waited for the operator on the other end of the line to answer. Five times I tried, and each time the call got dropped. I tried six more times before true panic set in. The color had left his cheeks and a sullen gray began to wash over every feature of his face. His lips began to turn a dull shade of blue. I punched the numbers in two more times. "I have Verizon, dammit. It's supposed to go everywhere! Why can't I get through?" I whispered into the stagnant air as his exaggerated breaths echoed in the hollow of the canoe.

I had a choice to make. I could dial… or I could paddle. I gave him the phone and told him just to hit redial as often as it took. Four tries in, he announced he could no longer press the buttons and slumped further in the canoe. With no cell service for the better part of those remaining miles, we could not reach 911 to notify them he was having a heart attack. With crushing chest pain and loss of breath, he did his best to remain conscious and alert while I was forced to frantically paddle the remaining miles of a river that drafted from as little as 12 inches to as deep as 20 feet.

In between stilted conversations and through Class 2 rapids with 256 pounds of dead weight wilting in the rear of the canoe, I said my prayers. After we finally got through to 911, the call was dropped six more times before they could tell us they would try to triangulate our location on the river, but to no avail. On the seventh contact, they informed us there was simply no way to access our location, and they could not reach us till we got down the river to the outpost.

How far is that now? I tried to calculate how far we had come before stopping for lunch and how far I had paddled since the onslaught of his pain. Without compass, map, or bearings, I paddled and prayed with the fury of a woman who refused to go down without trying. Had I known how far we were from the pullout at that point, I might have given up and slumped in the canoe beside him, but my ignorance paid off in huge dividends that day.

At each bend in the river, I was convinced it would be the last and whispered to the heavens over and over "C'mon Pocahontas...be the Indian! Be the Indian! Paddle, paddle, paddle." One and a quarter miles later I thought I heard the sirens of an ambulance and tried to pick up the pace. Don was still conscious but not by much, so I joked telling him faking a heart attack was a cheesy way to get out of paddling and that he would pay dearly for such shenanigans when we got home.

What in the morning seemed like generous accommodation soon became deadly handicap in the afternoon. Because our car had handicap tags on it and Don had told the girl about his recent shoulder surgery, she had opted not to leave our car in the general parking lot and relocated it down below the slough at the pullout field so we would be closer to the waterline when we got back. And, because we owned our own canoe and had not rented it, our canoe would not have been listed in their inventory. So when the ambulance arrived at the river outpost and said they had a 60-year-old man out on the river in medical distress, the Broad River Outpost employees did just what they were supposed to do. They counted canoes and matched them to the cars and their registry. In fact they matched everything all three times! Everyone in and still out had all been accounted for and confirmed.

Since our early morning host had left for the day ill and since each car in the lot had a corresponding rental agreement attached and none for the long run, technically we did not exist on paper. With no car in the lot unaccounted for and no canoe left out on the river, as far as the Outpost managers were concerned the ambulance dispatchers had gotten the wrong canoe outpost. Still, the paramedics refused to leave and asked for managers to double check with all the employees. With no other confuting information available to them, they told the ambulance driver they had no customers left out on the river on a long run and that there had obviously been a huge mistake.

Closing in on 6:20 pm, we had been out on the river since 10:00 that morning and in medical crisis for well over two. Having exhausted every ounce of energy I possessed in just getting the canoe to the pullout station, I did my best to scream for help, but nobody heard me. I helped my husband out of the canoe to the upper grassy area, laid him down, and screamed some more. Still nobody came. I ran back to get my phone and secure the boat and when he started groaning, panic kicked in again. In an effort to get to him, I stepped out of the canoe on the wrong side and fell in the thirteen-foot end, dropping my phone.

He laughed weakly, but with no way to call 911 again, I began to think it had all been in vain. Comedic moment lost, he laid back quiet on the ground, and I screamed as loud and as long in between tears as I could, but got no response. He was still conscious, but getting more unresponsive by the minute. I tried to find my second phone in the waterproof bag and dialed the Outpost itself to send help down. The call finally went through, but the line was busy! While trying to catch my breath, suddenly the thought of our old horse farm came to my mind. To this day I cannot tell you what prompted me to think about it, but two seconds later, hoarse from screaming, I did what I had successfully done for over 12 years to get the attention of horses from as far away as 30 acres. I whistled — not just once, but many times.

Finally I heard someone yell back, and within seconds two men loaded with EMT equipment slid down the slough meant for kayaks and canoes and were at his side. Meanwhile, the ambulance with sirens blaring from the ridge above followed the rutted side road down the hill. In a flurry of arms and legs, my husband was lifted onto a gurney, shuffled inside. They began hooking him up to monitors and IV's. They hollered the name of the hospital through the closing doors to me and climbed back up the dirt road out of the landing area and were gone. Standing with water dripping from both my life vest and eyes, I was left there on the shore with a 16' canoe, half a picnic lunch, and a huge hole in my heart.

An hour later with the canoe astride my geriatric ride, I entered the hospital still in wet and muddy attire. While they took him down for tests, the paramedics told me that they had packed back up into the ambulance and were about to leave the area when the lead EMT had heard a faint whistle and decided to follow the sound to the overhang of the cliff where he looked down to find me waving my hands and crying.

Still don't believe in divine intervention or synchronicity? If not for the fact that at the age of nine I watched every episode of Disney known to mankind and thought someday I might too become an English sheepherder, I might never have learned how to whistle like a pro and my husband would have died at the edge of the river.

So Charley…when you get a minute, please thank Walt for me!

CHAPTER TWENTY-TWO

Out of the canoe, but not out of the woods, I sat in the ARMC
Cardiac Intensive Care Unit family waiting area and contemplated
a future without his familiar smile and hazel eyes to wake me each
dawn. Over the last few hours he had told everyone who spoke to
him that I paddled like a mad woman, that I saved his life, that I
fell into the water with my phone at the end and made him laugh
till he thought he would die, literally. But most of all, he told folks
that I was his hero, that I could have quit, that I could have given
up without shame, but that I never once lost my stride the last four
and a half miles. He told people that I continued to paddle steadily
and even until we got to shore. Imagine that! In March we had
contemplated the merits of a divorce. Now less than three months
later, he was praising my name and telling complete strangers what
a wonderful mate I was. Still in a state of shock, I curled up in the
blue vinyl chair beside him and counted our blessings.

Like Kaye on October 8th, 1966, twenty-four hours before her
husband's death, I too had no idea what the next twenty-four hours
would bring me. Midnight rolled on through to mid-morning, then
complications with surgery scheduling set in, and it wasn't until the
next nightfall that they took him down. Hugs and kisses spent, I
sent the children home to rest and take care of the dogs, so I could
say my private goodbyes.

If Charley's death taught me nothing else, it taught me there are no
guarantees. Charley had counted on coming home to a hot cup of
coffee; Kaye had counted on another chance to make amends. In

194

the end neither got what they wanted. Bearing that in mind, I knew that once they wheeled Don out of that room there was no guarantee he would ever come back. No guarantee we would ever be given again the chance to say the things we had been avoiding for months.

Bloated by fluids and exhausted by circumstance, he looked so frightened and foreign, I began to cry. Between regrets over his job, his unhappiness with living under constant pressure, and the spiral of our marriage, life had put him in a place he no longer knew how to climb out from. He agreed his depression had placed our marriage somewhere it had never been before either, and while it didn't excuse my recent behavior, it had made him understand that if not for the children, moral protocol would never have mattered and I would have left him long ago.

I kissed his cheek and he kissed my eyes and told me again how much he loved me and we blinked our regrets and tearful goodbyes. God had granted us the second chance Charley had taken for granted.

As I watched his gurney blur behind my tears, I thought about all the little games we play and the bigger games that tend to take us out. I thought about Charley and Kaye, about vicious words and uncaring actions brought about because of broken promises and straying hearts. It was at that moment that I learned that sometimes the good Lord reaches down and either grabs you by the scruff of your neck or firmly holds you in His arms. As the gurney had just left the room, the jury was still out on what He planned to do with us both.

The days that followed continued to pass from dusk to dawn without time to think clearly or hold to personal agendas. In the absence of the anesthesia of absolute crisis, post-traumatic stress began to set in and it too had a way of taking its own kind of toll. The day Don had his heart attack everything changed for us. With hindsight to guide, we began to wade back into the waters of matrimony carefully, each with a keener eye as to what we wanted, what we would or would not accept from one another, and what we realistically needed to acknowledge about ourselves and try to change.

Summer had been brutal, but as frightening as the future loomed, I faced it with courage. My husband had cheated death, our failing marriage had beaten the odds, and we were holding tight to the things that had brought us together in the first place.

CHAPTER TWENTY-THREE

Ignorance may be bliss, but it's not the truth. While Charley's marriage had taught me that, it was something I found in his wallet that brought it home.

In Charley's first session with Spencer, he had practically wailed over the betrayal of G. You could almost feel the palpability of his heartache, confirming his breach of vows. In a subsequent session, Charley presented another time three years before his death that sent up a red flag about his and Kaye's marital discourse. He talked about a glass jar of something yellow that was thrown against the kitchen wall in an argument. There was something embedded within that impression that had to do with alcohol and a tragedy that caused a rift. He revealed that something terrible had happened between them, something that they could never seem to get over. It was a benchmark: a beginning of the end, a time when they began to drift apart. Charley is very clear about the divide, but not the cause.

In Kaye's journal she speaks about the several folks she interrogated to get information that day on her errands. She talks about the neighbors who told her things were fine, and one who told the truth and said they weren't, the only woman who had the guts to be honest with her: Bobbie Lee Fitzpatrick. And a comment made by one of the retired ATF agents that said an ATF superior had once said, *"I knew it wasn't suicide. Charley would never have killed himself over a woman. He'd had other girlfriends before and he didn't do it over them… why would he have done it this time?"*

It was a painful thing to hear, but then as I well knew, innocence is best worn by the guilty. Kaye must have known something about G and Charley, as in her journal she had alluded to an affair with another woman years earlier in Douglas. Maybe that was the explanation for the scene Spencer had previewed, where she saw Kaye smashing a jar of pickled peaches against the wall. The more I read and learned about Kaye, the more it became apparent that Kaye would have navigated a divorce with the aplomb and agility of an attorney if pressed, but it was clearly not what she wanted.

Kaye wrote in her journal about the bedtime scene between Jules and Charley, about him reading her the Halloween book and then dropping the bombshell about his moving out. Kaye discounted it in the next paragraph as a joke, but maybe not so. In a conversation with Jules, she told me her brother went on record talking about how his parents had fought all afternoon that day. She even said she remembered something about being told she could skip school the next day and go buy dresses at Sears to make her feel better about the impending separation. Maybe that was why Charley had them going through the Sears and Roebuck catalog for Christmas just before he left that night.

So, was Charley really about to bail on the marriage?

While preparing for a meeting with Spencer, I had cause to revisit his wallet one more time. Crammed inside the corner of one of the folds, I found a small piece of paper that at first I assumed it was a ball of lint. At first I dismissed it, but evidence is evidence, so I used a pair of tweezers to get it out. It was so balled up it took several minutes of careful wrangling to unravel it. The condition of the tiny bundle was so compromised that I was forced to remember Charley's wallet had been soaked in his blood and rain for hours that night. From the outside it looked almost unsalvageable.

Once I was able to separate it a bit, my efforts proved worthwhile. Flattened and pressed, it became legible and its contents floored me. It was an ad that had been clipped from a local newspaper for a two-bedroom home for rent in the Lake Park area. I was uncertain what to do with it. In one sense it provided further evidence that Charley had not intended to commit suicide that night, that he clearly had other plans that included a move sometime in the immediate offing. In another, it made one ponder if G had meant enough for Charley to think about starting a new life of their own.

Still, Kaye had recorded a conversation with Charley about a potential rental. In her journal she recorded that Charley mentioned they should consider putting their house on the market and rent while waiting for an ATTD transfer to Alabama or Tennessee to come through. Remember, he had already advised Kaye about the schedule to close Valdosta ATTD offices at the end of the year.

"While we were sitting there at the table, just before he left to take the children to Shoney's, he told me that he had either told Mike Bolton to sell the house or that he was going to. That was odd to me because we never bought a car or a piece of furniture without discussing it. I asked him why and he said that he thought that we could rent until the first of the year and see if he got a promotion. That just didn't make sense to me as we had often talked about renting the house in the event he got transferred... I told him that I did not want to sell it, that if he wanted to go to the next state when they started Operation Dry Up, let's just rent it and be paying for it. He insisted that we sell it. He could have sold it without my consent; it was the only house we had not owned jointly. At the time the loan had closed, my father had been in a very serious auto accident. I was unable to go to the closing."

Still, the fact that it was in his wallet and he had told Jules the night he was murdered that he was not going to live with them anymore left me saddened. Because of its placement inside the wallet and because it was still there for me to find some forty-odd years after it had been placed there, I sincerely doubted that anyone else had ever noticed its existence before. In a way, that made me happy. Had anyone seen it from the start, he or she would have tossed that onto the heap of evidence in favor of the affair and Kaye might have let this thing die as the scandal it was purported to be.

Unfortunately, its existence begged another question. If Charley had not been murdered that night, would he have gone through with his threat and moved out? Would he have taken the two-bedroom house in Lake Park over the home he had built with Kaye and designed to retire in? Or was this some sort of convenient love shack where he and G could go until things settled down? That is something none of us will ever know because that night everything changed for him and he never got to choose.

Academically I knew it would never matter. I also knew that solving the mystery of Charley's death would never gift him the wonderful years he has missed with his children, nor bridge the gap between him and his wife. But according to the medium, Kaye had been at his side throughout many of the sessions. Quiet and stoic, she let him take the lead and speak his mind. Perhaps she invites me to do the same within my own marriage, to wait quietly and patiently in the wings, not wasting time on the whys of love, but to enjoy the mysteries it brings to each of us.

CHAPTER TWENTY-FOUR

June had been a crazy month, but July looked as though it might be able to top it. Just as I was relearning how to hold onto my husband, Piper came waltzing home with stars in her eyes and announced that she was moving in with her new love the following month. With Nora gone and Piper packing down her world, the house seemed much too quiet. Cardboard box by box, my family was being deconstructed. Claire became somewhat depressed by all the comings and goings, and bit by bit I felt I was losing her too. On top of that, clues were flying in. Even though I thought I was getting pretty good at putting them all together, some continued to baffle the shit out of me. In addition to the mounting angst over my children leaving the nest, Winston Wahlberg began to keep rather steady company with me through email. The communications were awkward, and they made me nervous till I remembered the old adage "Keep your friends close, and your enemies closer."

Since the beginning Winston had not set right with me, so once again I relied on my gut to tell me what was right and what was wrong. Mr. Wahlberg had several strokes against him. First, he had been the one most anxious to keep me from getting a copy of Colbert's original file. Second, he had ratted out Gavin Eller without batting an eye. Third, he continued to give me misinformation. It didn't take much to figure out he was playing for the other team.

Curious, I sent Spencer a request asking what Charley presented when I gave her Winston's full name.

I get bootlegging references. Was he a "heavy" man during the time of Charley's death? Information presents as him in charge of distributing the alcohol. Not sure about an alliance between him and the Grim Reaper now, but for sure a bond when Charley was killed. Feels more like a drinking/smoking buddy kind of bond. They both got a cut from whatever shady business was going on.

For me that was enough. In light of the recent epiphany, I immediately began to taper my communications.

With so many empty moments to fill without the constant interruptions of children, I concentrated my attention on the new victim. In an email conversation in late July, these clues began to come through:

I get that Rox may have been strangled. There is a possible link to sexual behavior with this woman. She also feels younger like 18 to 22-ish. Dirty blond long hair. She may actually be related to the Grim Reaper somehow.

I responded to her information telling her I found out that a man named "Red" Wilson had smoked a pipe with mint-flavored tobacco.

His wife was the secretary for Jeb Finch, the Sheriff who went to prison and died. Your 'F' energy at the murder scene that night under the umbrella! Could V on necklace stand for Valdosta, as in a high school kind of tribute? For high school or college initial or do you think it is a name? Still working on the boutique thing. Will Rox speak to you? Can she tell you who did this to her, who dumped her in the lake? Was the strangulation sex-related and was it when she was with MOT when it happened or someone else?

Most of all, tell her I am so sorry for her. My girls are 18, 20, and 22 and my heart aches that she is not with people who love her any longer. Please tell her I can help her if she will allow me to. If she was my daughter, I would pray for someone like you and me to help her make her way back home.

Spencer responded:

It is possible the "V" could stand for a high school. I just don't know....sorry. She talks about two roses and the man who strangled her feels older than her. She feels very caught off guard, like she may have been lying down with him and he just snapped and choked her. She also mentioned a tiny white poodle that was around her a lot.

Gut feelings confirmed, I moved forward and threw him bait every once in a while, just to keep him coming back for more. A few days later and stymied, I sent S another email:

Could you please ask Charley the following? Did you know about the MOT before your death? Did you know about Rox before your death? Did the MOT know Rox and was the "V" from him? (Remember you said something about a watch being tied to him. He worked for Sears. Was it in the jewelry department?) Was it the evidence on Rox or the MOT that the shooter went after you for? Who else knows about "the lady of the lake"? Is the little blonde girl who fell in the ravine and the long-haired blonde girl with the roses and poodle one and the same? Is our pipe smoker the laundering factor in all this? Can you give location in the lake for searching guide posts? Did G do the introductions for Rox? Was the energy known as LT as lucky as his rabbit's foot charm would have us believe? And most importantly...What concrete evidence can you afford me so that I can finally nail the Grim Reaper?

When I got her reply, I almost died.

Ok, so I do not think the direct questions will work today. Here is what comes through...And don't kill the messenger!

The crow was threatening to tear Grim Reaper's eye out. Grim masterminded the plan. MOT tied to Rox and Grim tied to Rox. Grim would have had a gash under his left eye after Rox's death. He may still have a scar. Some politician would have flown into town right before or right after Charley's death. Rox made a dessert that looks like upside-down cake. She is in a bakery-type room. May have worked there or had a really, really nice kitchen. Three men conspired to kill Charley. It had to be done. He stumbled onto things he should not have. Grim was torn; he liked

Charley but not that much. Charley would have unknowingly implicated a lot of people. More later.

How the devil was I supposed to figure that one out if I couldn't get the flannel, mint tobacco pipe thing? If the cosmos had wanted to screw with my brain, it had most certainly been successful. After receiving that message, I couldn't have formed a cohesive thought if God had asked me to. And He did. In between the heart attack, the wedding, and the relocation of my middle child, I was running on empty and had no more patience for riddles from the great beyond. I would have shouted my frustrations at the sky, but we all know how ineffective that can be. So I whistled long and loudly.

"Ok, God, have I got *YOUR* attention now?" I began. "This time I talk and *YOU* listen!" The sky rumbled in disbelief, but refrained from pouring on me. "Alright... I give. You win!" And with that I was off to the races.

"I get that this is the end of a nine year cycle, I do. I also get that this is a process whereby the old is being shed to make way for the new. I get the fact that the universe has its own academics and that there is a method to YOUR madness and that in time the larger picture will emerge clear and make perfect sense and I won't doubt YOU anymore." The clouds churned, but held their tongues. "I get balance; I even get karma. I also get that it is important that I not fight these changes, but rather let them roll over my back and remain patient enough for them to establish themselves while I adjust to the new surroundings they are creating for me.

"I get all that. I do! I am just so weary of change and hope that in the process the universe and YOU get a few things too. Like... I am slow in adjusting to certain changes. And I am sometimes ambivalent about the wisdom of my own responses. I am filled with anomalies: moments of great enthusiasm for forward thinking and movement, all the while embroidering that enthusiasm with great angst. I understand the whys; I am just reticent that the universe feels the need to deconstruct me brick by brick, memory by memory, so that it can accomplish this. I understand that to alter one's path, one has to learn to fix one's sights on the horizon and not to continually dwell on the intersections already traversed.

"Above all, I understand that in the breaking down of the walls of my life, I am leaving behind building blocks for others to pick up, chisel into new shapes, and construct theirs and that that is always a good thing. But not always a painless thing. I also get that when it was all said and done I will be minus two kids, two cats, and a monthly bill of $115.00 for a storage building that somehow in its 12 x 20 space has contained more than half of my life. I get that...I do! But that doesn't mean that as one drives away a married woman and the other a starry-eyed kid eager to start a new episode in her life, a tear for each won't grace my cheeks.

"So yes, dear Lord, I am way beyond myself. And to my darling daughters, you may have the chairs and the tables that supported you in your youth. You may have the photos and the trinkets that I so carefully chose to display as part of my earlier identity. You may have the dishes and the pots and pans that held a hundred daily dinners and the precious few Thanksgivings where we were all still together around a table that hid its age better than I. You may even have the chair that held my mother when she was still young enough to rock you as grandchildren.

A cloud began to drool.

"Before you drown me once again, let me finish. You can give away the first real suite of furniture that cost me a fortune that told the world I was finally a real adult. My children may sift through my life and try out what suits and discard that which does not. They may have all these things I carefully polished and dreamed upon to build their new lives. Just don't forget...not a one of you... that in them lay a thousand dreams and memories of what it once was to be me. And just like my dear 8 x 10 friend, a part of me will die as you each pull away from my curb for the last time.

Oh yeah, and one more thing. Send me some God-blessed answers before You really piss me off!" And with that, God and I both declared a truce and the remainder of that Sunday a day of rest.

CHAPTER TWENTY-FIVE

Numerology had implied that July would render me hidden secrets and indeed it had. By the end of the month I knew exactly what "O.S.T.R.I.C.H." stood for. I knew with confidence what the anagram "MOT" stood for, and I could tell you where and what #19 and #1545 were all about. I could even prove my understanding of the document 1510.

By the end of that summer, I had narrowed down the address of the potential dump site of the second gun, and I was closing in on the names and motives of others involved. And thanks to the introduction of the young girl with the long blonde hair, the two roses, and the little white dog, I knew there was another victim I could tie to the Grim Reaper: a victim who lay strangled and maimed at the bottom of a lake. The only trouble was I just wasn't sure how she fit into all this — that was until the cryptic verse from Spencer about the crow and the MOT appeared in my inbox.

Excited over my acceptance letter from the University of Maryland to study Investigative Forensics, I wanted to share the news with Spencer. During our communications that day, the mention of the new victim came up again.

Could the crow be Gerri, or can I get more clues to that identity? And is the politician who flew into town Chandler Sorenson, the governor at the time, or the Speaker of the House Samuels? You said Grim had a tie to him. He was Grim's family attorney. Is MOT the strangler? Is the nickname "Rox" a short for Roxanne or unrelated and the "V" on her necklace for Valdosta maybe?

Spencer responded.

I feel like the name Rox is a nick name for a name like Roxanne or Roxy. Try to tie the MOT to Roxy. He was there. His hands were on her. Perhaps he did not kill her, but he was there. Was he blackmailed by Grim the ringleader? There are several men around Roxy. Did they rape her? V, Valdosta High School. Yes, yes that is it! She is younger, very cute, very well put together. She is tied to Grim somehow through a relative or something. Was MOT part of the club? Is this an initiation into the club?

I thought about the man with the crooked teeth who had sat not more than three feet from me, and a chill went down my back. Grim had been in this thing from the very beginning, and Charley had just been one of how many victims. What did our little lady of the lake have to do with Grim and the MOT? How they all were tied to one another? So far I knew Damon Cummings (Grim), Albert Fitzpatrick (muddy boots), and Hank Sloan (shooter) were connected to the MOT and he had been connected to Rox.

In another session, Spencer had mentioned that Grim had a scar under his left eye. Believing that it was tied to the message about the crow, I pulled out the photos from our first visit down to Valdosta. I held them under a magnifying glass, but because The Grim Reaper wore glasses, I could not verify the information. I could do nothing but wait for another face-to-face confrontation. As promised, other hidden secrets came through that month.

I can see her final breaths in the air just above her lips, bruised horribly, beaten, possibly raped, strangled, and thrown in the water. Look for the numbers 4, 9, 5, 2. The tree there…his hands on her throat. She is young, 18 to 22. Long blonde hair. Very put together, cosmetics, a family business, ties to the Grim Reaper and the MOT.

I stood aghast in the corner of my bedroom at the magnitude of what Charley had accidentally stumbled into. Who was this poor young girl? My heart ached. Her age was somewhere between my middle and oldest child, and I couldn't get that parallel out of my mind. What if it had been one of them? I begged for Charley's help and asked the cosmos to lead Roxanne to him for shelter and to Spencer for justice. Piece by piece, it began to come together.

A man dies of a heart attack one week after. A necklace with a "V." A pineapple upside down cake, two roses, a white poodle, 472, a gash under the left eye, a politician who flew in the night before or the night after Charley's death, September 29 and the four in flannel.

The revelations that came through from Spencer were daunting, especially since the reigning governor in 1966 was noted as being "Hollywood handsome" and a World War II, B-17 bomber pilot, known to fly all over the state during his tenure as the highest ranking official in the state from 1963 to 1967, not to mention an exceptionally close friend of Finch and Cummings. I was torn. The Speaker, Samuels, came with a gavel and had been a judge, but the governor, Sorenson, was the pilot in the bunch and was known for his adept navigating skills and ability to land safely in open fields and on ragged rural strips. As much as my pulse raced with that as potential corroboration of his presence in Valdosta the night of or after Charley was murdered, I still had a difficult time trying to place everything else received into a cohesive pattern of conspiracy.

True to what my Numerology report had suggested, the beginning of August had been a most unusual time filled with sudden experiences, unforeseen alignments, and a clear sign the cosmos had taken my pleas for information to heart. In session after session it began hurling images in my direction at random intervals and from all different directions. The two most important were the clues that tied the Grim Reaper to another victim and three other names to the reference "the four in flannel."

In going over files, there is a session where you talk about Al Fitzpatrick, VPD and later U.S. Marshal. You mention newspaper and his wife Bobbie Lee, that she was forced to go along with the "story" against her will. Then there is mention of him in boots — muddy rubber boots — he is angry that his wife has told Kaye about G, that he belongs to the boy's club. It is about fraternal protection.

Is Albert (Al) Fitzpatrick one of the four who wear flannel? And again, is Hank Sloan one of the four who wear flannel? That would leave me Damon, the MOT, and two others that were there with Rox that night/day. If Al and Hank are part of the four, then who else? The man with the pipe and mint tobacco? Possible list?

Damon Cummings*

Robert W. Chancellor (MOT)

Hank Sloan*

Al Fitzpatrick*

Something... Ganger?

George Wilson (pipe smoker)

I highlighted the names that jumped out. Again, the direct Q & A is challenging sometimes.

Why couldn't they just answer the direct line of questioning? Wouldn't that be exactly what the ATF, FBI, and GBI would do to me when this was all said and done, grill me like a piece of meat, turning up the heat till I answered every one of their questions? Or even worse, not talk to me at all if I didn't have enough hard information to pique their interest. I decided that would be even more humiliating, so I yelled into the cosmos "What gives you the right to be so selective?" The room remained silent. Apparently that was one of the selective questions they preferred not to answer directly as well... or had they? "Silence may be golden, but it's awfully annoying sometimes!" I threw back. Still nothing emanated from the great beyond.

"All right, I give. We'll try this again tomorrow and maybe you'll be in a more beneficent mood!" I grumbled.

The hum from the laptop began to grate on my ears and the glow to hurt my eyes. No direct questioning indeed! My head was pounding and my gut was tight with frustration, but I tried to remain grateful. After all, they had come through with an awful lot so far. I decided anger was not the better option, but two aspirin and a good night's sleep might be, so I shut my computer down, turned off my lamp, and made my way for the bathroom. Three steps across the room my path was interrupted by a wayward tennis ball.

Harley, my Westie, had been waiting patiently for hours to play a quick game of catch. I picked it up, hurled it down the hall, and waited for the familiar chase to ensue. But she began growling instead. "Wow... everyone's a little pissy tonight," I mustered. "Go on.... get the ball!" I urged, stripped off my shirt and pants, and motioned her to the opposite end of the hallway where a half-chewed tennis ball awaited her arrival.

Just as I was about to unhook my bra, she turned her head in the opposite direction, barred her teeth, and paced the four corners of the bed, all the while keeping whatever it was at bay. Slowly I pulled back from my release, grabbed my husband's T-shirt, put it on, and worked my way to the far side of the bed and looked out the windows. I saw nothing. We were two floors up. I motioned her towards the hall and the slimy green ball that baited, refusing to be both master and servant, but she held her gaze upon the ceiling. Again, I saw nothing.

"Goofy dog. Go get your ball! Mommy has to pee." Sensing all was calm, I unclamped my legs and made an attempt to cross the floor to the bathroom just eight feet to my right. Each time I took a step she shifted in her stance, followed the lines of the ceiling, and the growl came from deeper in her chest. I remembered how she had acted in April just three days before Piper had seen the evil entity with the red eyes in the corner of that same room. This time, I didn't bother to ask who it was. I simply crossed my legs, reached for the nightstand drawer and pulled out my rosary.

"In the name of the Father, the Son and the Holy Spirit..."

CHAPTER TWENTY-SIX

The pretty young blonde with the crooked neck continued to float through my nightmares and did her best to beckon us to find her in one of the small ponds at Saddle Bag Lakes. Hours were spent looking at maps and Google Earth to try and pin her exact location down. I knew the VPD clubhouse was near Brinson Drive. But the area was so full of twisted little dirt and paved roads that anchored the hundred small homes that dotted the shoreline of the five ponds that it was difficult to be precise. Then out of the blue one day, Roxanne came through and gave us the images she could see from her vantage point. We nailed the location where she was originally thrown into the lake. Amazingly enough, the area was not too far from where Charley's rental ad house would have been and incredibly close to the VPD lake clubhouse.

Other odd clues came through Spencer too, including the following one which introduced me to another new name and characters:

Theo Shelling had given her the purple orchid broach/pin. Her dad was not happy they were seeing each other. 1223 Bakers Way (hmmm… another baking reference) something was wrong with her hand or arm. She may have had arthritis in her fingers. Something that had her hand/arm stiffens up at times. Flag pole with a yellow banner/flag on it...

Every clue was always important. So who was this person mentioned by name: Theo Shelling? Rarely do they give both names as was blatantly obvious since Rox's last name was still a mystery to me. Since his name had not appeared in any other session and/or notes, I had to start from scratch. I turned to my go-to gal Erica at the Lowndes Historical Society for clues and had her search the Valdosta phone book from 1966. The last name of Shelling was nowhere to be found. I tried to have her find it in the Valdosta High School Year Book. Again nothing. The presentation *"her father was not happy they were seeing each other"* confused me. If Rox was this young gal of 18 to 22, could this Theo person have been an older bad boy type that her father didn't approve of?

If I added that to the other clues, it just got more confusing. Was this where the two roses came into play? And what about the little white dog and the persistent mention of her arm and her ailing of some sort of arthritis? The only other impression I'd received from Spencer that might be a believable fit for such an affliction was the clue about the young girl who fell down a ravine and hurt her arm. Beyond that, the habitual references to baking were driving me crazy. When I Googled the address that was given, it brought me right to the American Baking Institute website. Amazingly enough, the building had a yellow banner across the front of it just as Spencer had seen in her visions.

 With that kind of confirmation, I spent another two days canvassing the American Baking Institute's website, trying to get to the list of alumni students to find one girl in the bunch who might have shared the same first name of Roxanne. After 48 hours of searching unsuccessfully, I decided I was being too literal in my interpretations and let it go. Obviously baking was a guide wire meant to be followed, not the definitive location/institution. Setting aside my cravings for a pineapple upside-down cake, I went back to the business of living and work at the theatre.

As bits and pieces of the puzzle began to come together, an odd inquiry for a rental of the theatre placed me in touch with folks from MTV's One Louder Productions. After I consented to network for casting purposes, the production assistant told me the casting spots were for a new Oprah Network show about adults who gave up on something they had always wanted to do because life got in the way. For instance, you always wanted to learn to play the flute, but you went to business school instead. Or you always wanted to be a chef, but your parents wanted you to be a lawyer. This show would offer you support and an opportunity to go to Italy and learn to be a gourmet chef. You just had to be able to do it in say, ten to twelve weeks because that was the length of their scholarships. I thought it was a great premise, and so I offered her use of the theatre space as a networking tool, a sort of community outreach.

Towards the end of her stay, she offered me a chance to audition for a spot too. While it was a thoughtful gesture, I felt like Dorothy standing in front of the Wizard. I smiled politely and told this wonde̊ ful twenty-first century promotion wizard, "I don't think there's anything in that little black bag for me."

When the production agent asked me why, I explained. I told her about Charley, about Spencer, about going back to school for investigative forensics, and about what I had been working on for over eighteen months. Politely interested, she took my card and promised to read some of the blogs. The next day I drove her around the Athens area, scouting for publicity locations. We chatted casually about what I would wish for if Oprah could grant me one wish. Again, I told her twelve weeks would not be enough for what I wanted, but she insisted.

"If I could follow my dream at someone else's expense," I began and the gates flew open. Suddenly I had diarrhea of the mouth. "I'd want a real chance to do the work I do and share it with folks, not like on some of these hokey reality shows where they cut out the real work people like Spencer and I do for furniture polish commercials and make it seem like all it would take us was forty-five minutes, a magic wand, and twelve minutes of sponsorships to save the world."

I told her, "Victims and their families deserve their losses to be dignified and shown in real light. People need to know how much work and thought it takes, how much love and dedication goes into solving a crime, how many sacrifices must be made by family to allow the time and energy employed to plug all the holes in a cold case. I'd want to share Charley and Spencer with the world and tell the masses how Charley's death has changed the way I live, the way I think, the way I feel about who I am and what my purpose in life is. I'd want to…" and the litany of what I wanted and hoped to achieve was damn near endless.

Convinced my story was marketable, she asked if she could send an idea up the flag pole with her boss. For a few short weeks I felt there might be a shot at getting Charley's story out nationally. In those hours I kept my nose to the grindstone and worked tirelessly on building timelines and suppositions in order to present a tighter case. I talked with Spencer about the possibility, and we discussed dignity and proper formatting for such a potential project. At last, a real break.

In the back of my mind I hoped for the best possible outcome for Jules and Charley. Maybe then ATF, FBI, and GBI would take notice and give this thing a real shot. Maybe folks with greater skill sets and resources would join the cause and real headway could finally be made to bring Charley's killers to justice before any more of them died. Maybe I could be freed from the daily grind enough to go to school full time and finally find financial resuscitation for my checkbook. The optimism of "what could be" became infectious, and I grew lighter in my step and more confident in my future.

The original invitation morphed into several more phone calls, a personal meeting between the production assistant, Spencer, and me, and then eventually a conference call with the producer. A few adjustments, a few more negotiations, and a few promotional demands restructured and then the unmistakable epiphany: what they were asking for was fairly close to what we had wanted to avoid in the first place and certainly more than could be brought to bear at the time. They talked about a series, where together Spencer, I, and our introductory partner from C.C.I.R.I could solve cases, one every show or every two to three shows. We would be three women, all wives and mothers dedicated to solving cold case murders using paranormal avenues and twenty-first century forensics and intuition to put the guilty in jail and the dead to rest. We would be a new brand of *Charley's Angels*…no pun intended.

Collectively we saw the handwriting on the wall. No matter how many times they threw a new fleece atop it, the wolf of TV hype was always underneath. Charley was not a forty-five minute murder, broken up by twelve minutes of commercials and a three-minute resolution. Even if he had been, it wouldn't have been right. Irritated by the propaganda of exploitation, relations with C.C.I.R.I. cooled. Spencer and I still saw merit in trying to re-tool their vision and tried to edify by presenting a broader picture of what we did, but in the end Charley's murder couldn't be marginalized. In all fairness to his children and to our new found victim Rox, I needed to finish the job the right way, no matter the personal cost. The bottom line was Charley was an epic mini-series that refused fit into a thirty-minute television slot.

It sucked. Here was a chance in a lifetime and my overactive conscience was blowing it for me. How many times did I think an opportunity like this would ever happen again in my life? Oprah's folks were waiting to answer someone's dream and where was I? One by one I watched would-be soccer stars and post-partum polka dancers walk down the hall into the theatre and audition. It hurt knowing that some untested chef or some ballet-starved housewife would have a shot at twelve weeks of uninterrupted bliss following his or her heart's desire, while I struggled to pay the light bill, put gas in my car, and solve a murder. I didn't want to begrudge anyone a dream, but what about mine? Why couldn't mine have been so simple?

In the wee hours of the night I lay awake thinking. What if I could work double time on the case while I worked on the show and took leave from work to do it? What if they could hold production for another six to twelve months to help me get more of it solved? What if I quit school to have more time? What if they offered me a job and I could work on Charley's case and other victims' cases and nothing else? What if I won the lottery? What if I lost thirty pounds and grew six inches taller? What if an agent read my blog and just had to sign me? What if the sky were falling!? What if I got a tumor on the other side of my head and was finally able to get a real face-lift effect, instead of just slightly off-sided features from the first one? What if... what if... what if!

And what if this is exactly what Charley didn't want to happen? What if there was more to this than I had already discovered, and a premature eclipse into television history would bastardize everything and leave important issues unsolved? What if my perceived need to pay bills wasn't really greater than my need to be of service to another human being? I hated when the cosmos wanted me to be the bigger person! So as much as I needed the money, I promised to stick to my morals.

A month after it had begun, a secretary in New York called to set up the call we had been waiting for. I set my phone down on the desk and looked at the clock. In eighteen hours I would be basically pitching my book in TV format to a major production company. My hands were shaking. I could do this. I had to do this. If I could sell them on our version, Charley's case would go national, the four in flannel (those still alive) would go to jail, my bills would get paid, and my money troubles would go away! Emotionally revved, I closed the laptop and glanced at the 8 x 10 on my writing desk.

"Don't look at me like that! If you wanted it kept private, why in God's name did you pick a writer to talk to for Christ's sake? What the hell were you thinking?" I slammed. "You knew it would go public eventually, so why not now?" I blasted. "Look…I could really use this chance to make something of myself and help my family at the same time. Yours too! You don't think Jules would enjoy a little financial freedom?" I paused; his expression never changed. "I think she would." I applauded and rationalized my stance.

He smiled flatly, but then he was always smiling. It was obvious he wasn't buying into it. "Look…. I'm only trying to do this thing right for everyone involved. I don't make the rules; I'm just trying to survive them, ok? TV folks just have their own way of doing things: marketing, demographics…advertising slots…formulas for success, that's all. You're still stuck in 1966. Things are different now. They'll come around to our way of thinking," I said, trying to convince myself I was right. He just kept smiling and it was beginning to get on my nerves.

"People with money can afford to have morals, Charley," I rationalized. "And I'm not even talking about big money. I mean just pay-the-light-bill kind of money. Or get-the-extra-gallon-of-milk-this-week kind of money. Charley…I'm bankrupt and hanging on by a thread. I need this chance to start again." His smile changed to a smirk and his eyes stared me down with even calm. I thought about Kaye surviving on less than $200.00 per month and nearly smoking herself into extinction from worry.

"Ok, maybe not quite a thread, but it's not far from it. I'm hanging by a string… better?" I added and turned his photo around. "Stop judging me. I'm doing the best I can with what I've got and that isn't much these days, kiddo," I whimpered and left him facing the wall, but I could feel his eyes burning a hole in my heart. "I'm not dead yet, Charley. I still have to live in this world, pay the bills, make the meals, clean up the dog shit and the vomit, wipe my daughter's drool when she seizes and can't breathe through the mucus — and every other Friday I get to choose between buying gas to go to work and buying medicine to keep everyone alive. So don't get all high and mighty with me. I have my own private Hell to deal with, so…so…just give me a break!" I spat, rationalizing my obsession with money. Unimpressed with my meltdown explanation, he wasn't backing down and it pissed me off.

I thought about how he might have handled my situation and blasted his photo from behind. "So how would you deal with all this, huh? How about Kaye? How well would she have coped?" I slashed back and then remembered Jules's story about how Kaye had tried to handle her trials by taking her kids to the mountain, wrapping them in winter coats, and coasting down the side with the headlights turned off, hoping for a swift demise. I wasn't there yet, but I was getting close.

"At least I haven't considered suicide yet," I blurted. It was a low blow. When I thought about how it would have sounded if he were still alive and standing before me, my heart sank. How could I be such a shit? Of course he would have handled things with more grace. He'd have offered to come back buck naked and poor as a pauper if it meant he could have hugged Jules one more time and Kaye most likely the same. The back side of his photo looked as blank as the expression I knew he would be wearing on the other side.

"What is happening to me?" I barked. "When did money become so important?" I asked the air above us. His photo declined comment, so I answered for him. "Ahhhh...yes, I remember now. It became so important when it became so scarce... not that it was ever in abundance really."

I felt his look of disappointment through the back of the paper. "I'm humiliated enough by my own conscience. I don't need yours barking at me too," I mumbled. "Go to sleep. It's late." The photo quivered as the air flushed from the duct above my desk, but it somehow felt like more. It felt like Charley shrugging his shoulders with indifference, so I waited, hoping he might share a warmer response.

Five minutes went by and nothing. He was waiting for an apology. "I'm sorry," I whispered, "really sorry. I'm just so stressed out lately."

I placed a book at the back of the photo to insure he couldn't turn around and glare at me further. Stress was no excuse though, not even at the level I was experiencing it. What I said had been cruel, uncalled for. I left my desk for the comfort of nightly rituals and warm sheets, but the lamplight continued to bounce off the back of the plastic cover and bothered my eyes. No matter how many times I closed them, my conscience kept popping them back open and wouldn't let me sleep. Charley had crept into every part of my life and taken up permanent residence in my conscience, continually tapping out his moral code until I could take it no longer. Humbled, I crawled back into my desk chair, hoping he might engage further and forgive me.

"I'm sorry, buddy. But it's still true. I'm not dead yet, Charley. I have no idea the joys of Heaven or the judgments of Hell; I know only the hell of my family's here and now. I'm not blaming anyone; it is what it is. But I have to live in this world, and this world comes with a lot of price tags I am currently unable to pay," I muttered and waited for his smile to bleed through. "Nobody's stepping forward to finance my way. I have nothing left. No savings, no safety net, no inheritance: nothing. Do you hear me, Covington? NOTHING, Charley! NOTHING! Every penny we had has gone to keep us alive and afloat and now there's nothing left!"

The photo remained still, so I continued, "I'm it, kid. I'm the last line between here and a cardboard box and a graffitied viaduct. That's how bad it feels. I am the only breadwinner left in this house. While it may seem grossly unfair to outsiders who think I am trying to exploit this miracle, it might one day be necessary for me to do so in order for my family to survive. And I will survive, Charley. I will, because just like Kaye, I have no other option," I wailed.

Emotionally thinned, I listened to my heart to see if he had anything to say, but there was nothing beyond the dull throb of my pulse, so I softened. "You might be my guardian angel, Charley, but I am theirs. I'm all they've got, and my wings are tired, very tired…and I need a goddam miracle to save us." And with that I turned his photo around, kissed him on the forehead, and left him to his thoughts.

That night I slept facing the opposite wall, unable to look at him. How had my life spiraled so out of control? When did I become so lost that a stupid 8 x 10 glossy became my moral compass, making me feel so guilty about trying to survive? Was he right? Had the lure of financial security crossed my eyes and tempted me to compromise my ethics even slightly? I openly confessed a nice paycheck at that point could have eased the pecuniary tourniquet that was cutting off both my arms, but I took great offense to the word *exploit*. I was desperate; that was different. Exploitation was a luxury, a luxury fate was warning me I might no longer have. Still, if I was to be honest, a TV deal would not have been the guarantee that could have cured *all* my troubles. I still had issues with grief, misplaced hurts, family medical crises, and faith that I was doing the right thing.

That night I spent what was left of it tossing and turning. In the light of day, guilt and morals won out. The next call Spencer and I shared with the production company, we made our final pitch. Respectfully, we stuck to our principles and walked away. I know they say a person stands taller when he does something right, but quite honestly it felt like I was only standing a little taller in the metaphorical bread line than I had the day before. Disenchanted, I glanced at the photo again for support. He was smiling, though I was not. Just before they rung off they promised they'd look at another angle, but I knew it was just a line. Spencer finally clicked off. Left alone in my room with nothing but dial tone to fill the void, I cried.

A day or two later, the producers attempted to bridge the gap one more time. Spencer and I carried the torch of a re-tooled show's possibility a few weeks longer. With another call here and there sprinkled between brainstorms, the flame eventually died at both ends of the candle. It was no one's fault; apparently truth was only marketable in thirty-minute segments. Try as I might, there was no way I could distill Charley's death into such a tiny bottle. Poor but proud, I plowed forward on the case and hid within my studies to conceal my disappointment in the world and my disillusionment in God.

The last week in August, God threw me another lifeline. Someone who had found the blog had worked with one of the boy witnesses. I sent an email. Two emails later, she gave me the name of a former law enforcement individual. After another round of background inquiries and approval from Jules and her brother, I received the following.

Ms. Powell,

I have spoken with Jules and her brother through Facebook, and both have validated your efforts. I will be more than happy to assist

in any way I can. I worked with Damon Cummings as a Trooper in
Valdosta years ago and know him very well. I personally do not
know of "Roxy." However, I will speak to Cummings if you like. He
is an odd man so he may or may not be forthcoming. Has the name
Marjorie Church ever come up? Ms. Marjorie was married to GSP
LT. P.R. Church (deceased), is from Lowndes County, and was
very close to Sheriff Finch (he may even be kin, not sure). Anything
that had to do with Finch and that organized group she would
know about. Marjorie is at the Flagship Nursing Home located
about five miles outside of Valdosta. Her mind is sharp as ever and
loves to talk. Whether she will talk about this, I have no clue. Feel
free to call me anytime if you like.

And call him, I did. With his help, the mysterious clues about my
Southern debutante Rox began to come together. By the end of the
month my secondary contact had helped me divine the location of a
restaurant, the address of a hotel, and the identity of a person
Spencer had alluded to in a clue given me months earlier: *"Find*
the woman with the injured foot. Find her; she will talk. She
knows...hurry. She is in a care situation; she does not have long."

So far August had brought me from the edges of despair to images
of a young girl, several men, a seedy hotel room, hands about her
throat, murky water, and a necklace with a "V" on it.

I could barely wait for September to begin.

CHAPTER TWENTY-SEVEN

With the beginning of Indian summer, we celebrated our twenty-seventh wedding anniversary. That was a small miracle. Since all our finances were being consumed by medical bills, money was tight, so my sister said we could go and spend the weekend at her lake house an hour away. I was grateful as I needed new scenery in my life. Piper was now in the capable hands of her new love, and so I told Claire she could have her friend spend the weekend to help watch the dogs. The lake was perfect, far enough away for distraction, but close enough not to compromise. It was heaven. We spent the entire weekend on the water. Quiet and content, we lounged on the boat, mapping the shoreline while looking at homes we could no longer afford. As the clouds began to stretch and streak with color, we would curl up on the dock, watch the sun set, and wait for the fireflies to dance their way across the beach. At night we ate by candlelight and talked about what went wrong with our marriage. For the first time in years, we really listened to what each other had to say. By the end of the weekend we found we were still poor, but happy to be working our way back to where we had begun.

The Labor Day holiday had been wonderful, but the festivities soon ended and it was back to real life and real problems. My husband's short term memory loss, balance issues, and fatigue confirmed he could not go back to work. Humiliated, he filed for disability. Monstrous medical bills continued to eat away at our reduced dividends, and the loss of his steady income left us without buffer. In late September when the mortgage payments and household bills began to pile higher than the leaves outside, we had no other option left but to file for bankruptcy. I would have cried, but I had nothing left inside me to give. As my husband tried to comfort me, telling me thousands of people were in the same boat, I tried to comfort myself, hoping that God was breaking me down so that He could build me back up. After all, hadn't He shown me that sign the first trip to Valdosta?

"For I know the plans I have for you," declares the LORD, "plans to prosper you and not to harm you, plans to give you hope and a future." Jeremiah 29:11

By the middle of September, I wanted God to know I was already sick of the reconstruction process. Spirits dampened, I began to pack down the house and had no idea for where or for when. Confused and angry with God, I kept my distance from Charley and did my best with our *Haunted Honeymoon* Reader's Theatre production. Once we determined we could no longer afford to keep the townhouse or cut a deal to lower the rates, we began to keep our eyes and minds open for our next move. Exhausted, I remained miffed at God for the major inconvenience of poverty.

Emotionally at odds with both God and Charley, I began again to spiral in my faith. Criminology was teaching me that intuition had little place in the process, but at that point intuition was all I had. I decided it wasn't important if a handful of my professors thought all I did was toss about runes or splay cards with whimsical images to get information. In my heart I knew this was about a hardcore investigation and a process meant to break through the barriers of traditional methods.

By the end of the month, my hard-earned faith was rewarded. The man who had been introduced to me at the beginning of the month came through, and the payoff in information was huge. He knew someone who could confirm the existence of the young blonde girl who had been a party toy for local law enforcement. Even more, he was able to help me with information about where she worked, where she might have lived, and the possible connection between her and the MOT.

His contact told me Rox had worked at the American Legion Club serving drinks and providing backroom entertainment for local law with another young woman. My new contact told me Rox had been beaten and raped, that her body was so bruised when they pulled it from the lake they had to dump it somewhere else before anybody else saw it. She told me Rox had been strangled and then thrown into a local lake. They declared it a drowning, but when they pulled her out, nobody ever found any water in her lungs.

This woman knew things... shared things. And just when I thought it couldn't get any better, Charley stepped to the plate. On September 29th he whispered in Spencer's ear and gave her Roxanne's last name.

CHAPTER TWENTY-EIGHT

Just the like October of 1966, October of 2010 rolled in on a cool wind and an eerie note. Before the first week was out, my geriatric contact had proven her weight in gold. I sent an email to Spencer.

I did it! I got her...Roxanne Blithe (or Blythe, I have to check) was her name. Long blonde hair, very pretty, very loose. She worked in the bakery department at Harvey's grocery store in Valdosta. Slept with all the law enforcement types. She was not from Valdosta originally. Had an apartment somewhere there in town. Was found in one of the local lakes, I believe. Rumor said she drowned, but no water found in the lungs. Bruised badly, but no one checked for any other cause of death. My impression is that she was found and buried later, no longer in the lake. That's why no missing person issues to follow and research.

The MOT, Robert Weatherby Chancellor, died in a hotel called The Daniel Ashley Hotel on the corner of Ashley Street and Hill Avenue. His body was badly bruised too; he was left for dead, left in the room for a few days. Listed as a DOA to Pineville Hospital, then to Camden McLane Funeral Home. Info on Camden McLane death certificate suggests he was from Tifton, died in Valdosta, transferred out and buried in Augusta. Less than a forty-eight hour turnaround between discoveries of the body, transfers between two cities, and a burial. Seems overly quick, doesn't it? No time for embaliing? Hmmm... Somebody needed that body to decay awfully quickly so identification process would be a bust. But why? Roxanne may have been Damon Cummings' girlfriend. (The crow did try to scratch out the eyes of Grim. Roxanne Blythe was the crow, Damon Cummings the Grim Reaper.) She was quite possibly killed late September or early October '66 by strangulation. You mentioned September 29 as a significant day. It may have been only because we found out her name. But what if it was the day she died too? If so, yesterday would have been the anniversary of her death. I will try to verify through obits if one can be found.

Too old for games, I dug my heels in the next few days and went for Grim's jugular. Spencer called often, as sometimes the combination of our energies helped bring more information through. Emboldened by our progress, I began to state things in the blog I should have kept to myself. After we hung up, she sent me this:

I was going to tell you tomorrow, but after we got off the phone, they told me this: the shovel and the #7 are grave related, so stay on that. #7 may be a burial plot number. Four in flannel. Three hands on the throat — while 1 watched.

I was confused and wanted to be sure, so I fired back:

Three sets of hands or three hands, singular?

She responded in kind:

Three sets of hands...the four in flannel...three participate in the murder; one stands back and watches.

On October 12, 2010 we began a series of emails back and forth that lasted all day and into the evening. Roxanne continued to appear from under water, but now the peripheral images she began to present were different. Spencer sent me a Google Earth photo of the site she believed held Roxanne's bones. There was a Clip Art push pin stuck at the edge of a cypress swamp in the middle of a field with the question, *"Is this Robert Coleman's farm?"*

I studied the photo and noted that to the left of the pasture was a gated fence and across the road the working entrance to the Wild Adventures Theme Park. I remembered the clue: *"the property with the special fencing and carved sign is red hot property; something significant happened there."* I scrolled up a few inches and saw it to the left of the road. The fencing at the main entrance was wooden and spiked at the top like a fortress, and the carving in the wooden sign was striking. Bingo! She had nailed it on the head again and I told her so.

That patch of trees is actually standing in water. It is a swamp area, and that's why it could never be plowed under. Robert Coleman worked for the VPD in 1966, along with Al Fitzpatrick, Winston Wahlberg, and some of the others that hung out with Grim. I thought this was part of the original Coleman Farm, but that land runs in the other direction from the tree line. I found out this farm/land was actually owned by somebody else back then. Clint is trying to get the correct name for me. Could this be why Rox continues to appear to you from under water? Because she still is under water in this cypress tree swamp?

She responded with additional information.

I just keep being drawn back to the man by the carved fence who will talk. He has a lot to say. Have you identified the four in flannel? One stands back, remember? It is like he watches, knows it is wrong, but can't do a damn thing about it.

Was this carved fencing really what Spencer had seen in her visions? If so, was Robert Coleman the man who stood by it? My blood pressure began to rise. That son-of-a-bitch had been in several other clues, and his lack of cooperation was beginning to piss me off. I had spoken with him via phone several times and made three different trips to his house. I even met his daughter and yet he had never shared a single thing with me. The living players in this case were really beginning to grate on my nerves, but no more than the dead.

Spencer kept saying the man at the fence with the hay bales would talk, but apparently not to me and certainly not with Jules and her son in the room with me. Angry, I went back to my geriatric source and grilled her for everything she was worth. I spent an hour and half with Marjorie that day and then sent Spencer an update.

Marjorie referred to our young blonde debutante as a whore, said nobody gave a shit about her. That's why I would never find any paperwork on her. Nobody cared and since it was all law enforcement involved, everything was covered up. Nobody was gonna give any information on her 'cause then folks would start asking questions. One question would lead to another, and none of them could afford it to be known. They made her disappear. Can Charley help?

She responded:

The heads and tails game, like when you flip a coin. They played some kind of coin game. They are all laughing around Roxy saying "heads or tails" before they kill her.

I sent a reply back.

And what was happening to Rox while they decided? Was she drunk or did they beat her unconscious and that's how they got her wherever? Or were they holding her down?

I held my breath and waited for the voice on my laptop to inform me "You've got mail!" Several minutes ticked away and I began to bite at the corner of my lip. The familiar ding made me jump. I scrolled down and saw Spencer's words and gasped.

They were holding her down for sure. She was not drunk. They forced her down.

CHAPTER TWENTY-NINE

In the matter of a few days, Spencer and I exchanged more than twenty emails and phone sessions about the mystery girl Roxanne. The following began with my first email.

Talked to Marjorie this morning....hold on to your hat! Shovel and compass found, but she could not remember where. Shovel had blood on it. They said Rox drowned, but there was no water in her lungs and she was bruised all over her body. Marjorie says "those that done it got away with murder and have lived a life of lies since then." She hopes someone with the guts to do it will call them out and make them pay. I am going to see her on Saturday, driving down on Friday. Can you get any more info from Rox as to where the shovel and compass might have been found and does this have to do with her murder... or somebody else's? I do not understand the shovel segue if she was dumped in the swamp. Anything to help me dig further and help her move on?

She responded:

Here is more information for you. The name Jessica is mentioned. December 17th.

Rox's mom and dad may have kicked her out of her home after/around high school.

She may have been staying with an aunt. They mention the name Mitch (Mitchell).

One watched the murder; the other three participated. She was intimate with the three that killed her, but not the one that watched. The one that watched is soft spoken, really liked her. They mention the word Kingsville. Again...#7 may be a plot number.

Grim Reaper has dirt under his fingernails. A medium-sized black dog was present during her murder.

Again with the black dog. I thought my mind would spontaneously combust from sheer exhaustion and information overload. Being the anniversary week of his death, Jules and I decided to head back down to Valdosta for a short "fishing trip." I wanted to visit Marjorie in person, hoping that if she met Jules and sat face to face with me, I could pull more information from her. On the anniversary of his death, Jules and I made the drive to where her father had breathed his final breaths. The following is taken from a blog on that date:

10/9/10:
Just like in my dream... the road bent and bowed with little illumination once we made it out of town. The stars were thin and the crickets thick as they played backup to the whispers from the trees as we sped along the Clyattville-Nankin Road. There we were, counting the miles and adjusting the minutes, retracing his steps from that night each mile at a time. Only this time Charley wasn't at the wheel; I was. It was a pilgrimage necessary for us both. She — the daughter, I — the writer. Both needing to be there at the hour appointed to know and see for ourselves how black the night, how still the heart, and how deafening the silence. All day long we had made distractions of our own: research at the Historical Society, interview after interview, conversations upon conversations — all to fill the anxious hours before tonight.

Jules read from Kaye's journal before we headed out as a reminder that there was more at stake than just the rumor of a girl and a cup of coffee. It was 8:58 pm when we got on the road for the second time to where Charley spent his final moments. Mustang revved, top down, and nothing but the wind to keep us company, we drove quiet for the better half of the drive, passing a fence that now appears to be of special interest as it has been mentioned twice in Spencer's readings. As we reached the spot, we slowed to a crawl and turned off the lights. The deep velvet of the night folded in around us, and I could not imagine a more hopeless setting. Even with the stars above, the earth swallowed itself whole and you could not see two feet in front of your face. Fearful as we approached the second bridge, we cut the lights back on and inched our way forward to a stop. Jules got out of the car and walked in front of me down the side of the road, navigating the slim shoulder and then asked that I turn the lights out once more to embrace what her father must have experienced.

Checking both side and rear mirrors for other vehicles and finding none, I complied. Again, even once your eyes adjusted there was nothing but the unrelenting pitch. In silent vigil we each cast our prayers into the void and bid her father freedom from pain. "He would have been dead by now, I think," she said. Neither star nor human blinked a tear at the statement. No ghost exercised...or demon fought. Just the night, the two of us, and the endless silence.

I do not know what I expected of such a trial or that I expected anything at all. But there we were, the three of us, caught somewhere between 2010 and 1966 and there was nothing but the night to act as segue and nothing but the dawn to look forward to. It had been a long day filled with introductions and unexpected blessings and information. We spent many hours talking and listening, trying to engage others in our cause. I thought about Charley throughout it and Rox too, not trying to forget that Kaye too shared these last hours with him, not knowing if the marriage would last or fail, not knowing if the coffee would still be warm when he returned. And the children, how they slept in their beds unaware that the world would come crashing in all around them before the last raindrop fell.

It is now 11:53 pm and approximately the same time of night that the second set of witnesses (boys from Florida who had passed the crime scene) made the infamous phone call to the Lowndes County Sheriff's Department. They might stand at Sam Daily's store waiting for the call back to rejoin the Deputy Sheriff at the scene. It is also not long since J and I have returned from forty-four years ago. The minutes will continue to click by as we recount the hours and the events that carried the beginning of lies through the night and decades beyond. We could have easily stayed away, returned to the hotel, dug in for the night, and let the moment pass from where we were. But that would not have made either of us happy. We each had made a promise, for better or worse, to be there for that hour when Charley's world had come to an end and taken with it the infrastructure of a family.

May this trip and his death not have been in vain. I read something on a church sign as we drove back from the spot earlier in the day I wanted to share with you. I thought it poignant: "Nothing ruins the truth like stretching it." I will bear that in mind as I strive to tell his story without interjecting too much of my own. Goodnight, Charley.

The rest of the weekend was amazing and I could feel Charley's presence wherever we went. The next evening held what they call a Wolf Moon or a Blood Moon. Heavy with color, it hung low in the sky and dripped with warnings. They say that when that happens, there is blood on the moon and that one should look for trouble to follow within hours or days...and it did.

They never give me information which I cannot use, and they often bunch information around a single purpose, so I called Spencer.

"I finally received a return call from the woman with the injured foot; there was more information there. She gave me the confirmation of the location of the fort. And you once asked if I received a letter from a woman from Tallahassee. Then most recently you were given an impression of a letter inside an envelope. You said the handwriting was done by somebody with red lipstick and dark hair, that the address of 1711 Turn-bridge or Turn-ridge something... to a Mr. Ronald C... something was given. Get anything else on that or Roxanne?"

Spencer responded, and as usual it was cryptic in nature.

"Who lives near Roxanne's resting place... who knows who... who knows nothing and who lies? It feels like Roxanne was killed before Charley. It also feels like Charley did not fully understand the

contents of the tape, meaning he would not fully understand whom he would be implicating. As for the clue about the palm tree plate, it has a more specific meaning. Don't go digging for the letter; let it play out."

"Did you find out who Jessica is?" she asked.

"Oh yeah. Marjorie gave me some info about her too. Said she was a waitress/barmaid at the American Legion with Roxanne. Said she was pretty, had a medium build with light brown hair. The American Legion Club was near Wilson Street...or did she say Ashley Street and Hill Ave? She also said something about a large parking lot in the back. Maybe that was attached to the American Legion Club. I'll have to check my notes..."

"She has something to do with the shovel."

"Who? Jessica?"

"Yes... she has something to do with the shovel, the compass, and the number 7. This may be a grave plot or a lot number. As for the date of December 17th, I do not know if it is in reference to 1966 or 2010," she added and then informed me she had to go.

CHAPTER THIRTY

Forty-eight hours after the dark and bloody moon, more information began to pour in again. Spencer began.

They show me...they line the walls. They are gold... like mail slots... a goldish-bronze. There are many of them. The hands are shaking; he is nervous. Does someone see him? His hands continue to shake, palms sweat. The lock box reads #8099; he jiggles the key. He looks again to see if someone is watching him. The documents are inside...he must retrieve the documents without being seen.

Running on emotional fumes, it was all I could to keep up with what I was learning. She continued without break.

The shovel and the compass now fit within the picture. The heat was brutal on her...decaying...rotting her flesh before they buried her. Was it July? August?

Then the next night...

Elizabeth: name of woman with broken chandelier was hiding something in her house. Law enforcement came in looking for it. That is how the chandelier got broken. Two are searching through house and one is calmly talking to her. She knows all three of them. She keeps saying she does not know where it is. They can't find "it." Hinting to her that her husband might be in a heap of trouble. Feels like they are just trying to intimidate her and that her husband was never in trouble over "it." They show me 14 blocks from La Grange or at 14th and La Grange. Do you know this address?

And then next night...

Law enforcement entered the home without permission. She knew them, but that didn't give them the right. They broke the chandelier... "Where is it?" they kept asking. "Where is it? Tell us where it is or else..."

Again they show me the woman who holds the broken glass from the chandelier could not tell them, but that did not stop them from searching the house anyway. Again they, the three men telling her that her husband would be in trouble if he didn't turn it over...

And the next night I wrote this blog:

Multicolored leaves cuddle together in the street gutters in various levels of decay... much like the bodies of Grim's victims in Valdosta those long forty-four years ago. How many gone, how many murdered, we are forced now to ask? How many banded together to protect the guilty... to deny their own culpability in the debauchery of a town? And how many knew the secrets? How many whose lips remained silent while the victims lay gasping for air in the moonlight? How many whose consciences betrayed them on a daily basis?

When I write a book, I generally write it backwards... thus the delay. Every time I build the final few sentences... they whisper in my ear "There's more...so much more..." and I am stalled by my own curiosity to see this to the end. As you have read before, I build my stories first by creating a title, find the appropriate font, then write the ending and backfill.

Originally this book started as a historical fiction piece entitled The Coffee Pot Conspiracy. *But the more I learned (which now I see as so minimal, it amazes me I could fabricate a title at all), the more it became hinged on that one cup of coffee and then all the cups of coffee in Charley's life. While the working title of* The Coffee Pot Conspiracy *sends you images of Hugh Beaumont and Barbara Billingsly (of* Leave it to Beaver *fame, recently deceased, God rest her soul) sitting down to coffee with Ozzie and Harriet Nelson to discuss last night's episode of the* Jackie Gleason Show, *it now symbolizes so much more.*

Of course, I understand that you have not had unfettered access to Kaye's journal and so your impressions will be hindered greatly, but you do remember that that was the last conversation, the last words between husband and wife that night? The mutual consent to share a cup of coffee, delayed by the interruption of a by a drive-by moonshine investigation and an agreement to reconvene in the kitchen after his arrival home later that night? The time frame ETA of "shortly after the pot had percolated"? A projected window of forty-five to fifty-five minutes, tops? The cup of coffee they never got to share? The pot and the body that grew colder as the night went on? The unresolved marital issues? The breakdown of true communication? The uncertainty of a couple who had lost two children, been blessed with two more. Concerns about how they could navigate the future with new understanding and appreciation for each other's needs? And so it is not only fitting, but as I will explain to you the absolute thread that binds all in this mind-numbing ride.

Let us go back... not to the beginning, because in truth I cannot tell you when that is. I can only pick up the thread midstream and run with it. Let us begin with the summer of 1966. Our most recently discovered victim, Jessica, was most likely murdered somewhere around the 4th of July in 1966. It may fit the timing and the excessive heat she felt, the rapid sense of decay to her damaged face and skull as denoted by my dear friend Spencer. So let's conjecture for a moment, shall we, and find the common timeline for all this? Want to?

As Bette Davis once said, 'You better hold on tight... it's going to be a bumpy ride!'

Ok... so Jessica is murdered and beaten with a shovel somewhere around the holiday of the 4th. This fits. Then they move her from where she was murdered, which was near someone's home. (Just whose, I will not say as yet.) She lies there in the woods, but he can see her. It excites him...maybe too much. He can see her from his window. He cannot tell his wife or children... but he likes it. This voyeurism, this lust for the dead. He keeps it to himself. He shares this with no one but Jessica. She, lifeless... lies dead outside his window... him enjoying the site of her mutilation and decay.

Then the rumors begin to fly. Everybody hears, everybody knows... but nobody wants to get involved because they suspect certain law enforcement members have their bloody little fingerprints all over this one. They wait a few days; then they bury her, oh, let's just say possibly at a public works site. A friend reports her missing, but no one cares. She's a hooker and a whore. Nobody cares about the lower class, not in this town. It's all about the power and the money.

The four in flannel operate under their own power. The farther they get from the crime, the more they begin to miss the thrill. They plot for another. All the while Charley is working his AATD job and building houses on the side; they are pumping released prisoner workers on him, asking him to use them as "labor." Kaye is forced into running a prison farm atmosphere and she talks about this in her journal. The unease of having so many violators on their property. She is worried with Charley gone so much of the time. Now let's get back to the timeline.

Jessica is probably murdered in the early portion of the month, then buried at or under a local.... well, I know where and you will find out later. Then G suddenly pops into the picture much more often. If Charley goes for coffee, so does she. G works for the Parole Office at the Courthouse. My, how convenient! The same office whose prisoners work on public works projects, where Jessica is buried. Incredulously, they are the same people who are there that night at Charley's murder searching for evidence, or shall we say creating and destroying evidence. Stay with me now...

The town is dotted with cafés and tiny restaurants that border the Courthouse, "the then county seat of injustice," as I like to call it. State and Federal Treasury agents all working together for the common cause, with the local law enforcement in support. Like an 18-hour bra, they support only their own, though, and those that hang over the sides are left to fend for themselves.

The ravens hobnob and chatter. Who's cheating who in and out of the bed? In and out of the office. Suddenly now when Charley goes to drink coffee, everybody goes to drink coffee — at least everyone who is interested in what Charley knows and does not know about the missing girl. Take, for instance, the P.O. boss who suspiciously arrives every time Charley steps into the Plaza Restaurant. He drinks with him and maybe calls his secretary over to join them, or she meets Charley and then calls her boss to join them. How very cozy this all seems. This continues for weeks, this dance of tempting and teasing information from one another. Even more odd is the fact that in mid-July, G and her husband show up at Charley's home to drink coffee, talk about construction loans, and ask to borrow a gun of Charley's to go camping with that next day. Seems nice and friendly, doesn't it? Sure... if it hadn't been for the fact G had filed for divorce from her husband the April before. And that it was after 10:00 at night when they showed up unannounced to borrow a gun. And that they had left four children home alone at the time to come and do it. Odd, right? I'll say. Don't you find it curious that a woman who wants to divorce her husband so badly she has separated from him several times is willing to go into the deep, dark woods with the same man she is wanting to gift with someone else's weaponry? Hmmm....

Odd, but not even close to what else happens. G dogs Charley everywhere he goes. G loves sex, but apparently with everyone except maybe Charley. G continues to bait Charley with it, though, flirting and teasing. Charley falls, maybe not too heavy, but heavy enough for her to begin to have some emotional influence. The coffee drinking continues a lot and every day. It is the way they can be together and still be innocent. G knows everything about Charley. But more importantly, she listens for what Charley knows. She's been hired to keep tabs on Charley by people in high places, high positions. Where he goes, what he does, finding out who and what he knows. They get kinda cozy here and there; Charley gets comfortable. G hopes he will slip up and tell her things, but Charley is not stupid. Meanwhile Grim and Company begin to get a bit uneasy. They worry that the murder of Jessica may be a problem. But who is gonna dig up an entire pool to find her?

August rolls through, and the rumors still swirl about what happened to the pretty little girl from the American Legion Club. Rumors fly about cops messing with local ladies of the night, young ladies of the night, girls, and I don't mean arresting them. Girls go missing; people talk. Charley listens and finds out a few things. Not enough to send someone to the gallows, but he's got some dirt and he keeps quiet about it until September rolls on through. The heat waxes and wanes just like the Indian summer moon, and suddenly the boy's club gets a little braver. If one hooker can disappear and nobody gives a shit, then what about two? What about a club? The club of killers?

This is where poor Roxanne enters the picture. Dear sweet young Roxy — pretty little thing that works at the bakery, likes older men, likes badges and a man in uniform. The boy's club gets even braver. The pipe smoker and the Sheriff run a tight ship. The porn ring business seems to be just as successful as the illegal gambling and booze. High rollers from Hollywood like to fly into this sandy little burg and play high stakes poker. They like drinks, cigars, and pretty girls. So what the customer wants, the customer gets. If along the way the local boys club gets a few of the bread crumbs left over, who's the wiser?

Rox spends the night with one man that ends up being accompanied by three more. It is the initiation into the boy's club. She says something wrong. Before you know it, three sets of hands are on her throat, crushing her windpipe. She fights back, leaving a scar beneath Grim's left eye. There in the mud, they kick and beat her. The air escapes her lungs one final time as they toss the coin on who gets to finish her off, but the bitch dies before they can be satisfied. Angry, they kick her some more and when they are done with her, they roll her body into a swampy area. Where, you might ask? Oh, silly children. Did you really think I would tell you?

This is where the MOT comes in. The MOT (man on tape) was there with her that night. He sees, he knows, and he is scared to death that he is now involved in a murder — not just a sexual tryst. The MOT panics and makes a tape calling them all out by name, telling everything these men have done, who the mastermind is and who his minions. Grim doesn't know whether to shit or go blind he is so enraged and frightened. He, the fair-haired boy, the golden child, caught with his pants down and his dick so far from home. How can he explain this? Who will believe him that is was an accident? That he didn't mean to strangle her, just rough her up a bit? What will his darling little wife think? What will his church think? Funny, how he never seemed to care what God would think, isn't it? Funny how now that's all he thinks about.

The MOT gives a copy of this "spilling his guts" tape to Charley. Charley makes several copies and then foolishly takes one to a law enforcement official outside the city, thinking it the lesser of two evils. Poor Charley; he chooses wrong. G has done her best to keep Charley on a short leash, but he is fast becoming a problem for everyone. What if he digs further? What if he finds out where Jessica was buried or where Rox was dumped? What if he can tie the entire law enforcement system for an entire city to these two murders? What if it goes higher... say to high-ranking state officials? Then what?

Something must be done about the coffee-drinking ATTD agent. He is too smart to leave untethered for too long. The MOT and Charley meet. Charley begins to piece things together. Grim is young, ruthless, and stupid. He thinks he is clever and with the arrogance of youth immortal, the brotherhood bands together; they plot, they plan, they leave the sleaze factor to G. She passes money for the boy's club: hush money, bribery money. One hand washes the other. They are all dirty now — all but the guy who walks the line and drinks coffee, the one guy who could destroy the kingdom. But they have to be careful. They have to build the plan, set the mood. He has to fall for G, so that the affair will stick. So that when they do the deed, they can manipulate the press. He died of a broken heart... he couldn't live without her or live with the shame. It was almost too perfect. They could have it all and get away with it. It was the perfect crime.

A call is made. The hook is baited, the lure cast, and the black widow reels him in, nice and slow, so slowly he barely knows what is happening to him as she winds the thread tighter and tighter around his throat, pulling him closer, ever closer to her fangs. They meet, they gather, they murder, they manipulate, they lie and malign. Then forty-four years later they forget.

So we have Jessica in early July, Rox in the end of September or early October, then Charley on October 9th, 1966. It doesn't take long. They close the investigation in less than three weeks. They declare it suicide. But the MOT knows different. He holds up in a hotel hiding, hoping they won't find him, but they do. Six days later they demand he tells them where the other tapes are. "Where did Charley hide the other tapes? We know there are copies! Where are they?"

Their faces are red with anger, lips afire with cursing, their hearts black as coal. They have already committed three murders in their game; one more will never matter. But he dies of a heart attack before he can give them the location. They begin the search, house to house, intimidating and beating those who will not comply.

Have I got it right so far, Grim?

And that's when I received this email from Jules:

My brother just sent me a message. Very supportive of the blog and investigation. Said he remembers Dad borrowing his tape recorder in Sept. '66 and returning it with new blank tapes. Said if he could have gotten another one it could have been used to copy tapes.

And from Spencer:

Just read your blog. Charley says, "Bull's-eye!"

Ok... so that helped explain Roxanne, but what about Jessica? Emboldened by my pseudo success, I wrote back.

The thing I don't get is why. She was a hooker according to everyone, so no one cared. Everyone knew the VPD was crooked and screwed around, so no one cared. Was it the shovel that hit her face? Compass so they could know where exactly the pool would be built over her? And whose property was she first killed on? It must have been over the 4th of July. You had a session once where Charley was talking about the 4th of July. Jules thought it was for her, but I'm betting not a reference meant for her now.

So they kill her somewhere else, then let her sit over 4th of July and have her buried after that on a public works project. That's where the Park and Rec reference comes in. Does she say that the man who wears the boots is the man who wields the shovel? I will check into other facts today in between working...

As usual Spencer responded and with her came the wisdom from afar. Once again I was sent back to the boards and the internet to search streets and intersections I never knew existed before. Just before Halloween this came through.

Loved the blog today. Did you understand the tax reference from mom and dad? Can you email me a photo of your parents? They came through so detailed in appearance last night. They show me 777..."

I responded:

The angel number 777 means "You are definitely on the right path in every area of your life. Stay balanced and spiritually aware so that you can continue moving forward on this illuminated path." Thank you... I do not understand the sunflower from my mother and father, but I am happy to receive anything from them as even though I know they are with me, my hearts breaks at their inability to hold me one more time... Tell them thank you and thank you too for the message of love.

It was good to hear from my parents again. It had been so long I had forgotten why I had bargained to do this from the beginning. I understood the tax form thing... in the sense that my father had been executive branch IRS and for years it was a standard joke. We would try to do my taxes… at the age of 12 he had me begin recording my babysitting money and file taxes. I was proficient until line 11c. I could fill out my name, my address, and all the other non-mathematical information. Once we hit adding and subtracting figures, I was screwed! I could never quite get past "What's on line 11C?" without driving my father crazy. The sunflower had some peripheral meaning, but initially it registered as a no. When Spencer pressed me again about the sunflower, I replied, "Now if it had been sunflower seeds, that would have made perfect sense, especially in light of their nostalgic inclinations."

She began to laugh and when I asked why, she replied, "So that's what they were there for. She showed me a sunflower and seeds next to it, but I thought it all meant one thing: a sunflower, not sunflower seeds." And then I told her the significance of the seeds. Being one of ten my mother used to get very creative at filling in the gaps in our school lunches. One year for a full month we each got a huge individual packet of sunflower seeds in our lunch. My brother ate them constantly in class or out of class, it didn't matter. He would split the seed with his tongue, chew the guts, spit the shells, take a drink of water, and start the process again. The nuns would watch, fascinated that he could do that and read or write at the same time. Being somewhat ignorant, they believed the seeds must have been laced with something and were convinced they were a potential addiction. They made a big deal about the seeds and cautioned our parents that their children were becoming addicts. Ya' gotta love a parochial school!

October was ending just the way it began… on a cool wind and an eerie note. On Halloween night I sat quietly on the front porch steps of the townhouse, waiting for the last of the trick-or-treaters to come a-calling. Nibbling on a Snicker's bar, I looked up to the stars and wondered what holidays were like in heaven. As a gesture of good will, I raised the last bit of chocolate to the sky and offered it to my father. So far it had been an awesome month full of big moments and small miracles. The night I had finally pieced most of what happened together and realized *why* Charley had been murdered, I wept uncontrollably. Moved by his sufferings, I kissed his forehead and held him tight to my chest. Secretly I apologized that his life had been eclipsed for such sick and pathetic reasons.

Never had I felt such compassion for another soul. Not that Jessica, Roxanne, or the MOT had deserved to die the way they did; nobody deserved that kind of treatment. I would have grieved for anyone who had suffered the same, yet Charley had become so special to me it amplified my grief. His heart had been so parallel to mine at some points that it was hard to separate our collective angst. Choices had been ripped from his hands, and in their place only consequence remained. His wife, left unstable in the confidence of her marital vows, wandered this earth a shell of the woman she might have become. His children, without his guidance or benefit, followed paths that have kept them contemporaries, but not close. And his persecutors who still walk this earth lived lives without guilt, regret, or indictment.

It all seemed such a terrible, terrible waste. There had been no merit for the loss to comfort or console in the aftermath. Four lives had been squandered for desire of debauched fornication and it made me want to vomit. As I looked upon Charley's face, unfiltered sobbing racked my entire body, and I could not get over the collective loss. Without compromising his fragile framing, I held him tight until we could both breathe evenly again. Deeply moved, I brushed his painted forehead with my lips one more time before I returned him to a place of honor upon my desk. Emotionally spent, I slipped into the bed alone. I did not do homework that night, nor did I write. I simply lay there in the dark and pondered the reasons for the existence of man. What sort of experiment were we and why had it been allowed to go so wrong? Why would a compassionate and omnipotent Intelligence permit us to grace even one inch of His glorious universal stage? It was confounding to me. Humans can be such cruel creatures.

With such weighty thoughts, slumber was elusive, and I spent most of the night tossing and turning. By 4:00 am, I had only slept a total of two hours. Emotionally jetlagged, I awoke quiet and remained so the better part of the following day. Early in the afternoon I received a call from Spencer, and her words caught me off guard.

"Charley has a message for you," she began. *"Can you talk?"*

"Sure," I answered softly. Knowing that on any given moment on any given day I have asked Charley a hundred million questions, it was not odd that he came through with an answer. I reached for a pad of paper and a pen and poised myself ready to take dictation. "Go ahead...I'm ready."

"He wanted me to tell you..." and she paused, *"Thank you."*

Confused, I redirected. "For what?"

"Thank you for the kiss on his forehead last night." Without adequate sleep to buffer the edge of such raw emotions, I dropped my pen and immediately began to cry.

She continued. "He says to tell you, you are bound to one another forever."

"He was with me?" I whimpered.

"He was very touched by your compassion."

I had not told a single soul of the scene at my desk the night before and was aghast. Privately it had been a cathartic moment in which I shared the depth of my collective grief over the loss of my parents and his over the loss of both family and future, all for the likes of a woman who warranted only the use of an initial: G. If made public, I would have been embarrassed over how I had carried on and hysterically clung to a photo of a dead man I had never met for comfort. But since no one had been in the room either with me or even on the second floor of the house to observe my personal agony, I had assumed it safe to emotionally disrobe. For me it had been a moment of absolute clarity. Left naked with only my heart, his 8 x 10, and my Maker, I was deeply cut by the jagged edges of each of our lives and psychologically bled without salve. There was absolutely no way she could have known about the exorcizing

246

of my personal devastation or the kiss I had tearfully bestowed upon the cryovaced surface of Charley's photo. I never talked about it, never wrote about it until now. With absolute humility I whispered back, "Tell him..." I sniffled, "He is most kindly welcome."

"He is bending over you now. They are showing me what we perceive as angel wings... but they are his wings, huge and white enfolding you, completely engulfing you as you sit in your chair. He is placing a kiss upon your cheek and saying thank you... thank you...thank you..."

Slowly I stretched my arms towards my face, and then paused. Through heavy tears I asked, "Which cheek? I want to try and feel him." She instructed it was the left and I adjusted my palm and tried to imagine his cheek beside my own, but felt only the touch of my own hand.

"I want to hold him too... but I can't feel his touch," I cried softly. "Why can't I feel him, Spencer? Why won't they let me feel him?" I whimpered, instantly missing both the opportunity to feel his touch and the tactile connection. She told me he was there beside me, still holding me in his embrace as I cried unabashedly in the privacy of my office.

"I can't feel him...it's so unfair." And while Spencer tried to comfort me, I felt cheated that I had garnered such tenderness and yet was unable to access its sensation. "It's true... 'Hell is intimacy without proximity,'" I muttered under my breath. It didn't seem fair that she should be privy alone to such a sight. Though I would not begrudge Spencer a thing in the world, I wanted to be able to share in that moment on the same level as she. I wanted to see my Charley and make the connection real.

For over a year I had toiled each night in my efforts to bring him peace. The fact that I, for lack of proper divinity or deficiency of inner sight, could not share that one special moment with my chosen shepherd broke my heart anew. It is difficult to share the expanse of one's soul in the microcosm of an instant. Yet this was what the universe continued to ask of me on a daily basis. Overwhelmed by emotion, I needed several minutes to adjust. Grateful to Spencer for the message, I closed my eyes and wished him well, knowing what had been shared and what had been felt and heard was still more than most people ever receive in a hundred lifetimes.

CHAPTER THIRTY-ONE

Looking out my office window, I watched the trees and tried to adopt their grace in the changing seasons of their lives. One leaf… one thought… one leaf… one person… one leaf… one experience… one leaf… one adventure… one leaf… one loss at a time…gone. The year had been plagued by multiple separations, disappointments, opportunities, and colossal change — but it had also generated incalculable potential for rebirth.

As fate would have it, November entered with even gustier winds of bitter realities than the month before. Physically fatigued and psychologically compromised, Don had problems with equilibrium and disorientation continued. In addition to work and school, fate was now forcing me to become realtor too, as it was increasingly evident that vertical living was no longer an option. Stressed by financial worries and work-related betrayals, I grew tight-lipped and crusted with cynicism.

Each day a battlefield of unending challenges and retreats had buried parts of me as it allowed other parts to blossom. Bridges that had been built to stand the test of time fell prey to unauthorized decay. Yet I divined that the path on the other side might still be reached by digging deeper for new foundations and the chance for reconstruction. I realized that even as I had lost something that was better given away than kept, there was a keen sense of loss that still registered across my heart. Each damp wind, like a new experience, tested my resolve. Should I have clung to that which had brought me this far in my life… or should I adjust to the seasons in my life with grace and humility?

Again, I sought solace in the nature outside my bedroom office. Like the small maple tree that stood below, now barren but for seven turning leaves that clung desperately to its young mast, I realized I too needed to learn how to stretch my fledgling limbs to

249

the autumn sky and graciously allow those leaves meant for greater deeds than I could provide vehicle for, those leaves that still clung to me or those leaves to which I still clung… to separate and fall away as providence demanded. With equal timidity, I tried to center and embrace the new blush of another impending season.

After learning that the rumor of the dead girl being buried under a pool was in fact not rumor at all, I found more information that brought me closer to the potential location of her remains. Try as I might, Jessica had gone quiet and I could not understand why. In a conversation with Spencer, I expressed my frustrations.

"If she knows I can help her, why won't she talk to me?" I pleaded. "Why doesn't she just give you the address of the pool or landmarks that surround it? Why all the silly hide and seek shit? I just don't understand. Doesn't she know this is for her?"

"Maybe it's not really about her," she tested.

I bypassed her immediately and made some quip about staying on task. As always, Spencer spoke from a wealth of experience and wisdom. She explained, "Ok...as odd as this may sound, sometimes they don't want you to find them."

You could have knocked me over with one of my proverbial feathers. "How the devil do you get sexually abused by that many men, slammed upside the face with a shovel, beaten, thrown under a pool like construction waste, and not want someone who loves you to know what they did to you or where to find you?" I balked. "I'm sorry… that just doesn't make sense to me. There has to be another reason. I've obviously missed something."

"TA, it's not that easy for some of them. Take Jessica, for instance. How did she end up being buried under a pool?" Spencer asked.

"Well...if I freaking knew that, I wouldn't need her to tell me now, would I?" I joked, but my frustration was transparent and the humor lost.

"I'm serious, TA. Sometimes they don't want to be found because they don't want their loved ones to know how they ended up."

That thought had never crossed my mind. I was so stuck in thinking about them as victims that I completely forget that at some level they had actively participated in reaching their own final destination. "I can't believe they would choose not to be found," I stammered.

"Did you ever think that maybe, just maybe, Jessica doesn't want her family to know how she had been living the last few years of her life? Or maybe that her folks and her family are not emotionally ready to accept the life she led or the way she died? Think about how bad this has messed with your head. Maybe her family is not prepared for something like that."

"Maybe…" I stalled.

"Sometimes they give you the runaround because they know they have already caused someone so much pain. They don't wish to add to it… see?"

I shuffled in my seat and pulled the phone from my ear for a minute. Once again, my ignorance of the process overwhelmed me. "So, crossing over doesn't give you all the answers either, I take it?" She confirmed that indeed it did not.

"Jesus, she probably thinks I'm a shit for barking at her about not giving me more information. Roxanne too."

"No. They don't judge us from that side. They know you are trying to help them, but they do not all process their passing at the same rate. She and Roxanne may not be ready to tell you everything yet because they have not learned how to deal with it all yet. Sometimes they get stuck, just reliving things over and over," she added.

I hesitated. I could not imagine reliving such horrors and thought better than to push again for more details. "Please tell them both

I'm so sorry. I had no idea what I was asking of them. I'm so sorry. Please tell them for me."

"You just did," she replied.

Suddenly I understood the magnitude of what I had been asking. The two victims became more real. I rationalized that even on the other side they had no more emotional maturity than that of my own girls. Places deep within my soul began to hurt. How different Jessica and Roxanne might have been if they had had been mine. Still very much out in the cold as far as identifying an exact location for her remains, I asked Charley for help, but with the caveat that Jessica be ok with my search.

Later that evening with the words of Marjorie about a bloody shovel and visions of Jessica obsessing about the damage and decay to her face, I asked for ethereal guidance and a chance to follow the four in flannel as they committed the crime. I know that my rest that night was unsettled; alas, the only thing I can recall from my slumber was standing inside a small room that had not been finished. Sheetrock mud and taping were still exposed; floors were covered in sawdust, tidbits of lumber lay next to nails and huge clumps and drizzled tailings of caulk. The window openings had been cut, trimmed, and framed, but actual windows not installed yet.

I remember it was a shell of a room inside what appeared to be apartments or offices of some sort. The place felt like a two- or three-story building still under construction, a building that looked out over an area with scattered construction debris and large piles of sandy-colored dirt heaped at various junctures. Standing inside the room, I could feel the breeze through the window. I sensed someone near me, but was not frightened. The person did not know I was there watching. I leaned out the open window and looked down. Construction equipment, stray lumber, wheelbarrows, and shovels littered the ground directly beneath me, but beyond the immediate area things seemed to clean up a bit as though further along in the construction process.

The person with me bent forward into the window to look farther out. When I followed his gaze, I saw the gaping hole. It was rectangular. While the earth surrounding it held a honey brown color, deep within its cavity the shade became more reddish in pigment. At the time I did not know if it was meant to be the footprint of another building. But after comparison to others, I soon realized that it could not have been a basement as it was more than one story deep. When I questioned my ethereal company as to what it was, there was no answer. I glanced back towards the door and saw the shadow of my escort pacing in the hall; he had left me there alone to contemplate the view. I turned back towards the window and stared at the shape below, its dimensions, and the proximity to a clump of woods. This was new construction in an area that was sparsely populated. The template of buildings was laid out, and the one I was in was the closest to completion. I looked down again, gauging and deciphering the shape of the cavity beneath me. Uncommonly large for private use, it became instantly clear that this was for public use. When I suddenly realized what it was I was looking at, I woke in a cold sweat.

I was given a name as guide wire. When I Googled this name, the internet gave me more than fourteen different possibilities of location and name combinations to review. Searching Google Earth and Google Maps, I discerned by population density and locale several plausible sites. But when I sent the list to Spencer for perusal, the very address I had made the personal exemption for a variety of reasons was the only address that jumped out at her from the list. Keeping an open mind and because she has thus far never been wrong in this case, I Googled it.

The satellite zeroed in and the images of two- and three-story buildings began to come into view. The closer the satellite got and the higher the resolution, the more clearly the images of a complex came into view. But it wasn't the template of the complex that caught my attention so much, though the address gave me the exact same perspective as the one in my dream. It was what lay just north of my perspective that gave me chills.

It was the image of a large pool.

CHAPTER THIRTY-TWO

Finals were fast approaching and I spent copious amounts of time with my nose pressed between the pages of criminology and psychology books, praying that my brain would hold enough information to get me through with passing grades. I know you think, "Dear God in heaven, woman, get a grip! Eighteen- and nineteen-year-olds constituted 98% of the freshmen in colleges all over the United States; surely at fifty-two you could intellectually compete with them." But that is the funny thing about age and school: sometimes they don't always mix. That long removed from pencils and protractors, my brain sometimes panicked. But just about the time I would decide to toss in the metaphorical towel, I would see my daughter Claire wander down the hall in grungy gym shorts and a torn T-shirt with a bowl of Captain Crunch, and I would regain a healthy perspective. I could do this. If she were in school, she would be my contemporary...Captain Crunch and all.

One morning while I was working on a paper for psych, Spencer called. What began as a quick casual conversation about her move soon spilled over the dam of consciousness, and Charley flooded the room with information that covered more than seven pages in my notebook. In an effort to show you how abridged information is given, I will record in the same fashion in which it was distributed that morning:

Charley. He is showing me trains. They are loading and unloading, heading NW. He keeps talking about the trains. There are two or three energies involved with this, the train scene. Grim and Winston. They are involved with the moonshine and protection of the train. They get paid from profits. They are in charge of distribution and protection...

I asked who else was there with them at the trains. Who else in the stable of names we are now familiar with might have hand their hands in it as well? I recalled Kaye's journal and a section where she mentioned someone in her house the night Charley died, and Spanks Mavry who held a position with the railroad as Trainmaster.

"What do they show with his name?" I asked.

He is frightened he will get caught. He is very nervous. Why did he get involved? What if they find out he was involved? He is wringing his hands...very afraid.

I asked if they saw Beau Colbert as he lived near Winston and seemed to be attached to this whole moonshine/railroad mess. Spencer had already given me other information, so I knew he was there the night Charley was murdered. When she began to focus on Colbert, this came through:

Hmmm...very interesting. They show me he has blood on his hands, literally and figuratively. He is very upset... frantic. Outside he looks calm, but inside he is freaking, like "Oh my God, I just saw something!" He is scared, shaking now. Oh my God, what did they do? He is young and naïve in spirit, cannot believe they would do this. Attracted to G; would have done anything for her, agreed he would help. Sick with love for G, he declares he can do it; he agrees it must be done, is willing to participate. But that is just his bravado talking; he did not think they would ever go through with it, so it didn't matter. He was trying to impress G. He sees Charley's body and freaks. He cannot believe they did it. He is physically shaking, petrified. What now, what now?

There was a lull and my blood raced, remembering something in the statements made by one of the young men. "Spencer, hold on a sec."

When the boys called the incident in, they first called Brooks County and then were instructed to call Lowndes as Charley's body was on the other side of the river. Waverleigh said he had overheard the call from LCSD dispatch to the Colbert home and clearly heard the dispatcher being told that "Beau was taking a bath and would get dressed and be on his way to the crime scene as soon as possible." With that, my theory was confirmed. Colbert was there when it went down or shortly thereafter and was part of the crew who had manipulated the crime scene. He, Cummings, and Sloan are the three along with G who must have staged the car, fired the second shot through the underside of Charley's chin, and relocated the body. Then one of the idiots placed Charley's hat and the flashlight from the car onto the road for the crime scene photos. Waverleigh said he never saw either of those when he was there. I suddenly recalled something from way back in the beginning: a list of names given to Spencer and her response that three names rose from the paper and appeared in red: Hank Sloan, Beau Colbert, and Gerrilyn Baldwin. I was just about to remind her about that when she continued without warning.

He must get home to clean up. He is still freaking out. The blood, Charley's blood, is on him. How could they have gone through with it? What are they supposed to do now? Charley is dead. It wasn't supposed to go down that way. He comes later; he knows what went down. Still petrified. He never thought they would go that far...

My hands began to shake. Beau Colbert's son was the man who had given me the original file and I was indebted to him. Now I was beginning to freak inside my own skin knowing I would not be able to bring myself to look in his eyes and tell him his father was complicit. How could I tell him that his father, the man he claimed was Charley's good buddy, was there the night he was murdered and did nothing to stop the insanity? And even worse, all this because he was in love with Gerrilyn Baldwin who had helped lure Charley to his slaughter.

Spencer left me no time to consider.

He is freaking. He was there before and had to come back; he had to take a bath. The blood... the blood. He is being forced to finish the job. He is young in spirit, naïve, corrupt, but not malicious. He could not have gone through with it, all for G, all for G. What have they done? What have they done?

In my head I saw that karma had been met. While in his earthly station, Beau Colbert had done nothing to stop the insanity and the cover up that followed. But karma demanded that he correct the situation as could be done from where he was now. Thus, the file he saved forty-four years ago to cover his ass could now be used to uncover everybody else's. This, I thought, I could sell to his son when the day of final reckoning would come with the publication of this book. *[Thank you, Beau. Thank you. May you be at peace when all this comes to light. Charley mentioned in his first session that he forgave Colbert. He refers to the young energy in law enforcement. He understood the manipulation of you by G and he forgave.]*

Oh, the things we do for lust…we might never do for love. Appreciating the lengths to which the cosmos was taking to get me this information, my hands became steadier than Colbert's must have been that night. But before I could ask if his were the fingers that held back the head for the second wound or the bloody fingers that wrapped around Charley's to pull the second shot, Spencer jumped ahead. Harried, I tried to keep pace.

Do you understand the arrest on the train? Do you understand the man, the staff; there is a worker from the train's staff. He is the scapegoat. He was arrested. Look for information on him... an arrest. The train goes further NW of Valdosta; the arrest is there.

Charley remained consumed by the train scenario. While she repeated some of the information several times, I asked for a redirect and introduced the lockbox #8099 again and hoped for further information.

They are showing me...8099 lockbox. They show me the numbers 2223... 2223. These are street numbers. There is more: 2223 East Thund... something. It is a specific building... the roof is wood... shingled, wooden shingles... thick shingles of wood, like a hut or a shack appearance. This has to do with the lockbox.

As I recorded the new influx, I asked if Charley was open to other questions. She said she would try. So I told her I believed Charley had been too smart to have just made just one copy of the MOT's tape. Charley would have covered his ass too. I asked if there was another somewhere... anywhere that I could still retrieve for evidence. I told her about Jules's brother's confirmation, that Charley borrowed his tape recorder sometime during the later portion of the month of September of 1966. With pen poised above the paper, I tried to steady my hand, hoping he would grant me this one wish.

"C'mon, Charley, c'mon, I whispered to his photo. "Just this once, buddy. C'mon. One direct question for one direct answer." I heard rustling at the other end of the line as Spencer adjusted herself.

"Do you know who lives in Charley's house now?" she asked. I told her a priest. The irony was not lost on either of us. She continued.

Charley is showing me underneath his kitchen floor...dug something... dirt... they couldn't find it...wood floor... small hole...

I caught my breath and took a sip of my coffee, now cold.

They couldn't find it...standing facing the pantry... directly below the ground or beneath one more level down... he digs the hole with his finger nails with hands... covers with loose dirt... they could not find it.

I asked if she is getting the impression it still exists.

There... still there... copy to Finch destroyed by Grim. One copy circulated, one copy kept hidden... kept hidden... the house... the dirt below...

I asked to redirect to the lockbox, hoping to get more.

They show me the lockbox again... documents rolled up inside... 8099 ... gold in the hall... they are all lined up...

I asked if the lockbox or the documents still existed. She said she can't say. I asked if he thought I could find the tape. She continued.

He is standing in front of the pantry... opens the door and looks down...there... it is there.

I asked if this was the tape he made with his son's tape recorder.

Yes, the tape. Yes... the recorder.

I wrote like a mad woman; choppy words ran all over the page, but there was more to come.

He tells me that... ace of spades... black...tell her that... do you understand the black ace of spades?

Again my heart broke in two. "No... I don't. I'm sorry, Charley; I don't understand....you have to help me, Spencer. Anything else he can give me to help me understand the car reference? This is the second time he has used a card...I'm not getting segue. Can you help me?"

She was silent. Then in a thin whisper, "No, sorry. There is nothing said about it further."

I told her again, "This is the second card reference I cannot divine. First there was the seven of spades just before the information about Jessica and now the black ace of spades when we are talking about the lockbox and the tapes." She asked if I still had his wallet. I did, but it was not in reach. She continued, regardless.

Do you understand the wallet? He is showing me the last thing, the last thing in the wallet. It is in the very back, paper like...

Before I could even reach for the plastic bins that held my Charley and all his paraphernalia, she moved on and I was hit between the eyes with the next revelation.

Jessica, they show me... a previous suicide attempt... cutting of wrists... blood... admitted to the hospital... it is more an emotional cry of pain than physical...Any family in the area? It does not feel like it... she stayed overnight... they kept her, watched her...research this... there is more for you here.

I tried to redirect and asked if they used the shovel to beat her.

She is very fixated on her face... what did they do... why does it look like this?

I broke in to ask another question, but she cut me off and continued.

From Jessica. She shows me the man who watches her body in the dirt from afar has a fire in his backyard...in July. It has something to do with her, but it is odd. It is too hot for a fire...no leaves. It is a large fire...but too hot to have a fire... what is he burning?

I scribbled the information as fast as I could. In the midst of everything Spencer blurted they have a personal message for me. I hold my breath, certain it will be as riveting as the last six pages.

They are showing me the pantry... they have a message.

I was convinced we were now back to the tape Charley had hidden, so I turned the page to start anew.

They are telling me to tell you to...

I was certain this would be the big moment I had waited over a year and a half for. "C'mon, Charley, you can do it!" I pled.

They say... to take out the trash.

I wrote this down before my brain had time to process what I was writing. My heart pounded with adrenaline as I read what I had written: "To take out the...do what?" I asked.

"Take out the trash," she repeated flatly.

"Are you shitting me? " I retorted.

"They say… you need to take out your trash," she responded and broke into peals of laughter.

I was amazed and hugely disappointed. I told her that it was now Thursday afternoon and that trash pickup was on Wednesdays. She told me they insisted and reiterated about the trash. I volleyed their serve and told them I always took out the trash myself and it went out Wednesday mornings before I would leave for work or Tuesday, the night before. Again she confirmed their adamant demanding and plowed through with another stellar communication.

They want to know if you understand the bowling reference.

"Bowling?" I heard myself say and could not comprehend how we had gone from crime scene information to random nothingness in less than sixty seconds. "What the hell, Spencer? Are they kidding? Trash and bowling?" I hear myself ask again and then threw my pen at the wall. "I give! What the crap am I supposed to do with this?"

Spencer, as always, remained on an even keel and laughed to lighten the mood. "Just be aware. You know how this works, girl. Sometimes they just want to let you know they are current in your life. Just be aware and" she giggled, "…and go check your garbage!"

By that point I was so undone I assumed that the spell was broken. "Ok… I'll check the garbage, but I am sure it went out. I couldn't get to it, but I told Don to haul it out just before I left yesterday morning." And with that I eyeballed the clock and decided it was time for me to get off the phone and get ready for work, but she began again.

Charley wants to know if you understand that the murder is about the tape, that it is not about the moonshine. The tape… it is all about the porn: the tape. He is showing me it is coming to a close. Charley is at the scene, watching the cars… walks away… turns back… walks some more… closure is coming…closure is coming.

Inside I screamed, "Spencer, no! I am not ready to let him go," but she continued.

Charley is smiling. He is moving on — he is beginning to distance himself. Moonshine... money... murder of law enforcement... the MOT is forced to make the tape or makes it on his own. Charley made the tape, the copy. Elizabeth was a fishing experiment. They wanted to see if she had "it." They were just getting information... Charley could have gotten the tape from the MOT and then used it to make the copies. It is all about protection: the porn, the tape, the murder...

When the conversation was over, I hung up the phone, took my shower, and went downstairs to make a sandwich to take with me to work. While I stood looking in the refrigerator, I noticed one of the bottles of juice was all but empty and annoyed that someone had not had the decency to finish it off and throw it away. I poured the few drops left in a glass and then opened the pantry door to throw it out.

Garbage was piled so high the bottle rolled off the top of the heap and onto the floor beside me, and I all but choked on the chuckle that flooded upward into my throat. They had been right. Don had forgotten to take the garbage out. After picking it up and putting in a bag, I crossed the room to turn on the TV for the dogs so they would have something to keep them company till Don got home. The TV came on, and I turned it to their favorite channel: ABC's *Family Channel*. The sitcom that was on was one of my favorites, so I watched for a second, not recognizing the episode.

It was about spending "quality family time" together...BOWLING! I laughed all the way to the garbage can and into work.

CHAPTER THIRTY-THREE

So who was in charge of the railway back then? Who was the one who coordinated with law enforcement to get hundreds of gallons of hooch to travel across the South, traveling northwest out of Valdosta?

And what of the lockbox, lockbox #8099 that held the precious papers? I continued to search for that, but there was so much more to find for before I ever got there, like the black ace of spades and the seven of spades which still hold significance, or the name of the hotel/motel where Jessica lived and her last name so she can be identified. Previously I had received information that brought me closer to where she is buried. At first the #7 made no sense at all, but now I believe I have narrowed it down to a small concentrated area. In another session I received information that confirmed my suspicions about her location and also her last name. The confirmation came through Spencer, who had directed me to seek a slip of paper stuffed inside Charley's wallet.

Having reviewed documents, credit cards, and various other wallet paraphernalia a hundred times, I could not think of anything I had seen before that would provide such an epiphany. But Charley has never proposed something without delivering. I promised Spencer that I would look as soon as I could. An hour after our conversation, I finally arrived home and went to my office to begin my search. I pulled his wallet carefully from the plastic bag. The leather was old and crusted. With absolute attention to its fragile condition, I took extra care in opening it. Spencer had told me that Charley instructed I should go to the last piece of paper in his wallet. I should disregard anything that was plastic or laminated. Charley's wallet had two sides and a bill area once fully extended, but she told me to trust my own instincts. She said Charley would guide me and that I would recognize what he wanted to show me as soon as I saw it.

The leather creaked as I opened it. Once it was splayed, I chose to let Charley guide me. I slid the contents from the left side out onto the plastic bag to keep it from compromise. Slowly I began to deal from the bottom of the deck, so to speak. The first was a plastic card from Shell that had the calendar on it. Recalling Spencer's instructions that neither plastic nor laminate would contain what it is I needed, I pulled the next thing from the bottom. As crazy as it seems, I had no idea what it was that was to be answered by this action. I had given so many questions to Charley of late that I had no idea what clue I was even working on. Spencer had promised that I would know "it" when I saw "it," so I kept going.

The red cardboard had been handled so many times that it felt like flannel under my touch. I read what was printed on one side. It was a State Farm Insurance card, the kind you fold and keep in your wallet. I looked again at the card in disappointment. What was Charley trying to tell me?

He had clearly instructed it would be the last thing in his wallet; in fact, he had been precise, stating it would be the last paper document in his wallet. Not knowing what to do, I rolled the folded card over and over in my hand, contemplating my next move. Maybe it was in the other pocket. Maybe I had chosen wrong. Maybe my connection to Charley was not as strong as what I had felt it to be. In the moment I resolved that the error must have been mine and that I had somehow not understood. I went to set it down. As I did, I realized I had flipped it wrong side up. Wanting to keep everything in its exact order, I began to turn it over. Just as I did, I saw what was printed on the tiny lines before me. My heart leapt within my chest. There it was… black ink on red cardstock: State Farm Insurance Agent, Thomas P. Sorenson.

The last name of this agent had been meant as confirmation of the last name of the first victim: Jessica.

CHAPTER THIRTY-FOUR

Life wasn't giving me much time to breathe in between jolts, and the emotional spiral of endless uncertainty was consuming. In psychology we were reading about the "Lucifer Effect." This is a fascinating concept, and I learned more about how normal, compassionate humans, when instructed to, would inflict increasing levels of pain on innocent strangers if told to do so by a person they perceived as being in authority. Beau Colbert had been just like one of those people in the test. Taking orders from someone he perceived to be in charge, he did the unthinkable. On the other side, perhaps he was finally able to see what remedy could be made by leaving the file behind for his son to discover. Maybe Beau hoped that one day someone would bother to ask the right questions so he could finally provide the right answers.

Criminology was teaching me a great deal. Even though I have scoffed at the excesses in psychology, I was learning something from it as well. Edified by both book and counsel, I spoke with an ATF agent about the case. All throughout the course of the investigation I had kept in contact with various agents as to my progress and intentions. I reminded him to check the blog if he wanted to catch up with my findings. I seldom heard from him, so I assumed he was engrossed in discovery. While most of what Charley had told me confirmed other suspicions, some sent me on other paths. In a conversation with Spencer, I explained my frustrations with some of the more random clues and several of the partial addresses given.

"Every time I try to type in '2223 East Thund...' and attach it to a Valdosta address, the address Google search picks up is '2223 Thunder Bowl Road,' which is near some kind of racetrack for stock car racing, I think. If they have more of the address to show you, that would be great. Also, I asked Jules to describe the kitchen back then. She did not recall a pantry; is Charley showing you then or now? Apparently the kitchen was remodeled in that house three years ago: new counter tops, new cabinets. So I need more help in locating the tape burial spot. When he showed you the pantry door and said a hole was in the floor, was he meaning at the bottom of the 'pantry' there was a board loose or that area of the floor in general?"

"Whatever Charley was showing me regarding the kitchen would be current. He shows me the bottom inside the pantry and down below. Remember it might be a floor below, but it is that general area. I will check out the Google address and get back to you."

On the 10th of that month, Kaye finally decided to join in the fray. Her journal chronicled the last few months of Charley's life: who he talked to, what he did, projects he was working on. She talked about the house building and how she was tired of having prisoners forced on her. She said she felt like she was running a prison farm at the end, but was it really? I called Spencer from my car on the way from one meeting to the next. She was on her way to a meeting as well. We talked briefly about the events leading to the MOT. I arrived at my meeting a few minutes early and, as I was organizing my briefcase, she was getting her car washed. This is what I love about what we do.

As the water began to blast her windshield, she apologized for the noise. A large school bus pulled up next to me, and I apologized for its noise. Two seconds later, the cacophony quieted. In the midst I began to speak about my gratitude for Charley's help and that certain agencies now seemed to be stepping to the plate to help in re-opening this case. In my soliloquy I marveled at how Charley has been able to help alter the course of his history, change the timbre of his legacy from one of suicide and marital discord to one who was trying to do the right thing by helping me follow the bread crumbs to solve his murder and find Jessica and Rox. As we were comparing notes, Kaye broke in.

Go to pages 19, 26, and 42: there is information for you there.

That part of the journal dealt with the prison. Kaye began sharing information with Spencer about an energy known as Carlos, a prison worker.

They show he is a tall, thin young man there at the construction site where Charley built his houses. He is between nineteen and twenty-three. Only been in prison a few years; the kind who hurts animals, then moves on to humans. Convicted of possible assault against his mother. He is very discreet, watching, always watching. Soft spoken and smart. There is money... money in his hands. He is part of those who watch and inform.

So a prison farm it may have looked like, but a network of spies is what it was: prisoners who got paid to watch Charley's every move, paid to keep tabs on what he did, where he went, who he talked to when he was not working or with Gerri. It was all staged. Everything began to fall into place. In the beginning it all seemed so disconnected: Charley having an affair, Baldwin working for Parker, prisoners being forced on them as wanna-be carpenters, the big come-on by G since April (two weeks after Jessica allegedly tried to commit suicide). Everyone it seemed was up to the eyeballs in coffee, booze, pornography, and blood. Good Christian men pounding their chests and speaking about honor and the sanctity of brotherhood all rotting from the inside out with evil and lust. Lust for money, lust for power, lust for the sake of lust. Disgusted, I worked on my psychology and criminology papers the rest of that month and tried to keep myself distracted from our impending bankruptcy.

One night while looking through the archived bills from Judge Eller (Kaye's attorney), I found an entry for the billing of depositions. The name beside the entry was for a Mrs. Elizabeth Middleburgh. Shocked, I read the name again. Could this be my Elizabeth, the Elizabeth with the broken chandelier and the palm tree plate? The Elizabeth who was interrogated by the three officers who went to her house and told her that her husband would be in trouble if he didn't give it up? The "it" had been the tape that the MOT had made! My heart began to race. I was having another "Holy shit" moment.

That night, released from academic strongholds, I dove back into fulltime investigation. I read and read every billing entry by Eller and noted that the FBI agent's name had been omitted from the page. I found that a curiosity and pulled out another bin to dig for my Crime Lab Report. There at the bottom I found the agent's signature and wondered if he could be noted here on the Death Certificate, why had Eller purposely left his name off the other? Somehow, my Elizabeth was connected to the tape and the three law enforcement individuals who were searching for it. Had Eller known? Was this part of the deposition of the FBI agent or were they two separate issues?

What is it they say? No rest for the weary or no rest for the wicked?

News about the existence of the tape the MOT had made as insurance had bolstered my spirits for a time, until the rescinding information that Grim had destroyed it came through. Numbed by the epiphany, I floundered in my hope until I realized that Spencer had said "Damon destroyed the tape." When I added that to the fact that Jules had said her brother recalled the night his father had borrowed his recorder to make copies of something… my joy returned.

Spencer's exact words were "the tape," and that meant only one thing to me literally. She never said "the tapes" were destroyed; she had said "tape," as in singular. It was then that hope sprang from the decay of my dreams. I knew that Charley, regardless of how ignorant he might have been about what it contained or who might have been implicated by it, he would have never made just one copy. Not my Charley. He would have made at least three if not four or five. The night before Thanksgiving with visions of pornography tapes dancing in my head, I drank a cup of coffee and toasted my darling boy in the 8 x 10 as I shoved a fistful of stuffing up the ass of a twenty-four pound turkey I had nicknamed Grim.

When I woke the following morning, before lighting a fire or putting on my classical music to bake by, I recorded my dream in a blog:

Last night I had a dream. But it was like one of those dreams where you feel you are awake as you are having it. In my dream I was writing the Prologue to the book and it began something like this...

Slivers of warm breath escaped from her mouth and hung in the cold air between us. Her eyes, gray like her father's, fixed on the spot just to the right of my foot. The next sixty seconds were going to be crucial. What if it wasn't there? The latex gloves rubbed and made odd sounds as I pulled them across my skin. I wasn't crazy about the way they felt, but I had been warned that in order to participate I must follow standard procedure. I waited patiently as others complied, then punched Spencer's number into my cell. Once the line had been secured, I nodded to the agents beside me. They initiated both the film and photo sequence, recording the first grid. I spoke softly to the psychic/medium detective on the other end. She implied I needed to reposition the small hand trowel closer to the left side of the opening, grid #2, and begin my excavation there.

The agent took my lead, and with a glorified paint brush began to sweep small mounds of sandy surface dirt to the side. A few clicks of the camera and a constant hum from the video cam kept vigil in the background. I placed the trowel to the earth and moved about an inch of surface fodder away from the grid line. Another round of photos ensued. The videographer motioned that I back away a few inches to allow greater access for the camera. I did. I didn't care what they asked me to do. I would have painted myself like one of their dimestore hookers and danced naked as bait for Grim in the middle of the town square if that's what it took to be there when they pulled it out. Nobody was going to keep me from being present after all I had been through to get there — no one. I held the trowel up while the agent to my left used the long lashes of the brush again to clear for the next entry. As he did, a section of synthetic tines ran interference with what appeared to be the rusted edge of a can. This was it. It had to be. Charley had promised and had delivered so often I could not conceive of failure.

Hands shaking, I gave the trowel over to the agent in charge. He took the tip of the trowel and tried to break the clay around an extruding piece of metal. Heart pounding, I realized this was our moment of truth. It had taken 78 weeks of intensive research for me to get this far, but for Charley and his family forty-four years. Together, however, it had taken us a lifetime. I gave Spencer the description of the object; she confirmed and I motioned for the activity to continue. The agent made several gentle stabbing motions at the area surrounding the lip of the can. Fragments of clay shifted and fell away. Another round of clicking broke the silence. I chanced to look up at Jules for just a second. Her breath ragged, she smiled weakly and then returned her gaze to the earth below us. Larger chunks removed, the brush returned. Long, slow strokes like elephant lashes slowly began to erode the years, and another few inches of the canister was revealed. What color had not been compromised by dirt and rust shown blue under the camera lights. I recognized it immediately. A small, inappropriate laugh squeaked from my throat. "I'll be damned," I said. No one seemed to catch my drift but Charley. He knew. He had always known. Two more strokes with the trowel brought the moniker into view and confirmed my guess: it was a nostalgically painted coffee can. I crossed my fingers and said a silent prayer that their slogan was not in vain. The brush and the trowel worked in tandem for another seven minutes and then with somber voice, the agent announced the can appeared to be intact and that it clearly showed signs of the possible remains of something inside. It was there. Now the question was what condition was it in?

November had been a heady month thus far. While its locomotion had steamrolled its way through my bravado, the holiday slowed the train of information to a crawl. I was allowed to take a deep breath and celebrate with family and friends. Grateful for the epiphany of the night, I moved throughout the day with lighter heart and a hope that balance would soon be restored to my personal life. Surrounded by my husband and my children and their respective significant others, I ate and drank the last of my week's pay until it was too late to do anything but stare at the newly erected Christmas tree and enjoy the flames of an artificial fire.

CHAPTER THIRTY-FIVE

In between my anguish over budget cuts at work and the encroaching sea of cardboard boxes that began to line the walls of my townhouse, I did my best to chronicle recent information. Granting that it was the holiday season, I contacted Spencer only when my back was up against a wall. As fate would have it, my back hit that wall about the 7th of December and stayed there right up through the New Year's Day. I made a call to Spencer.

"Anybody talking out there? Feels like I'm losing the thread."

"I am sitting in my car waiting to pick up my kids. Got a pen? Ok... record this. They show me Jessica is tied to the attorney. By the way, did you find out anything about the insurance guy from State Farm, Sorenson?"

"Still working on that, but I did find another red-colored card in Charley's wallet from another State Farm agent. His name was Robert W. Langdon. I'm trying to find out if he is still alive, but Clint hasn't called me back yet so I..."

"Hold on... what's this?"

"What's what?"

"They are showing me Jessica being treated for abdominal pain. Wait... she may have been pregnant."

"Jessica possibly pregnant?" My head began to reel. "Wait...you said they showed her trying to slit her wrists?"

"Yes...and with abdominal pain, remember?" she added.

"That's right. So are we talking about a pregnancy... or a miscarriage?" I asked, but Spencer couldn't say.

"They show me Route 44. Not certain what this has to do with it."

"That agent was listed in Moultrie on Route 44."

"They say Jessica may have confided in Charley and that the date of December 21st is significant. They keep mentioning the name Maxwell and...and..."

"And what?"

"Sorry...that's all for now."

Her response amazed me. "That's all for now?" I muttered under my breath.

If Spencer's impressions had been right, there was a strong chance Jessica had been pregnant and that potential pregnancy could have been the reason behind her suicide attempt. Even more, if it was somebody who rejected her, it could have been the incentive for someone to do her harm. What had the other clue been? *Jessica tied to attorney.* Immediately my suspicions went to the attorney Gavin Eller. Shortly thereafter, I was forced to cross him off my list. Charley said that Eller had not known about his murder beforehand, and I felt certain whoever had gotten Jessica pregnant would have eventually been involved in her murder and the others too. So what other attorney had been involved with her? Discouraged for the moment, I concentrated on other information.

Since Charley had been murdered in October, I made the assumption that the December 21st date Spencer had mentioned was significant for the upcoming holiday. The other information had been about Route 44. Other than the second State Farm agent's address, I had no idea why it was important, so I looked it up. Route 44 was relatively local to Valdosta, and since the ethereal only point out dates and/or locations if a noteworthy event and/or other clue can be divined, I tried to pay greater attention. I pulled up Google Earth, plugged in the address, and found that County Route 44 ran off Highway 133, bisecting several smaller roads before it ended at Burton Road. Since it is also known as McAllister Road, I tried to find a segue to Charley's case. Two roads in, I found said segue. Just past Griffin Road, the next offshoot to the south was County Route 43, a/k/a Trussman Road.

Immediately I recalled the name of an ATF agent listed on the documents from Beau Colbert: a Mr. Hubert Trussman. Agent Trussman had been there the night Charley was killed. Understanding the shorthand of the dead, I realized something must have happened between Jessica and the man who bore that road's name. If memory served me well, there had been another clue from Spencer earlier about a note that was passed from Damon Cummings to Hubert Trussman. It simply read *"Sorenson."*

Knowing Trussman had a reputation for violence and alcohol, I worried. Was this the man attached to the clue below?

The man who drove Jessica to the "love shack" drove a little red sports car. He delivered her like pizza. A call would come in... or a note and he would light out to pick up the entertainment for the afternoon or evening. He drives to a place out in the country and then drops them at the end of a long sandy drive.

Curious, I moved to the only other name mentioned: Maxwell. Trussman's name had been familiar and the connection immediate, but this new name never hit my radar. Was this someone I had somehow missed in all my previous research?

For days I obsessed about finding who this person named Maxwell was. I tore into the plastic bins with a vengeance and searched every document I could find, but no Maxwell, not as a first name or a last. I even sent emails to the Lowndes County Historical Society asking for copies of every page of the 1966 phone book that either listed names beginning with the letter M or the yellow pages who listed attorneys, thinking the bundled information meant my Maxwell was an attorney's name or firm. It wasn't until I wrote a blog several days later about other unprocessed clues that I finally understood what Charley had been telling me by using the name Maxwell.

The blog:

My disappointment spreads. While there were indeed many shifting of directions on the 17th, they all came through the umbrella of my job. Dramatic shifts being thrust upon me in my programming, unorthodox and unplanned directions, which I am still pondering and trying to digest with Herculean effort. But as for the case, I am now quite flummoxed.

Charley has never mentioned a date as significant and then not followed through with some sort of revelation. Now, as I said, if it had been a generic sensitivity to this date, then buddy he was right on the ball because I was ambushed by my superior. My job description is all over the map at this point and my frustrations at an all-time high. And so I wonder was the misinterpretation mine? Did Spencer misinterpret? Furthermore… do the dead get angry at us?

Maybe Charley did not like my re-enactment of days ago. Maybe he did not wish for me to speculate so close to home. Maybe my mentioning G and her dismissal of his affections brought about too much angst. Or maybe… maybe my obsessions over my job and finances of late have obfuscated the more intuitive fingerlings I usually receive when in a much calmer state. If so, then the error is mine, Charley, and I do so apologize for being less the vessel than needed. In spite of all the wonderful achievements and accolades received thus far, in spite of the release of my novel and the great networking system that has resulted, in spite of going back to school and working hard to get straight A's, in spite of the incredible if not phenomenal advances made in this case since January last — it has been a most difficult season. Hell, who am I kidding? It has been a changeling year, pure, plain, and simple. I am doing my best to crawl out from under its heady weight. My saving grace has been this case, this incorporeal relationship, this absolute immersion of soul and intellect and the opportunity of diversion it has afforded me. So now what, Charley? Now what?

You hold up four fingers... four fingers. You obsess about your wedding band and Grim's inability to remove it. I know about G. I know about B and D. I know about the shooter...H. I know who the MOT is and I understand the numbers 19, 1545, 1510. I have walked through your description of the murder a hundred times. I know where and when. I know how and who. I know about Jessica and Roxanne, the four in flannel, the evidence, the ballistics, the evidence, the MOT. Unless something has transpired within the respective agencies unbeknownst to me as of today, I continue to wait with bated breath. Is it something in the pictures, Charley? Did you see something I did not? Can you tell Spencer what it is? Was it something from my dream the other night, something slumber has hidden from my conscious world? Break the veil, Charley. Tear through and tell me what it is I am meant to look for now. Is it another girl? Another victim? Who is Maxwell, Charley? Who is he? I need you, Charley. I need you to help tie the ends together.

By the way, I keep one of those single coffee bags with me at all times as a talisman. It reminds me of you somehow. It's from Maxw...

Holy crap! I just answered my own question. Stream of conscious writing is amazing. I don't know why I didn't see it before. It was right in front of me and I totally missed its meaning. OMG.... Damn, boy! You're good! How could I have been so stupid? I love you, Charley... I freakin' love you! What a sense of humor, you rascal. Mrs. Olson would be so proud of you. I'm still laughing, and now I'm going to make myself a cup of coffee. Jesus, Charley, you crack me up!

No sooner had I hit the keyboard and punched out the cap for the letter *M* than the meaning hit me like a ton of bricks. Maxwell had never been the name of a person, place, or thing...per se. It had, however, meant a brand. Charley had hidden the final tape inside a Maxwell House coffee can and then buried that can under the pantry of a home whose address I had yet to divine. The dream was not a dream at all: in fact it was a vision. Charley was showing me where and how he hid the evidence. Always amazed at the process of intuition, I flashed back to my recent dream and the first day I blocked my cover page. Remember when I told you back in the beginning of this book how sometimes I just know things before I can possibly even consciously know things?

More than seven months before I began the blog, before I ever met Spencer, I had recorded several chapters under the working title *The Coffee Pot Conspiracy.* But even more than capturing the essence of this case in a title, I had written about how I pulled a Maxwell House Coffee can from a pantry in an old abandoned farm house and used it as my secret weapon:

"I know about the affair, Charley," I pressured and leaned into the counter. "How it all started with a couple of innocent cups of this..." I flashed my secret weapon: the can of Maxwell House coffee from the pantry. His eyes seemed to follow me as I began to pace the floor again. Finally, I had his attention. My anxiety started to build. Dead people knew things, saw things. They took dirty little secrets to the grave. Theirs, their families', their friends', sometimes even complete strangers'... possibly mine."

Can you imagine the impact of the moment when I opened that file on my laptop and realized that from the very start somehow Charley had been directing me to the MOT from even before I knew the MOT existed? Key words jumped off the page: *coffee can, Maxwell House, secret weapon, pantry.* My heart nearly beat out of my chest. The rest of the clues of course held allure, but no connection to anything I could lay label to at the moment. Even if they had, it was going to take more than a few minutes to unwind enough to pursue them.

CHAPTER THIRTY-SIX

As fate would have it, the epiphany of the Maxwell House Coffee can would not leave me alone. I plagued Jules and her brother about the layout of the house, but neither could recall a pantry. Even the priest who now owned the home had not mentioned a pantry in the restructuring. I should have been discouraged, but the more I thought about it the more I became convinced that Charley would not have left it there anyway. He would never have placed Kaye and the children in such danger. It had to be another house, another pantry. While I pondered which home it could have been, other clues came through.

There is a receipt in Charley's wallet. Is something circled on it? Check… also, they keep showing me the date July 11th. They show me that Roxy and Jessica both served drinks to the men at the clubhouse. There will be a big shift in the case in four days. They do not say what… just a big shift.

I wrote as fast as I could. "Got it."

"Did you have a dream about Charley last night? He says it was a visit. Also, something about an agent Vasquez, someone who will be helpful. Do you know this person yet? Oh, and is Jules planning some type of memorial for Charley? Don't worry: Charley is with you."

I barely got a chance to respond before she had to take another call.

Later I checked the wallet and found the receipt.

Morris Pawn Shop

Chas Covington bal on accnt. 79.50

Saw 35.00

Head Guard 6.50

Zippo lighter 3.00

30 Carbine 35.00

Nothing, however, was circled on it. But it was dated October 6, 1966 — just three days before Charley was murdered. I knew the lighter was significant because it had to do with Gerri. There was a big to do over that in court and in Kaye's journal. Gerri had testified she gave Charley a lighter for his birthday back in September. But in Kaye's journal she wrote Charley had told her that wasn't true. Either way, the lighter must have been extremely important because later in Kaye's journal it came up again when she had been questioned about it by Bob Callenwald, Charley's regional superior.

Why would Mr. Callenwald have demanded that Kaye hand over the bag of items Charley purchased at the pawn shop three days before his death, telling her that one of the things had belonged to him?

"I cannot say."

Left without segue, I turned to the other clue about Maxwell. Bound and determined to close in on the whereabouts of the coffee can and the final missing tape, I grilled Spencer for more. Spencer cautioned that finding the gun or nailing down the location of the missing tape might not become what would most help bring the case to fruition. Inside I knew she was right, but I was desperate for something to offer the feds. I also knew that neither could happen without the proper legal procedure, which I could not effect without other hard evidence to prompt. Wanting to add more eggs to my basket, I went back to my notebook.

"What about the person who has the huge bonfire in their backyard in the middle of summer? Was this in July? As in July 11th? The day Jessica is murdered? Was this in Grim's back yard? Trussman's back yard? Hubert Trussman was an ATF agent who

helped investigate Charley's murder that night. He drove in from Moultrie with Bill Hardy. Kaye talks about him in her journal too...get anything?"

"I get 41. Was he 41 at the time of Charley's murder? I get a lot positive energy around him, like he was highly decorated with awards and what not. Again they are talking about Trussman putting a folded piece of paper in his pocket. Feels like Grim handed it to him, but he is quick to fold it and put it in his pocket. It has the name Sorenson written on it."

Again I wondered, was this confirmation on Jessica's last name? Or was it about the governor who shared the same last name?

"Charley is holding up four fingers."

"Is this for the Trussman being the fourth in flannel or to tell me 'in four days...the case will shift,' blah, blah, blah?"

"I cannot say...sorry."

I was becoming desperate. "What about this? Rumor had it that another agent from Atlanta had a thing for a lady in Moultrie real bad, a cosmetologist/ beauty operator. They used to have meetings there in Moultrie. Men from all over would come there: Columbus, Albany, Atlanta, and Waycross. They said Sal had an apartment out there somewhere in Moultrie and they would drink and party. They said Agent Rogers, Sal, and a Mr. Haggard got in a bit of hot water. Rumor had it Haggard was an undercover agent who stayed with Sal occasionally when working a bust. They said Haggard started sleeping with a woman named Maria Autry. Later, they moved in together. Folks said the Moultrie gang used to party all the time. Rumor also had it, Ropers and Haggelslip screwed up a huge liquor deal just a month before Charley's murder because of that."

"What do you mean?"

"You see, back then they could get government money advanced to them to fake a buy for moonshine, like a sting. Most times it was just a couple of hundred bucks, but sometimes they could receive up to a thousand in cash if the bust was worth it. A retired agent told me that Labor Day weekend of 1966, they got a call on a huge deal. Sal picked up the money to pull it off and then met with the 'go-between guy' to set up the details; where they would meet, what time it would go down, who would be there, etc… Everything was set. They would buy the hooch, take the seller down and make a big bust and score major points with the ATTD and maybe get a huge promotion. While they were waiting at a hotel for the appointed hour, Sal and his comrade Haggard began to play cards and drink. The later it got, the more they drank. By the time the bust was supposed to go down they were so drunk that they just gave the 'go between guy' the bag of money. No deal ever got made. Nobody was arrested… but the money was gone! They were so inebriated, the snitch had to drive both agents back to Sal's apartment and put them to bed. It was a total screw up."

"Are you kidding?"

"That's what I heard. That's why Kaye was so convinced Sal was in on Charley's murder. Folks said Sal had a gambling problem on top of his drinking problem and the screw up with ATTD that day didn't help any. Kaye thought he used the money to cover his debts and that the story was a cover. She wrote in her journal that she thought Sal was getting back at Charley for writing him up."

"It sounds a little over the top if it was just over a couple of hundred bucks. But if we were talking really big money, then maybe a plausible motive to get Charley out of the picture…but that's not what they present."

"Ok… so what does Charley say about this? Kaye wrote that Sal's girlfriend moved out of town two years before Charley was murdered. Two weeks after Charley was murdered, she showed up on Kaye's doorstep and told Kaye that Charley had called her a few weeks before his murder and asked if he could bring G to Albany with him. She said he [Charley] begged her to let them stay

there a day or two as Valdosta had gotten too hot for them to be seen together."

Without hesitation Spencer retorted, "Not buying it. Charley says that's not true."

"Ok...how about this. Kaye's journal said they told her Mrs. Mavry came to the house the night Charley was murdered. They claimed that Mrs. Mavry brought her husband. But Kaye writes she never saw the wife, only the husband. And how odd that he would have come with the ATTD agents anyway, because Kaye states there was no close bond or association to warrant either the wife or the husband being there. She added that Mr. Mavry was the Trainmaster for Southern Railroad, the same RR that runs NW out of Valdosta. Could this be the other person who was involved with the moonshine on the train? The man you saw before who was incredibly nervous, wringing his hands?"

Spencer responded:

"You are on to something here. My heart is racing like someone's adrenaline is racing. Stay on this."

"Ok," I blundered and reached for my notebook. "What about these names?"

"Mr. Dowser, Tag Agent from Valdosta?"

"Sly and cunning, but not connected."

"Mr. Thornton, Atlanta?"

"Businessman, straight laced."

Just for fun I threw Callenwald's name back out there. "Bob Callenwald?"

"Possible connection to moonshine."

Next I tossed Charley's immediate supervisor out there. "Bill Hardy?"

Again she came back with, "Possible connection to moonshine."

"What about Agent Rogers, in charge of undercover work?"

"Nothing...sorry."

I thought about a few other names both from the journal and from interviews that had been bandied about and presented them as well.

"Who is Albert Moorefield? He had a dance band, told dirty jokes, and was a parole officer in Moultrie."

She came back with, "They present dirty, into illegal numbers rackets, booze..."

"Was he involved in illegal moonshine on the trains running NW out of Valdosta, or peripherally with Charley's murder?"

"They show me, not involved with Charley's murder, but possibly involved with the moonshine. Also became a sex offender."

"They show me the numbers 321 or 342, numbers for a train conductor or route. This is a clue to help you narrow down something."

Convinced there was more information to mine, I redirected the conversation back to the Trainmaster Mavry. "He was involved, wasn't he? He had to be! He must have been sent there as a precaution, an extra pair of eyes for Grim? Protecting Grim and Winston and the railroad moonshine deal? Was Callenwald involved in the moonshine train deal too? You know he never told Kaye what was in the pawn shop bag that supposedly belonged to him, but I bet it was the lighter. And I'll bet too that it wasn't his in the first place. They wanted it to help cement the affair."

Spencer's breathing came in short spurts. "From Kaye ...go to page 32 of the diary. The corn husked. I have no idea what this is about. Something like the man that husks the corn knows it all."

Again, the man who was the farmer seemed to grab the spotlight. As days went by, I began to doubt as much as I knew. On the 21st of December, Charley had promised a clue or a shift. Seeing as I had not been able to figure out what the 17th of December was, my confidence was at an all-time low. Confused and needing approval, I sent out a message, uncertain if holiday festivities would preclude its receipt:

Today is the 21st. Charley said it was a significant day... I sent you a huge thing in the last email, but just realized something. The governor of Georgia in 1966 was Chandler Sorenson. You said there was a tie between Grim and the governor at the time of Charley's death. Was the victim Jessica Sorenson a relation to him? Is that what Charley wanted me to figure out?

Spencer responded:

"Page 32 has yet the biggest clue. Very direct message from my spirit guide as I ask, 'How can I help TA?'"

Naturally I flew to Kaye's journal. I quickly counted out to page 32 and then counted again as a page was loose and I was uncertain if that would be counted as one of the numbered pages. When I got there, I devoured every word in hopes of securing the confirmation implied by Spencer's spirit guides. I cannot tell you how often the name Bob Waverleigh was written upon that page. I will paraphrase part of the storyline of the page and then enclose a brief excerpt. Bob Waverleigh was a farmer too. Here is the excerpt from Kaye Covington's 1966 journal, page 32:

I told them about the man that called that Sunday evening and his telling me his name was Bob Waverleigh. I started thinking that he [Charley] had been framed as it seemed odd that a Bob Waverleigh called that night and one of the men who found Charley was also named Waverleigh. Whoever I talked to said they

*could not locate any man named Bob Waverleigh, and then I was
told that Sal [Charley's partner] said a Bob Waverleigh did not
call him, but Sal has lied on this thing so many times.*

And in truth they could have set Kaye up. There was no way she
could have confirmed a Robert or Bob Waverleigh had existed if
she had gone by the listings in the Valdosta phone books. Why?
Because Waverleigh was from just across the state line in Florida.
Kaye would not have known to get a Florida phone book for
Cherryville Lake. I deferred to Charley, but hedged my bets that
his partner Sal Wheaton knew more about the farmer from Florida
than he was saying and was trying to keep his name out of things. I
thought it odd how they never mentioned Sal being at the crime
scene that night. His name is only mentioned in the journal as Kaye
described him and again with Claude Kirby at his side delivering
the news to her that night that Charley was dead.

I chewed on that thought for a while, but kept coming back to the
lie about the farmer from Florida. How could Sal have sanely
suggested no such Waverleigh existed when the entire Covington
Case file was based on witness testimony and he and his son had
already been accounted for? It made no sense.

I had already talked to Stevie Waverleigh, Bob's son, once before.
Odds were his original statements had been manipulated to reflect
the same information as everyone else's. After all, the young
Waverleigh had been pretty forthcoming about the fact that he
never saw one photo taken in his presence. He also stated that the
rain was horrible that night while he, his friend Martin Buckley,
and Stevie's father Bob Waverleigh were there with Deputy Sheriff
Beau Colbert. And again, he'd had no reservations in telling me he
heard the dispatcher's conversation that night about Deputy Colbert
being in the bathtub when they called him in. All in all, I think
Stevie had told me what he could and turned a blind eye to his
father's odd behavior after.

Deep inside I felt his father knew more than he had let on. His
name had appeared too many times in Kaye's journal and
Spencer's visions to warrant the moniker of coincidence. Like a

shark smelling blood in the water, I continued to circle his name. Maybe that was why his wife refused to let me talk to him on the phone. She was very polite, but just kept repeating the same thing over and over: "He's a good Christian man, a good Christian man. He doesn't know anything. He's just a farmer, that's all. Just a farmer. You can't talk to him. You need to talk to our son. He's the one that was there that night. Robert can't talk to you about this, but maybe my son will. I just don't know…I just don't know."

Common sense and academics unmistakably obligated me to get more evidence before I could risk proclaiming anything publicly. Still, it didn't look promising for this "good Christian farmer" to have been innocent of everything. At the very least, he was culpable. At the very best, he was convictable. That was where I was headed.

According to information, Bob Waverleigh knew Gerri Baldwin. Rumor suggested Bob Waverleigh had been involved with the Woodsmen of the World Insurance Company and its local lodge. A Mr. Bob Waverleigh had also called Charley's house several times, including the day of Charley's murder. Since the boy Stevie Waverleigh was a minor, he was presumably present when he and his son's friend were interviewed on the 18th by Colbert. As the statements clearly read, they were taken at the address of his home in Cherryville Lake, Florida. Here you had officially recognized witnesses and yet Kaye was told no such man existed. They had presented in another session that Bob Waverleigh was the key to the triangle between him, Gerri, and Charley. They had mentioned the cheese cutter clue, and its use was most likely why Kaye was never allowed to see her husband's body; in particular his lacerated arms.

As I put the rest of the clues together, a warped roadmap of what I thought happened that night began to take shape. Just before Christmas, I decided to take all the information to date and formulate a theory about what I thought had happened. Eager to get Spencer's reaction, I fired it off in an email, hoping to smooth out the wrinkles of my suspicions and more importantly try to prompt further information and/or confirmation.

Late December 2010:

With the information I have to date…I think I know how it all went down now. I propose the following:

The then Governor, Chandler Sorenson, was known to travel between ATL and Valdosta regularly, partied with Finch and several other folks during the spring and summer of 1966 at the American Legion Club and/or the Eagles Club. Jessica and Roxanne were most likely a part of the entertainment package afforded them afterwards. Though Marjorie suggests Roxanne may have been prettier, the Governor went for Jessica in a big way. The Speaker sidles up with Roxanne. The Governor and Jessica slept together at the designated "Love Shack" every time he came into town. True, both girls sleep with several other men, but the fact remains. She and the high-ranking official had had sexual relations and when she ends up pregnant, she has to let him know. His counterpart steps in and puts her off. She becomes distraught, gets scared, and slits her wrists (March of '66), and ends up in the hospital. They treat her, keep her overnight, and then send her home. Uncertain what to do, she either tells her father (unknown at this time) who tells Charley, or she tells Charley directly about the porn ring and her troubles and asks his advice. Charley tells her to lie low, starts looking into the porn thing and the association between Valdosta and high-ranking state officials. (This may have been the "other work" Charley was working on that Kaye alluded to in her journal.)

In the meantime, the Governor panics and has the Speaker call Finch to see if she can be bought off. Finch tells the Speaker/Governor not to waste money on a two-dollar whore; he will have it taken care of. The Speaker then enlists Grim to do the dirty work. Jessica is handled by Grim through the four in flannel. Meanwhile, agent Trussman (in Moultrie) is part of the railway moonshine deal; he along with agent Callenwald out of Atlanta, who is also Charley's Supervisor, are involved in the railway deal.

Jessica is taken out of the picture on July 11th. Roxanne becomes worried that something has happened to her because she knows about the pregnancy and who Jessica thought the father was. She also knows that Jessica told Charley. She keeps quiet about things until the night she is in bed with one of the four in flannel and foolishly asks what happened. When they press her for information as to how much she knows, she refuses to say anything more. They beat her and demand to know who else knows, and she finally says that Jessica told someone in law enforcement. They begin to strangle her to get his name out of her. When she confirms it as Charley, they continue to beat and strangle her to find out if there is anyone else. But she dies somewhere in the later part of September or beginning of October. They set everything in motion from that point forward.

They have been trying to find out how much Charley knows since the early summer. Between G and Jade, they have his construction sites covered and his home monitored. When Charley gets a little too close and things get a little scary, they get a snitch (Henders) to tell Charley about a moonshine deal that involves the railroad on Sunday nights at about 9:30 as bait. They wait for him that Sunday night, October 2, three days after Roxanne is murdered. But he doesn't make it because he is out of town at his mother's. When he doesn't show, they hatch another foolproof plan, but this time they have to involve more people. By now, everyone is getting a bit panicky. The Governor is really nervous as the presidential primaries are only a month away, so he calls Finch to get it taken care of immediately. Finch gets with Grim; they get Callenwald to fake a potential moonshine bust for that next weekend on Sunday, October 9.

Charley's week Monday through Friday is fairly normal. He stays about the immediate area, works on the houses. Thursday he goes to the pawn shop and picks up a few items, one being the lighter. On Friday he goes to Moultrie to qualify. Things go well. He stays a while and talks shop with several agents. One is Edgar Patterson. He finishes up and then goes home. Once there, he gets a call from his boss Callenwald saying Atlanta called, telling him that they are tracking a truck with raw materials across the state and that he and Sal (C's partner) must be on standby because all other state and local agents are already sitting on stills. So he instructs Charley that he cannot leave his house without getting permission and telling them where he is going. Charley is told he must check in every two hours. In this manner they can track his every move.

He stays home Friday night after getting home from Moultrie where they have had qualifying trials all day. During the daytime he is with Bill Hardy, Hubert Trussman, and several other ATF agents, all so they can keep tabs on him. Saturday he spends at home doing yard work and checking in. Again, they are watching his every move. Sunday they watch the house. They watch his and Kaye's every move to set up the alibi/deal with G to be used later in her testimony. They know every time Kaye leaves the house. They have her followed and recorded everything she does outside the home: where she goes, what she does, who she talks to, which roads she takes on her errands, and what times she comes and goes from their home. Even when she goes to get milk to finish making her chocolate cake, mailing a bill, and also when she goes to Bobbie Lee Fitzpatrick's house later that afternoon to ask her about G. Every single move, every phone call made between G and Charley or anyone and Charley that day is noted.

The others, including our farmer/cheese cutter Bob Waverleigh, call several times to check on Charley. Even the snitch (Wiley Henders) calls his house a few times that day to remind him of the moonshine deal on Sunday night. Kaye and Charley spend the day arguing about the alleged affair. Then after dinner Charley suddenly gets a call from Callenwald, telling him that the truck is parked in Athens and that they can go out for a while but to keep checking in. Charley is tired of fighting and wants to get out for a bit, so he decides he might go check out the snitch's info. He reads his daughter a story, tells her he is moving out. Jules cries and Kaye does her best to smooth things over. She wants to question Charley, but this is when he gets another call about the "moonshine van" and decides to head out of town to check it out and/or see G. Kaye offers him coffee, but he cannot wait or he will miss the moonshine deal going down. That's when this whole thing goes wrong. They want the tape. He refuses. They murder him, and the cover up begins with inside help from the Governor's office. The team pushes documents through so the feds won't get their nose involved. Six days later, they find the MOT hiding in a hotel and beat the shit out of him for the other tape. They demand to know if there are more copies out there. He dies from a heart attack as they beat him, and he is left for dead. It is days before he is found in his room by a maid.

The Governor has everyone on standby. He has his buddy the Speaker (Damon's family attorney) handle things. No information goes any further than Atlanta and the lawyer. Gavin is being paid to keep Kaye in line. But she won't comply and so they start playing rough here and there. That's why Gavin tells her he will get her the money, but to let it go after that. Kaye can never get anybody to help out of Atlanta. The Governor, the Speaker of the House, and Finch own them all. The reason why Callenwald is skittish about what was in Charley's pawn shop bag is because Charley got hold of the lighter. I propose the lighter was either found at one of the murder sites or in Jessica's apartment. Or maybe Jessica pawned it for money and Roxanne told Charley to go get it out of hock to prove Sorenson was with her at some point. It possibly belongs to the Governor or someone else who cannot afford the scandal. It's engraved with his name or some telltale sign that will point to him, and Callenwald has to retrieve it quickly to keep suspicions away or keep it from becoming potential evidence.

Every one of the ATF agents involved, along with GBI, State Patrol, Sheriff's Department, and the VPD are up to their eyeballs in this thing. Pull one string and it all unravels to show them all complicit with drug running, moonshine, illegal gambling, homicide, and pornography!

So.... what do you think? Do I join the witness protection program yet?

Spencer responded, but the response only brought more questions, not confirmations.

I am shown Stein/Steinbaugh. Can't say if this is Jessica's last name or if this is tied to someone else. Again I am shown the man that dropped Jessica off to see the man she was sleeping with drove a red sporty type car. He was like a delivery boy if that makes sense. She had to walk down a long gravel road to get to the house. It was a borrowed house, a place to sleep together and not be seen. I see a street sign that says 21st intersecting with a "C" named street, possibly a county road. The delivery boy gives her a ride home afterward. Sorry, this is all they show for today.

Who knew they played reruns in heaven? With no new information, it was back to the dry erase board and Google Maps.

CHAPTER THIRTY-SEVEN

By the time I was ready to hang the calendar for the New Year, I was also ready to pull my hair out. Even though I thought I had figured out what had happened that night, something felt off in my calculations.

Jessica had had many partners, but who, other than the Governor or the Speaker from Atlanta, would make a late night trip to Valdosta? I already knew about actors like Jack Paladin and Omar Sharif, who occasionally flew in from California for high stakes poker at the Eagles Club. But this was something else. According to an impression from Spencer, a high-ranking official had made a special trip down that night because of Charley's murder. But why? We knew Jeb Finch had deep ties to Sorenson, who was a WW II pilot and Damon Cummings to Samuels. Hoping for more guidance, I said a prayer for confirmation and at the end of the month I received this from Spencer:

When I ask if you are on the right track, I get... continue on the path. A gavel (like a judge would use, but not to say it is a judge's gavel). In regard to the lighter...they described a silver lighter with an engraved design throughout.

While I was definitely on the right path about the lighter being significant, I still couldn't say for certain whose it was. As to the gavel clue, it only provided the necessary weight to tip the scales in the opposite direction of the state capital. Originally, I limited myself to the person of interest being a judge, but I had been wrong. It wasn't about a judge; it was about the gavel. Who else among the listed person of interest used a gavel? The only other high-ranking state official left in 1966 who would use a gavel that made sense was Jack T. Samuels, the Speaker of the House, who would use his gavel to bring a session to order. Strengthened by this realization, I continued to pursue his possible involvement. As far back as the first session of recorded interviews, his connection to one of the four in flannel was made evident. Damon Cummings had openly admitted Samuels was "his man in Atlanta" at the time, "his family attorney." When you coupled that with Damon's suspected involvement with all three peripheral murders, it became increasingly obvious that Samuels would have to have been the one there that night.

Think about it. The governor was a pilot, but could he have afforded the chance of discovery and scandal? Hmmm…but the Speaker? He was free to move about at will and had ties that went both up and down the line. He was the bridge between the murdered hooker Jessica and the governor of the state of Georgia and the young Trooper Cummings who was desperately trying to help cover up the hooker's death, the porn they were all involved in, and the reason for Charley's murder. It had to be him.

Who else could you ask for advice, political and/or legal favors, confess to and still feel perfectly safe? Survey says…BING-BING-BING your attorney! Especially if your attorney was the number two guy at the state capitol. Why? Attorney/client privilege, my dears — that's why. Damon could spill his guts about dead hookers and murdered ATF agents until he was as blue in the face as Charley was in the morgue that night, and it wouldn't have mattered. Samuels would have been bound by duty and forced by professional obligation to keep it private. The more I thought about it, the more it made perfect sense. And since Samuels was at the state capitol, paperwork could be pushed through or removed without anyone batting an eye. Even more, the pharmacist at the State Crime Lab could be coerced into signing off on death certificates, all without raising eyebrows. No matter what Damon did, asked, or could tell him, Samuels would have been bound by legal obligation to his client and loyalty to the governor, a governor who had just tossed his hat into the ring for the presidential race.

Although the matrix on this thing was bizarre, it became more believable once you threw all the clues together. Still, what if I was wrong? What if I was giving Damon too much credit for the manipulation and Sorenson and Samuels not enough? Could it have been shit rolling downhill, instead of up? Like Samuels trying to protect himself from associations with G and thereby Charley's murder? Or maybe even Samuels trying to keep free of taint from Sorenson's dalliance with Jessica, her suicide attempt, her pregnancy, and murder as his boss approached the November presidential primaries?

The more I thought about this new arrangement, the more the loose strings of the case began to pull together. For instance, what about the removal of the second page from the Crime Lab Report with the ballistics on it? Who else could float in between all those departments in Atlanta and pull the strings necessary to bury documents, hide the truth, and manipulate the cover up that followed?

Suddenly the images of the shaky hands in the great hall in front of the bronze P.O. Box 8099 slot with the documents inside took on greater meaning. Who would have held P.O. Box # 8099 in 1966? What postal office would have had numbers running as high as 8,000+? Whose sweaty palms took the documents from that mail slot? Were these the same hands that removed the second page from the original GBI Crime Lab Report and circulated the remaining single page to help further cement the effects of the conspiracy?

Suddenly it became all too clear. Samuels could handle the manipulations necessary at the state level, but who better than a young State Trooper outside the loop to help act as go-between and bark orders from on high about how to best clean up the mess locally? The Speaker would have legal prowess to help govern his counsel and political power behind him to push through any agenda. Who would tell the number two guy in the state to go to Hell? Cummings could fly under any radar, demand any favor, and commit any crime with backers like that. Cummings became Samuels' mouthpiece. Since the relationship between the two was already well established through his family, it was a no-brainer. Who would question it? Cummings could be kept in the loop, but also in the clear in case things went down badly. And he was. The family attorney/Speaker of the House could orchestrate things easily from his throne on high, including other law officials and/or agencies in Atlanta. Cummings was right: with that kind of protection, he became untouchable.

Can you even imagine the kind of power that would have funneled into Cummings' 26- year-old ego? Just think: you're a young rookie still wet behind the ears making pittance a year and calling the shots on the ground for the state capitol. That's the kind of egotistical high he would never come down from, and that's the ego that showed up that first interview at the Lowndes Historical Society. But at that time, his "man in Atlanta" was still alive. Now with him dead, the conspiracy theories surrounding this became endless. My brain was beginning to feel like soggy spaghetti.

Each day I tried to get a cleaner trajectory for my theory, but kept hitting a proverbial snag. What if I was wrong? What else had Charley said in his first regurgitation that I still needed to quantify?

It was between LT, G, and the younger law enforcement. But it all goes back to that woman… that woman… the black widow… porn… a triangle between LT, G, and the younger law enforcement.

What more was I missing? I returned to my notebooks and files. What else did I know about this LT energy? There was something about a medal, a lucky rabbit's foot, a wheel chair, and a scar on his left hand. All these clues would help, but since several other men I had suspected as the LT energy were now dead, I didn't see anything happening without some sort of legal intervention. With nowhere else to turn, I was dead in the water with no wind to ferry me ashore.

Frustrated, I sent Spencer a message. While I waited, I Googled my way around the net and discovered Samuels had become the Lieutenant Governor of Georgia shortly after Charley was murdered. So was this older, socio-economically higher person named by Charley in his first session that had an association/relationship with G the Speaker? According to the internet, the Speaker's sudden rise to Lieutenant Governor of the State of Georgia within less than three months of Charley's death meant I could now add one more mark in the pro column under his name.

Parsing semantics with the dead had never been easy, but lately it was beginning to give me a chronic migraine. What if Charley had really meant the Lieutenant Governor? What would I do then? I held my breath. It was insane to think such an iconic figure would have allowed himself to have been so tangled up in this mess, but murder makes for strange bedfellows. Major hush money would be required. Was that the possible connection to G, the Governor, and the loose diamonds clue?

I knew if I brought up such possibilities at my formal presentation to ATF, FBI, and GBI, my credibility would instantly fly out the window. Still I clung to my gut instincts that I was on the right track. Maybe the lighter was the key to more than I thought. Maybe the lighter belonged to one of them. I thumbed through Kaye's journal. Somebody was definitely threatened by its exposure, or Callenwald and Gerri wouldn't have wanted it back so badly. Trouble was, who could I ask? No matter how I attacked this thing, I was screwed.

That night as I pushed myself away from my laptop, the futility of what I was trying to accomplish slammed me in the gut. How would I ever be able to convince the ATF these people may have been involved without an actual confession? Defeated, I went to bathroom to take a bath to soak my weary bones and consider my limited options. Forty-five minutes later I re-entered the bedroom refreshed, but not resolved. Don was already in bed, so I plopped down beside him and asked how he felt about Montana.

Curious, he raised an eyebrow in concern. "Montana?"

"Yes... Montana. I'm thinking that's where they'll send us in the witness protection program if I'm right. Some nice little sheep farm out in the middle of nowhere. My name will be Betty Jean Schumacher and yours can be Chuck. We'll be a lovely middle-aged couple from Lincoln, Nebraska who decided suddenly to retire and explore the great Wild West and raise sheep."

He never batted an eye; he merely adjusted his fingers on the remote and asked, "What have you done now?"

"Nothing much…. just tried to accuse the Governor and the Speaker of the House from 1966 in a series of extra-marital affairs with prostitutes and then find them complicit in the cover up of their murders, not to mention Charley's and the MOT's. That's all."

"Oh… that's all?" he smirked and then changed the channel three more times before settling on a war film.

"Well, maybe not the Speaker of the House. Maybe he was only involved in the cover up. Still," and I ran the towel across my hair one more time, deep in thought, "don't you want to know why?" I asked and shook my hair free.

He wiped his glasses and calmly surrendered. "Ok… why?"

"Why?" I blathered. "Because everything points to their being involved. That's why. Think about it. Why would those two girls have to be killed? According to Marjorie nobody gave a shit about them. So why if nobody gave a shit did the four in flannel go so far out of their way to erase them? Especially Jessica; she was possibly pregnant, you know. Somebody else would have known about that, like the hospital where she tried to commit suicide. So why her? Why risk it? Why kill two hookers and then beat the snot out of a man in a hotel who is the only connection between the killers, the pornography, and the victims? Who does these things, unless they have something major to lose? Or something really major to hide? And I mean *really, really* major. Don't you agree?"

He clicked the remote another five times and landed on an infomercial while I gathered my hair into a bundle at the nape of my neck.

"So?" When he refused to take the bait, I continued. "And then, somebody pretty high up flew from Atlanta to Valdosta that night. Who gets their butt out of bed in the middle of the night to travel to a place like Valdosta?"

I looked at Charley's photo, remembering it was his home. "Sorry, no offense, pal... but what's the big attraction?" I continued to pontificate. Don didn't answer. He was busy watching some guy paint the underside of a rowboat with a can of spray rubber.

"I wouldn't fly to Valdosta in the middle of the night. Shit, I wouldn't fly to Valdosta in the daytime. So what's their reason, huh? Gotta be something big, really big. Folks don't go out of their way to protect other people's asses; they do it to protect their own," I proffered. Then another thought hit me: "Unless, of course, they were being paid to protect it and not protecting it left theirs even more vulnerable."

His eyes never budged; he just clicked the remote again and moved on. "Hmmm... I never thought about it from that angle."

I buffed my damp shoulders with the towel and extrapolated "Maybe that's where the extra money they show G couriering came from. Or maybe...the loose diamonds."

He clicked the remote one more time and sat up in bed. "Why can't you just bake pies and do laundry and like other wives? Montana...really? I hate snow."

"I love snow. Ok, then...no Montana. How do you feel about rain?" He frowned, so I mentally roamed. "How about Astoria, Oregon?"

"Why Astoria, Oregon?"

I couldn't believe that the answer wasn't totally obvious. "They filmed the Goonies there...duh!"

"The Goonies? What are you talking about? Why should I have to spend our golden years with the Goonies?" Frustrated, he hit the remote again and landed back on the rubber man who was now fixing holes in somebody's roof.

I wanted to explain that technically we would not be living with the Goonies since they were a fictitious bunch of characters, but it was a moot point. As to the other part of the question, I would have responded, but it was a damn fine question. Why couldn't I just leave sleeping dogs lie? Why couldn't I have just let Jules's family history alone and become the domestic goddess of his dreams? Why make death and paranormal activities more important than pastries and dirty laundry? He changed the channel two more times before I moved from the side of the bed.

"Good question...I'll get back to you!" I said as I pulled an oversized T-shirt over my head. Suddenly I noticed the loving faces of my parents in a photo on my nightstand and remembered if not for Charley, I might never have connected with them again. "You're why...you're the reason why."

"What was that?" he asked.

I wiped a small tear from my eye. "Never mind," I winced and shook my head again to get damp out of my hair.

He noted the change in my tone, looked at the corner of my nightstand, made the correlation and softened. "So when we move to live with the Goonies in…Astoria, are you going to remember to put your laundry in the dryer?" he chuckled.

I looked at the clock. "Shit! I forgot to put the clothes in the dryer again and I need a shirt for the morning," I screeched. "And to answer your question…no. I will most likely suck at laundry in Astoria just as badly as I do in Georgia, and you might as well get used to it."

"Do the Goonies do laundry then? Somebody's got to iron my shirts," he chuckled.

"No, they do not," I sneered back and wandered half naked down the hall to toss my work shirts in the dryer.

CHAPTER THIRTY-EIGHT

Calendar pages continued to peel away. Ankle deep into a new year, I felt like the case had slowed to a crawl. But as January 2011 began to mature, so did I. More comfortable with my divine purpose, I noted that the world became more comfortable too. Each morning my walks got longer and my list of worries got shorter. The winter chill that had bit at the inside of my nostrils and burned my lungs for the past month seemed warmer and less offensive. Things were getting better, and I was able to tolerate the silences from Charley with more grace. Reconnected with my higher self, I was happier than I had been in over a year. Occasional snows dusted the lamp posts outside my bedroom office, making it postcard perfect. Though I was sad to think of leaving that view behind, the lake house promised a new start and a better chance to heal.

In February, Jules notified me that she had read in *The Valdosta Review* one more of the geriatrics of that era had passed: Robert Coleman. Coleman had worked for the VPD before, during, and after the time of Charley's murder and owned the farm just kitty-cornered from the Wild Adventures Theme Park. Of course I was sad for his family, but again felt cheated that he had shared so little when I felt he had known so much. With another witness gone, I was down to spare change as far as peripheral sources of information went. It frustrated me. Aside from that, complications with moving and work kept me hopping, and so as much as I hated it, Charley continued to take a backseat to the rest of my life.

After a few weeks of silence, though, my heart began to ache. Where was he? Why had he not made an effort to make his presence known or sent me signs to follow? Concerned, I fired off an email to make certain I had not lost my connection to him.

ATF called earlier and will call back in a little bit to go over dates for my presentation. Does Charley have anything he wants to weigh in on date wise for this? I hate that he is AWOL and miss his guiding hand. I will do my best, but really want to do this with his blessing and input.

Spencer responded:

Charley is not AWOL. He is just allowing you to learn a lesson. Only you know what that is and perhaps you have not even figured it out yet. That being said, let's have a chat, he says. There is one person that is off. Three are correct. To find the fourth, the one that smokes the strange-smelling pipe/cigar, you have to look in the car. He winks and starts to walk away, so I ask him to wait. "How can we figure this out?" He replies, "You already have. Tell my daughter I saw her by the river. Tell TA that paper cut was a doozie. Trust yourself." Kaye and I are off to go horseback riding. Kaye is with him, smiling. He blows a kiss and is gone.

I looked down at my hands and laughed. "Nice try, Charley." At the time, I had not suffered a paper cut, but two days later I sliced my thumb on a packing box. I hated it when he did that. "Ok, paper cut handled…let's get down to some real work," I blathered and returned to the email.

"Charley is not AWOL. He is allowing you to learn a lesson," was the first thing I needed to deal with. Other than daily frustrations over academic deadlines, work, and home life, the recent disloyalty and abrupt and disrespectful manner of departure of my assistant still stuck in my craw. Truth was she had been wrong for the job from the start. She was an actor at heart, not built for administrative duties, and I should have realized that early on. Emotionally exhausted, I decided I would let the issue slide and move on.

"So what's next?" I moved my eyes down the email. "Ah, yes! *'Let's have a chat' he says."* Since when did you suddenly turn British, my good man? I chuckled. "What the devil, Charley? Shall I serve tea with this next clue or will three-hour-old coffee be sufficient? After all, it's Maxwell House and you know what I always say: Maxwell House Coffee; *'Good to the last confession!'*"

 I giggled at my cleverness and then moved the cursor further down the email to divine other information.

There is one person that is off. Three are correct. To find the fourth, the one that smokes the strange-smelling pipe/cigar, you have to look in the car.

Charley knew I was pressed for confirmation about the fourth in flannel. The fact that I couldn't definitively place Wilson the banker in that role and walk away without hesitation bothered me. Since George had never really blipped on their radar until I put him there with the moniker "the man who smokes the mint tobacco," I felt I needed more to justify my supposition.

"I need a better clue than this, Charley. Your *'Look in the car'* clue leaves me another hole to plug. Think...whose car?" Was Charley referring to my car? His car? Kaye's car? And if so, how do I get access to a 1966 Ford or a Buick that no longer exists? I knew the mint tobacco pipe/smoker moniker could be traced back to Wilson, but lots of men smoked pipes and cigars back then. Wilson was the president of the Southern Bank of Valdosta, a potentially perfect place to launder illegal gains. Combine that with the fact that his wife Lucinda had been the long-time secretary to Lowndes County Sheriff Jeb Finch, and the situation made the prospects of a cover up even easier. But was that enough for anything more than supposition?

By late February 2011, the townhouse was nothing but one big blur of tape and brown cardboard. The owners of the lake house had been great and given us keys early so I could get some painting done before the furniture arrived. For over a week I made the trip one hour each way down and back after work to get rooms painted. With the help of my husband and my two law enforcement buddies Lana and Don Rutledge, we started to move. By the time I had to return to work, most of the house was put together. As payoff for good behavior, I received a phone call from ATF offices in

Atlanta to schedule a target date for my presentation. Burdened with several meetings within my own government agency, I noted that several conflicts and schedules were switched numerous times before we settled on a final date.

As the appointment for my formal presentation approached, I tried to get as many ambiguous clues solidified as possible. Those I could not I left out of the report altogether. Even though Spencer and I both knew they would look with callous eye upon anything psychically garnered, there was no way I could not include her contributions. To date, both Spencer and I had been under the impression that the pantry location had been in the home that Charley had lived in until the night of his murder. But soon complications began to set in. Spencer was able to divine through another session with Charley that the final tape had been buried beneath one of the "grandmothers' houses." Naturally, since there were two of them, I called Spencer to narrow the choice.

"So hey, I hope Charley can do this one more thing to help me out before my meeting."

I heard Spencer shift in her seat. "Ok…let's try."

"Alright, here goes. Can he confirm that his mother's place in Millen was the house? Because I'm concerned that area may have been bulldozed and rebuilt since back then. You see, they had a fire. So if that's true, the tape may be lost to us. I will try to Google the address from an old letter and send it to you if that helps. Does he feel like it's still there in the dirt somewhere… or is this the wrong grandmother's house?"

Spencer's breathing could be heard over the phone. "Ok, so I asked and the response I got was… 'The one by fourth.' Do you understand?"

"Got it! It was his mamma's house, then. Her house was located near what was then referred to as the Four Points. Maybe it hasn't been destroyed. Maybe…."

"They do not say one way or the other," she added, and that was all.

Prayerful, I gathered steam with the remaining evidence and put together a fairly impressive 97-page (plus peripherals) presentation for the ATF, FBI, and GBI's collective review. Each night when finished with the theatre and my studies, I worked on the presentation, editing and re-editing to make certain I didn't end up sounding like an idiot. I knew the first time I mentioned a psychic detective, eyes would roll. I wasn't willing to let all the hard work Spencer and I had done become little more than reality TV fodder. I made certain that every plausible scenario suggested rang true with some sort of hardcore support for its supposition. After three weeks of constant grooming, all my binders were ready.

Sitting in a meeting about the county's new computer programming, I noticed my cell was buzzing. Proper meeting etiquette is to turn off all electronic devices, but those in the room were familiar with my family's medical idiosyncrasies, and so I am allowed to keep it on vibrate in case my middle child or husband might have a medical emergency. As my supervisor spoke, I eyeballed the dashboard. The number was not Piper's. In fact, most of the number was not even present. So when I saw the first three digits and nothing else followed by my caller ID registering the origin as ATF, I excused myself to take the call.

When I was safely in the hall and had closed the door, I answered.

"Miss Powell? This is Agent Garvey's secretary. I just wanted to confirm your 10:00 am appointment this morning. Are you still coming to the meeting?" I looked down at my watch, noting the date and the time. It was 10:17 am.

"Miss Powell? Are you there?"

CHAPTER THIRTY-NINE

My heart sank, and I rushed down the hall to my office and grabbed the calendar. There it was, circled in black ink. And right next to it were three more dates circled in black ink. How was this possible? I double checked my calendar the week before and swore the correct date was the one on Tuesday. I flipped back through my notes. As mentioned, there were two or three dates initially recorded, but because we had to accommodate both my and several agents' schedules, only one of the dates fit. With school and the move, I thought I had given myself enough room to meet everyone's deadlines. How could this have happened? Before I hung up, I closed my office door and apologized profusely. When I checked the calendar more closely, I noticed the small red checkmark near the date and died a thousand tiny deaths while she tried to help me chart a new course.

"I'm so sorry. I had so many dates circled before we settled…"

"Could you hold please while I see if Agent Garvey and the others can stay through lunch? Will that give you enough time to drive in?"

I had been waiting patiently for this day for over two years. Damn and double damn!   While I mentally chastised myself for screwing up the posting with another meeting from my own government job, she kept me on hold to see if there were any other options.

Her extra efforts made me feel even worse. The logistics were simply impossible. I worked an hour from home. We lived an hour from Atlanta. Even if I left then, it would be over two hours before I could reach them. While I berated myself, she assured me it was no problem and that we could re-schedule it in another month. Grateful for her kindness, I whimpered my apologies for the one hundredth time and climbed off the phone. How could I have gotten the two meetings so confused? Disappointed, I sent Spencer an email that afternoon, hoping for some kind of cosmic comfort.

Ok, so the dates got switched so many times, I had three different dates, including the first date written down for tomorrow, but it was scheduled for today! They offered to postpone it till the afternoon after lunch, but my files were at home, I was an hour away in shorts no less, and they were downtown and no way to get it all done in two hours, So I was not able to meet their immediate alternate schedule either. Now I have to wait till April or later to get in. Maybe there is a reason why, huh? Maybe I'm going to find something else that will help the cause better than what might have been helpful today.

Spencer responded:

Always a reason...

Weeks after the first fiasco, ATF called and gave me a new date in April. This time I circled the date in hot pink highlighter. Satisfied I had garnered a second chance with the ATF, I tried to broker my way into a second one with Charley.

I keep hoping Charley will lead me to the tape. I know he thinks I can figure it out from green paint and old pantry floors, but... it's just not that easy and I really want to do this thing right. Folks are dying down there, and it's important we get the information to the right people before they are all gone. Jules is getting edgy.

Spencer responded:

The conversation you had with Don last night was a step in the right direction. My right hand is hurting between the thumb and pointer finger. Did you hurt your hand? Mention of Georgetown and an attorney who currently lives/works there.

The conversation I'd had with my husband was merely an honest exchange of where we were and where I hoped we'd eventually end up. As for the comment on my hand hurting between the thumb and forefinger, it did. It was sore from writing all my school notes, gripping the steering wheel too hard on my rides home late at night, and unpacking boxes. The Georgetown attorney clue was a new one, and I had nothing to piggyback it to.

A day or two later, Spencer told me if I wished or needed to work with other psychics on any of my projects, including Charley's, she would understand and that I should feel free to do so. It was such a random statement that I laughed it off, unable to imagine this kind of chemistry between victim, psychic, and writer anywhere outside the three of us. Prompted by her invitation, though, I told her she was fee to work with any other intuitive writer and then added the postscript that of course, I was joking.

A week later, March 2011 came to an end and so too the successful rash of rehearsals of another production. With finals looming on the immediate horizon, I put the final polish on my lighting design for the show and then buckled down and hit the books. A few days before the show opened, cast and crew confirmed their desires to have the cast party at our lake house. Unable to say no, I agreed. Since it was so far away and the cast all female, I suggested a slumber party might be a better bet and set about to make arrangements. The idea was infectious and so was their laughter. Plans made, we ran the show the following night while I calculated the hours I would still need to grocery shop, finish painting the kitchen, and unpack extra linens for beds.

Laney, who was a member of the cast stayed after the dress rehearsal that night and asked for directions to the lake from the other side of town. During the course of conversation, we got to chatting about life and such. One thing led to another and the next thing she asked about my books. Immediately I broke into casual discussion about the Moore's Ford Bridge story and then sidestepped my way onto my favorite topic: Charley. When I mentioned working with a psychic, Laney's eyebrows dipped and her eyes went dark. I'd seen that look before on folks whose religious fervor felt threatened in the presence of someone who spoke with the dead. Fearful I had offended yet another Southern

Baptist in my circle of theatre friends, I eclipsed my conversation and simply gave her my card.

"Here. If you get bored some rainy night, check it out. If not, this card will make a great bookmark," I rallied and climbed the risers to the light booth to shut down the grid.

Impatient, she mounted the stairs behind me two at a time. "Did you say you work with a psychic detective?"

I stalled. So far I had been accused of being grossly sacrilegious. I had been called half witch, half Satan worshipper and was grossly uninterested in acquiring another moniker to add to the pile.

Worried I had not heard her the first time, she reiterated. "Seriously, so you work with a psychic?" I shuffled more equipment about the desktop till there was nothing left to shuffle and then sheepishly collected pencils trying to delay the onslaught.

"Yep... I do. And amazingly enough, I've yet to go up in smoke, so I'm thinking God doesn't have a problem with it yet. But you'll know the minute He does because my hair will burst into flames and I will turn into a pillar of salt." Convinced I had headed her off at the pass, I crossed the room and held the door open for her departure.

Suddenly she backed away from the door to allow me clearance. "Turn into salt! You're funny... but seriously. You work with a..." and she held her breath.

"Psychic," I offered, plugging the holes in our Swiss cheese conversation. "Yes ma'am, a real honest-to-God psychic."

"Uh-hmmm," she grunted.

I brushed her aside and turned the knob before setting my key. The lock clicked over and the silence remained awkward. "So, you good to go?" I invited.

"Oh my God... it's you."

"I beg your pardon?"

"You're the one we were supposed to tell. I had no idea at the time...I'm so sorry. I just never put it together."

Confused, I shoved her out the door and smiled. "Sorry. I have to set the alarm."

I would have stayed inside long enough to discourage her wait, but the alarm only allowed for thirty seconds after setting before it would scream "Intruder!" When I joined her on the outside, she hit me with another zinger.

"About the girl..." she hesitated. "There is a girl in your story, right? I mean... your murder case about Charley? There was a girl in it, right? A blonde girl...youngish...very pretty. Worked in the adult entertain..." she left off the rest of the word, waiting for me to either confirm or take the bait.

I balked and remained silent.

She took it as disclaimer. "I'm sorry. Maybe it wasn't for you. I just thought maybe she had something to do with your dead man, but..." and she hung her head and began to move towards the steps and into the night. "See you tomorrow night, then," and she offered a weak wave as she hit the top of the stairs.

I held my key rigid in the lock, paralyzed by her remarks. "What about the blonde girl?"

Recharged by the inquiry, she bolted back up the steps into the light. "There was something about a girl in the lake... but she didn't really drown, did she?" She tilted her head away from the direct lamplight and waited impatiently for my response.

I slipped the key out of the lock. Had I mentioned either Jessica or Roxanne to her in my diatribe? I couldn't remember, so I casually sloughed it off.

"What about her?"

"There was a girl then. Hah! It *was* you I was supposed to tell," she rallied. "I just knew it!"

"Yes, there was a girl…a young blonde. Her name was Roxanne. She was the first one I found out about, but she wasn't the first female victim. She was actually the second victim."

Laney's eye danced in the dim. "The second victim? You mean there was more than one girl killed?"

"Yes. Another young woman named Jessica was the first girl they murdered. Beat her face in with a shovel and then buried her under a pool." I wasn't trying to talk out of school; I just wanted her to know that for me this wasn't a game.

"God bless, that's horrible! How sad, how very sad," she muttered as the light left her eyes. "And your second girl? She didn't drown you know; my psychic said they killed her. She was a hooker. I mean, she said the girl worked in the adult entertainment film industry, right? Pornography and doing tricks?" she proffered delicately. When I didn't stop her, her eyes popped and she plowed on through.

"Oh my God! It's true, then?"

"What's true?" I stalled and held my gaze, not understanding exactly what she was building to.

She continued to pull information from her memory as we walked down the steps. "She told us in a session this last August or September. You remember…when I auditioned for that Readers Theatre show with you. But I didn't know at the time it was about you. She told me it was for somebody working on a murder and then somebody I knew with a theatre association, but I didn't realize she meant you until tonight when you told me about your Charley."

I smiled at the possessive term. "My Charley?"

"Yes, *your* Charley! She told us this person, you apparently, was in danger. But we didn't know who she meant at the time, so we couldn't tell anyone. I mean… we couldn't tell you that you were in some sort of danger because I didn't know it was about you till now. Jesus, this is so weird," and she took a huge breath as if more oxygen would bring more clarity.

"Did something happen to you last fall, somewhere around September?" she asked and ran over her own words trying to recapture something else that had been told them. "And there were other things too. I just can't remember everything. I'll have to ask my sister. She recorded the readings. So maybe I can get her to meet with you. Her name is Samantha."

"Samantha…right." It was getting difficult to keep up with her. "Who told you this again?"

"Our psychic."

"*Your* psychic told you *I* was in danger?"

"Well… yes. Not that I knew it was you back then. We just knew *somebody* who was working on a murder was in danger."

"*You* have a psychic?" I asked, curious. Suddenly Spencer's words came back to me. 'If you need to talk with another psychic about this case or any case...please...feel free. You may receive information from many sources; do not cut yourself off.'"

I looked at Laney. Straight-laced and proper, she was the last person I would ever have suspected of dipping in the hokey-pokey pool, which made this all the more intriguing.

"Wow," she snickered, amazed at the epiphany. "It's you... it has to be you. And to think I could have told you about this months ago, but I didn't know about your other work then. Ok, let me start from the beginning and then maybe it will make more sense for you."

I watched her pull out her keys, though they never got near enough to the car door to have quantified the effort. The air had chilled considerably since the sun went down, and my shirt was too thin to protect me, so I grabbed a jacket from inside my car as she spoke. Suspicious after the sudden loss of their father, she and her sister had contacted a psychic to ascertain if their father had died of foul play or natural causes. Satisfied it was from the latter, they kept the relationship between psychic and survivors going, for once contact had been made, they could not emotionally let him go. I understood their plight and continued to empathize. Her story picked up somewhere after she had auditioned for a Readers Theatre production of mine. During the autumn of 2010, her psychic began to receive information from one of my victims and without appropriate destination, she kept it to herself. In her second show with me, our acquaintance grew into a friendship and now she could barely contain herself.

By the time we ended our conversation, the hour was too obscene to broach a call, so I sent a text to Spencer for her perusal the following morning.

All the way home I tried to recall the dates of the fall show and calculated whether the received information had come through about the same time my middle daughter had her paranormal episode. Sleep did not come easily that night. If I had been in danger then, was I in danger still? And if they had gone through Piper to get to me once, was she still a vulnerable target for them to manipulate again?

The next morning I got up extra early to see if Spencer had gotten my message. She had.

Yes, it was Samantha. I did a reading for her on Thursday. Here is other info. It has to be Roxanne. Roxanne may have relatives living in Hanover Park, Illinois. Roxanne says something fell from your computer area either yesterday or today. Feels like a piece of paper; it may have felt curious. Whatever it was, you eventually dismissed it. Feels like Roxanne was trying to show you something.

Do you recall? You may have even crumpled it up and thrown it out or to the side.

Last name Jaegers is mentioned. Pipe smoker did it. Mention of a small clock, the kind with the silver bell on top. Is this yours? Just a confirmation of being around you. October 13. Not sure what significance this date had or will have. The district: is this an area in Valdosta?

I tried to recall a piece of paper that I might have handled during that time sequence and could come up with nothing but a small yellow Post It with the name Cooper written on it that seemed to get shuffled about my desk waiting for recognition. I had gotten the name from Clint during one of my visits down to Valdosta. I assumed it was tied to the name of a J.T. Cooper that had been in a list of folks I'd gotten from Clint. This J.T. had worked for either the VPD or the Lowndes County Sheriff's Department during the time just before and/or during Charley's death. Obviously this man's last name held some importance to Roxanne, but why?

Aggravated, I experienced doubt seeping in and plaguing my mind. You'd think I would have been used to it by then, but with my formal presentation so close, the ambiguity of new and untethered associations made me nervous. Jules must have sensed my trepidation as her calls suddenly became more frequent. Early on she had said she wanted to go to the presentation. One would think, "Sure…why not?" It was her father after all. But that wasn't the purpose of the meeting, and I could not afford to blow it again. Erring on the side of caution, I kept the potential schedule to myself, fearful dates would either get changed again or something else might interfere. One humiliation had been enough.

As it turned out, the meeting scheduled was finally confirmed, but it landed right in the middle of her trip to pick up a horse. Since she was already headed out of town, the social breach was irrelevant. I wasn't trying to be difficult. I understood the way these encounters worked and knew from the get-go this was going to be no social call. The agents' attention could not be split, and mentioning that I worked with a psychic detective would be enough of a major distraction without dangling Charley's daughter in the wings.

Jumping back to Spencer's email, I mined for more corroboration.

"The mention of the small clock, the kind with the silver bell on top" made me smile. Not more than five feet from my writing desk was an antique dresser I use to store old quilts in. On top sat an antique alarm clock that I bought for $5.00 at a yard sale twenty years earlier. If Roxanne knew the clock, then she knew my office and that warmed my heart. No longer frightened by the proximity of those I was desperate to help, I took comfort that they shared my long nights and troubled sleep. Working what clues remained, I fired back…

I tried to find Blythe or Jaegers in Hanover, Illinois. Nothing. I did find a piece of paper on the floor the other day that said "Cooper." Anything? Ask Roxanne if she can help further. And did the MOT hurt her ever? Is Jaegers the last name of the MOT's daughter? Can they help me? School is done and I need to get back on this thing hot and heavy before ATF schedules again.

Spencer responded:

Cooper? What is that? It feels so familiar. MOT never hurt Roxanne. I get no on Jaegers being the last name of the MOT's daughter. Seventeenth by the lake… Mention of that suicide attempt again and being in the hospital (briefly). March 11th may have been the date she was checked into the hospital.

Again with the 17th by the lake. The only thing I could garner from that was that Charley had once shown Spencer a meeting he had had with Jeb Finch when he gave Jeb the envelope with the tape inside. That meeting happened out by Saddle Bag Lakes. Was this what was being referenced? Or was this the night they strangled her? The date for my ATF formal meeting would soon be upon me, and the hysteria of not wanting to look like a complete amateur started to seep through my composure.

Not wanting to be a pain, but I have ATF, FBI, GBI meeting on Thursday! Can Charley, Jessica, or Roxanne confirm the four in flannel as Hank Sloan (shooter), Damon Cummings (Grim Reaper), Albert (Al) Fitzpatrick (rubber muddy boots), George Wilson (mint pipe smoker)? And what about Trussman, who was given the name Sorenson on a small piece of paper from Damon? Was he the driver of the small red sports car that picked Jessica up and delivered her to the love shack for Sorenson? Ask them to help me clear this up before I print the rest of my report.... please. Tell them I just want to help and be clear.

As usual, she did her best to calm and edify.

OK, first take a deep breath. You got this. Charley says, "Move forward." Trussman seems on the outside. What happened on April 21st? Can you remember what you experienced this that day, something pertaining to this case?

That was a good question. What had happened on April 21st that had to do with the case? I rummaged back through a few of the blogs to jar my memory, but found the blog of April 20th mostly anticipatory of more information from Roxanne and the 22nd to have been in regards to my parents. Then it hit me: *The pipe smoker did it!* That's what happened. The clue I kept trying to diminish was the clue that just wouldn't die. *The pipe smoker did it... the pipe smoker did it... the pipe smoker did it!*

CHAPTER FORTY

In the beginning of May I received the best birthday present ever: a note of confirmation about my ATF meeting. Overjoyed, I responded enthusiastically, confirmed I would be there, and then posted the damn thing everywhere so I could not possibly forget the date and time. I sent a copy of the invite to Spencer and asked her to ask Charley and my parents to stay by my side. Her response was brief and to the point.

"You just did!"

That night I went through everything I had. Each binder had its 97-page report filled with multiple disclaimers, interviews, and research information. In addition to that there was a copy of the original GBI (Georgia Bureau of Investigation) Crime Lab Report I received from the GBI headquarters in Atlanta and a copy of two CD's, one containing the entire widow's (Kaye R. Covington) journal and one with the recorded interviews with the gentlemen from the first few chapters. Next, I had copies of the original funeral registry from the Camden McLane Funeral Home in Valdosta, the entire file from Beau Colbert, Deputy Sheriff of Lowndes County Sheriff's Department, which contained the witnesses' statements and Colbert's copy of the original GBI Crime Lab Report which included the mystery page two with the ballistics information that confirmed the use of two guns. I also had a copy of the death certificate of the MOT (man on tape), a/k/a Robert Weatherby Chancellor, and six of the eight crime scene photos from Clyattville-Nankin Road that night, as well as copies of several other documents I thought might be pertinent.

Everything else was in my head. I knew that no matter the question they might ask, I could pull the information from memory. Bearing previous disappoints in mind, I left nothing to chance and made two extra binders. Just after midnight, I loaded a box filled with everything into the trunk of the car and closed the lid, satisfied that I could do nothing more to prepare.

Nine hours later, I donned the outfit I had chosen for the occasion and drove into Atlanta with Don. The coffee in my cup was left untouched as the butterflies in my stomach held no taste for caffeine. I went over everything in my head and grilled Don about how I would drop the bomb about Spencer. In the end I went with the standard phrase "information suggests" and let the rest of it fall where it would. By 12:00 pm we were parked outside the doors of the building, and I was busy checking the mirror for lipstick blotches on my teeth.

My husband had expressed a desire to go in with me, and I told him he could come for the ride, but not to the meeting. It made me sound cruel, but I wasn't. It wasn't about him or Jules, or even me. It was about the evidence, the timelines, and the supposition. It was about how Charley went from being father and agent to deceased and forgotten. It was about everything the original investigators had ignored or hidden and everything I had unearthed and suspected. I also knew I had one shot at this. Neither Jules nor Don could have added to anything I was going to say. All the information the family had possessed had been in my hands for nearly two years. Through no fault of their own, they had been unsuccessful to move the case forward. Truth was, everyone had helped along the way, but everyone had also given everything to me for a reason, and that reason was to solve Charley's murder.

On May 5th, 2011 there was no one more prepared or more qualified to champion Charley's cause than I was... and I needed to remember that.

CHAPTER FORTY-ONE

Leaving the parking lot and entering through those large double glass doors was one of the bravest things I had ever done. With Don beside me, I walked to the front desk and signed in. When the security guard asked who I was there to see, I rattled off the list of names from the formal invitation as I scrawled my name on the next empty line, hoping I had pronounced them all correctly.

"Wow," he responded. "You've got a couple of the top guys in that list."

I raised my head. My eyes glazed over. That was good! Oh shit... that was good and bad. "Top guys" meant they had the power to move this case forward if they saw merit. "Top guys" also meant they had had the power to bury this thing deeper than the first set of agents had, and they would have no time for pure conjecture and little patience for common hearsay if they thought I was a fruit loop. What if I screwed up? What if they laughed at me once I introduced Spencer into the equation? Worse yet, what if the evidence I did have wasn't enough to hold their attention long enough to get to Spencer and the hundreds of hours of distilled links to everything else?

I had already been warned to play her role down as much as possible, but at some point there was no way to avoid bringing her and the information received from her into the mix. Grateful for the info but more nervous because of it, I tried to hand the security guard back the pen. This gesture proved to be my first blooper as it was already attached to the clipboard by a chain.

"Sorry," I whispered. He grinned and moved the clipboard to the center of the desk.

My husband echoed his previous statement. "Did you hear that? You've got the head guys. That's impressive!"

The man stuffed inside the white shirt behind the desk leaned forward for effect and sniggered, "What'd you do... rob a bank?"

Don stood there holding the box smiling and piqued an eyebrow at me, uncertain how to respond. Normally I would have quipped back something completely inappropriate like "Noooo... that was yesterday. This morning we blew up the courthouse, but we had a few minutes to kill before lunch so we decided to drop in here and case the joint for a job this afternoon." But that was well before I noticed the gun on his hip and the five or six other folks buzzing around the elevator who also wore holsters as accessories. I smiled back at the man who reminded me of a crème-filled cannoli and shook my head. "Hah! Good one!" I drooled. God, I sounded like such a schmuck!

Two seconds later the guard's smile broke out like a rash all over his face and he chuckled again. The harder he laughed the faster the pink blotches blended together upon his chubby features and his eyes sparkled.

"Just kidding…but seriously, Ma'am," the man's voice dropped an octave and the smile left his face as he motioned to Don's arms, "What's in the box?"

Apparently the kidding was over. Don lowered it for his perusal and immediately began to explain that the binders were for each of the agents and the other files were evidence. I kept an eye on all the folks coming and going with guns attached to their belts while Don continued to tell the man about Charley, about my research, and then about his heart attack. The two exchanged medical histories as I made mental notes of my opening statements. A few minutes later, a new crop of folks came through the glass doors and a bevy of holstered weaponry and security tags dangled from chiseled and not-so-chiseled chests as they crisscrossed the lobby heading in different directions.

Each person who came to the desk to sign in or sign out shared chirpy banter with the guard who never budged an inch other than to manipulate his pudgy fingers which toyed with the pen on the chain in between autographs.

"What time did you say your appointment was for?" he asked.

"Not until 1:00 pm."

You do know you're early, right? They're all out to lunch," he noted as another person clocked back in.

"Yes, I know. I just wanted to make sure I was here on time... traffic and all. You see, the last time I..." I began and then thought better.

He nodded his head and then shared a joke with another man who crossed from the other end of the lobby and exited through another set of doors camouflaged with frosted glass. That was the sixth or seventh person I'd seen wearing a holster pass through that way.

"What's behind those doors?" I asked, sounding like a tourist.

"I could tell ya," he sneered, "but then I'd have to kill ya!" and for a second his tag line hung in the air between us as I tried to rationalize whether he was just trying to be cute or serious. "I'd have to kill ya...get it?" Another huge pause and then his eyes popped and his face broke into the humor rash again, and he was all a giggles.

"James Bond? The famous saying 'I could tell ya, but then I'd have to...' you know."

I couldn't believe he even thought it was necessary to explain at this point, but I nodded just the same that I got it. He said it again, and this time my husband joined him. With the two of them yucking it up, my entire vision of the day began to melt, and suddenly my dignity felt like baggy nylons gathered at my ankles.

How was I ever going to get anyone to take me seriously behind those frosted doors if I couldn't get the security guard to see me as anything other than as game show fodder? Before I could answer myself, another group of folks rushed the front glass doors and descended upon the desk to sign back in. In a sea of office personnel, one woman stood out. Her hair was cropped short, her makeup sparse but striking, her purse (tastefully leather appointed) matched her shoes. She was official looking. When she stood up after clocking in, all six feet of her slender frame shifted and drizzled down into bright red pumps that rose up on stiletto heels to meet her.

As a matter of courtesy, she acknowledged our presence. "Good afternoon," she said and then chattered with the guard as she scribbled her name. Suddenly I recognized the voice as the woman who had tried to salvage my dignity over the phone a month and a half ago. Intent on making a good impression, I moved from my chair and crossed the two feet to the desk.

"Beverley?" I asked and thrust out my right hand.

She looked down at my open palm. "T. A. Powell? The writer?" she queried as she finished autographing the sheet, noting the time I signed in.

"Yes, I'm T. A.," I nodded. Finally someone who would give me some respect and knew I meant business.

She placed the pen down beside the ledger and with one fell swoop gracefully raised her head and looked down to reassess me.

"You're shorter than you sound over the phone," she stated flatly and then smiled. I stalled by grinning back. Shorter than I sound over the phone? How the hell do you sound short over a phone? Just as I was about to say something brilliant, cannoli boy chimed in.

"Yeah... for a short stack, she's a real pistol according to her husband," the security guard added, piqued his eyebrows for effect, and winked at me. My husband began to open his mouth to join in the fray, and I gave him the stink eye.

I tried to regain my dignity. "Yes, well... I sound much taller in print," I quibbled back and then realized the absurdity of what I had said.

"Cute. Ok. So... you're about forty minutes early," as she leaned back into the desk to double check my arrival time.

"I didn't want to be late," I responded.

"Fine. I can take you up with me if you'd like, but you may have to wait till I can gather everyone together."

I nodded, sensing silence would serve me be better at this point.

"What's in the box?" she asked as she pointed at the box.

Six binders, six manila envelopes... all containing my formal report and additional supporting evidence plus photos for their review," I offered and tried to sound official. "I have one for each of the agents and an extra binder with duplicate information as backup just in case another agent may want to join us," I said as professionally as I could. My husband nodded and held up the box, grinning like he was trick or treating for UNICEF.

"Good," she applauded and began to peel away from the group. "Well, if you've signed in, grab your things and follow me." I returned to my chair, grabbed my binder, and placed it inside the box with the others.

"Is your husband coming?" she asked, turned and grinned like an airline stewardess.

He stood up quickly and held the two front corners of the box, drumming the sides of it with his fingers waiting for her ok. I tried to catch his attention, but his eyes were fixed on our escort and he was grinning like a puppy who had just been asked to go outside and roll in dead possum guts. That was until he caught my gaze. All it took was one eyebrow slightly elevated to dissuade.

"No. No thank you. I'm good. I'll just give her the box and hang out down here and wait if it's ok."

"That will be fine," she glared. "It will be a while, though. Her appointment was for an hour, just so you know, in case you want to change your mind." She proffered a polite smile and in response his eyes twinkled. My eyebrow took a slight dip. Message received, he let his eyes dull. She might have changed his mind, but I hadn't. I reached for the box, sighed, and he got my drift. He rolled his fingers from the underside of the box and stuffed them back into his front pockets.

"That's ok. I'll wait here." I dipped my other eyebrow. "Or in the car...I have a book and a banana out there," he added, blinked hard, and then pulled out his keys as though surprised they had been stuck in his pants the whole time.

"Someone will escort her back down when she's through," she added. "It was nice to meet you."

"Great. Good to meet you too. I'll just read my book or run an errand till then," he said.

"Good boy," I thought and mentally patted him on the head. "Sit...stay... stay." I balanced the box on my hip for a moment and tried not to look like a UPS man as we crossed the lobby away from the frosted doors to the stainless steel facing of the elevator. Apparently those rooms were for something else. As I waddled carrying the awkward container, I realized a briefcase would have looked much more professional, but I couldn't have fit everything I needed inside one. We crossed the remainder of the lobby, and I tried not to look like my boobs were resting on the rim of the box. But it was a moot point: my arms were not long enough to lower it, and raising it was out of the question.

As we stood in front of the elevator, I caught our reflections. She was tall, stately, and dressed in a designer outfit that made her look like one of the girls from the James Bond series. Next to her reflection was a woman I did not recognize. The white and navy blue outfit I had chosen that I thought would make me look very Ivy League and posh was blocked by the box. What little showed made me look a geriatric Shirley Temple in a sailor suit.

Just as the elevator binged and the doors slid open, she smiled broadly and motioned with her hand. "Please... you go first." She stepped aside for me to pass. I shifted the box to see where I was going and stepped over the threshold, tugging at the back of my sweater as I went, trying to make my waist look longer.

To break the awkward silence, she made small talk as I climbed in. "I never met a writer before," she sighed. "How exciting...Hmmm? Do you write other kinds of books, or just murder mysteries?" she peppered.

I tried to lower the box and prop it on my knee, but it was too heavy and my legs too short. "Well…" I began.

She poured herself in beside me and her long, slender neck loomed inches above my head, so I was forced to look up.

"Yes. You were saying?" she prompted.

Suddenly I heard the small sarcastic voice in my head bring me back to earth, "Yes, you go first, Ms. Powell. You know what they always say...age before beauty." I ignored the dialogue in my head and that fact that I might be a few years older and more than a foot shorter than my host and concentrated on her fascination with my being a writer.

"Thanks. Yes, I am a published playwright and novelist and a professional theatre director. And I work on cold case murders with psychic/medium detectives," I said, beaming back at my husband who gave me thumbs up.

"Wow," she muttered with what sounded like sincere awe.

Dignity restored, I hoisted the box on the opposite hip and adjusted my chin a little higher to meet her gaze. Just as the doors were about to close, she looked down at me, reached across the box to push a button for a floor that didn't exist, and exclaimed "Gosh, I just can't get over it!" she gasped. Thinking it was in response to my professional dossier, I began to craft something pithy to come back with, but before I could, she finished her thought. "You really are that short." And that was that.

Temporarily humiliated, I rode silently to our appointed destination, the floor that does not exist. The elevator slowed to a stop and gave a slight hiccup before it settled. When the doors finally opened, I found myself suddenly surrounded by people who carried files and guns on their hips as big as the box on mine. My host apologized for the chaos, explaining that renovations were underway. After a brief remark to another colleague, she led me down a hall past painters and carpenters to a room and then asked me to wait. Seven minutes later, I was shuffled through another set of doors and was led down a longer hall to a pristine room with a mahogany conference table, leather cushioned chairs, and motel room art. The secretary showed me inside and asked if she could get me anything to drink. When I declined, she left me to prepare for the others who had already been informed I had arrived.

No sooner had the door latched behind her that I sized up the situation. I had delayed our first meeting with a scheduling snafu and now, early and eager for the second, I had already been told four times how short I was. Chances were they would not see me as any taller, so I had to think of the best way to appear greater in stature if only a ruse. Ah yes, thank God for theatre! How to come from a point of strength that would forgive all that had happened before?

Suddenly the director in me took over and I set the stage, placing the largest file at the end of the table where I assumed the head ATF agent would reside. Each chair placement after that received a binder and several files in front of it. Minutes later, agents flooded the room. Once introductions had been made, I motioned them to sit, starting with the head SAC ATF agent. The others moved to their respective chairs, and then I went to the opposite end of the table and stood waiting for their attention. The SAC for ATF acknowledged me and the reason for the meeting. He politely waited for me to sit. I thanked him and motioned that they should all do so first, as I needed one more second to begin. They obliged. Once they were all seated, I pushed the chair behind me into the corner and proceeded to instruct and edify from a standing position the rest of the meeting. Without giving anything away, I will say that Spencer had warned me that one person in the group would play the devil's advocate. This person had, but I was prepared.

I began with a general overview and orientation of the binder contents, followed by a breakdown of the additional files before we even opened the covers. One particular agent who later became my strongest advocate fought me every inch of the way with cynicism and apathy. When I introduced Spencer into the equation, you could have heard a pin drop. Every agent in the room made eye contact with another, and you could see the grins begin to break at the corners of their mouths. That's when I discussed some of Spencer's first impressions and then backed them up with hard copy evidence when I dropped the photos into the mix. One look at those and the atmosphere in the room changed dramatically.

As they previewed each photo, I lectured about the initial denial of evidence proving it was a homicide. I pointed out that the statements had been taken almost two weeks after Charley's death, all at the same time and not one of them mentioned rain, even though it was a matter of historical documentation that Valdosta had received a record-setting amount that night.

Later I directed their attention to anomalies within the photos. I reminded them that the investigation lasted only 18 days. Then I blasted that the widow's attorney, then a former Superior State Court Judge, had refused to reopen the case based on lack of physical evidence even though he had confessed to me that two detectives had shown him evidence to the contrary seven to eight years after. I recalled for them the statute of limitations on murder cases, which of course was unnecessary but theatrically effective as they stared at page 2 of the ballistics report, which screamed that the bullets had come from two different guns. I reminded them that all parties of interest to the case were still alive at that seven to eight year benchmark and viable for prosecution. With deliberate measure, I topped off the ensuing silence by reiterating that this same former Superior State Court Judge had obstructed justice and denied not only Charley's widow the information but also the state and federal agencies represented in the room. Cautiously these men eyed the photos, each other's expressions, and then me. Questions began to pry loose from their lips slowly as we metaphorically pried back the coffin lid of Charley's case.

Convinced I had finally gotten their attention, I stretched an inch or two taller in my comfortable flats and my middle-aged sailor suit. I allowed them to talk among themselves for a few minutes. When I hit a lull in the questions, I moved the conversation forward and instructed them to go to the binder sections containing the original witness statements taken by Beau Colbert, the Lowndes County Deputy Sheriff and then back to the original GBI Crime Lab ballistics report hidden on page 2, which dramatically conflicted with the incomplete report I had paid $19.86 to retrieve thirteen months earlier from the GBI Crime Lab headquarters in Atlanta.

With the hard evidence of the ballistics report and the blaring disconnect between Colbert's report information and photo discrepancies, true discussion finally broke forth and I began to breathe easier. The hands of the clock had moved many segments, and I feared I was about to be cut off. But the SAC for ATF held out his hand, broke into the dialogue, and pointedly asked if the person I suspected as the shooter was still alive. My heart sank. Finally I had them all engaged, my credibility established. Now this. If I told them I knew Hank Sloan was already dead, it would pull the plug out of the bottom of my boat. Then everything I had worked for over the past two years would go down the tubes. Every agent looked towards the end of the table and the little woman who had finally awed them, waiting for her reply.

"I believe Mr. Hank Sloan to be deceased," I said and watched as fingers that held the photos of Charley's broken and bloodied body began to go limp. "But before you dismiss this case based on that, please consider that I believe there were three other victims in this case that deserve to be recognized, their remains found, and causation of death vetted. The room remained silent for what seemed like an eternity as each exchanged a notable glance with one another and then graciously turned to their host for guidance. The SAC for ATF nodded pensively, visually canvassed the remaining men, and then asked that I continue to present the rest of my case.

A huge sigh of relief escaped my lungs and then filled them once again as I heard myself say, "If you all turn to page 62, I will tell you about the other three victims in this case: two young females and one male, whom I believe are directly connected to the murder of Charles Gordon Covington and part of a now forty-five year cover up. The following individuals conspired to hide their malicious and illegal activities. Gentlemen, if you are ready? Page 62, then? At the top you will see the list of persons of interest in direct order of their assessed involvement with this case... "

The first hand on the clock continued to move while I spoke, and this time they intently listened and not one person interrupted me until I was done telling them most of what I suspected and everything I could prove. I listed the victims one at a time, along with what information I had that would tie them to one another, to the shooter and his accomplices to Charley. When I finished, I gave them my verbal supposition how everything I had found pointed to a variety of illegal activities, but predominantly a pornography ring involving local, state, and federal law enforcement agents, who committed a series of murders to hide their involvement and then conspired to conceal evidence for over forty-five years — a conspiracy that may have employed the influence and favors of two high-ranking state officials in 1966.

When I finished, the six agents who had questioned my every utterance remained in active conversation as the door closed behind me. A hundred and thirty-three minutes after a middle-aged woman in a sailor suit had walked into a building as a desperate housewife seeking not to do laundry, she walked out of an elevator a half an inch taller in her flat shoes, leaving agents scratching their heads and wondering what to do with the information she'd presented them.

As I heard the click of the doorknob behind me, I knew I had nailed my mark. I'd never been so proud of me before in my life. The agent at my side escorted me through halls and onto the elevator where I assessed my reflection in a new light. He returned me to the desk, handed me back my box, and signaled cannoli boy that the meeting was over. They watched as I signed my name with a flourish and then, mission accomplished, he shook my hand and wished me well.

"That's an autograph there. You'll want to hold onto that. Someday it's gonna be worth something!" I applauded. He smiled and wished me a good day. I wished him the same and then watched as he swaggered back to the elevator and mentally critiqued my performance as he waited for the doors to open.

I had done Charley proud. Hell, I had done everyone who had ever met or loved Charley proud. Once the silver door swallowed him whole, I sighed and let the adrenaline ease from my veins. The voice of the security agent called me back to the present. I realized Don was somewhere with a half-eaten banana and a paperback, waiting for me to return.

"So, how'd you do up there?" he asked and nodded his head in the direction of the elevator.

"I rocked the shit out of it!" I beamed.

"Do you think they'll reopen the case?" he asked.

"They don't have a cold case department from what I understand, but with what I just gave them? They'd be crazy not to. The book will be written either way. I'm just giving them the opportunity to help clean up some of their own mess first. It's up to them now to decide whether to do it or not," I blurted.

"Your husband's waiting outside. He was right. You are a pistol," he chuckled.

"Damn straight, I am! A 53-year-old pistol in a sailor suit," I confirmed and hiked the box up onto my other hip.

Sunlight flooded the lobby as I put on my shades, adjusted my sweater, my ego, and my course of direction in life. I had done it: accomplished just exactly what I had set out to do almost two years earlier. Whether they reopened the case or not, I would always know I had kept the promise I'd made to Charley and to myself. Emotionally amped, I let myself out through the double glass doors to join my husband who stood patient and anxious waiting by the car.

I gave him a big thumb's up as I crossed the parking lot. He smiled. I winked. After he popped the trunk and slid the leftover box inside, he tossed me the keys to my chariot and we rode home with the top down. I told him everything I could remember. When we pulled into the driveway, I still felt the thrill of what I'd accomplished two hours prior. In light of the number of trained personnel involved in the first investigation and the level to which evidence had been destroyed, it would always remain that what Spencer and I had managed to pluck from the cosmos was nothing short of a miracle.

That night I went to bed a different person, blessing the cosmos that had changed my life. Four nights later the cosmos had its turn again and returned the gratitude by sending me an astounding email from someone who'd found my blog.

Dear T.A.,

Who are you? Why are you interested in this case? Very dangerous. Assassination was set up by his trusted colleague. Shooter may have been a Samuels who was either the ex-boyfriend or ex-husband of the Tolbert woman. This assassination can give a black eye to more than one law enforcement agency. Moonshine still was not involved. Probably about guns, dope, or counterfeit money. Samuels warned a person to leave Valdosta and stay gone. My mother went to pick them up in Valdosta. Why would the coroner rule it a suicide? Why would the local Sheriff's Department rule as well? As I said before, still very dangerous. Just so you know I know something, there was a heavy rainstorm the night of the assassination. Many now dead, but some may still be alive. My information is that Charley Covington was a straight arrow who loved his family and talked about his children all the time. He was one of the good guys. I am bringing this up as I think it is the right thing to do. Perhaps a little late, but I did not have all the knowledge I have now. I want nothing for this except our safety and perhaps if the information proves fruitful, the FBI would be kind enough to look into a crooked Sheriff's Department in Texas and reopen the case of one of my murdered relatives. I support our law enforcement officers, but I also know there are crooked cops out there. Good luck to you. Scared, but willing to talk...

The email was forwarded from an unknown Internet address that read Roland Snodgrass.

CHAPTER FORTY-TWO

Just when I had stopped second guessing myself and was comfortable that I had given ATF every plausible tool and angle to move forward from, some stranger muddied the waters with strange and foreign images. What was I becoming — the Pied Piper of payback for every lost soul who ever got screwed by a shady law enforcement agency? Since receiving it, I had read the email no less than 43 times and still drew a blank as to who this Snodgrass fellow was or how he could have possibly been connected to my Charley. Where had Mr. Know It All been for the past forty-five years while everyone innocent rotted in their graves and the guilty flourished in their lives?

Concerned about my evasive and cryptic deliberations, my husband began tracking reverse emails trying to divine who our mystery contact really was. Since every reverse trace came back for some professor dude in California who was well under forty years of age, we figured the moniker for a ruse. Knowing that the universe does not waste its time with superfluous messages, I offered my help in exchange for his. Apparently my host was not impressed. Several days went by without any word. Irritated I had wasted so much emotion on this guy, I backed off. A few nights later he called, said he had sent the message on behalf of somebody else and that he would pass my number on, but no promises. I asked for a return number; he declined for a second time and hung up on me. Frustrated with Snodgrass, I took a glass of wine and sat at the end of my dock staring at the stars. I didn't mind working hard for information, but I wasn't about to be the star in somebody else's dog and pony show. If the cosmos thought he had worthwhile information, let them chase the son of a bitch.

The lake has always been a good place to sort things out for me, and that night was no different. Sounds in the cove drifted in and out of my auditory perusal; then a radio in the distance broadcast a favorite contemporary tune and brought things to a head. At first I slightly hummed along, but the more I listened to the words the more I realized that the song was just a musical version of my own angst. Inspired, I downed the wine and shuffled my way back up the dock to the house. That night I tore through the keys on my laptop, intent on sending a message to the universe through my blog:

Ever have one of those weeks when your life feels more like that new song by Adam Lambert "What Do You Want from Me?" Well after three years of that and a couple of glasses of wine, I looked to the stars and asked God and the universe the same question: What do you want from me? Haven't I asked every question, followed every lead, and sacrificed every rational thinking cell in my body to blindly follow where it is you lead me? Haven't I done enough to warrant some direct guidance? Well... haven't I? Have I not devoted the last two years of life to my divine mission, forsaking everything else in my path, including my sanity to do so? Have I not made enough personal sacrifices to warrant a wink and a nod when asked? Tonight I am spent. Charley feels distant, my guides seem to have lost their train of thought, and I grow weary of guessing my way through this phase of my life. So, my dear light workers and those on the other side, I now ask you point blank...What do you want from me?

And do you know what they answered? This was a message I received back from Spencer the following morning.

Just read your latest blog entry and was told to pass on to you, "It's not what do you want from them. It's what do you want from you?"

WOW! In response, I posted this:

What do you want from yourself?

Wow...I know it was meant to be a profoundly inspiring response and the impetus for thought-provoking therapy. And it will be... just as soon as I get over the fact that I have just been summarily bitch-slapped by the universe for throwing a publicly private pity party and daring the world to join me.

Right now, though, I am still slightly aghast that of all the situations I have asked direct responses for lately, this is the one they return. I am caught between laughing at them and laughing at myself, even as I struggle to let go of the original question: "What do you want from me?" In the interest of not overreacting, let's take a deep breath and then center ourselves, shall we? Ok.

After all, laughter is the best medicine, and these are the same "they" that reminded me once to take out my garbage because they thought it was too full. So... did I really expect less of them? Did I really expect them to ignore my literary temper tantrum and not have a clever quip to come back at me with? Noooo! Did I not throw that crap out to the universe as way of showing my current displeasure with recent short-term trials? Yes, but was this not the emotional Nemo cast into the ethereal waters to prompt and elicit an immediate response? Yes, but...Drat! I hate it when they call me up short and turn the tables. Ok... therapy time.

Soooo...all right, I'll bite. What do I want from me? It's a good question, not as easily answered as one might think, but a good question nonetheless, so here goes. Ok...honestly? Honestly, at first I just wanted to bury my life in Charley's death because mine had become so convoluted and misguided. In the beginning I wanted to spend all my time thinking about his hurts, to either let go of or avoid of a few of my own. I wanted to find the mystery and intrigue that no longer appeared to be part of my life. I was an adrenaline and information junky that needed the high of somebody else's chaos to make up for the fact that my own life of motherhood and daily mundane duties reflected a life that did not seem to fit with where and what and who I had always thought I would be. I thought... if I could just find Charley's killer, that that would be journey enough to plug the potholes in my own path.

But then I got hooked. Then it didn't matter so much about my journey. It became about Charley and his journey. I did more living in his death than I was doing in my own life. While it built a bridge between us, it was the wrong kind of bridge to build. So again I ask myself "What do I want from me now?" For now... I want my journey to be a truer reflection of my own in finding his. To learn how to better navigate the emotional obstacles he did not. I want to write this book and not only tell his truth but tell mine in the process. I want to be the person who stood up for the two girls that had their young lives mangled by circumstance and ripped from them by men who had every intention of fully living out their own in comfort and false glory — even if they had to lie through their crooked teeth to their adoring wives and their innocent children to do so. I want to stand tall at the end of my day and know that what I have done here for Charley is not just tell a story but to have made a real difference for him and those who were left behind, ignorant of the truth and ignorant of the cost he and three other people fatally suffered for others' comfort and lack of conscience. I want to know that what I do and what I say from this point forward will be divinely guided and that I will be emotionally compensated for the sacrifice of rutting my way through this horrible thing with fledgling intuition and hopeful prayer. I want to know that I am exactly where I am meant to be and exactly who I am meant to be: a writer who speaks for those who can no longer speak.

What else should I want from me? Only a few things: things like the confidence to know that this journey has not been in vain and that I have done right by those who were brave enough to place this in my feeble fingertips to begin with. The creative tenacity and inspiration to craft a way to make this my life's work and to be able to devote the necessary time it takes, but not risk family or finances in doing so. To know in my heart that all of this is real: Charley, my parents, the MOT, and the two young girls. To trust that all those who litter my path each day with signs understand my need for confirmation and support this tremendous call to serve.

What do I want from me? Hmmm....not much, huh?

How about you? What do you want from you?

And it was a good blog. But I'd left out the one thing I really wanted from me… from the universe…from my husband and from my mother: absolution from the universe for not being profoundly good enough to warrant direct intervention. Absolution from my husband for making self-appointed freedoms and evolutionary ambitions more important than my vows. But most of all, absolution from my mother for being thirty-one minutes late the day she died.

That night I went to bed emotionally exhausted and physically spent. It was the night I had the dream that was not a dream.

Cognizant that I was awake but obviously asleep, I simply appeared behind the wheel of a car, driving to somewhere that felt familiar but not recent. Sensing more than seeing my children about me, I sent them off to play and then parked the car in the driveway of a house I knew was home but had no memory of. The house reminded me of one my parents had owned in New Orleans, so I got out and walked to the door. I knocked and heard someone call from within to enter. I did. Seeing no one in the entry, I wandered from room to room until I got to the back of the house and the kitchen, where I found soft music playing and a middle-aged woman putting away groceries. It was my mother.

Conscious that she was dead and that this should not be happening, I immediately asked her where my father was. She snickered as she put away an oatmeal box and said, "He isn't very good at this yet, so I left him at home." Confused, I reminded her she was dead and she simply laughed again and then bid me sit at the table with her for a minute. Slowly I pulled out a chair and sat while she put away the last items from the bag into a tiny fridge. As she turned and started walking towards me, I immediately blurted out how much I missed her, how dearly I loved both of them and that I was so sorry I had not been there when she died. She casually pooh-poohed my theatrics and moved to the table and sat. Overcome, I crawled to the floor beside her and laid my head on her knee just as I had done as a child. When I was finished blubbering, she patted my hand and her blue eyes beamed with love.

"You need to let this thing go and forgive yourself," she said.

"What thing?" I asked, sincerely wanting to please her.

"This thirty-one minute thing you have stuck in your head that you think is so important."

Tears rolled. "But it is important," I wailed.

"Not to me it's not," she said and rolled my face upwards to see me better.

Tempered by her gaze, I brought myself under control. "I'm so sorry. If I hadn't gone home to take care of the kids... the farm ... meet that stupid realtor... I could have been there. I could have... held your hand. I could have..." and lingering tears choked both my throat and my reasoning.

"And what?" she whispered. "Kept me from dying?"

"Noooo... I guess not," I rationalized. "But I promised you I would be there. I promised I would be the one to hold your hand at the last minute, and I wasn't there, and it wasn't right. I'd been there for everything else, dammit. The midnight runs to the hospitals, the surgeries, the moving..." and the list seemed endless. She listened until I exhausted myself, and then took my hand in hers while I continued to vent.

"It was cruel of God to do that to me. I had been there for everything else. Why wasn't I special enough for that?" I wallowed. "It wasn't right that I was not allowed to be present at the most important moment in your life...I was a *Looper*, for Christ's sake, second in command," I cried and apologized profusely for letting her down. In my grief I explained I was convinced that God had seen all other eight children fit to be there, except me. I could not fathom what infraction had been committed to warrant such.

"All ten kids came home, all ten of us. And eight stayed. My baby sister and I were there for three days, but we had to go home. She couldn't stay because of work and kids. I couldn't stay because of the farm, my kids, and other professional duties. They said you'd be fine. We were coming back Friday for the surgery. I wanted to stay that extra day, but there were the kids and the farm animals to take care of. I had a realtor showing the house. Everyone said you were fine, but they lied. As soon as they called, I drove as fast as I could," I sniffled. "I got pulled over for doing 110 mph just outside of Birmingham. Did you know?" I asked and she smiled. "I made the four-hour trip in just over three," I added, though in the end it didn't matter.

"I know... I know," she said, though she couldn't have possibly known because at that point she was dying. I know because I knew the moment she died. There was a thing with the clouds and a rainbow in the sky that happened that I still can't explain, and I felt her tugging at my heart. I remember because I looked at the clock on my dashboard at the time and like an idiot I whispered to her if she needed to let go, it was ok, that I would be ok with her leaving without me, but I lied. I lied! I found out later that that was the exact time of her death. Even though I'd promised I would be ok with it, I had never been ok with it and it had rotted me from the inside out for the past five years.

"I missed the most important moment in your life, in my life, by thirty-one minutes, and I will never be able to forgive myself," I keened and openly wept at her side.

"There is nothing to forgive." She smiled and wiped a tear. "Do you know why it wasn't necessary for you to be there?" I shook my head no, overcome with emotion.

"Because you had been there for all the other moments in my life that were *equally* important. All the midnight runs to the hospitals, the surgeries, the moves... the birthday parties, the shopping sprees, and the funerals. All those moments when I wanted or needed you by my side, you never let me down. You were always there. Had you been there in the room that day and had I been forced to look into your sad eyes and say goodbye, it would have made it all the harder to leave and I could not stay any longer."

I squeezed her hand and exhaled slowly, trying to lower my heart rate.

"You never needed my forgiveness because you never did anything wrong. You weren't meant to be there because you had always been there. That was my gift to you."

Absolved of a crime I had never committed, I remember collapsing into the warmth of her hug. I do not know how much time passed tucked inside her touch, but it was enough to heal the hurt. I kissed her small hand again as she wiped a wisp of hair from my cheek and said, "Now... let this nonsense go and move on." And with that she kissed me on the forehead, told me she loved me, and faded into the night.

The next morning I woke with such peace and stillness in my heart that I knew it had been real. Just like the night she'd died, when the living room had filled with the scent of gardenias and she whispered in my ear that she was sorry she was late, but that nobody in the hospital would tell her how to get out and she could not find her way home. That visitation had been real too. The nuns had it wrong all the time. People and animals we loved could remember us on the other side. They could reach through the veil of grief and hold us tight and honor what we had shared in corporality.

From the very beginning I'd thought that it was the miracle of Spencer and Charley who had brought my parents back to me, when in fact Charley and Spencer had been a gift from my mother and father to help me find my way back to them. Realizing that, I was humbled beyond comprehension. This case hadn't been brought to me so that I could solve a murder and write a book. It was brought to me to learn to ease my pain by setting it aside and serving another human being. By focusing on Jules's loss and Charley's heartache and not on mine, I had allowed myself to put another soul first. Selflessness and the miracle of faith were the gifts my parents had gifted me with from their heavenly home in an effort to accelerate my divine evolution. Altered by the epiphany, I spent the pre-dawn hours in quiet meditation on the dock, staring out at the lights as they flickered atop the water. Eventually the illuminations began to fade with the dawn, so I wandered back to the house and my desk, seeing everything in a new light: the light of self-forgiveness that taught me that I had not been late. I had been spared and given the opportunity to use all my God-given talents as a way to honor them. Charley had been the gift sent to help in my spiritual development, and in return, I was being asked to help solve his murder to help aid him in moving forward in his.

With hot coffee in hand and drizzled sunlight laced upon the shoreline, I was finally content and happy just to breathe. No longer threatened by the lack of omnipotent corroboration, I sat at my laptop listening to its familiar hum, comforted by the memory of my dream. Reading the post from the night before, I hummed a bit from Adam Lambert's song and knew the spirits had accomplished their mission all in one night. Like Scrooge, I had been shown the error of my ways and granted a new lease. I wanted to sing it from the rooftops! I could do this thing. I could learn to trust and follow what was being given and not look back and live in the past. Happy to be free of my self-imposed prisons, I yelped the final verse out loud and did an air-guitar move that would have impressed even Clapton!

Unimpressed, my youngest daughter Claire entered my office and announced she had a message for me. I was fairly certain considering the hour that it was to inform me I should not quit my day job and to shut up, but it was something quite the contrary.

"Suspicion…Conviction…Salvation!"

"What?"

"I don't know. I was asleep and somebody kept whispering this in my ear. It was most annoying."

Astounded, I sat back in my chair and wrote it down just as she had said it. "Are you sure this is what they said?" I asked, opening a new email on my laptop and typing furiously.

"Yes… they just kept whispering it over and over. I told them to shut up, but they don't listen very well. They just kept repeating *Suspicion…Conviction…Salvation!*"

"What does it mean?" I asked.

She looked at me with her wrinkled T-shirt, hair askew, mascara run eyes, and drooled. "Are you freaking serious? You really think this was for me?"

"Well… it was your ear," I sneered and giggled.

"Yeah… ok. Well, it was my ear, my sleep, my bedroom… and my day off, I might add. But it was definitely your friggin' ghost people, so tell them the next time they want to send a message to you they should just text it. I'm going back to bed." And she staggered down the hall, turned, and added, "And turn your stupid radio down! I'm sick of that stupid song!"

"Radio?" I chuckled and hummed a few bars just to piss her off. Once I heard her door slam shut, I returned my attention to the message and fired off my email to S. I was amazed at how many channels the infamous "they" used to get information to me. Poor little Claire. She had been up half the night and not happy to have been on the other end of the ethereal phone line, but what the hell.

"Suspicion…Conviction…Salvation!" Had the message been a sign for me that things were moving forward? Or a sign from Charley that he was well on his way to a new level of spiritual evolution? Or could it have been a warning for Grim that his days were numbered? In the end I surmised there was a bit of information in it for all of us. In light of my recent dream, the forgiveness of my mother, and my promise to trust more in the process, I sent out another email to Mr. Snodgrass. This time it was a nice one and my contrition paid off.

Three nights later I received a mystery call from a woman who claimed to have been the frightened girl Mr. Snodgrass had written was rushed out of Valdosta that night. Our conversation was politely cryptic at first, but once my intentions were clearly conveyed, hers seemed to become a bit muddled. Her confession, as it were, was filled with erratic information that felt even more fragmented and vague than the disjointed email her cohort had sent the week before on her behalf. She said she wanted to tell me everything, but said she couldn't because she was afraid the KKK would find out it was her.

It didn't make sense. The KKK had been mentioned only once in reference to an impression Spencer had about George Slidell when he'd argued with another man out in an open field and then shot him to death. It was a disconnected presentation that Spencer and I were never able to find segues for, but that was way back in the beginning and I had not thought of him since. Was this a new way to tie him to that night in a role other than as the red-headed go-to man? Confused, I contacted Spencer again and asked for intervention.

Think with me. What's with the KKK influence? What if Rox's last name was Tolbert, not Blythe, and the connection he's making was between Roxanne and Samuels? Maybe she dated the son of Samuels or maybe it was Jessica? What if when she was killed they got a hold of Daddy Samuels because they didn't want it ever being potentially tied to the Samuels family in Atlanta and by proxy the governor? See what Rox says. Was one of Samuels's kids a boy who used to date either of them? That could be the tie between Grim and Roxanne. If Samuels, could that be why he would be crazy enough to be involved in the first place? Think with me. Call when you can.

As always, half my diatribes went unheralded and she answered my questions with more questions, an approach which only served to increase my confusion.

Did Samuels die in 2010? Ok...is there a way to find out if Samuels had a big scar on the inside of his left hand? Something about a fax on December 12th. I know you have a lot of documents, but possibly one dated December 12th. It has Gerri all over it (not sure where they are going with this). One of the girls feels like Rox.

Her dad may have been an herbalist or really into Chinese-type medicine. Henders' farm — you will find more there. The half tire, like a car tire that has been cut in half or half is buried in the dirt.

Did you have a nose bleed?

The intellectual vertigo caused by such random statements was becoming increasingly intolerable and should have given me a nosebleed, but it hadn't. Understanding that Spencer can only deliver what's presented, I took the cue and studied everything about Mr. Jack T. Samuels you could track on and off the internet: his career, his relationship with Chandler Sorenson, and his attorney's law firm's ties to Cummings. Article after article, obit after obit, and portrait after portrait all crawled across the screen, but none with an angle that gave me any clues or showed me the inside of his left hand.

My mystery caller had confirmed the last name of Samuels. Unlike my candidate, his candidate turned out to be a Floyd Samuels of Valdosta who was some sort of local kingpin, fresh up from Florida. This fella had been into alleged counterfeiting operations, moonshining, and drug and gun running.

When I asked Spencer which Samuels I was supposed to be following, she said Charley signaled that the Valdostan-related Samuels held little importance in his actual murder. When I asked for confirmation if it was Jack T. Samuels (who also had been an attorney, a judge, Speaker of the House and promoted to the Lieutenant Governor of the State of Georgia six months after Charley's death), Charley implied I should be looking at the bigger fish and gave Spencer a big thumb's up and then disappeared as she walked through the sliding doors of the local retail market. Amazed that Charley would appear at the entrance of a Wal-Mart store to Spencer, but not within the sacred confines of my home reinforced the insult of second-hand confirmation. Nonetheless, I took the slight in stride and continued to move forward with the high-ranking official Samuels as my main person of interest.

Why would the cosmos bring up another Samuels if my original choice was correct? And why would this woman bother to reach out now? But most of all, why would you promise to do whatever you could to help solve Charley's murder and then do nothing for over four decades? That was the endgame for me. Why would she have gone out of her way to contact me only to dump me when she found out I talked to a psychic... unless she had something else she wanted or needed to hide? Curious, I traced the cell number back to the New England area and recorded her information. The call lasted about forty minutes in which time she had told me about her clandestine meeting at a restaurant with Charley Covington the afternoon of his death.

According to Kaye's journal, the only restaurant Charley had visited the day of his death had been the Shoney's Big Boy where he took Jules and her brother for spaghetti around 4:30 that afternoon. I knew that, but I wasn't going to volunteer it. When I asked what she had discussed with Charley, she claimed the conversation had been about her estranged husband. She said he had been thrown in jail the week before for bootlegging and she was trying to negotiate a deal for his release by giving Charley inside information about a potential gun-running deal that was going to go down on Clyattville-Nankin Road that night. That was the first time I had ever heard anything about the guns. When I asked her if she knew anything about the local porn ring, she nearly hung up on me.

"Porn?" she blasted. "There was no porn involved! This was about illegal guns and drugs...and possibly counterfeit money. I don't know what you're talking about. Charley would have never been involved with something like that," she pounced, obviously not understanding the inference.

"I didn't say Charley was involved in it; he discovered it." I backpedaled and told her he had been investigating a lead about law enforcement being involved with making porn. When I asked her if she'd ever heard the names Damon Cummings, Hank Sloan, or Albert Fitzpatrick before, she said no. When I asked if she had ever heard the names Jessica or Roxanne before, she declined knowledge of any of them. But when I asked about the name Gerri Baldwin, she immediately described an attractive woman with long legs, dark eyes, and dark hair just as Winston Wahlberg had done. She said this woman had approached her at the restaurant where she worked and asked if she would go across the street for $50.00 to the trailer park and have sex with a man who was distraught over his wife's extramarital affair with a lesbian. She said he needed to bolster his confidence by being with a real woman.

I thought he needed to file for divorce, but blindsided by the absurdity of the statement, I waited to hear more. She then told me this woman (G) was a friend of Samuels's. She said the woman had told her it was just a sexual favor to give this man back his verve and raise his spirits and that there would be good money in it for her. Ms. Moorey (my mystery caller from New England) said she refused and then immediately refocused my attention back to her meeting with Charley about her husband. She claimed Charley's death was all her fault. Then she confessed she'd carried this burden of guilt for over forty-five years and that it had really messed her up. That's why she couldn't begin to deal with the psychic stuff. She just didn't want to drag all that back to her surface memory.

I assured her that she was not the reason why Charley was killed, but she felt certain Charley had died because she told him to go out there that night. She said when she heard Charley had been murdered, she ran into the woods to hide and somehow a Mr. Schmidt (another local kingpin who dealt in guns, drugs, and moonshine) found out about it. She said Schmidt found her and warned her she better get out of town before she was next. Then she said he went to a phone, placed a call to someone in Florida, and told them to come pick the girl's sorry ass up and not to say a word about it to anyone. In a way, I was irritated and in another, amazed. One more mention of Spencer, though, and she abruptly ended the conversation saying she would only communicate with me further through Jules.

Tolerant of religious fervor, I accepted the offense but wondered if that was the true reason why she bolted. Conversation abridged, I never got to tell Moorey that Kaye's journal talked about Charley being at the Shoney's Big Boy that afternoon or that I never thought she was making that part up. She had explained in the condensed discussion that she had had two different waitress jobs at the time. Descriptions suggested the first one was at the S & K and the second at the Shoney's. I never really got to question the other parts of her story before she cut me off. Obviously she had made contact with Charley at some point, but her limited reasoning for his death and the overwhelmingly broad scope of other offenses I had researched were on two different hemispheres. Still, it bothered me that she felt she had been violated when I asked her to tell me the truth about who Roland Snodgrass was and what her relationship to him was. After all, how did either of them expect me to trust them with what I knew if they told only half of the truth of what they knew from the very beginning? Hadn't I had been as transparent thus far as possible about my intentions and my associations?

Whoever this Roland Snodgrass was, he sure knew an awful lot about the kingpin Schmidt confrontation. Why, you might ask? So did I. It wasn't long before I got my answer. The very next call I received was from Mr. Snodgrass himself, stating that the woman who drove to pick the girl Ms. Moorey up from Valdosta that night and brought her back to Florida late that next morning had been his mamma. He said she was gone about four hours and took her gun. The whole affair had been very hush-hush. He also told me his parents were part of some other investigation at the time, something about CIA men trying to talk to his father. He even called back a second time and gave me a list of names and numbers of CIA folks who had tried to contact them. Both Snodgrass and Moorey had talked about some big shot from Florida with the first name of Ray. When I queried Spencer, she said they showed her a man with a mole or freckle on his upper lip when the name Ray was presented. Other than that, she had nothing more to offer on him.

Looking for background information, I went to Clint and asked about a 1966 Ray powerful enough to make a woman like Ms. Moorey want to duck and cover. At first he couldn't place anybody, but when I mentioned the Florida association, his tongue cut loose and he told me all about a Ray from Florida who moved to Valdosta in the 1960's and bought a car dealership not far from the S & K restaurant where G had allegedly approached the Ms. Moorey girl.

I reviewed my notes and some of the things jelled. In a short email I sent an abridged edition off to Spencer.

V is for the road that separates the AFB from the trailer park, Castlepark bakery for Rox and trailer for Jessica S &K restaurant, Greek, a/k/a The Fort, same place where this mystery woman (Linda Moorey or Floyd, as she could have been known by her maiden and/or married name). Says she met with Charley that Sunday and gave him info about the guns. Same place where this woman claims potentially G asked her to go for coffee and to talk her into having sex with someone else. She also says she signed the funeral book and was at the funeral home on the Tuesday after to be with him, but that there was nobody there. Very odd. Also, she said a man named Don Schmidt ran guns and that that was the info she gave Charley the day he died to get her husband Randy Floyd out of jail; said this Don Schmidt guy offered to take her home from work and then took her to some woods on the outside of town and told her to get the fu... out and stay quiet. Said KKK would find her if she ever talked.

Floyd family home was just doors down from Beau Colbert, and they had a huge car dealership just down from the VPD lake house where Rox was dumped in the lakes behind there.

Your black/white pepper-haired Asian lady at the Harvey's grocery store bakery that Rox worked at fits description of your lady and her maternal instincts towards Rox. A Miss Williamson who was the owner, dead, but there was another girl there at the same time as Rox, about the same age: Linda Peeves. The S & K rest was also owned by a man with the last name of Slidell; not certain if he is related to the red-headed go-to guy Slidell, a George Slidell. Do I have this all wrong?

I hope this helps. Things feel off for me and I am uncertain. I was hurt by what that lady said. I do this for Jules and for Charley. Isn't what I have done so far enough for them to appreciate? Am I on the wrong track or is this some kind of test? It almost feels ungrateful, but I am too sensitive right now to be a decent barometer. Tell Charley... he and I are forever. I follow his lead.

Adding that to another email I received from my theatre pal and her psychic, Moorey's may have made more sense:

*The message was a general warning to be cautious. The message was something about a young woman in the entertainment industry. She was murdered. The murderer was her boyfriend or lover. Is that right? Was she a singer or a dancer or something? My sister is reviewing tapes looking for the segment. She has three years' worth of tapes. She has a session lined up with Muzette tomorrow. If there is **any** update, she will let us know!*

I am confident you are being looked after. Has Spencer said anything about danger?

When I canvassed Spencer, explaining my concerns about the Moorey and theatre friend's info, she insisted that Charley presented the excess information as peripheral. The real impetus for his murder was the porn and the cover up at the clubhouse. Still, I couldn't ignore what had been proffered by the two new strangers. Adding their information meant adding another set of circumstances to the investigation. My concentration was already thin, and injecting possible lies and further suspicion into their tale only made their impact more convoluted and unworthy of my time. Tempered by Spencer's warning, I tried to move past it, but it haunted me just the same.

Why would the universe have sent such a detour? Had I unintentionally blown this case out of proportion and a local scandal was the pinnacle of its true significance? Because I could not mesh the two scenarios, I began to worry about my formal presentation to ATF, FBI, and GBI. What if her two-bit gun runner Schmidt was the real identity of the man in this case and not the Speaker of the House? Charley had said it was the bigger of the two fish, but if Grim was involved with both …how was I ever going to make the right choice?

After a restless night, I responded to Spencer's email.

Spencer, my head is about to explode! This whole thing doesn't make sense. Yes... Jack T. Samuels died August of 2010 according to obits. But what about this other man Schmidt? I have no idea when and/or if he has died. Still trying to find out about the scar. Will check my faxes and emails for 12/12/10. Is the clue "one of the girls feels like Rox" attached to this 12/12 doc? Also, was this Henders the felon/snitch the same man that lured Charley to the road that night with this misinformation?

What the devil does a half-buried tire have to do with this? Nosebleed was my daughter Claire. When Charley gave you the two thumbs up at Wal-Mart, was that for Samuels being the judge that got Jessica pregnant? Or was that a possible Samuels's son/child that was involved with the shooting of Charley? Help!

Sidestepping the whole Samuels debacle, she responded...

Fax feels like something that might be in your documents you passed on to ATF, GBI, and FBI guys. Did you enclose a fax as evidence? Two thumbs up was just confirmation of heading in the right direction with the judge thing in general. I feel like the tire is just a landmark. Does/did this Henders snitch have a farm?

So I responded...

"Will *check on Henders owning a farm. The only fax I have is the one about MOT's death certificate*

So she replied...

Focus on that for sure!

If the fax with all the information about Robert Weatherby Chancellor's death had been authored by Gerri, how much if any of it was true? The MOT had been brutally beaten to death in the Daniel Ashley Hotel and found by hotel staff. The body had been transferred to the Pineville Hospital Morgue, to Camden McLane Funeral Home, and then on to the Platteville Funeral Home in Augusta, Georgia where it was immediately buried — all this within 72 hours. Mentally I flashed back to my files and the two-page certificate and one of my first sessions with Spencer. Charley had described the Coroner at the time, a Mr. Colquitt Cross, as a crooked drunk with no work ethic. And so the dance between what I knew and what I could prove began again. Later when I sought Google Earth for the area Henders' farm was near, I was flogged. Not more than a mile from there, four roads either connected to one another or ran adjacent to one another. It was like a spider web of coercion.

Sarah *Trussman* Road.

Robert *Wetherton* Road.

Sorenson Field Road.

Jack *Henders* Road.

Now… you might think, Jesus, TA! They are just road names. But are they?

CHAPTER FORTY-FOUR

Weeks later I learned from Clint that indeed an agent or agents from the GBI had been in the Valdosta area recently and had spoken with him, reviewing the list of interviewees and those persons of interest I'd posted in my formal report for appropriate order of priority. Encouraged by their action, I continued to work on the outline of this book and the parsing of archival information in between work and research. Spencer and I kept in contact, and peripheral information began streaming on various other players in the mix, one of which was a young man named Carlos.

Carlos was the one of the young prisoners pawned off onto Charley's constructions sites by Darwin Devonshire and Parker Jade that summer before his death. He was a young Latino. I knew very little about him other than he warranted a brief mention in Kaye's journal as the young murderer who gave her the willies and made her feel uncomfortable with the arrangement. Late one afternoon while talking with Spencer about other impressions, I accidentally dropped my notebook on the floor. When I went to pick it up, a pink piece of paper fell out. As I was reading the information on it that dated back to May of the year before on the same day I had deciphered the anagram of the MOT, it said this:

Carlos...short-term prisoner...nineteen to twenty-three years of age... he watches, he observes. His body language is discreet. He is slender, holding money that is handed to him by Gerri. He is soft spoken, smart, and began by injuring animals, then moved on to people. Domestic assault on his mother. Look to prison warden (Darwin Devonshire). He assigned him... worked for Charley...not very good at carpentry.

No sooner had my eyes finished canvassing the page than the last name of "Rodriguez" appeared. Nothing is ever an accident. Realizing that this was a prompt, I asked the natural next step:

Is this the last name of the young prison worker named Carlos whom you saw accepting money from G for watching Charley almost a year ago? The one who was placed on the construction site to spy on Charley?

Spencer stalled for a second and then said,

This is interesting. Yes... this name is tied to the young man who worked on Charley's jobsite: quiet, alert, took notes and made observations. And yes, a spy so to speak...paid informant. His father worked or died in Atlanta, owned a gas station. There is a tie to his mother when the word "murder" is mentioned. They show me he was incarcerated after Valdosta, and the two states that are mentioned are Tennessee and Oklahoma. He would be in his sixties now. Cannot say if he is still in a prison, but it feels as if he is still alive. He knows everything. He might talk. See what you can find about him.

I jotted down everything she said and then folded the pink piece of paper and slid it in next to the day's information. Another angle to pursue, but one that would take the ATF or some other agency to accommodate. There was no way as a civilian I would be made privy to that information. I had forgotten all about him, and as I began to shove the pink paper back into my notebook, I noticed another scribbling tucked in the upper fold of a corner. Apparently somewhere about the same time I got the info on Carlos, I had also written something else.

Go to Kaye's journal... go to pages 19, 26, and 42. Read them. Read them again.

And so after I hung up with Spencer, I did. Page 19 was completely dedicated to the conversations Kaye had had with Bobbie Lee Fitzpatrick, Albert Fitzpatrick's wife at the time. I knew I had read this before, months ago in fact, when the muddy rubber boots were mentioned. So why would they be sending me back there again? As usual, mine is not to quibble why; mine is just to follow orders and figure out why. Bearing that in mind, I picked up the notebook and read again for anything I had missed.

It talked about how Kaye had gone to her to ask about the alleged affair and how she begged Bobbie Lee to tell her the truth, and Bobbie Lee did. Hours later when she went back to question Albert directly, Bobbie Lee answered the door and pleaded with Kaye not to let Albert know she had been the one to tell her that there was something going on between Charley and Gerri Baldwin because Albert would get very angry. Folks said he was quick-tempered, liked to kick and hit. It made me think about my conversation with Marjorie. She told me that Roxanne's body was black and blue all over, even though they claimed it was a drowning. Spencer had said that they had tossed a coin to see who got to take her out. Strangled and beaten black and blue, literally. Coincidentally, I'd heard the MOT's body too had been badly bruised. I was beginning to sense a pattern in the signature boot kicks of our suspected assaulter.

Picking up three quarters down the page, the diatribe also mentioned another man, a Mr. Eugene Spinnaker who had supposedly talked to Charley as well and warned him to let the affair go. Even though she had never met him, Kaye eventually called him too and he told her not to worry, that it was just coffee drinking, that Gerri Baldwin was always part of the coffee-drinking crowd and usually showed up there with Parker Jade. Remember, Parker Jade worked in the Parole Department with Gerri Baldwin and was involved in placing the convicts like Carlos to work on Charley's construction site. Eager, I hopped to page 26. It spoke to the hours just before Charley had left home that night and then in the calm after he left. The widow wrote about how she had called Ashley Hill's wife to tell her that she would not be able to pick up their son Craig the following day as she had to run to Moultrie the next morning because the pants she'd bought for her son didn't fit. An entire page was dedicated to the issue of pants.

In the beginning her desperation to find long pants for Jules's brother seemed to be an obtuse obsession, but not so. The very fact that Kaye was consumed with purchasing long pants for the boy just days before Charley's murder only enhanced the importance of the observations about the weather taking such a dramatic downturn in temperature that first week in October. Her concentrated attention on the weather spoke volumes. It gave me the direct segue I needed to bridge to Spencer's annotations about the final moments of the second female victim. Spencer said she could see the last few breaths hang suspended in the air just above Roxanne's blue lips. With each nuance from Kaye's journal, the totality of what had happened continued to jell.

Moving to the next page, page number 42, Kaye wrote about speaking with Bob Callenwald about the alleged affair between Charley and Gerri. First she asked if Charley had been fired.

Callenwald emphatically responded no. Then she asked if Charley had been transferred, and he told Kaye that Charley had asked to be placed on the best qualified list, which put him up for transfer availability. That's why the Friday before he died he had gone to Moultrie to qualify. Next, Callenwald absolved himself in this conversation with Kaye, telling her he had talked to Charley either that Wednesday or that Friday just before he died. He told her he let Charley know that people were beginning to talk…that things were being said about him and the Baldwin woman in an unflattering light. And that if the shoe fit, he should not only wear it, but do something about it. He also told Kaye he had tried to spend some time in the coffee-drinking coffee crowd with them, but had seen nothing he thought uncomely in their behavior. Callenwald further denied knowing anything about the affair that allegedly had started between the two back as far as April of 1966.

When Kaye asked if the "bag" had ever shown up, the bag from the Morris Pawn Shop, Callenwald told her no, but that if it did she should notify the boy at the Morris Pawn Shop immediately. Callenwald told her there was something in that bag that belonged to him. He refused to tell her what it was and then ended their conversation. When she pressed for more information, he rather flatly referred her to Bill Hardy. This was Charley's immediate supervisor. Kaye warned Callenwald that she had already tried to talk to Hardy several times and that he too was avoiding her. Kaye threatened that if Hardy would not speak to her the following Saturday, her next visit was going to be to Senator Russell.

The journal goes on to report that when she returned the following weekend, Hardy told her he had asked permission to speak to her about Charley's case, but was told that she would have to get direct permission from the Deputy Director in Washington, D.C. before he could ever speak to her about it. Kaye wrote she was furious with his stalling and so before she agreed to leave his office, asked if he would at the least try to respond to certain things Deputy Sheriff Beau Colbert had told her attorney Gavin Eller. He hedged, but she begged, saying she just wanted to know if he could confirm as to whether or not they were true. Below you will see a partial list of the questions Kaye posed and the answers she received. The *K* stands for Kaye and the *B* for Bill Hardy.

K: Is it true they were going to marry in December?

B: That is what Mrs. Baldwin said.

K: Had he made arrangements for a divorce?

B: No. Not that we were able to find out.

K: Had he ever been out to her house?

B: No.

K: Is it true they met at Sal's apartment? If so, when Sal was always at home?

B: Sal cannot swear that they did. He leaves his house key on the air conditioner outside. He has never seen them there, though he thought so.

K: What about all those pictures she [Gerri] says she has of Charley? Were they made with our camera that Parker Jade had?

B: I don't know, but I can tell you that Parker Jade is very uneasy about this whole thing.

K: What about the box of anniversary cards they sent each other?

B: There was only one card. It was card that read "Me and my big mouth." This came about one day when they were in the restaurant drinking coffee and some other person in the crowd asked Charley how his son got to be so smart. Is his mother smart? To which Charley replied, " 'Course to hell she is smart; she married me." Mrs. Baldwin got mad and he sent her that card.

K: Where are all of the clothes she gave him?

B: There were two shirts; they were in the office in a drawer. Sal took them home with him; he figured you did not want them.

K: Why in heaven's name would Sal want them? Mrs. Baldwin told me that she wanted them back and told me again to get the .38 mm pistol for her. I told Mr. Hardy to tell her I better not hear anything else about that pistol. I asked if it had been fired.

B: There was no reason to test it.

K: Why does she always seem to be in the possession of a pistol? First the .22 and I don't know how long she had it. Does she feel insecure without a gun? She is already married to her husband. How does she explain all of Charley's things to her husband?

B: I don't know.

K: How did she remarry her husband so soon if she was so in love with mine?

B: He said he had been trying to get her to go back to him and figured there must have been another man. She said that she realized that her children were the most important things in the world.

K: Do you know she has a reputation of always being after someone's husband, then running back to her husband?

B: I know something about it.

K: Is it true he took her up in the plane in Lake City?

B: She came out to the airport. They did not go up to together. I did not even take a statement on that.

K: What about this bootlegger's wife from over around Douglas that he was supposed to be involved with?

B: That is all lies, nothing more.

K: If he did it, Bill, what happened in an hour and a half to make him go to pieces?

B: We don't know. Mrs. Baldwin said he came by after church and saw her and her husband together and probably thought they were getting back together.

I now had gone two pages beyond page 42, but could not stop as the questions were too important not to take note of and the answers even more telling.

K: Where did she go to church, Bill? It was 9:00 pm when he left home, and it started raining like mad. Who is going to stand outside and talk after church in the rain? Do you think that shook him up, but he still had sense enough to go to the office, clear out his things, get a pistol, and go out there and fake a suicide?

B: We just don't know.

K: I can tell you one thing: if he had that much sense, he had sense enough to know what a mess I would be in, that I would not have enough money to educate these children, that he had no will. You know how he felt about these children. That theory is fantastic. If he was going to do that, he would have gotten his business in order. Which shot was fired first?

B: The one under the chin.

K: Where was he when this happened?

B: By the front tire.

K: Was there any blood there?

B: No.

K: What position was he in when the other shot was fired?

B: I think standing up.

K: Why did he not drop the gun instead of having it under him, and why were there no broken bones?

B: I don't know.

K: Do you think he could have fumbled around with a gun, shooting himself twice with no prints?

B: It is possible.

K: Did you ever find out who was in the truck?

B: No.

K: Who did the car belong to that was pulled out of the ditch close to him?

B: It had no connection.

K: Did Charley ever give Mrs. Baldwin any gifts?

B: No. There were no gifts except a cigarette lighter she says he gave her.

K: Bill, when we get in the court, is there anything in the way of evidence that you are going to spring on me that I have not asked you about?

B: No. You seem to have heard what I have, and I can assure you there is no box of pictures or cards. Do you mean to tell me you are still going ahead?

K. I told Mr. Hardy that I intended to proceed, that it wasn't that I had no confidence in them, but that they had missed something somewhere and had been too wrapped up in the love affair to come up with a reason. I told him that was the only way to get these people on the stand and see who would get up and point their finger and say "I saw it and he loved her so much he could not live without her and he had to kill himself."

That is the last contact I have had with them except my phone conversations with Mr. Thornton in Atlanta.

I was becoming confused about the statements about the lighter. Here in her questions to Hardy, she asked about the disposition of the lighter with a different slant. Early on, they said Gerri had given the lighter to Charley. In this section of the journal, the shoe was on the other foot, and Kay was being told that Charley had given the lighter to Gerri. And there were various other issues mentioned before she brought up the bombshell question about the alleged pregnancy of Mrs. Baldwin.

Officers Kaye had questioned simply told her they heard the two were very much in love and that Mrs. Baldwin had made it known that she was "late." The rumor of a pregnancy was later corroborated by a conversation with retired ATTD Agent Patterson who recalled he had also heard that Baldwin had miscarried two times in fact and that one of those incidents had taken place while she was in the office of an ATTD agent.

June was beginning to wrap up certain parts of the mystery, even as it shrouded other parts. All in all, it made it more difficult to understand the images of December 2010, when Spencer said Charley was beginning to walk away from the scene... turning... smiling, and insisting closure was coming.

CHAPTER FORTY-FIVE

One year earlier in May of 2010, I'd received the following notation from Spencer.

The ostrich is tied to the farmer by the fence. The farmer is tied to the pipe smoker. The pipe smoker is tied to Roxanne. And Roxanne is tied to Grim. October 22nd. Stay focused on Roxanne. You are so close.

At the time I understood the general outline, but was unable to apply actual identities with aplomb to other information and dates in my coffers because of the confusion still surrounding my choices for the fourth in flannel. That was until the final week of June 2011 when I received a message from Spencer and it all finally began to fall into place.

They mention Wilkes. Could be a nickname. The number sequence 777 for you, Google it to find out what it means. The scarecrow goes up near this location during this time of year. Where the pool used to be could be on somebody's farm/ property now. They mention the name Henders again. The metal unicycle, a decoration in someone's yard. Have you seen this?

I began to visibly shudder in my chair. The only reference to a pool had been about where the decaying body of my first female victim was buried. If what I was reading was in direct reference to that, then Spencer had just been given the final location of her remains. Somewhere on the farm of the snitch Henders who had lured Charley to his death, at the site marked by the tire half in and half out lay all that is left of my young girl Jessica. My heart began to race. What to do now? I couldn't just send this kind of information out, and yet how was I supposed to keep it to myself?

Waiting on Clint to get me the address of the Henders residence now almost trumped the potential misidentification of the MOT, but I couldn't stop just yet. There was more to her message.

As always, direct questions are a bit tough, but when you mention the farmer…they show me the farmer who stands by the fence with the burning hot property. They show the special fence with the carving in it. It feels as though this person has recently passed. Do you know who this is? He feels familiar. He says he heard them, watched them as they moved something, the men in the field who shouldn't have been there…on or about October 12th. They were out in the field, a small group of them. It was very late, after midnight…shoving something into the water…he knew they were doing something wrong, but did nothing to stop them.

This was the piece I was missing. Even though Waverleigh had been a farmer too, Robert Coleman was the only farmer whose fence was near the burning hot property with the special fence. There was no doubt now about where that was. That property was Wild Adventures Theme Park Surrounded by the "special spiked fence." And the property in question was directly across the street from it and just on the other side of Coleman's fence! The men in the field were members of the four in flannel, and what they were doing was more than obvious. They were rolling the bloated body of Roxanne out of whatever vehicle they had transported her in into the cypress swamp that dotted the middle of the cow pasture, a pasture that sat directly adjacent to Robert Coleman's back yard and barn, the barn with the ladder leaning against it, just as Spencer had described. Spencer had done it again.

The image on Google Earth she'd sent showed exactly the same type of swampy area filled with cypress trees as the space Roxanne had described. Coleman had lied when he said he knew nothing. Had openly denied knowledge of Roxanne, of the four in flannel, and of any wrongdoing by his fellow officers. But he had lied — lied to me, lied to Jules, and to Cole, Charley's grandson who had sat in his living room and listened to his vague ambiguities and banal denials. Coleman had watched that night as the four in flannel had rolled the mangled body of my second female victim into a pasture bog. He'd held his tongue listening as the four in flannel stood back, jeering at the sinking body as the dark waters of the marsh swallowed her whole. It made me sick. The hallowed ground that would forever hold her remains sat not more than a thousand yards from Robert Coleman's back door, and he had never said a word.

My skin rolled with disgust as I remembered his hug thanking me for trying to do the right thing by Jules and her deceased father. Immediately I was pulled back to several interviews inside his home. I can't imagine what he was thinking as I asked those questions. How smug and self-righteous of him to sit there beneath a tapestry flag, with Jules and her son in the room and not share with us so much as a misgiving about what might have happened. I had even asked about the young blonde debutante that was rumored to have slept with most of the VPD and Sheriff's Department. Asked about her by her many names: Roxy, Rox, Roxanne, Blythe, and — nothing! I even described her in both flattering and unflattering terms, and still he talked about everything but her...and in the end nothing at all about any of the victims. Not a word about what he had seen or heard about Charley's murder. Not a word about a young prostitute being buried under a pool. Not a word about the young girl who'd been dumped in the moonlight three nights after Charley's assassination.

It made me physically ill. How could he have hugged Jules and told her how much she resembled her mamma and not spontaneously combust right there on the back porch steps? Jules was Charley's daughter and he had lied right to her face. I recalled meeting his daughter. It was during that last interview. His generous smile had made me feel so bad about my suspicions and my consistent pressures to get the truth. I looked at her and his flags upon the wall and thought "He's somebody's father, grandfather...how can you think such things of him?" And then I would think of another man, Gavin Eller, who was somebody's father and grandfather too and recanted my compassion. Now in the aftermath of recent epiphanies, I could have cared less what shame was brought to his family. After all, the sin of omission was his, not mine. Just the same I felt badly for his daughter, but I could not use that as default to keep his part in this silent.

By the time my pulse slowed and my heart regained its rhythm, I had already pulled up his obit to confirm something, and again it made me want to vomit. Nothing was presented but hyperbolic accolades for his many years of public service and dedicated valor — nothing less than what I expected, but little of which he deserved. How many more involved in this conspiracy had gone to their graves with such unwarranted honors? My blood ran cold with antipathy, and I realized I could not write this book fast enough to uncover all those who parlayed crimes within the shade of their public service. I also realized legal prudence would force me to change some of the names, and you the reader would never know the true identity of Mr. Coleman, but I could not allow that to poison my desire to publish. After all, I had a duty to Charley, Jessica, Roxanne, and the MOT to tell the truth. Even if Coleman had never laid a hand on any of them directly, he had never used a hand directly to help them either.

Trolling my way back through Spencer's messages, I tried to concentrate on the second part of the text. When you broke it down, it made perfect sense. The OSTRICH — *Officers Sex Tapes are in Charley's House* — was also tied to Coleman somehow. Because Coleman had been VPD with Hank Sloan, Albert (Al) Fitzpatrick, and PJ Church at the time of Charley's murder, segue was easy to discern. It gave me the willies to think about how twisted everything appeared. While still trying to digest the Henders farm epiphany and Coleman's latent confession, Clint's call came through and interrupted my thoughts.

"Hey, baby girl, I've got some really big news for you," he sighed. I took his breathy punctuation as unbridled fatigue and not disappointment.

"Great!" I blurted, bypassing his prompt, "Because I've got some freaking incredible news for you too," I panted, anxious to share what I had just divined.

"I got a call a few minutes ago about Marjorie Church."

"And?" I baited, eager for him to share his news, so that I could share my news about Jessica's remains and Coleman's involvement. "Does she want to talk again?" I asked and immediately began to scan the calendar for my next open weekend. "I can't get away for at least three weeks, but I might be able to get down there in..." I flipped the page of my calendar to the next month and saw an opening. "Or, I could just call her... Wait! Do you know anybody that can get one of those ground sensors? Or ground sonograms I think they call them?" I asked as I ran my finger through dates marked in red. "Shit. Looks like I'm booked through...Ok, here's a date. First chance is Monday, the week of..." and he flatly cut me off.

"She died this past Saturday morning."

The air in the room suddenly felt too dense to breathe. "What did you say?" I gasped.

"Marjorie died this past Saturday morning."

My heart plummeted into the pit of my stomach, and the calendar slid to the floor at my feet. The information about Coleman and Henders now took a definite back seat. "Oh my God, no! Not now...not now! Shit! She can't!" I yelled into the phone. "Not now when we're so close, Clint."

"I know. I know. They said she started having trouble breathing Thursday night, so they took her on to the hospital and...I don't know what actually happened, but they said she passed this past Saturday morning."

Even though I hadn't verbalized it, the first wave of compassion went out to Marjorie and her family for their collective loss. Simultaneously, however, her passing also generated another tsunami that was far less compassionate and barreled its way straight towards my gut. A wave that roared "It will never matter about Coleman or Henders now. What if the agents who had visited

Clint the beginning of that week had not gotten to her before she died?" Suddenly Clint's pronouncement sounded more about the death of my case than about the spitfire woman in the scooter I'd befriended. I began to panic.

"Noooo...not now, dammit!" I muttered, all the while trying to recall everything Clint had told me about the visitation the week before. "Do you know if the agents got to her before Thursday then?" I asked, trying not to sound incredibly disrespectful.

"Well, let me see. The day they saw me...that was last Monday, right? They interviewed me, then asked me to look over a list of interviewees inside a black binder and asked if the priority of the listing was correct." Clint's mention of a black binder meant they were actually using my presentation package as guide. "You had Marjorie listed as one of the ones at the top along with Waverleigh, Cummings, Eller, and Fitzpatrick, and when they were getting ready to leave, the agent asked how far it was to Marjorie's nursing home, and so I gave them directions."

"So it's possible they might have still made it out to her before Thursday, right?"

"Yes, it's possible. I saw them on Monday morning, so they could have gone out there after lunch, but I don't know. They didn't tell me if they weren't leaving right then or if they were going to wait till the following morning. Either way, they still would have easily gotten to her before Thursday's troubles if they followed your list, unless..." and he let the doubt hang in the air between us.

When I didn't respond right away, he added, "I'm sorry, kiddo. I just don't know what to tell you. They didn't confide in me."

"I know, I know. Of course they wouldn't have. Why would they?" I blathered, and the epiphanies of Coleman and Henders began to fade in importance. "Of course they wouldn't have told you what they were going to do next." I thought about the old adage "loose lips sink ships." They might have asked for directions, but they would not have advertised their next move. That was for rookies like me who baited through blogs and couldn't keep my yap shut.

"You ok? I'm sure they would have stuck to the list, just the way you had it ordered."

I bypassed his compassion and tried to work through what he was telling me. "But what if they didn't? What if they went back to a hotel to go over your notes and got sidetracked with something or someone else? What if they didn't make that drive out there on Monday... or Tuesday or even Wednesday, Clint? What if they decided her interview could wait till the weekend? Or that the nursing home was too far out of town for their immediate schedules or they should call on folks in geographical order instead?" Doubt gripped my sanity in an alligator death roll and refused to allow me to come up for air.

"I just don't know..." he kept repeating to my endless queries. I knew he was trying to be helpful, but his helplessness wasn't helping at all; it only made me more nauseous.

"What if they decided not to even bother, Clint? Or even worse, she gave them that Rain Man act and they wrote her off as senile?" I heard myself say. And then my heart did a flip flop and sank again to the bottom of my gut. "Dammit! They just had to have gotten to see her!" I whispered. "She was my brass ring." Marjorie had known everything, but you had to know how to work her. She wouldn't have just let things fly if she thought you were clueless or unworthy. You had to bait her every inch of the way and then even if she would spit out a morsel, she would still make you pimp for the rest of it. She liked to string you along, see what you knew and what you didn't. Then she would tell you something and repeat it over and over like an idiot savant until you would get so frustrated with her you'd want to scream. And just when you would think she was about to drop the mother lode, she would run off in another direction. Trying to redirect her back to topic was like trying to redirect the freaking Colorado River. It was as if she was testing you. When your patience ran thin and you were ready to quit, she would suddenly tell you every name, date, and location you needed easy as pie.

Her death was almost impossible for me to digest. Yes, I knew she was old. Yes, I knew her health had been greatly compromised and she was tired of hurting, but she was a fighter, a pistol full of piss and vinegar. I had counted on that to keep her alive long enough to give her testimony to those same men who had sat around the table and listened to me not more than a month earlier. While Eller had been the first major coup in solving Charley's murder, Marjorie had been the one in Jessica's and Roxanne's. She not only confirmed what I'd heard about the two girls: she even gave physical descriptions of them. She had been the one who told me all about the parties at the American Legion Club, about the blonde bombshell Roxanne, the light brown-haired Jessica, and the stream of uniformed men that enjoyed both their company and their sexual talents. She had been the one to tell me about the bloody shovel and the compass that was found, tying the four in flannel to a specific community pool where the remains of the first female victim (Jessica) were rumored to be buried.

Marjorie had been such a wonderful source of information and such a colorful character; I'd almost wished I'd been her contemporary back then. She knew her husband drank excessively and cheated indiscriminately, but she said she didn't care. He just better never drag whoever or whatever it was home or flaunt it out in public. As long as she didn't have to hear about it, she would keep her yap shut, adding the caveat that didn't mean she couldn't and wouldn't do the same. And she did, though she refused at the time to out the name of her favorite indiscretion. But since I wasn't a priest, I could have cared less thinking it would have had nothing to do with Charley...but I was wrong.

Marjorie was married to PJ Church who was with the VPD, and he used to get together with others in the brotherhood on a regular basis. They would party and talk all night long, oblivious to the fact that she could hear every word. "That was their mistake," she said and tried to warn me to be careful. "Those that had done the deeds have gotten away with murder — not once but several times. They would not think twice about killing one more to keep them safe from discovery."

She reminded me that while Albert Fitzpatrick had been a good friend of her husband's, she knew he was not a good man and had done horrible things. She attached his name to Roxanne, talked about her bruised and strangled body. She warned there were others still out there that knew the truth about how Roxanne died, knew that the drowning was a farce. She said Albert knew everything, but that he'd most likely never confess to knowing anything. Then she went off on a diatribe about how former law enforcement officers never bothered to ask her anything all those years ago and how mad that had made her. When I asked her why, her guttural response shocked me. Sitting in her scooter, the crumpled figure of a gypsy shod in slippers, toyed with the bangles on her wrist, cocked her head, and slurred back, "Why?"

I nodded. "Yes…why?"

"No point asking questions when they already knew why. They was the ones that done it. By the time anybody got around to missing them two whores, they'd already been disposed of. Ya' understand me?"

I nodded again but held my tongue.

"They'd already disposed of their own garbage, wiped everything clean."

When I pressed her if that was why I couldn't find an obituary for either of the girls or even an article about them having gone missing or drowning as they said Roxanne had, she grunted and rolled her eyes.

"You ain't never gonna find out anything about those girls. There won't be no paper trail for you to find, little miss. The two of them was whores. They did stuff they shouldn't oughta and they did it with every uniform in town. They didn't care, ya see? And in the end, that's what done them in," she exhaled. Her chest rose and fell with equal composure. But her eyes were clear but blank as though the cataract of culpability had finally fallen from her eyes.

"They thought I never knew what happened, but I did." She sighed and I waited for her to catch her breath before she stared out the window and began again.

"The uniforms? They were gonna protect themselves no matter what, 'cause they were all involved in it up to their necks! The whole lot of them. Wasn't anybody gonna give a shit what happened to those two hookers, so they took 'em out. Nobody cared what happened to them. I know I didn't." She drooled from one side of her mouth and went back to fiddling with her bangles.

"But Marjorie..." I began.

She rolled her eyes. "There were two kinds of folk in this town back then. Them that knew and them that I would never know. You see, the folks that knew about them two already knew what happened to 'em and pretty much knew who done it. But they didn't care. And the folks that didn't know they existed? Well... they didn't know they died either. It wasn't part of their world anyhow, so what would they care?"

I remembered how upset I was at her calloused nature and could not fathom her lack of empathy. "But they were just kids... so young."

"They were whores!" she blasted. "Kids don't do the things they did."

"But Marjorie, I have girls that age. Surely somebody went looking for them?"

"Didn't matter. They didn't find out anything, and you... you ain't never gonna find nothing 'bout those two either. The brotherhood...they covered their tracks pretty good when they was done with them," she volunteered.

I remembered everything she said that day and that was just one of the conversations the GBI and ATF would never get to hear from her own lips. Marjorie had been so anxious to finally set the record straight. By the same token, she hadn't been quite as anxious to sell herself down the river to do it. She was afraid of what Albert might say, what he might do. The timing of this couldn't have been worse, and I wondered if the GBI had gotten to her, just exactly how much they had been able to get. Without her alive, how was I ever going to be able to validate our conversations or get authorities to look further for the two young females' remains?

Clint had graciously allowed me to process the information and then pulled me back from my reveries with another apology. "I'm sorry. I wish I could tell you GBI made it out there, but I'm not even certain I was allowed to tell you they made it out to see me."

"Is there any other way I can check on that? Ask family members... check with the nursing home staff?"

"Let me see what I can find out for you. Sorry. I just thought you should know." And with that another phone rang unremittingly in the background and he was forced to excuse himself to answer it.

I hit the *END* button on my cell and sighed. "Shit! Now what?" I muttered as the air chilled around me. "Charley? Are you there?" I asked, but the air remained stagnant. "How can I prove anything if everyone keeps dying on me before they can give anyone a freaking statement?" It didn't seem fair, mostly for Marjorie. Finally she could have had her say and cleared her conscience, but now she took whatever she had known with her to a place only Spencer could access.

I had Jules as backup, but unfortunately Jules had only been with me the day of the second interview, and she had never been privy to any of the additional conversations Marjorie and I had shared via cell since Richard Chapman had first put me in touch with her. With Marjorie gone as my ace in the hole, how was I going to be able to prove that the four in flannel had murdered Roxanne and

Jessica? Half of the people involved were dead, and who among the living was going to corroborate her testimony?

Marjorie's late husband P. J. had worked for the VPD at the time of Charley's death and had been buddies with Fitzpatrick. Marjorie told me they drank together and talked about their loose women when they did. With P. J.'s death, Marjorie now had the courage to sing like a canary and she did. She warned me to be careful, said Fitzpatrick was a loose cannon and her allegiance to him had vanished with the death of her husband. I promised I would keep Clint informed of all my actions just in case. Marjorie told me she prayed someone would call them out before her death, but without knowing if the GBI had made it to her, it was likely the remaining four in flannel could still stay in the shadows and live out their lives in a lie.

I said a small prayer for Marjorie's soul, and the air shifted around me. I knew it was nothing more than a slight breeze, but I thanked her just the same and then reached out for the comfort of my friend.

"Charley? Now what?" I begged. "What do I do? Where do I go from here?" I pleaded, knowing full well he could hear me, but had no immediate conduit for instructions. It seemed every time I got five steps forward, the cosmos went out of its way to drag me back another thousand. I was growing weary of the dance. Staring at the silent phone and the piles of papers on my desk, I was numb with devastation. The breakthrough with Spencer's previous clue had made me all but giddy until the news about Marjorie. Suddenly it didn't seem to matter. All that work I'd done on the formal presentation? Worthless. All the research and timeline work to support Marjorie's statements? Pointless. Without her validation, the GBI would be stalled in their tracks and the ATF, if they ever even bothered to join in the fray, would most probably see any agency's resources invested in this as a waste.

One week ago I had been given a glimmer of hope and quantifiable endorsement for my investigative efforts. Clint had been contacted by at least one Georgia Bureau of Investigation agent and Marjorie had still been alive and able to talk. Now, seven lousy days later,

Clint was contrite and the stakes had never seemed higher. It was bad enough when I had had to confess that my alleged shooter Hank Sloan was already dead, thereby taking ATF's dog out of the fight. But now I was going to have to inform them that the only major witness willing to talk was also deceased. Knowing now they could neither confirm nor deny the information Marjorie had granted me in either phone calls or personal interview would leave me dead in the water. Disheartened, I sent S a message and waited for her reply.

Why did this keep happening? Everyone involved with this case either died or lied his or her way into eternity. There was no way GBI, ATF, or anybody was going to fork over resources of time, energies, and money to investigate if all I could proffer was hearsay and innuendo. Confident Charley would not have let me down, I filled my head with fantastic scenarios where agents flooded the nursing home and made it to Marjorie just minutes before she was wheeled away on a gurney. Or that they had spent hours over the two or three days before that, gathering even more than she had shared with me, lying to myself that soon my fears would be calmed. Each scenario crafted was more theatrical than the next, but no matter what I envisioned, every one of them felt fleeting and improbable.

Two hours later, Spencer saved me from myself and wrote back that she was busy with company but would get back in touch as soon as she could.

The rest of that Sunday I walked under a black cloud, trying to concentrate on other information as a way of staying positive.

CHAPTER FORTY-SIX

Spencer called back late that night and extended her condolences about the loss of Marjorie, though there had really been no reason to do so. She said not to worry and that she would contact me if anything else came through as to whether the GBI had made a connection or not. I knew in my heart that if there had been anything presented to give me hope she would have told me, so it was a moot point to bother her further. Tired, but still emotionally wound, I decided to stay up for a while.

Once again, Kaye's journal came to the rescue with plenty of distractions. After fumbling through a few pages, I detoured to the day of the murder and read and re-read her notes about the last few hours both before and after Charley's death. On page 49, she recalled that a man by the name of Spanks Mavry had come to her house that night shortly after Sal and Claude Kirby had broken the news of Charley's death to her. In her journal she wrote that though she remembered Spanks being there, she could not recall ever seeing his wife (Eve) and that seemed odd to her.

For me, the mention of Spanks Mavry's appearance was very important for several reasons. Charley had shown Spencer the information about the railroad runs with illegal moonshine, and Mavry had been the Trainmaster of the railroad segments in question. Charley and Spanks were acquainted, but not close, at least not so close that he would have been the obvious choice for folks to call for comfort's sake to come to Charley's house that night. Nor was the relationship between Eve and Kaye so strong that she would have been the obvious choice either. And the fact that Kaye does not recall ever seeing her adds credence to the fraternity conspiracy issue. Otherwise, why would Spanks have just shown up out of the blue at 3:00 in the morning to assist Sal Wheaton and Claude Kirby? Mavry's sudden appearance on the stage without precursor made it easy to perceive his role as something more significant.

Had he been peripherally involved in the murder, or was he part of the damage control/cleanup crew? Whatever, his position there that night without wife in tow and un-requested by Kaye was indeed a red flag. Likely he was called to either protect his own ass or the others by observing and occupying the widow while they searched the house for Charley's guns and presumably the tapes as well. Convinced, I sent Spencer a message to explain my thoughts.

The next morning Spencer called and told me that she read his name in regards to that night. She explained they often allow her to feel what they felt, and in this case Spanks was apparently on the verge of coming completely unglued. He was petrified he would somehow be connected to the murder of Charley through his associations with Damon and Wahlberg and the railway hooch. He was shaking, palms sweaty, panicky, heart palpitating. Spencer said they made her feel nauseous. The two who had skimmed profits from the illegal railway deal as payment for protection were not foreign to Mr. Mavry, and Mavry was fearful of discovery. Perhaps Mavry had been on the take as well and had blood on his hands too.

Sunday night's disappointments over the loss of a major witness eventually rolled out of bed and into Monday morning's chaos without leaving me an inch of sleep to buffer. Just shy of 9:30 am, my phone rang and it was Clint calling to see if I had heard anything back from Spencer about Marjorie. I told him Spencer was busy with family, but had promised to connect later. Before I could ask anything else, he abruptly changed the timbre of his voice and promised he would call me right back with the information I had requested. Dumbfounded, I asked what he was talking about. I hadn't asked for anything yet.

"Clint? You ok?" I asked.

He cordially thanked me for my time, calling me by a different name as if I was a complete stranger, and then the phone went dead. Confused, I sat at my desk and wondered what the devil had just happened.

"Has everybody gone off the deep end?" I mused and returned to my work. Forty-five minutes later he called me back to apologize and explain.

"I hated to hang up like that, but somebody walked into my office and I couldn't talk anymore."

"That's ok. I totally understand," I replied and granted him forgiveness, though it was completely unnecessary. "You were working. No biggie," I proclaimed. He had no obligation to break up his work day to babysit me or my emotions after Sunday's disappointments.

"No... You don't understand. I said *somebody* walked into my office while I was on the phone with you."

"Yeah... I got that!" I chuckled. Shit! First everybody goes wacky; then they go deaf. What the crap was going on? "I said it was fine. Really, I don't expect you to..." and he cut me off again.

"Don't you want to know who that *somebody* was that walked in?" he pressed.

"Oh... charades, I get it. Sure. Who walked in and made it necessary to talk all official sounding and then rudely cut me off like I was some kind of two-bit crack whore?" I playfully asked.

His breath got all heavy and I thought he was just playing along with my ghetto talk when he flatly whispered "Damon Cummings."

The color drained from my cheeks so fast it made me dizzy and I had to lean back in my chair so I could catch my breath and salvage my equilibrium.

"The Grim Reaper?"

"That's right. The devil himself walked right in while I was on the phone with you. I thought I was gonna have a heart attack."

"You?" My knees were banging the side of my desk. "Shit! I could be having one now!" I confessed, and my heart continued to lurch inside my chest. "Damon Cummings...Wow!" I muttered.

"Yep. He was acting real strange, too. Said he was just in the neighborhood, so he thought he'd stop and ask me a question about a program at my church."

"Your church?"

"Uh-hum."

"But I thought you said you hadn't seen him there in over eight months."

"That's right. Folks tire of him pretty quick and they pretty much ran him off."

"Hmmm. Said he was just in the neighborhood, eh?" I chuckled.

I knew where Cummings lived. I also knew where the Courthouse had been moved to. I also knew there was no neighborhood that big in the state that could accommodate both. The absurdity of his statement reminded me of a scene from the movie *Arthur*, the scene where Liza Minnelli, a/k/a character Linda Morollo, shows up at Arthur's engagement party and tells him that she was "just in the neighborhood and decided to pop in." Of course two sentences later she had to explain that it took her three bus transfers and a $20.00 cab ride to get there. But that wasn't the point of her character's explanation and neither was it Damon's. The trip had been early, direct, and intentional. But why?

"So what did he really want?" I asked.

"Well... at first he started asking me about some program at my church, which didn't make sense to me because like you said...I hadn't seen him there for over eight months. But I didn't know what to say, so I answered his question and gave him somebody else to call for info."

"And?"

"He just said ok and continued to hang out around my desk. I didn't know what else he wanted, so I asked him if there was something else I could do for him.

"And..." I pushed again, becoming a victim of my own suspense.

"Suddenly he starts asking me if I ever talked to some blonde lady that was down there a year ago asking questions about some old case from the 60's."

"No! What did you say?"

"Well, at first I didn't know what to say, so I asked him what case. And then he said some old revenuer, a guy named Covington. Had I ever talked to you, I mean the blonde lady about that?"

"And," I hammered for a third time, "then what?"

"I asked if you were good-looking," and I could hear the grin in his smile.

"What the...? Why did you do that?" I giggled.

"Well... I was stalling, trying to think of what else to say. Anyway, he said, 'Yeah, she was good-looking.' So I told him...I think I'd remember if some good-looking blonde had talked to me or not."

At that point I wanted to reach through the phone and given him a wedgie, but he was having so much fun with it I let him be. "Ok, ok. Cute. Go on."

"Well, he just kept plugging me with questions. Had I talked to you? When was the last time I heard from you, blah...blah...blah. So I told him I had talked to you when you'd come down that day and eaten breakfast with Winston at Denny's."

"Clint..."

He wanted to know what I told you, so I said, 'Hey. I was just twenty-two or twenty-three when that happened, and all I did was pick the body up from the middle of the road and put it on a gurney, then transport it to the hospital morgue. What else could I tell you about other than that? This thing didn't involve me."

"So what did he say? What did he say?" I badgered, like a school girl in the bathroom waiting for information about an intended crush.

"He just thought it was funny I hadn't heard from you in a year. Said he'd been hearing things lately and thought I might know something more than what I was sharing. He said he hadn't heard from you since you were down there, so I asked if you were supposed to have called him back or something. He said no, that he had refused to talk any more about it. So I laughed and asked then why he would be upset you hadn't contacted him back if he wasn't gonna talk anyway."

"And how did he respond?" I blathered.

"He just shrugged his shoulders. Then he started telling me about his sister in Tallahassee and how she has Alzheimer's and is filthy rich. Said he was gonna inherit a million dollars and shit."

"Then what?" I asked, making a mental note to ask S if this was the woman who would be sending a letter from Tallahassee she kept seeing coming to me from an unknown woman.

"Well, he just sorta wandered around my office touching stuff. When I asked him if he needed anything else, he just walked out."

"Whoa. That is weird. Talk about synchronicity! I can't believe he walked right in while I was on the phone with you."

"Yeah, me neither," he said.

I was about to ask him something else when my cell alerted me to an incoming call. It was Spencer. "Clint? Now it's my turn to cut you off. I'll call back later. It's Spencer."

I clicked in on the other call and let Spencer know everything that Clint had just told me. We both let the information sink in.

"Do you think the GBI has been to see Grim?" I asked.

"I can't say for sure, but it would fit with the scenario," she responded.

We talked about Marjorie's death and how disappointed I was that she had passed before we could have gotten more information. Without compromising things, I could not just pick up a phone and start asking nursing home employees questions without raising their eyebrows as well. We chatted about other clues, and then she promised to keep in touch if anything new came through.

As fate would have it, I received another call the following Monday from Clint about another early morning visitor to the Courthouse office: Albert Fitzpatrick. This time he was audibly shaken. "What's going on, baby girl?" he asked. "First Cummings shows up here last Monday asking questions about you, then this morning Fitzpatrick shows up asking questions about you and about Cummings."

"About Cummings? Why would he ask questions about Cummings?" I wondered out loud.

"I don't think they see each other much, but he wanted to know when was the last time I saw Cummings, so I told him."

"What did you say? What did you say?" I repeated like an excited four-year-old.

"He wanted to know what Cummings wanted. I told him and then he did the same thing Cummings had done. He wandered around my office and picked up things and then as an afterthought asked me about you."

"Why? I never got to meet him. I tried the last time I was down, remember? They said he hung out at that seafood shop out by Castlepark Shopping Center or thereabouts, the one where they sold fresh fish and scallops. But he had already left by the time Jules and I found it. So what did he want to know about me?" I asked, now more curious than I had been about Cummings.

"He wanted to know if I had ever talked to you. Said that you were down there a year ago asking about some old suicide case. He couldn't remember whose, just that you had talked to some folks including Cummings and he wanted to know what I knew about you and why you were digging around about it. I told him the same thing I told Cummings, and then he said he had been hearing things too. People were asking questions, and he was curious about who I was and what I was interested in that old case for."

"So he just turned up out of the blue too?" I asked.

"Not quite out of the blue. He's a private detective now, and sometimes he comes to the Courthouse to get updated information of folks he is serving. But I don't think that was what he was fishing for today. He used that as his excuse, but I'm pretty sure he was lying. It was clear what information he really wanted and that was information about you."

"Shit." My heart pounded. First Cummings, now Fitzpatrick were getting nervous and asking questions. My pulse raced. These two were the last alive of those I believed to have been part of the four in flannel. If they were following the blog, they knew I knew murder was definitely part of their repertoire.

"What should I do?" I asked, knowing Clint would have no more idea what to do next than I did.

"I don't know. But you sure have folks getting nervous down here, including me. These men aren't right, girl. No telling what they might do. Albert's always been a violent kind of guy, and Cummings is just as unpredictable."

"Winston Wahlberg probably told them about our conversations that morning at the Denny's when I asked him about Roxanne and figured you and I might still be in contact."

"Could be...could be. They just seem real convinced that I know more than I'm telling them. And I do, but I'm not going to share anything you've told me with them. Don't worry about me. Just *you* be careful. Ok?"

I ignored his concerns about my safety and apologized for putting him in such an awkward spot. Then I told him he was the only pair of eyes and ears I had down there that Spencer had given total clearance to, and I felt I could trust him, even with my life. He warned me again about Fitzpatrick being a private detective. We talked for a few more minutes about the inconsistencies and similarities of the conversations he'd had with the last two of the four in flannel who had come to see him one after the other. When I felt I'd garnered all the information I needed, I rang off. My next call was to Spencer to check on my safety. Then I followed that with an email to SAC Agent Garvey with the ATF to let him know about the recent events and my personal concerns. His response was polite but generic, and it left me feeling odd.

Was I making too much of the visits? Was I really in any danger? At this point I had no idea if the GBI had actually gotten to Marjorie before she died, but it was becoming more and more clear they had gotten to both Cummings and Fitzpatrick, and their nervousness made me nervous.

By the time I got home that night, I was emotionally exhausted, so I gave Don the car to go pick up some groceries while I took a hot shower and tried to release the worries of the day. Mission accomplished, I crawled from the shower feeling like a new woman, toweled myself dry, and then traveled into the adjoining bedroom to get clean underwear. The clock on my nightstand read 8:24 pm. Since Don had gone to the Kroger in Covington (ironic, huh?), I figured I had a good hour before he would be home. Underwear secured, I flipped my damp hair up inside a towel, slathered on some lotion, and decided to bypass casual evening clothes and got straight into my pajamas. I knew Don wouldn't mind, so I decided to go for the whole nine yards and poured myself a glass of wine to sip on as I checked my emails.

While the laptop was booting up, I crossed back into the bathroom and drug a comb through my hair. The dogs began to bark. Convinced Don had somehow made the journey in record time, I rushed to the windows of my office to motion I would grab some slippers and be right out to help unload groceries. But Don was not the person who stood outside my door. This person I did not recognize. I shied from the windows and retreated back into my office where I could grab a housecoat and get a closer look without being discovered.

The car in the drive was a two-door white sedan with teardrop headlights, and the person at the door was a white woman, young, in her mid- to late thirties, brown hair, dressed in blue jeans and a light colored T-shirt. She knocked on the door several times. The banging sent the dogs into a frenzy of chaotic barking. Inappropriately dressed to receive company, I made no motion to go to the door, but watched from my office vantage point. She stood at the side door for more minutes than I would have, considering the unrelenting barking of the dogs and the fact that there had been no car left in the drive. In fact, the more I thought about it, her appearance and reluctance to leave made no sense. I pulled a knot into the ties of my housecoat and then went to the front porch to observe her actions further. She went back to her car, used her cell phone, and then amazingly got back out and re-approached the door. This time I answered from another location, a deck at the front of the house. I asked her what she wanted.

She explained she was trying to find the house of a friend on a Blue Heron Way, but that she was lost and her friend would not answer her phone. I told her a road with a similar name was several streets up, left from the bridge and bid her a good evening. As I walked back into the house, she made another phone call, then pulled out of the drive slowly, made a notation on a sheet of paper, and then eased her way slowly up the street and turned.

One would not think it so odd if it hadn't been for the fact that mine was the only driveway out of the three homes on this short street that did not have a car in the drive, had dogs barking incessantly at the intrusion, and no front room lights on. And the driver, having received instructions, turned her car in the opposite direction of where I had instructed her. Nervous, I locked the front door and ran to my office and jotted down everything I could remember about her appearance, the car, and the conversation. Once completed, I took a long pull on my glass of wine and proceeded to worry about who she really might have been and who had really sent her.

CHAPTER FORTY-SEVEN

With holiday festivities over and the close of the second week of the month in sight, things remained hectic but doable. Work schedules had stabilized thanks to summer camp daytime hours, so my evenings were free, and Don and I got to play. By the third Monday in July, I was golden brown and happy to have made the move. Early that evening when I got home, I was pleasantly surprised to find that Don had already made a picnic dinner and gotten the boat ready for a romantic evening cruise, complete with chilled wine, cheese, and crackers.

With several hours of sunlight still left, I enthusiastically jumped into a swimsuit and ran down to the dock to meet him. As the boat eased out of the slip, tensions began to slowly ease out of my shoulders, and I turned my face into the sun and relished the evening breeze upon my cheeks. Ten minutes and half a glass of White Zinfandel later, we coasted into our favorite swimming spot, put out the anchor, and then tossed out a few floaters for us to lounge on while we caught up on the day's events.

This was the first summer since being a child on a family vacation at Clear Lake, Iowa that I recall truly enjoying the break from cooler weather. I decided that for a couple of poor folk we were living mighty high. Grateful to God, I whispered a small prayer of thanks as I lowered myself into the warm water and allowed myself to unwind. No sooner than Don had handed me my glass than my phone back on board began its familiar ring. Since Piper had recently suffered some minor seizures, I hedged my bets against a crisis and swam quickly back to the boat to check for medical emergencies. With towel in hand, I was happy to see the familiar number and so relaxed again and took the call. It was Spencer. Knowing how rarely she reached out without prompt, I knew the call would be important.

"Yesterday I saw a feather," she began. "This morning Charley showed up and tried to channel through me."

"He what?" I blurted.

"He tried to take over my body to channel. He got halfway through and I kinda freaked, so he stopped. I never had anyone try to channel through me before. A lot of psychics channel, but I've never done it."

It was good to know that after all this time Spencer could still be spooked. Feathers were big harbingers of great messages or events, so I thought that was the end of her tale, but not so.

"He left and I felt bad, but...then they showed me Grim moving money around. Not like transferring $100.00 from savings to checking, but like transferring major money from one account to another. Big money! Shuffling it around like he was trying to hide it. Not certain what this has to do with things."

"I do. He's getting nervous!" I answered and buffed my hair to keep it from dripping into my earpiece. "I'd be buying stock in Depends if I were him because eventually this thing is gonna bust wide open and he'll be shitting in his pants by the truckloads!" I giggled. "What else ya got for me?"

A few minutes into the conversation, my hair began to drip again, so I put her voice on speaker and continued to try and towel it dry. While she was catching me up on kids and whatnot, I poured some more wine.

"So Charley did a hit and run, eh?" I chuckled to fill the space and grabbed a pen from the dashboard of the boat along with some random papers from my purse, just in case. Her just in case showed up about two seconds later when the conversation turned from pleasantries to poltergeists. I signaled Don I'd be a minute or two and began to take notes.

"Ok, down to business." I put down the glass and sat poised for the onslaught.

"Do you understand the boy of the farmer? Do you understand the boy, the staged witness...the farmer there too. Do you understand the boy, grown, his wife now worried; she whispers in his ear 'Tell the truth... tell the truth. Your father is dying. Tell it now before he dies with a lie on his lips...tell the truth.'"

I knew there had been two farmers: Robert Coleman the recently deceased and Bob Waverleigh. Yes, I knew exactly who she was talking about: Stevie Waverleigh, Bob Waverleigh's son, the same Bob Waverleigh who had called Charley's house that fateful afternoon and spoken with Kaye, the same Bob Waverleigh who was shown tied with G, the same man with the cheese cutter who had lacerated Charley's arms.

"Yes...I know who this is."

"They are showing me...The farmer...his wife is blind...not literally, but blind to all this. The first wife knows. She knew. The second one, she is scared. She knows something is wrong, but does not know for certain what. The son knows, though. He saw something the day it happened. Something he saw in a silver lunch box, the old-fashioned kind that is shaped like an old barn. It is silver, a silver-gray. The boy opened it. He saw it. It did not make sense, but his father kept that lunch box with him all day long. He moved it with him from room to room. When he walked out of the room, the boy looked inside. What was in it made no sense. He could not ask his father why he had it. He was not supposed to see it; he was not supposed to know.

I drank half the glass in one gulp and motioned for my husband to come into the boat as it felt like more was to come.

"They show me," she continued, *"The wife is in his head, like the voice he hears inside his head. She whispers for him to tell the truth."*

"What was in the lunch box?" I hear myself say in between her thoughts.

"They are not showing it to me, but it is odd whatever it is. They show me...the boy does not understand why his father would have such a thing. There is someone in the room with the boy. He is now a man in his sixties. There are blinking lights; the lights are going on and off."

"An interrogation?" I blurted.

"No, not literally. But this is the way they show me it is like in an interrogation. They show they are in a room and they are asking him questions about what he knows about the murder, what he knows about his father."

I recorded the information as fast as I could. Now on board, Don leaned over my shoulder to read and dripped water onto the page. The ink began to blur and I grimaced. Spencer continued and I accidentally knocked over my glass as I reached for another piece of paper to continue. Contrite, Don tossed his towel to the floor and retrieved my goblet.

Spencer continued. "He is in a room. Someone keeps asking him questions, pushing him for answers. They want to know more about that night. The boy, now man, hears his wife's voice in his head telling him to let it go. His father is so old, he is dying. What can it hurt now if he tells the truth? They cannot harm him. He will not go to jail; he is too old and too sick...tell the truth... tell the truth!"

My husband, now dry, began to read the paper from the floor and then watched my expressions as Spencer continued to deliver more information.

"An arrest will be made on July 21st... July 21st... look for the arrest..."

"What?" I stammered. Alarmed, Don looked up from the first page to see what I was writing. I wrote the word and then underscored it three times. "An arrest? In this case? But Spencer, this *is* July. This is the...what the hell date is it today? What? Like the 18th already?" I looked at Don and he confirmed.

"That would make it someday this week, Spencer. Shit! That would be Wednesday!" I calculated and my heart beat even harder. "How can that be? Clint said he had just been contacted by the GBI, what, three or four weeks ago?" My heart was lodged somewhere in the middle of my throat and my hands were visibly shaking. Don, hearing only half of the conversation but understanding I was outside my normal calm, became concerned.

"This July?"

"They don't show the year," she answered. "They just keep showing me a calendar with the names of the months flipping over and over and landing on July. The date of the 21st is circled and there are big bright red letters scrawled across its facing that read ARREST... ARREST...ARREST... in capital letters. They keep showing me this over and over."

"Holy shit…" was the sum of all I could think to say and my handwriting began to look like a three-year-old's.

"Wait," she continued. "This is interesting. They are showing me an article in the newspapers. Damon Cummings has been in an accident of some kind. A car accident. Not killed, just injured."

Don handed me another glass of wine and I took a sip, then handed it back.

"Does this take place in July, too?" I asked, spastically trying to keep up with her dictation. Getting near the end of the paper, I motioned to Don to grab anything from my purse that didn't look important so I could keep writing. He handed me an envelope and shrugged his shoulders. I motioned for him to pull my purse closer and began to search for something else myself.

"Did you say this accident was going to be in July, too?" I reiterated as I found a small notebook.

"No. They don't say when. They just keep showing me the article. I know this is a lot…"

"Man, I'll say," I sighed and finished my narrative.

"I just knew today was going to be crazy," she laughed. *"I saw a feather!"* And we both laughed, knowing that every time I saw a feather an important message was always delivered.

"It must have still been attached to a whole freaking flock of birds then!" I laughed. *"This is the motherlode! I cannot believe all this shit."* And I set down the pen to give my hand a rest, but wanted to press them for more on the arrest. *"Still nothing they can tell you about the year of this arrest... or if it's Damon or Waverleigh or Fitzpatrick?"*

"No. You know how this works. They give me what they think will help to point you in the right direction...or confirm something. Direct questions are always difficult, but I can try. Do you have a specific question you wish to ask?"

Still stunned about the calendar/ARREST thing, I was trying to think of what exactly was most important for me to know. Spencer sensed my hesitation and broadened the scope.

"Ok. Do you have anything in general you want me to ask about and we'll see if they can help out that way?"

I thought about some of the other clues that had escaped me while I tried to formulate a specific question about the arrest scenario. As a bone I threw out several unhinged phrases that I had not found segue to. "All right, take your pick. What about the infamous 'the black ace of spades' or the '77 and North Lawn' address in New Hampshire that got me nowhere... or how about Gerri and the 'one ruby and the loose diamonds' presentation that makes no sense? Or how about 'the barbed wire around Jessica's ankles'? Was that before they beat her or after when they were trying to bury her under the pool?"

"Ok...ok. Let's see what comes through," she suggested, and I could hear the beginnings of her familiar soft sigh and rumination on the other end, but no words. Eager to fill the silence and help

her out, I tossed another question into the air. "Or hey... what about that Theo Shelling kid? There's one I haven't figured out yet." I heard Spencer shift her breathing on the other end, which usually signaled someone coming through. "That one never made sense to me. They gave you both names, but no segue. It didn't make sense to me that they would go out of their way for nothing."

"Ok... this is interesting," she whispered as though only to her, and so I hushed myself, preparing for another assault. When nothing immediately broke forth, I acquiesced and went back to the bigger fish she had just tossed into the fry pan.

"Really, I just want to go back to the calendar/ARREST thing. Can they give you any other information? Like who will be arrested? July 21st is next week. While next week would be a friggin' miracle, even a year from now would be awesome at this point," I chuckled. "So can they tell you? Just so I know how much longer I get to look like a schmuck to friends and family. Not that it matters. I pretty much am gonna look like a schmuck for this whole thing from here to... well, eternity at this rate," I giggled. "But really, can they say? One year? Two years? Ten years? Can they give you a hint how much longer?" I baited. "Pretty please?"

Another few seconds went by and then she announced that a woman with dark curly hair and an injured foot was trying to come through. "She says she knows you came to see her. She is presenting the letter M. Do you understand who this is?"

I rummaged through my standard list of characters.

Then Spencer added "She keeps showing me her slipper. Why does she keep showing me this?" I waited as Spencer mentally adjusted to what picture was being presented. "Oh... she has only one slipper. The other is a shoe, maybe? She keeps repeating herself over and over. Do you know who this is? She must have recently crossed; sometimes they repeat themselves a lot when they do."

But I knew in an instant who it was who wore slippers like shoes and repeated herself annoyingly often, recently passed or not.

Marjorie Church had worn slippers and spoken in circles, often repeating herself till it drove me to distraction. Each time I had seen her in the nursing home, it was the same way. I was dumbfounded. Marjorie had just died not more than two weeks earlier and already she was making herself known from the other side.

"Oh my God, Spencer... I know who it is! And yes, she did just pass, but the repeating thing? She did the same thing when she was alive," I squealed. "She would say everything two or three times."

"She says that she is sorry she didn't get to tell them more about...what is this?"

I was at the edge of my seat. "About what? What is it?"

I could hear Spencer adjust herself. "She's trying to show me a picture of something. No, someone. Turn it... turn it... turn. What? No, just a little more...who is this?"

I had no idea what Spencer was seeing, but I could tell from her voice she was trying to get the woman to focus or bring something she was trying to show her into focus. I was getting as frustrated with Marjorie dead as I had on occasion with Marjorie alive.

"C'mon, Marjorie.... show her!" I encouraged.

"Do you understand... the picture of... of...turn it a little more...?"

I could hardly catch my breath. "Who? Who is it?" I asked anxiously.

Spencer's voice did that funny scale slide thing that people do when they are suddenly presented with something that has no immediate segue. "Albert... Einstein?"

"Excuse me?" I slammed. "Albert who?"

"Do you understand... the picture of Albert Einstein?" she repeated, almost as incredulous as I.

"Am I supposed to?" I asked in return and found myself mentally adjusting to nothing to get a better view. "Albert Einstein? What the devil does he have to do with Charley's death?"

"She says she wished she could have told them more about...then she shows me the picture of Albert Einstein. Maybe she is trying to give me somebody's name. Do you know an Einstein?" I had so many great comebacks for that, but chose silence instead. "Or maybe just somebody named Albert or Al? Do you understand who this might be? An Albert or an Einstein?"

"There was only one that came to mind that both Marjorie and I would have put into the mix. Bingo! She's talking about Albert Fitzpatrick! So she did it! She did get to talk to the GBI before she passed?"

"I cannot interpret, but she says she talked to them, signaling it is who you think, but she should have told them more about Albert. She is sorry she did not tell them more."

My heart was racing. Thank God. Marjorie had talked! Marjorie had talked! Knowing now that she was that close to death, though, I had no idea if what she had said to them made any sense or if she was cognizant of who they were and why they were asking her questions. And what if they didn't ask enough questions? Or the right questions? Nobody knew this case like I did. Why didn't they take me with them? What if they didn't know how to play Marjorie? What if they allowed her to ramble on and on, but didn't rein her in and take her to task? What if...what if? Spencer cut me off.

"She is trying to show me something else, now."

I was all ears, but still concerned and with a battery of questions lined up like 747's just waiting on the next tidbit of information to filter through. "Ok...you go first."

"It looks like a pin...or some kind of a small piece of jewelry. She has a lot of jewelry this one," Spencer observed and I agreed.

Marjorie reminded me of my middle child Piper. Very eclectic, always adorned with bangles and bracelets galore, very much the gypsy lady with curly brown hair and eyes so dark they almost looked black. Spencer continued and I reminded myself to pay attention.

"It's some kind of pin. It's small, round-ish. I wish she would hold it still. I can't get a good look at it when she moves like that," she said, forgetting I could not share in her visions. "It's a deep blue or deep purple, with a plant or a ..."

"Flower? Like an orchid" I belched into the phone.

"Yes, I suppose. The piece itself is small and round and...Why does this feel so familiar?"

"Oh shit... you mean familiar like the brooch?" I asked.

I don't know why the images of a previous summer impression came flooding through to me at that exact moment, but it didn't matter. My arms were ablaze with goose bumps, granting me confirmation before Spencer ever said another word.

"It's the brooch!" I squealed again. "I know it is! It has to be! I'm having an 'oh shit' moment!"

Spencer laughed then continued to coo at the woman with one slipper, but could not confirm.

Suddenly I felt like an idiot. "Oh shit" moment indeed. What was I thinking? The brooch had nothing to do with Marjorie. It had been a clue presented about Roxanne and some pimply-faced bad boy her father didn't approve of. And besides Charley's wedding ring, the two pennies of G, and the MOT's watch, this was the only other piece of clandestine jewelry that had ever been mentioned... so it couldn't be the same heirloom. Could it?

"Scratch that. I'm probably wrong," I proffered, wanting to cut my losses ahead of time. While Spencer debated on the exact

configuration of the piece, I snagged a cracker with cheese on top and waited patiently for the object to display itself more clearly.

"It could just be a pin..."

"Yep, I knew it! Skunked again!" I proclaimed and took the rest of the cracker in one bite.

"Wait... no, you're right. It is a brooch." I heard the words through the phone and then what happened next shocked me. "It's the same brooch!" Spencer announced and then all hell broke loose in the heavens!

"She says 'The purple orchid brooch was mine, the brooch that Theo Shelling gave to Roxanne was mine. He stole it out of my bedroom, the son-of-a-bitch! That whore... that lousy little whore. She had no business keeping it. It was mine! He was mine! The fu...ing brooch was mine, and he gave it to that whore while he was sleeping with me!'"

Spencer was trying to keep up with the dialogue and I was trying to keep up with Spencer and damn near choked on the cracker I had been munching on.

"She's ranting like a crazy woman, yelling and screaming at me, saying she was in love with Theo and that Roxanne had stolen her man. She's absolutely livid. She hated her, this young blonde, Roxanne. That's why she was so heartless when she was telling you about the way Roxanne had been killed. She was happy about it. She's showing me...Roxanne being beaten, strangled. Saying strangulation was too good for her. She deserved to die. Boy, this is incredible. You should see this; she's absolutely incensed."

Instantly I remembered how casual and callously Marjorie had spoken about the young woman's death, as though Roxanne had been nothing but a mangy stray. Marjorie had said it didn't matter about either Jessica or Roxanne, but there had been something cold in her voice when she talked about the younger blonde. "She was a whore. Nobody cared if she died. Good riddance to bad rubbish, I always say," she had claimed. I could see the whole thing happening in my mind.

"She's still swearing!" Spencer stated. "Though now she seems to be concentrating on how much she hates Theo for the moment."

I almost gagged. "So Marjorie was having an affair with Theo while he was sleeping with Roxanne? Shit! And I thought Theo was some young high school heart throb, not some dirty old man. Remember? You said, 'Roxanne's father was not happy that they were dating.' I just thought he was a punk biker or something, not…. Oh my God! That's just icky," I blubbered. My eyes grew three sizes and I made a motion to Don that I was fine, but freaking.

"Remember, he wouldn't have been that old then… well, older than Roxanne certainly, but only in his late twenties or early thirties at that point," she reminded me. I tried to spit out the dry fragments of cracker that wanted to get caught in my throat. "They show me he is still alive, maybe two towns west of Valdosta. Very sick… blood in his spit. Has something to do with his lungs. Very ill. He will talk…he will talk."

"Holy shit…I can't believe this," I muttered and Don climbed back up onto the boat, motioned to my wine glass while he watched my fingers furiously record the rest of the conversation.

"Whoa… wait. I wish you could see this. This is really something," Spencer giggled. "You know how when people get so angry, they go into a rage, cursing and yelling so manically that they end up spitting at the same time?"

It'd been a while, but I could. I imagined the dark-eyed gypsy woman forty-five years younger, out of her geriatric scooter, throwing her dark wavy hair about, clanging her jewelry as she paced the heavens; blaspheming the name of the man she was cheating with.

"Wow... she is really pissed!" Spencer added and then giggled again at what I imagined was the equivalent to a child's temper tantrum.

It was then that it hit me: Marjorie had been the woman in the clue given me over a year before.

"Is she the 'woman with the injured foot' from a session of last May?" I asked, curious to see if Marjorie had been the infamous "she" they had foretold us of. And the woman with the curly brown hair who has information for me.

"That would be her." Spencer confirmed. "She is really... Wow. She just flew out of here like a bat out of Hell! She was really furious!"

Frightened it was my entire fault for having asked about Theo to begin with, I was concerned that Marjorie might permanently cut me off. "Will she be back? Can you tell her I'm sorry for bringing him up?"

"Don't worry. She'll be back when she cools off a bit."

Frightened that I had alienated myself from further information, I spent the rest of that night telepathically trying to apologize, all the while dumbfounded at how the endless pieces of this puzzle were being aligned to come together.

CHAPTER FORTY-EIGHT

Once again my worries of being abandoned were short lived, as
Marjorie returned in a day or two and had much to share with
Spencer.

*Marjorie was not upset at you, just about the brooch. Of course
you could not have known about it. Regarding Waverleigh (the boy,
now man), again mention of the wife encouraging him to talk. He is
conflicted, feeling like he will free his dad and imprison (not
literally) him at the same time.*

*Showing me the name Phillips and 77 again. Gas station, maybe? I
do not wish to interpret. And what's with the number 77 again?
Over and over. So who had a curly bang? Sounds weird, I know,
but dark hair and a natural curl in the bang. Was it Albert? Do you
know what he used to look like?*

The letter opener with the flame on top...this is significant.

I was glad Marjorie had not held a grudge and even happier to
know that Waverleigh's conscience was working overtime. As for
the gas station, the continual showing of the number 77 was
confusing. I always thought it was a Phillips 66 gas station, so why
does the number 77 keep appearing? What is its significance? As
for the black curl, it could have been Hank Sloan. The letter opener
with the flame on it, though, was a new one, and I had nothing to
refer it to. Just as I was researching that, another email came
through.

This is from Marjorie...The 7th is mentioned and possibly a 77.

*It happened (death of one of the girls, the one strangled) by the
side of the oak tree where all the names were carved. You can see
the clubhouse off in the distance behind the tree. If facing the tree,
clubhouse will be in the distance to the right.*

The name Rachael is mentioned, possibly tied to Marjorie Church...a granddaughter perhaps...Two cherries like on a slot machine...8491 Willow Street (address directly from Marjorie).

To which I replied:

Is 77 a badge number? If Roxanne was murdered on the 7th, then Charley on the 9th and the MOT on the 15th of October, that might make even more sense. Because Charley made the extra tape the week before and then buried it at his mother's house that Sunday before they killed him. If Sunday was the 9th, then Thursday was the 7th and Charley was out of town in Moultrie qualifying on the 8th. He may have not even known about Roxanne's death before he died. Unless that was the day they finally pulled her out of the lake because they left her in the lake for a few days. That's where Grim's patrol lights were seen whirling in the night. Remember, his call number impression? The disco-police swirling lights clue?

Can you ask Charley if this fits his timeline better? Or even Marjorie...

We know Grim was at the lake when they pulled her out...but is this date of death or date of the pseudo discovery? Anything else?

As I waited for more information to trickle back through, I did my best to look up the address Marjorie had given and was amazed. I posted this to Spencer later that afternoon.

Got it! Here is the address... it is at the corner of North Oak Street and Willow Drive... Family Attractions (229) 263-........8491 Route 4 Ln, Quitman, GA 31643

What does Marjorie want me to do with this? Is this where they had the slot machines, the two cherries reference? Because they used to have them at the Valdosta Amusement Company, which may have even been what they called this back in 1966. Again... why send me there? Thought this was about porn. Does Marjorie confirm Albert Fitzpatrick, Hank Sloan, George Williams, and Damon Cummings as the four in flannel? And does our mystery woman's last name Moorey mean anything to her? Does she know about the Speaker of the House?

I know, I know! Slow down... slow down!

Spencer's response was quick and brief.

Ok, just looked at it. I do not want to interpret, but it looks a lot like the house I saw when I was shown the "meeting place" for the political guy to have sex. Remember that?

Yes, I did remember. That and other clues with specific addresses had something to do with the love shack street numbers 21 and another with Cherry Street. But still... what did this all have to do with Charley, other than this was where high-ranking state officials got their jollies? Unless this was where some of the porn was shot too. The Love Shack was used by many: the high-ranking state officials, local law enforcement, and two of Hollywood's high rollers for adult entertainment with Jessica and Roxanne. I continued to work each clue as I could, but the profiles of the four in flannel always stayed in the back of my mind and worried me that without a solid fourth I might name an innocent man guilty for another man's crime. The name Ganger had come up several times along with Cooper too, and I just wanted to be certain that they were completely out of the mix before declaring Williams the final suspect, so I fired off another message asking for confirmation.

It took a few days, but Spencer finally answered.

I feel a stronger pull towards Williams. The four in flannel feels more like verbiage used to help you understand there were four of them, not so much that they actually referred to themselves as the four in flannel.

From Charley:

The 19th by the river.

The answer is coming.

77th precinct.

The person that puts on the makeup at the funeral home, Alexa or Alexandra, something like that. A spouse...possibly of the funeral home guy.

The curtain will fall.

Were you sitting on your front porch tonight?

Seeing Damon's name in the newspaper

I did not instantly understand everything that came through each time. Still, I comforted myself with the fact that I was still at about an 89% success rate and that was nothing to be ashamed of. Again the number 77 was implanted. I became curious as to why they felt compelled to repeat it, other than it has significant meaning in numerology terms and angel numbers. (The number 77 signifying one is on the right path in their endeavors.)

With another name for Clint to investigate, I moved on. Summer was nearing its end and school for me was just weeks away. With little buffer left, my leisure time would be cut by half. Beyond that, I needed to get the book started, yet I realized I could not finish it without knowing first how this investigation would end. As I worked my way through things, another email from Spencer with information from Marjorie came through.

From Marjorie...

The neighbor next to Charley...talk to the neighbor. Ask about the coffee can, about the coffee grounds everywhere.

Showing me Albert Einstein again, trying to use as a reference for the name Albert...she says I was going to tell them more (the GBI) about him. Then she shows me Einstein again.

The loose cannon...the guy who used to play Russian roulette mention of him again...is he one of the four in flannel?

Charley says on the 17th a shift happens (pertaining to the case).

Keeps showing me ice skating references. This is personal...for you. One man goes down literally, not life threatening. Feels like a knee injury or something that affects the leg. Does your stomach hurt? Just made my stomach hurt.

I responded:

Ok... I was writing in the book the other night about Bobbie Lee Fitzpatrick. The coffee grounds incident was G wreaking havoc in the kitchen two weeks after Charley was dead. The Russian roulette man? That was Hank Sloan, the shooter. Yes, he is one of the four in flannel.

A shift on the 17th?

ANSWER: Hmmm! Bring it on! That would have been the Sunday just before Fitzpatrick turned up in Clint's office wanting to know about me.

Ice skating? Or maybe just showing you ice?

ANSWER: Don fell on some ice on our porch and severed his quadriceps tendon and had to have his knee rebuilt. That was in 2004, I think.

Stomach hurt?

ANSWER: This could either be from my husband's colon surgery and his diverticulitis or just too much stress from work. I do not understand how it is that I have become such a target for chaos.

Beyond that and the copious amounts of information I'd been receiving, the summer had been good to us. The house on the lake had been just the thing to allow us to breathe in between our own chaos and allowed our hearts to heal. I needed to find my way back to normalcy. Having this many weeks off from schoolwork on top of my job had allowed me to really get my feet back under myself. Tensions in the air were gone. The kids came and went, enjoying the summer sun and the lake, and Don and I were closer. Still, I worried that we might slip back into old patterns. If that happened, I knew that would be the end of us. I did my best to keep things moving emotionally and tried not to dwell any longer in the past. While the theatre ate up the hours of my days, the lake and the research ate up most evenings and the gentle roll of the rhythm was comforting. Still, sometimes when you least expect the reassurances of angels, they deliver a message without prompt and you know that they really are a part of your day.

Spencer:

They just want me to say they know Don has been on your mind a lot and that everything will truly be ok. Jessica's dad tied to Sorenson, the insurance guy. Mention of a ring you keep looking at.

The ring I kept looking at was my wedding ring, but it was good to hear from those on high that things would continue to fall back into place for us. Even more incredible, I parsed each of the clues and paid particular attention to Charley's insurance agent.

Pete Sorenson was the State Farm Insurance Agent for Charley (remember last card in his wallet not plastic). He worked in an office at Castlepark Shopping Center next to Harvey's, the store with the bakery Rox worked at. Just down the road from the Bailey's Trailer Park. Ask Marjorie about that. Ask what hotel/motel Rox and Jess worked out of, the Red.... what? Had there been a Red Roof Inn in the area maybe? Does Marjorie know about the MOT and who and where he was from? Does Marjorie know about the watch?

Thank them about Don... been looking at my wedding rings. Clint checking into makeup artist Alex or Alexandra. He told me that men usually did the makeup in the funeral homes, and beauty parlor ladies were hired to do the hair back then.

Precinct and 77, huh? Don't think the two are related. GBI, ATF, FBI, and Sheriff's Department used zones or districts. VPD used precincts, but none go that high. Is this a badge number? Or is this in a huge metropolitan area that I should be looking... like New York? Or maybe just the Angel Number's reference that I am on the right path. As for the 19th at the river? Hmmm. Still thinking. Any news on Stevie Waverleigh the boy/man witness?

It was important to me to continue to work the clues, but in the back of my mind I was hopeful that either of the Waverleighs would crack and tell the truth about the night Charley was killed and everything that led up to it. It didn't matter to me which one; either father or son would have done nicely. Because of the *July 21st/ARREST* images and the recent loss of Marjorie, I prayed that the GBI would make certain they got to them before something else happened. As fate would have it, I was informed four days later that the elder Waverleigh was not doing well.

On July 31, 2011 I talked with Spencer on the phone and even more information came through. She told me that Charley was there and that he kept saying *Open the envelope, the white envelope! Just open it!*

"It may be an old or a new letter," Spencer said. "He just keeps saying for you to open the envelope."

That was great, except that there were probably a hundred thousand white envelopes in those plastic buckets of material. I made a note to go through them all again and continued to take notes. Spencer suggested I talk to Albert Fitzpatrick. Then she suggested I talk to his ex-wife, Bobbie Lee.

"I'm not certain talking directly to Albert at this point is such a wise thing. Remember who he is? Marjorie called him Mr. Crazy-pants, Mr. Loose Cannon? And as far as his ex-wife, Bobbie Lee? Clint can't find her. She had some medical issues and went into the hospital, and now he doesn't know where to find her and doesn't want to send up a bunch of red flags trying to ask questions.

"Ok...let's move on. Do you understand the name Veronica? Is this an agent? Feels like a younger agent, female, who has really

bought into this thing. In her forties maybe, somebody working the case? Does this mean anything to you?" she asked.

"Not to me. I have not been privy to who and/or how many GBI agents have been working this thing at this point," I answer.

"Ok, just be aware. They say you need to go to page 14 of the journal, page 14, the 7th line down. Read what is there."

I made another note and added it to my list which was getting longer by the minute.

Next she hit me with, "Is Bob Waverleigh sick? The man with the son? They keep showing me the letter A. Is he in assisted living? They show me a hospital, and they keep flashing 'THREE DAYS, THREE DAYS, THREE DAYS...' they do this very fast. They keep repeating it."

I wrote as fast as I could, amazed that her information was so on target. Three days earlier Clint had called me to tell me that the elder Waverleigh had had an aneurism. That was my letter *A* confirmation. Then for some odd reason, they brought up Carlos again and said to ask Jules's brother about him. They thought he might remember Carlos being around the house. The odds of talking to Jules's brother were slim, and him remembering something from that long ago even slimmer, but I added that to my list as well. Next they told me *"to go to page 21"* in the journal and read that as well.

That night I did read both pages. Page 14 referenced a Phillips 66 gas station and some moonshine folks the ATTD was interested in. The address given was thought to be in Valdosta, but later proved to be a location in Vidalia. The men in question had been showcased in a newspaper clipping that Gavin Eller had in his possession. Uncertain of segue, I moved on. When I read the 21st page, it brought me back to the doorstep interview and denial by Albert Fitzpatrick as well as the mysterious phantom phone calls made that weekend by Bob Waverleigh. Obsessed about fitting it all together, I went over my files and every email for the past year or so, looking for missed clues and wrong assumptions. Through it all the photo on my desk remained silent but constant in his company. By the time I was ready to call it quits, it was after 1:00 in the morning.

"I'm still here, Charley, still trying to put it all together for you." I sighed and pressed the final button on my laptop to shut it down. "Talk to me, Charley. Help me figure these last few things out," I challenged. Then, as usual, brought my fingers to my lips and transferred the kiss to his forehead. "Goodnight, little man. I love you," I whispered and shut off my lamp.

Physically exhausted from sitting at my computer for so long, I took longer than usual to complete my nightly rituals. My eyes were tired, my legs heavy. I felt weak as I dragged the covers up and across my body and settled my head into the pillows. Mentally I was exhausted too, but my brain refused to shut down. Even though I had pretty much nailed the big picture, the smaller fragments surrounding Charley's murder still kept me second guessing myself. Without other recourse, I closed my eyes and said a small prayer that I might find whatever else was out there to help the authorities nail the remaining four in flannel and deliver the true identity of the man Charley had called LT.

Sleep finally settled on all in the house. Somewhere hours later, I felt warm breath on my left ear. As my husband and I sleep with all four dogs, it was a given that one of them had made his way to my pillow. I brushed a stray hair from my temple and then rolled, anticipating connection with the white muzzle of my Westie, Harley, but that was far from what I encountered.

As I turned, the air around me began to feel heavy. My eyes slowly adjusted to the dark, and suddenly I was face to face with the black silhouette of a man looming just above my head. I gulped for air and then finally screamed.

CHAPTER FORTY-NINE

Hyperventilating, I jerked the covers back and forth, pounded on my husband's chest, just as the figure pulled back and then disappeared before my very eyes. Don, of course, jumped into action and by the time I could explain he was halfway through the bedroom, switching on lights and making threats.

"It was a man. He was here...by the bed...here," I pointed. "Right here at my side, bent over me... and then I screamed and he was gone," I managed to explain, still catching my breath and searching the corners of the room for evidence.

"A real man?" my husband asked as he noted not one of the dogs had budged until I had yelped for all I was worth.

"Yes... I mean...no. I don't think so. I don't know. It happened so fast," I backpedaled, trying to decide if I had seen anything at all or just dreamt it.

"Did you know who it was? Was it Charley?" he asked, as he calmly paced the confines of the master bedroom and bath.

"I... I don't know. It was the figure of a man all in black and right in my face. I freaked. I've never seen anything like that before," I panted and clutched at the corners of his shirttail as if they could protect me.

"Let me just check the rest of the house, just in case." He managed to tug his revolver from its sleeve and yanked on a pair of jeans. "You stay here."

"Like hell," I said and got up to go with him, grabbing my housecoat as I went.

After touring the house and letting the dogs out to void, we went back through the residence room by room and shut things down, checking all the locks twice just in case. Together we crawled back into bed, and I snuggled close, hoping proximity would keep me safe.

"Thanks," I managed and he patted my shoulder, rolled back onto his side, and drifted back off to sleep. I spent the rest of the night tucked into the side of my husband and kept the covers up over my ears, barely able to breathe, but too frightened to expose any more of my head than necessary. The next morning I got up and then sent a message to Spencer, telling her I had had some sort of visitation.

"It could have been Charley," I wagered, "but I was so tired and the figure was so close to my face that I freaked. Literally...I screamed like a little girl," I giggled. "Scared the shit out of Don and almost gave him another heart attack in the process," I added, trying to be casual and flippant about the whole event.

"Don't worry. It happens," she comforted.

But I still felt like an idiot seeing as Piper had squared off with the devil himself and shown more courage than I had. "It just caught me off guard...I wasn't expecting anyone to be there," I said and then realized how stupid that statement had sounded. It's not like ghosts send out calling cards first announcing their scheduled visitations. "I'm such a schmuck!" I laughed. "I beg for it and then weenie out when it happens...Jesus!"

"Ok...ok. Just start at the beginning. What were you doing before it happened?"

"Sleeping," I smirked.

"No... I mean, were you working on something... or thinking about something before you went to bed? Often they appear in response to something, like a trigger."

"I was working on the book, trying to figure out some of the clues from the last session."

"Ok. Tell me what you remember and don't leave out anything," she instructed.

"Alright. Well, first of all it was totally black," I started, "which was really odd when you think about it because the room was dark. But somehow this figure was even darker."

"That's very common. Most often they manifest in black silhouette. Sometimes full color, but this may be the best way whoever it was thought he should appear to you. What else do you remember?" she baited.

"I don't know... it happened so fast."

"Now think. Was it a man or a woman?" she asked.

"Definitely a man," I responded, surprising myself.

"Why do you say that?" she asked.

"Because... because of the shape of his head."

"And why is that?"

"Because ... it was like..." and I began to pull things from my memory that I didn't realize had been imprinted. "Because the person was balding. You now, like when a man has his hair on the sides cropped really short because he has almost no hair on top?" I explained. "Like a military cut or something."

"So this person was male and balding? Anything else that makes you think it was a man?" she pressed. "Start from his head and work your way down. It will help you remember things in order."

Suddenly the image froze in my mind, and I listed everything I could recall. "There were a few short hairs that stood out on the top of the head. Very G-man looking. And the shoulders were broad...

but maybe not as broad as they appeared because..." and I stalled, as I pulled together more of the impression.

"Yes... because why?"

"Because…because the person had on a suit. Yes! A suit. It made the shoulders look square and wide. And the collar was high. High and stiff, like an Oxford button down," I heard myself say and was amazed at how much I had taken in, in such a short amount of time.

"Was he standing... what did the rest of him look like?"

"I couldn't tell. He was bending over the bed. You know, how like when a child gets sick and stand by your bedside just breathing into your ear until you wake up and notice he is there? It was like that, but I didn't register anything below his waist because I was so scared when I realized what was happening."

"Was there anything else about what you did see that seemed odd? Was there anything that you can remember that stood out?" She encouraged me to review my image for some other detail that could help me narrow down the identity. "Anything that struck you as unusual or special?"

And it hit me! "His ears! Oh my God, his ears. They stuck out from the side of his head, not ridiculously so, but they looked so familiar." I knew in an instant the silhouette which had hung over my bed the night before was the same silhouette that had shared my writing desk for almost two and half years.

"It was Charley," I whispered. "Oh my God, Spencer... it was Charley." And I smiled to myself until I remembered that I had screamed in his face. "Oh shit!" I exclaimed.

"What? I thought that would make you happy. You always said you wanted to have him..."

"I know, I know," I muttered, thinking how awful he must have felt having me screech in his face like a wild banshee, especially after he went out of his way to grant me my wish.

"This is not the first time he has visited you, you know. But this is the first time you were either tired enough or open enough to see him. Do you remember anything else?"

Still mentally flogging myself for being such a twit, I missed the implication. "I'm sorry. What?"

"Did you see anything else? Like a notebook in his hand?" she lured.

"I... I don't remember. I just remember rolling over and having this dark frame of a man bending over me with his face right next to mine and then..." I could feel the warm breath and the density of the air about him. "And then I screamed like an idiot and scared the shit out of both of us."

"You didn't scare him, but he was worried he had frightened you."

"He did. Why didn't he just come to me as Charley... in the daytime? And why was he bending over so close like that? That would scare the shit out of anybody to roll over and have some strange man in your face," I rationalized.

"He came to you as the figure of him he thought you would recognize first, the photo you talk to on your desk. He had the notebook to signify writing, and he was bending over you," and she paused either for effect or to make certain I was listening, "because he had just given you a kiss on the cheek."

"A kiss?" My hand went to my left cheek and I wanted to cry. "So I yelled at him? God, I am such an idiot! I beg for this shit my whole life and when it finally happens... I punk out. I'm such a turd," I chastised. "Can you tell him I'm sorry? That I promise if he comes again... I'll be more... more," I had to think. "Crap, what more would you be about something like that? Cool? Yes...more cool about it."

"Don't be too hard on yourself. I still wake up in the middle of the night with people trying to come through and call out," she laughed. "My husband has learned to ignore it. It's just a natural reaction. Eventually you get used to it... and they don't scare you as much," she edified.

"But it was Charley, my Charley. I have been begging him to come to me and then what do I do? I act like a moron and scare us both back into eternity." And that night I promised I would be open, I would be cool. I promised I would hold my breath and count to ten before I screamed. I promised the world to bargain for his favor again and then I went to bed, keeping one eye open and my mouth shut. In the end, I accepted that the moment had passed and he would most likely not return.

The next morning it was back to reality. Problems with the theatre never rested, but neither did the research. So it was back to the salt mines for both. Contented that Charley at least was trying to grant me my wish, I dug my heels in deeper and tried to keep an open mind so he would feel more welcomed. I had no idea what might happen next, but I'd made myself a promise after the other night that I would do my best to be more prepared. While Spencer took a few days off, I pulled various segments from earlier months and quizzed myself on those emails that had been returned unanswered. Once I had diluted things, I fired off another email.

Can Marjorie or Robert Coleman give me any information as to whose truck or car they used to carry Roxanne from the Saddle Bag Lake to where they dumped her across from Wild Adventures Theme Park? Also... what was the compass used for? Locating the spot for Jessica's murder or Roxanne's?

Spencer responded:

I am not going to respond to direct questions but just open it up to anyone and anything...

Who was the sheriff at the time of Charley's murder?

Fitzpatrick may be the one who entered Charley's office that night.

Fitzpatrick may be the one who killed MOT.

Fitzpatrick had an "if you want something done right, do it yourself" attitude. He volunteered to do these things like he was the one who could do it right.

December 23rd.

Grim may get in a car accident, but will only be injured.

Ok, I know this sounds weird, but is there a piece of paper in Charley's stuff that looks like it has weird symbols like hieroglyphics? It's something Kaye had that she put in with other items. She keeps saying, "The whole time I had it."

I responded:

I have found several letters. Two are from Kaye, in shorthand, but there is a white envelope that has squiggles on the front. Inside is a worker's job insurance claim for a Will Wetherton, age 61, signed by Charley on May 2, 1966. Is this the real MOT?

I checked Google Earth for your Cherry Street in Valdosta and got nothing but a street full of little shit houses. Did she live there at one time? Was there a love shack there or was that where she used to meet the MOT? I don't think the letters in shorthand are the hieroglyphics... they are Kaye's shorthand, letters to Lonnie C. Johnson, a Commissioner, and the other to Herman Talmadge.

Do we think this Will Wetherton is the real MOT and not Robert W. Chancellor who they say on the death certificate died on 10/15/66? There is another article in the bin, a card/letter from a Wilches Company. It has a Trussman and a Wetherton signature on it. In fact, Will Wetherton's signature on it. The card/letter was sent to "Dear Friend," though there is no date on it. Must have been important or why would Kaye have kept it?

While I was still disappointed about the mishap with Charley, I was tortured at the possibility that my MOT was not who I thought he was. Was it possible that they had been able to kill somebody and have his death certificate falsified and body transferred to Augusta

415

and everything else manipulated and handled without any interference from people with morals and scruples? Or had they processed the documents themselves, changing names and information to hide who they had really killed? My brain was on fire! Was my MOT somebody else? Had they buried some other man in his stead and lied about his identity? Had they even transferred a body to Augusta at all?

More information came through. Whoever this Will was, Spencer said they presented that this man had a clear connection to Charley and to my Elizabeth with the broken chandelier and the broken plate with the palm tree on it. Since I had already sent Clint on another wild goose chase searching for the exact address of our snitch Henders so we could check Google Earth for the precise location of the tire clue, I rattled the chains of my other connection Ricky. He was able to plug a few holes for me on the Elizabeth clue.

I sent this email to Spencer.

Ok... have Clint on the chase for exact address for Wiley Henders, the tire half in half out guy. Also was working on my blog and things are starting to come through.

You/Marjorie gave me "the 17th by the lake." Is this September or October of 1966? Very important to know what month for my timeline and what it refers to. Can they give you a nod one way or the other?

Will Marjorie or MOT confirm he is Will Wetherton and what the relationship between him and Elizabeth was? Did Charley send him/the MOT to her because she worked for his best friend, Judge George M. Tilly and thought they might keep a copy with them for protection? Did she take a statement from him? She was a court stenographer. Get it? Hieroglyphics. Is there something in the box/bag Kaye is referring to that came from Elizabeth to her?

Also...Marjorie gave you October 7th in relationship to Rox. Is this when she was strangled or when she was found? They strangle her on the 17th of September by the lake, then is she found floating in the lake on the 7th of October? Or is the 17th by the lake about something else? Maybe the date that the copy of the tape was given to Finch? In which case, the MOT made it way before October 3rd when Charley finally buries it under his mother's pantry.

And what is the 19th by the river about? The lake is one thing, but the river? Who is that tied to? See... the places and timelines don't fit unless I get some clarification. Was Rox's body found in the lake before or after Charley was killed? And then reburied when they rolled her into the swamp on October 12th after he is already dead and gone, which would explain their not being in Millen for the funeral.

Sorry...sorry! It's just things are flying through my head and I have to ask questions before I lose my train of thought. Also, got information back on Elizabeth Middleburgh. Husband's name was Warren and he was an attorney. She was court recorder for the Southern Judicial Circuit which covered Brooks, Lowndes, Thomas, Echols, and Colquitt County areas. Brooks County was across the river from Charley's death. Lowndes was Valdosta. Echols County was where the snitch Henders was from, Lake Park area.

Why would Elizabeth's husband have been in trouble for hiding the missing tape? Do you remember when they broke into her house demanding to know where "it" was and told her that her husband would be in trouble if she didn't tell them? You said it was just a fishing experiment on the four in flannel part, so what is the tie between Wetherton and Middleburgh?

I could barely keep pace with the all implications this new potential MOT would bring to the table. Adding a few other exchanged pieces of information, I crafted a blog that I could not publish...until now.

The blog:

Never underestimate the power of a feather.

While Sunday's feather brought the tantalizing tease of a plausible identity swap for the MOT, it also brought other information that finally closed the circle of how the MOT was introduced to this situation to begin with. You know, it has always bothered me how this man Charley and I refer to as "the MOT" was seemingly dropped into place from out of the blue. Think about it. You have a man who supposedly comes from Tifton, travels to a hotel less than 30 miles from his home, is randomly chosen to be beaten to death in a hotel, and his body is then immediately transferred out of the area to Augusta to be buried — all within 48 hours! And who says government officials aren't expeditious and efficient? Now, while all this should remain suspect, it is not too far out of the realm of plausibility, but bear with me.

The part that has always gotten me is that there has never been never a solid segue from Tifton to Valdosta that would realistically explain the MOT's sudden appearance as a player or why, when he got his knickers in a wad, his gut instinct was to run off and find the first nice ATF guy he could find. Add to that the incomprehensibility that he would share hidden information with a complete stranger, and you have a Nancy Drew mystery on steroids. See my quandary? What is the catalyst for this first foray into the murder sequence and what is the previous connection to Charley that made him so approachable? After all, the man was not asking directions to the local mall. He was giving Charley the dirt on every corrupt agency and law enforcement officer in the area: federal, state, and local. So Sunday's feather not only revealed to me that the potential MOT had worked for Charley for three months, but also that he may not have been who was written on the death certificate. We must remember that the County Coroner was just one of a hundred folks in local law's back pocket, so altering or just outright lying on a death certificates was mere child's play for these folks. To be more specific about my find, Sunday's feather was not your atypical feather. Unlike the lighter, more petite feathers I am generally accustomed to, this was a huge feather, a long, black, heavy feather lying right there on the beach in front of me as I crossed to the water. It could not have been overlooked even by a blind man. So you know me. Immediately I say to myself, "Wow! Whatever the forthcoming message, it must be big." And guess what? I was right because after I got over the "Oh, shit!" moment of the MOT possibly not being the MOT, I called Spencer and told her what I had found.

Now this is what I love about Charley or the infamous "they" from afar: they love to bait and then reel you in slow. Or maybe I'm just stupid and it takes me longer to process. At any rate, upon hearing my news, Spencer immediately sensed a connection between my new MOT and my Elizabeth of previous months. You remember Elizabeth, don't you? The woman whose house was entered by three of the four in flannel? The woman who stood holding broken shards of glass from her chandelier because she would not or could not tell the three where "it" was hidden? The woman whose pretty palm tree painted plate got smashed because the three were impatient and decided they would tear up a few things to help loosen her lips? The same woman who appears in deposition papers by Kaye's attorney? The same woman who worked for a judge friend of Charley's north of Valdosta? Oooooh, that Elizabeth! Yes, now you remember!

Well, when you put it together that way, it all makes sense. Think, my dear readers! If we believe the MOT was originally from Tifton, where we know there was a lot going on with the WOW Lodge #1545, including moonshine, gambling, and the ever popular porn ring G and the four in flannel were involved with, segue is easier to see. Then add in the MOT's known connection to both Jessica and Roxanne by getting them legit jobs at the American Legion Club as waitresses/adult entertainment. Then you close the connection to porn. Then to top things off, you simply toss in the unbelievable fact that in the same month as Jessica tries to kill herself (March of '66) this man at 61 suddenly desires to do construction work outside in the hot, blistering Valdosta heat. Hmmm...now you can see how everything fits. He was a plant on Charley's construction crew, just like our dear friend Carlos. But something went wrong.

Things weren't supposed to get out of hand. Everything was going great; money was flowing; folks were horny and happy...till Grim

419

and higher-ups got greedy. That's when they branched out. They went beyond local and it got messy. Jessica got pregnant; then she got scared. She ended up slitting her wrists somewhere around March 11th and did an overnighter in the local hospital trying to pull herself together. Higher-ups who had slept with her got nervous; she became unstable. (Oddly enough, this is about the same time that the MOT suddenly seeks employment or may even have been sent by Parker Jade for employment with Charley on his houses.) With Jessica becoming a walking threat, they had to take her out of the picture. Then Roxanne got either brave or stupid and brought her up one night months after Jessica's disappearance while hanging with the MOT and the boys. It gets ugly; she is taken out of the picture.

What's a MOT to do? He runs to Charley, his old employer, for help. Why? 'Cause his ex-employer was the only law enforcement man he could trust. Charley would know what to do to help protect him, and he did. They took the MOT's tape and made copies... then he hid one the first Sunday of October 3rd when they expected him to show up at the designated place set up by Wiley Henders. But he can't 'cause he had to visit his mamma who had surgery that week. Making the tape as insurance wasn't enough to keep them safe. Roxanne gets taken out of the lake just up from the VPD lake house by the Grim Reaper on the 7th of October while Charley is just getting back from Moultrie and his round of qualifying. Then he is told to stay put all weekend, but just him and his partner. Amazingly everyone else is allowed to roam free. Then after they have tracked his and Kaye's whereabouts and goings-on all weekend long, they call and cut him loose at 8:00-8:30 pm, but only after they have inundated the house with calls all day reminding him about the big moonshine deal at 9:30 that and every Sunday night.

Grim pulls Rox from her watery grave. Charley gets taken out. Then they dump Rox's body and go after the MOT, beat him, kill him, and his body is carted out of town so nobody knows what happened to anyone else. He is immediately interred which means no embalming, which means faster decomposition and less opportunity for post mortem identification. He can't talk about

Jessica, Roxanne, or the four in flannel and neither can Charley. So they search for the tapes. They go to Charley's house, his office, and then to Elizabeth thinking Charley might have sent the MOT to her for safety. She says she has nothing; she keeps quiet for her husband's sake. And with all four murders committed and everyone buried or dumped by the end of the third week in October, everybody who could have ratted them out is either paid off or dead. Thus, they can effectively end the investigation just 18 days after Charley's death. Done.

Now that's the kind of segue that makes sense.

Just writing about the possibility that the MOT had not been who was written on the death certificate got me so fired up I could scarcely breathe. Think what this would mean to the case. How could I possibly explain this one to ATF or GBI? Still, no matter how many times I tried to parse it, the scenario made more sense this way than any other. Not to mention the fact that Spencer had said G's fingerprints were all over this one. My head continued to spin out conspiracy theory after theory, but they all funneled into one main question: Why would someone from Tifton be murdered in a hotel in Valdosta and then be transferred to Augusta to be buried two days later?

Curious, I returned the remaining pile of white enveloped letters and then fell to my knees. Stuffed in between the ledgers of a yellowed bank statement was a white envelope that was addressed to "Chas Covington" in black type and underlined. Opened, the lined parchment inside held two holes punched at the top as if pulled from a chart or ledger. Pale with age, the scrawl of someone relatively uneducated ate the entire page and left me breathless. This text appears just as written, misspellings and all.

June 9, 1963

Dupont, Ga

Dear Mr. Charlie

I want you to come to my house by your self an I can tell you a lot you don't know for the man at the lake an it is all on all of this. So I want you to let no one no nothing about this but you so you come to my house any day about 12 o clock an I be at home. I live out on the withers road 2 miles south on the hard road till you come to Box 10-A an turn left an I live at the first place so you don't let no body no anything till you get this sateled

yors ears

Joe Chauncey

Dupont, Ga

R1 Box 10-A

My mind went blank. Chauncey was a name specifically mentioned once before by Spencer, but I had never found anything to attach it to, so let it fall to the side. Confused as to what I should do with it, I decided to call Clint in the morning to try and find the person or at the very least the location of the home it mentioned. So which person was I to follow? The author of this new cryptic message? Or the envelope with squiggles that housed the paper that quite possibly gave the MOT a new identity?

It was shortly after 1:00 in the morning when I finished my deliberations and decided that I could not publish the blog as I now had another clue to decipher. Since everyone had long since gone to bed, I tried to be as quiet as possible as I went through my nightly routine. Teeth brushed and face washed, I gripped the handle of the bathroom door and eased it open. I adjusted my eyes and silently crossed into the room. The ceiling fan was whirring, Don was snoring, and the dogs were randomly dispersed about the bed, unaffected by my entrance. Grateful, I slipped out of my shoes and then my glasses. The numbers on the digital clock rolled over one more minute as I went to get undressed. Menopause was screwing with my personal thermostat. Too hot for pajamas, I pulled my shirt off over my head and flung it to the floor. Still bound by my bra, I tilted my head to the side as I unfastened the strap. Finally released, I heaved a small sigh of relief and lifted my head. Slowly I reached out for the covers. As I turned back to crawl underneath, there in my face was another black silhouette of a man!

The next morning I sent Spencer a message:

Spencer… I did it again! Ok, so basically I suck at this thing. Charley appeared to me again last night. Here I was trying to be all quiet and not wake up Don or the dogs when I went to bed…and then when I pulled off my shirt and went to crawl into bed, I and my bare tits faced him off, and I screamed loud enough to wake the dead! Literally!

No wonder the Blessed Virgin hedged her bets and steered clear of me as a child.

I can still hear her laughing.

CHAPTER FIFTY

As July's chaos slipped behind the first clouds of August's angst, work at the theatre went back into to its normal cycle of productions. I was happy for the distraction. First up were auditions for the season opener, Disney's *My Son Pinocchio, Geppetto's Musical Tale.* Beyond stressing about the budgetary process beginning again, I was blessed with a resounding response of people to cast from and could not have been happier to be back within my comfort zone of theatre. The budget process would take whatever victims it would, and just shy of winning the lottery and building my own theatre there was nothing I could do to divert its agenda. Outside my office I was well aware of the realities facing my position; inside those four walls, it was all about the magic and I was so in need of grease paint and illusion.

Since the *Pinocchio* cast was male heavy, I made several great choices and then struggled to try and fill the last available principal but smaller role. With music and choreography rehearsals going into their second week, I was still minus one man and that situation began to make me nervous. I never like to double cast someone in a show if I can avoid it, but I was beginning to get desperate. After canvassing regulars, I found that everyone I asked was either too busy or already in another show. Time was becoming crucial. It looked as though I was going to begin blocking without a full cast until another theatre favorite of mine, Lynn, found the perfect man to play the mad scientist. Happy for the potential plug, I brought him in for an audition and promised to work around his schedules. Because he was a minister and a hospice chaplain, his hours were somewhat erratic. But because his voice was solid and his character acting spot on, I didn't mind the sporadic absences and felt an immediate kinship with him I could not explain.

Charley remained constantly in the background, though I knew his appearances would become less and less as he became more ready to move on. I was the delay in his departure and I knew it, but there was so much still I felt was left unanswered. Why hadn't the MOT come forward to set me straight? Who was buried in his grave? Why hadn't Gerri ever come to the table and finally told the truth about what happened and whether or not she had ever loved him? Who or what did the initials LT really stand for, and who the devil was Ganger? The elusive man who wore an olive green Parks and Rec uniform was somehow tied to the *O.S.T.R.I.C.H.* affair and presented as having similar strong ties to Grim. Why did this man's name continue to pop up whenever Roxanne's was mentioned?

These were the questions that plagued me and kept me from making final headway. Weeks later I revisited an idea I had for an opening for the novel and failed. Several pages in, I knew it wasn't the right fit and tossed it out. It was the second time since I had tried to begin this story that I had been stalled. Finding the proper voice for the book was imperative; its elusiveness kept me from writing. Desperate to defend my talent, I used my production as an excuse to further avoid my laptop. Sometimes late at night I would arrive home from the theatre and stare into the night sky, waiting on the blue screen, afraid that I had nothing left to give. Each time I committed to write, my head got fuzzy, and I couldn't formulate an intelligent thought. Had Terry Kay been right? Had I wasted all my words on the blog? Or was there still more to discover and this was the cosmos's way of preventing premature departures and suppositions? Professionally paralyzed, I was lost, adrift in a literary fog that seemed to congeal with each passing day.

As August gave way to September, I struggled even more to find the proper narrative voice. In seven weeks I had gone through seven different openings, but nothing felt right and I couldn't seem to get any traction. I worried that if I wrote it from my perspective, Jules or my bloggers might get angry, convinced I had commandeered the story for emotional profit. In my dreams I saw crowds of ill-defined faces at book signings screaming, "It's Charley's story, not yours! We don't want *Eat, Love, Pray* — we want *Eat, Love, Pray and then Prosecute the Sons-of-Bitches!*"

Catatonic, I sat at my desk and contemplated the effects of my apparent writer's block and was dumbfounded. This had never happened to me before. I could blog my way into perpetuity, vomit in ink at a moment's notice. But asked to form a cohesive opening sentence for the book of a lifetime, I became obstructed. Fearful that I had come so far to surrender so little, I cried and paced the floor of my office. The floors creaked beneath the oatmeal-colored carpet. Frightened I had lost the magic behind my craft, I begged the 8 x 10 on my desk to guide me back to sanity. Once again, within twenty-four hours I received a return message through S.

They said to pass this on to you: "There is no wrong in write... just write!"

Although somewhat more tender in their delivery than the infamous reverse Adam Lambert, "What do you want from you?" bitch slap, the universe's message was still pretty much the same. Get over yourself and get on with it! Cattle prodded for a second time by the cosmos, I decided to plow forward and see what poured forth. Believe me, I still went through several paragraphs before I finally realized that to tell this story I had to tell my own, starting from the beginning. And once I found my voice, Charley's began to blend in, and I felt his strength and inspiration behind every word.

The rest of the month followed suit with brilliant budding colors and crisp winds that wound their way around the tops of Georgia pines and then slid across the calendar into October. With the first weekend taken up with the startup of my new semester, I had little time to do anything other than react to academic requests. Coursework was getting harder, but then that was the point. As the nights got longer and the days shorter, I thought more about Roxanne. Not just because it was October or because the old fashioned alarm clock in my office she likes so much continued to fall without prompt. No, I thought more about Roxanne because every morning I awoke after October 3rd the fog was thick upon the lake, and when I stood there in silence concentrating on the rigors of the upcoming day, I noticed I could see my breath.

Spencer had talked about seeing the last breaths of air escaping Roxanne's blue lips as the four in flannel beat and strangled her to death. For over thirty years I had taken note that the first weekend in October usually brought about a cold snap. Kaye had obsessed over much the same in her journal:

When I picked Martin up from school that afternoon, we went to Brookwood trying to find some pants in a husky size for Martin. Sears did not carry them in the store, and the weather had turned unusually cool, too cool to wear short pants. I could not find them there, so I went to Taylor's and they could not fit him. I went on to Castlepark and bought Jules a Halloween costume at Playland and then went to Irene's Tots to Teens to try to fit Martin. She did not carry husky pants, but I took two pair of regular pants to have him try on at home. I told Irene that I might go over to Moultrie on Monday to Friedlander's and try to find some husky pants there. She told me if I found some to let her know as she needed some for her son, I think his name was Wally. We tried these pants on Martin on Sunday and they did not fit. We thought about ordering some from Sears, and Charley measured Martin. He then made an order out for Sears and ordered two pairs of corduroy pants. We came home about 6:00 pm Friday night. Charley came home right behind us and he seemed in good spirits. He told me that we were stuck at home all weekend — that the whole state was put on alert because of a truck that was being tailed from another state with raw materials on it. As the truck left one territory, another group of officers would pick up the trail. He told me that only he and Sal were on standby because the other officers were working a still in Clinch or Echols County with state agents.

Having independent corroboration of such, I felt better about my timelines for Roxanne's murder. Later on that same page, it appeared that there may have been an unsuccessful attempt by higher ups earlier in the summer of that year to get Charley out of Valdosta and out of the four in flannel's hair.

He also told me that that Friday night he had asked his supervisor, Mr. Callenwald, to put him back on the list of best qualified. You had to be on the list to be considered for a promotion. Around the end of May or beginning of June, the Atlanta office called to get Charley to take a promotion and a transfer. We talked it over, and he decided he wanted to stay here as we had just built our house and wanted to think about retirement. When he had started this job, he worked with J.K. Stuart, and there were no federal officers. As a result, he and Mr. Stuart worked just about the whole Middle District. He refused the promotion and asked to be taken off the best qualified list. Later when I asked why he decided to get back on the list, he explained, "Well, I have been thinking that Operation Dry Up will be over in Georgia around the first of the year and they will be closing offices and move into Alabama next. Valdosta will more than likely be closed and this area worked out of Moultrie."

It made me wonder. Was it possible that my two high-ranking state officials and other suspected higher ups within Charley's agency tried to keep Charley from discovering anything further about the porn ring by offering the transfer out of Valdosta that May as bait? The timing was too convenient to be a coincidence. With the thought of wispy ribbons of air rushing through the maze of unnatural kinks left behind in Roxanne's throat by the four in flannel, it became harder to enjoy the season.

Each day I left the lake surrounded by fog, and each evening I drove back to it under deep blue autumn skies that danced above roadways embroidered by the bristled stubble of freshly harvested cotton fields. As October 7th faded into the night, I thought about the synchronicity of my connection to Roxanne and my role within her mystery. Later that night, I finally made the connection to a clue about a piece of paper that had fallen on the floor of my office a year ago, the one that Spencer had told me Roxanne had tried to get me to notice. It was the clue about the name Cooper. All along I had made the assumption that Cooper had been a standalone name from all the other names on my list. It was a natural mistake. Thus, I extrapolated that perhaps I had made the same mistake with another name, Ganger, in assuming it a standalone name.

While having a conversation with Clint that evening about the anniversary of what I believed to be Roxanne's death, I mentioned Coleman's ethereal confession about seeing the group of men at midnight the night of the 12th rolling something into the cypress swamp on the farm to his left. When I asked if Clint recognized the name Cooper or the description of a man named Ganger, both names which had an association to Roxanne, he asked for a moment to think. When I added that Ganger always came through with the added impressions of a male energy that wore an olive-colored uniform and had an association or tie somehow to Park and Rec and Grim. He deliberated for another minute and then announced he was sorry he had not put two and two together before. The two names I mentioned, Cooper and Ganger, had not been separate. When I asked him what he meant, he replied by telling me that where the something had been rolled into the swamp was on property that was once owned by a man named Ganger Cooper. Not separate, they had been the same person all along. I was floored.

"But when I asked you who owned it, I thought you said it was owned by a Rayland or Rutland or a Kirkle…something?"

"Yes. It is now and probably since the 70's, but you didn't ask that. You just asked who owned the property. Back in the 60's and earlier, it was owned by Ganger Cooper. Why? What did I say?" Suddenly it made perfect sense why Roxanne had dropped the POST IT to the floor twice that day. She had been trying to tell me where to find her.

I remembered laughing and told him that from now on, I would do better to just let him ramble on, as I received more information that way. With the mystery of Roxanne's POST IT name and its meaning now deciphered, I was able to set the names Ganger and Cooper aside and felt more confident in the exact location of her remains. Two mornings later on October 9th, I was plunged back into 1966 with the anniversary of Charley's death and prayed for similar revelations.

Forty-six years ago Charley was still at home on standby, mowing the yard, swinging children on swings, and being the man he had become. Kaye was still married and determined to make her marriage work. Jules still had a father and a world of joy ahead of her. That night I paused to reflect about all the small and large things that had happened since I stood at the appointed hour with Jules, in the middle of a blacktop road just one thousand feet from the Withlacoochee River one year ago and then asked the heavens that Charley be spared the reliving of his murder. All day long I carried a photo of Charley with me as a constant reminder and constant companion.

The next day Spencer received an early morning visit from Charley. He showed her papers he was going through in the back of his car and the name of who he was gathering the papers for: someone named Glorious Bundles. I halfheartedly wanted to post it to prompt a response, but had learned I must be able to vet the information first. Having never seen or heard the name before, the only thing clear was that Charley still had information to give me, and I was still happy to receive it.

Work and school continued to drag me across the calendar. One day while working on my anthropology bone quiz, I was asked to identify a set of slides. I got them all right, including Roxanne's favorite: the hyoid. The hyoid bone is the thin bone that lies suspended in the neck and remains intact unless severe pressure is applied. Severe pressures like from… strangulation. It seemed everywhere I went that autumn I saw young, beautiful blonde debutantes walking the streets of Athens and realized that if not for death and forty-five years, any one of them could have been Roxanne. Her spirit followed me at every turn, and her essence seemed to fill the air whispering in my ears *"Look for me…look for my hyoid… find me…find my bones. My hyoid has been broken. Find me and prove to the world what they have done."* Again I recommitted my efforts to school and promised to do my best.

Three weeks later with fog on the lake and a fire burning in the fireplace, I took the morning off and celebrated the successful completion of a course on *Mapping and Exhumation of*

Clandestine Graves. With another feather in my educational cap, I was that much closer to keeping my promise and that much more confident I would. October ended and November picked up its thread without skipping a beat. The sun rose later each morning, like a painted lady exhausted from the follies of the night before. The rides into work seemed longer.

Happy to be on the downside of studies, I eased in my tensions and enjoyed the pastoral display, playing the same game in the car I always do with Charley. It is a little game of hide and seek we play, mostly for me to know he is current with me. I hide a wallet-sized photo of him driving a boat inside the pages of my Angel Numbers book without looking. Then as I see numbers on license plates of cars ahead of me, I flip to see if his photo is there on the same page as the corresponding number. Some days he likes to hide more than seek, but on that day he was spot on.

The ride into work is one hour and ten minutes. So he has that much time and five counties of roadways and intersections in which to find me. This happened four times within the course of my ride. Tickled, I rose the next morning anxious for the ride. Thirty minutes into my trip, I had nothing. Confused, I pulled the photo from the book and whispered that I missed him. Then I returned him to a new page and said, "Tag. You're it!"

Having gone into work later than usual, I saw traffic that was almost nonexistent, and I assumed that was the delay in our game. No cars? No tags! Just about that time, I looked at the digital clock on the dash. The clock rolled over to 11:02. Disappointed because of the significance of the date, I felt the desire to contact Spencer and share. The date was November 11, 2011 or numerically 11/11/11. Understanding the potential spiritual and numerical connection, I grabbed my phone and then stalled. Surely it would be even better to wait till the bewitching hour of 11:11 to call her? That would make it 11:11 on 11/11/11 and might bring me something more than a childish game of hide and seek or a fleeting feather.

Cautiously I continued to drive, keeping one eye on the road and one on the digital clock. As the minutes clicked by, I rounded the curve just outside Newborn and saw something huge and feathered squatting in the middle of the road five hundred feet or more in front of me. Annoyed that the deceleration or potential detour might compromise the remaining Verizon link, I tapped the brakes. I had two choices. I could just accelerate, honk my horn, and blast through the feathered mess at sixty-plus miles an hour, or I could test my theory that all things happen for a reason and trust that the cosmos was sending me a sign. In the back of my mind I heard Spencer's familiar mantra, *"You must trust the process."*

I looked at the clock and slowed my approach. Quickly losing any hope to make my 11:11 cellular connection, I decided to just go with the flow. "Ok, so it looks like I'll miss my call to Spencer, but maybe this little asphalt aviary is my consolation prize. Maybe instead of placing just a feather in my path, the cosmos is having fun with the day and sending me a whole freaking bird!" I chuckled. The ridiculousness of my thought process amazed me. I shook my head and sighed. "I need a freaking vacation."

Frustrated, I slowed the car another five miles per hour and turned off the radio. The feathered monster in the road ignored my advance. Irritated, I glanced at the clock on my dash. The digital display rolled another minute closer to the magical combination of 11:11 as the 'Stang rolled another hundred yards closer to its back. Just as I was about to resign myself to the fact that the universe had invited me to be just another buzzard at a road kill buffet, the head of the creature lifted and turned. Dumbfounded by what I saw, I slammed on my brakes. I couldn't believe it.

Curious, it cocked its great head, and the white crest undulated in the simmering autumn light. Its beady eyes trained on me and the yellow of its beak glowed as if polished. I gasped in amazement as it flexed its muscles and the breadth of its wing span took up more than two thirds of the broad side of my Mustang. Stunned, I sat and watched as it maneuvered its great girth about the road, assessing the threat level of my mechanical horse. Decidedly it was unimpressed by my intrusion. It crooked its neck and eyed me for another second and when I didn't move, it dismissed me and lowered its head to pick at the carcass beneath its talons. When I pulled my foot from the brake and inched my way forward a few more feet, it abruptly turned its attention back, hopped two steps towards the hood of my car, and then unfolded its wings as if to threaten.

Startled, I jammed the brake pedal back into the floor. Challenged, it cleared five more feet and then flew directly over my head to a high limb. I shoved the gear of the 'Stang into park, held my breath, and then hit my hazard lights. Mesmerized by its sheer size, I became cataleptic. It adjusted its stance on a towering limb fifty feet above me and cocked its head again. I exhaled in measured breaths and then waited to see what it would do next.

A minute went by as we considered one another. When I lowered my driver's window and adjusted my head outside its edge to get a better view, it dove at my ragtop, scratched at the fabric, and then returned to its post on the ground. For another two minutes I watched as it ripped into rotted flesh with total disregard for the ensuing encroachment of another car. I raised my arm and reached outside to take a photo with my cell phone as the approaching car honked its horn. Frightened by the foreign sound, the creature leapt into the air. As it passed the side of my car, its wings gulped in what air was left inside my lungs to raise it high aloft to a neighboring pine. In the thirty-two years I have lived in Georgia, I have never seen a mature bald eagle in the wild, let alone been less than twenty inches from the reach of its dagger-like talons.

The time of this event? You guessed it: 11:11! Convinced it was more than mere coincidence, I took note of time and placement and recorded it in a text. Shortly after, two more cars entered the highway. Frustrated, it made another swoop and left the area. The car behind me honked with irritation. I motioned the asshole to go around. After shutting off my hazards, I re-engaged my car and drove the rest of the way to work in absolute silence. No radio, no phone, no tag numbers, no Angel numbers, no breath. Awestruck by the event, I made a promise to call Spencer later in the day when I could tell her everything that happened, but I wasn't forced to wait long.

At exactly 1:11 my phone rang. It was Spencer. She said she had been thinking about me all morning, asked me if I had a few minutes. Still emotionally high from my earlier experience, I excused myself to get pen and paper. Five pages later, I emerged from a spiritual coma and hit the END button on my phone. Vindicated, I looked at the expansive crawl of ink that wandered its way across on the pages before me and took a deep breath. The consolation prize for the lack of my customary game of hide and seek had been huge. In the midst of the numerical abnormality of the day, the heavens had seen fit to deliver not just a feather, but a whole bird: the bird of Justice, a bald eagle. The significance of the day brought forth another blessing. Energies that had previously shied from filling out my cosmic questionnaires stepped forward into the light and gave Spencer a rare glimpse into their process.

Dazed, I set down my pen and re-read the pages of our recorded conversation in the privacy of my office, still caught up in the rapture of revelations.

The shooter Hank Sloan displayed himself for the first time. Bending to wash blood from his hands in the lake where Roxanne's final remains resided, he went mad with frustration. Each time he would dip his hands into the water to wash them, they would come out red... stained by the circular ripples of crimson that continued to roll towards the shoreline with a vengeance. No matter how many times he dipped them in, the procedure repeated itself again and again as though they could never be cleaned...he was trapped in this eternal process for what he had done...

And there was more. Spencer told me the MOT had finally stepped forward.

The MOT, heavyset and panting, was sweaty and panic stricken, revealing his golf association with the insurance agent who was somehow connected to Jessica. Miss Marjorie told Spencer that Theo was just two towns outside of Valdosta, coughing up blood and then reminded me what she told me when we first talked at the nursing home before she passed. A message about one of the four in flannel that was still alive. She said. "I meant what I said. He's a real loose cannon, dangerous, unpredictable... DANGEROUS... be aware."

I knew the reference to mean the ethereal anagram of Albert Einstein. Spencer continued.

She told me, "Chapter 13... your answers are in Chapter 13 of your book. Look there."

Then she told me her car began to fill with the familiar smell of pipe smoke.

It's him: the pipe smoker. Miss M is showing me the man who smoked cigars. Spencer's lungs begin to fill with secondhand smoke and she has trouble breathing. He is the man with the silver engraved lighter tucked inside the bag from the Morris Pawn Shop Charley had on him back in October 6th, 1966.

"I have the receipt in his bloodied wallet!" I blurted and then frantically continued to record what came through next.

They show me...Roxanne is rising from the bloodied water, unstained by the blood it now holds from the hands of the shooter and is ready to move on. She walks up onto the shore and waits. Jessica rises from the dirt, face intact and not a speck of soil on her; she too is anxious to evolve to the next level. The shooter walks with his two dogs, his hands wet and dripping with the blood he cannot escape. Charley is showing Spencer an hour glass. He tips it over and the sand begins to run. The time is running out. Closure is coming. Closure is coming. The shooter, the girls, and the MOT begin to walk away. Charley follows, then turns and says, "You did it... you did it."

Spencer whispered, "I wish you could see what this looks like, T.A.... It's so beautiful, so beautiful...the light...they are walking towards it...just beautiful!" Then she added.

November 17th is significant.

I recorded the final message and told Spencer I was worried that the time to put it all together was running out too fast for me to be ready for closure and that the clues were becoming more than I could ever possibly process. How would I ever know when enough was enough and when to let go and let God?

"You will know when you get to the end of the book," she said, "when to stop writing and let the world read the story. You must continue to trust the process."

Not surprisingly, her words were the same I had heard whispered in my ear just hours earlier. Stunned at the enormity of the information, I returned to my work and spent the better part of the afternoon in silence. Deeply affected, I decided to take the rest of the evening off. At 5:55 pm while passing back through the exact area where the eagle had made contact just hours before, I finally made the bigger connection. The eagle Charley had sent me truly had represented justice. I slowed my car to enjoy the ride and process the epiphany. At 6:05 I played the hide and seek game with Charley's photo again, but he refused to stay in between the pages. Every time I opened the book to search the numbers, his photo fell in my lap. Convinced he had something more he wanted to share, I held the picture in my hand while I drove and thanked him for the many blessings and information of the day.

As I fondly rubbed the edge of the photo thinking about the eagle, I was suddenly drawn to think about two clues I had thought meant something else: Charley's clue *"The answer is in the car"* and Kaye's clue *"I just threw it into the box. It's been there the whole time and I never knew."* As the autumn sun began to dip behind the Georgia pines, I remembered that the photo I was holding in my hand had once been in the box she spoke of. Suddenly it made sense. I held the snapshot up to the light and noticed two partial fingerprints that remained raised at the bottom right hand corner of the small photo… as if someone with something viscous on his or her hands had once held the photo at its edge to inspect it. A photo that had been buried in the box from 1966 until I had found it and rescued it to carry with me. Was this what he was trying to tell me? That I had been holding the most crucial piece of evidence in my hands all the time? The fingerprints on the bottom of the photo danced in the sunlight. Is it possible they belonged to someone who had been involved in his death that night? Maybe they had accidentally pulled it out as they searched for the P. O. Box key?

I didn't know... I couldn't know. All I knew was that the day had held more magic than anything I had ever experienced before and I had to trust. Why had I plucked it from Kaye's box? Of course I was pleased by the expression on his face and had chosen it as my personal talisman... but why? There were other photos. I tried to rationalize the whys and wherefores of my actions, but I could not. All I knew that day was trust.

I held his picture into the bent sunlight and watched his smile. I had fingerprints! I didn't know whose, but it didn't matter at the moment. I had fingerprints! I called Spencer and told her and we sealed the conversation with a promise that we would call each other at 11:11 pm later that night and see what else might come through. I hung up the phone and the theatre rat inside me gave way to joyous song from *Sweet Charity*, "If they could see me now, that little gang of mine."

****

At 11:11pm Spencer began the reading. At 11:12 pm a female energy made its presence known and I began writing.

Spencer's familiar breathing pattern kicked in. Seconds later she announced, *It's in the blood,"* she says. *"The energy explains she is just like her mother... just like her mother, manipulative, callous...it is in their blood. It is their way. She mentions her childhood...her mother's boyfriend. Age 8, age 8... age 8. It began then. Age 8, it all went south; so did his hands. Sexual abuse...good girl gone bad. She never loved Charley. It was a ruse.*

I wrote as fast as I could to keep up and asked Spencer for confirmation that it was G.

"It's her. Dark brown hair, long legs, red fingernails, red lipstick: it is G."

I took a deep breath but the oxygen had gone to my head and not to my lungs. I grappled for air, while Spencer continued.

"Who is this? Who is this?" she asked. "Is this someone new?"

She described what she was being shown and I recorded.

Gray hair, long, bushy mustache, very thick. Tall, slender...older man now... walks with a cane. Looks like a professor. Lots of hair for his age, thick, gray, his mustache full. Triad. G involved with this man, the younger law enforcement, and Charley... there is an association. He is a farmer. He has the initial W in his name. He has a son. He knows everything. He is still alive.... still alive.

I knew who this was and G knew that I knew. I asked Spencer again to ask Gerri if she ever loved Charley. A resounding *"No...Never"* is returned. It is all I can do not to crush his 8 x 10 to my chest and protect him from the evil bitch that floated in the ethos above us. The next few minutes were spent in scribing impressions.

Kaye brings you roses as a thank you. My parents tell me to hang my holiday wreath. The shooter continues to vomit, spewing his guts in an effort to cleanse his soul. Roxanne, who shows us the bakery and bids us speak to a woman named V, the mistress who says this is who she was. Cruel, cold-hearted. She knew no other way, but has made her peace with Charley on the other side. She admits to using men as stairs, stepping one to the other, getting what she wanted for the moment and then moving on. She makes no apologies, no excuses for her behavior. In her family it is tradition...her legacy...their way.

Silence crept into the air for a moment while Spencer's breathing adjusted. Then suddenly she broke in again.

And what is this? Someone new? Someone else who knew the four-way very well? Someone who always wore a brown suit.

Now it was time to adjust my breathing. I flipped the page and began a new one. Her use of the word "suit" and not "uniform" meant we had a new player in the mix: a civilian.

They are showing me...Someone else... a black man who remains stuck in his untimely death. Hmmm...he is showing me the four-way...the intersection...he is hiding...he sees Grim take the money from G.

In my mind I saw Damon's greedy fingers grab and tear at the bills he cherished more than others' lives. She continues,

He saw Grim double cross him. He was furious. He was hiding in the woods as the money changed hands. "You lied, you lied," he says. "It was not supposed to go down like this! I know what you've done. I know and I will tell."

I knew immediately who this was. It was Bugman McFallon, the black nightclub owner who had owned the Ten Oaks Country Club property just below the four-way. The nightclub owner whose property after death had fallen into the hands of the known felon snitch, Wiley Henders. The property that held the burned remains of Jessica under the tire halfway in and halfway out. Grim had insisted they were the best of friends...the black nightclub owner who asked Grim to count his money for him, to help buy farm equipment. The black nightclub owner who said he would tell the truth, but never got the chance because he was run over at his mailbox by a car shortly after. That too was called an accident. So just how many necessary accidents could there have been in Valdosta back in 1966 without Grim's name and the four in flannel's fingerprints all over?

Spencer said it was clear he had not moved on. "He is of ghost, not spirit. He continues to live this betrayal over and over."

In the wake of such an epiphany, I remembered Deputy Colbert's son once told me it was a hit set up by Finch to keep Bugman from squealing. Just the same as Hank Sloan's head wound had been the product of a botched hit and not a personal accident. I made a note and then asked Spencer to redirect. We asked G about her LT. She replied.

Who is the man who had a thing for feathers too? A man who had a special feather? A lucky feather; it was brown and white. He put it in the band of his hat and kept it there even in death. Was in a wheelchair at the end? Buried with his hat. This is G's LT. She shows us the plow. He is a farmer too perhaps. It is an old plow. He has an affinity for them, collects them.

Before she was finished, Charley came to the forefront and gave her a message about a ship in a bottle setting sail. Spencer told me the message was specific to me, that I would understand. She said he presented with his ship in the bottle and that suddenly the waves inside began to swell and overtake the tiny vessel; piece by piece the mast and bridge of the ship broke apart. In one fell swoop, the ship was dashed upon the sides, the glass broke open, and he was drowning. Then our connection was made and the ship began to repair itself. Slowly but surely the mast was returned to its original stature and station. The bridge and rigging regained their place of honor. The glass sealed about its craft, and the water rose within the confines of its transparent margins, but no longer threatened. Spencer told me that he wanted me to understand the impression: setting sail, sailing away. I knew what he meant, but was very frightened that this was his way of saying goodbye.

Spencer assured me it was meant for me as in "set your sails; now you can sail off into another adventure," that it meant something wonderful.

Tearful at the other end of the phone, I acknowledged the metaphor and did my best to expel a quivering lip, not ready to let him go. She cautioned that I would understand, saying "You know how this works." And to be certain I do. But as happy as it made me to think that Charley was now ready to set a new course for his sails, I was overcome with a wave of longing for the days when he used to appear in desperate measures and need my help. I felt just like Dorothy in *The Wizard of Oz* standing on the platform, with air balloon and passage home waiting, tugging at the tufts of curls that brandish the chest and shoulders of the Cowardly Lion and saying, "I'm gonna miss the way you used to whimper and wail for help." And that's the way it seemed: like one more letting go in my life, another tear in my heart, another loss.

For a day I wandered mentally about the memories of our journey and tried to be happy for my dear friend, to know that he was finally on his way to where and when he should have been forty-six years before. I was sincere in my desire to see his sails swing wide with wind and determination. Still, a part of me wanted to board that ship and go with him so as not to break the bond. As he and Kaye left Spencer's vision hand in hand and all together, a piece of my heart went with them. I comforted myself that Charley wanted me to set my sails too, that he was freeing me for some great next adventure. But the perceived loss of his heart as my ballast left me without an even keel.

Two days after his message, I left my house and began my long ride to work. Annoyed with the same agitating excuse for music on our airwaves these days, I popped in a CD of old 70's music (my glory days) and began to ease into my day. As the sun broke the horizon and the light fell softly on crisp pastures and brittle fences, I finally understood the message. Delivered in typical Charley style, song # 8 on my CD came on. It was an old favorite, redone in recent history by Brooks and Dun, a song called "My Maria," written by Daniel Moore and B. W. Stevenson. As I was singing along, canting the words by rote, it suddenly hit me.

There, with brilliant sunrise, hot coffee, Mustang in the wind, and a lighter heart, I heard the words coming out of my mouth. I laughed and then repeated the song another seven times just to hear his message and smiled, knowing my Charley had not left me as I supposed, that his message was not meant as goodbye, but as a thank you. "We are forever," just as he had promised.

"My Maria...There were some blue and sorrow times

Just my thoughts about you bring back my piece of mind

Gypsy lady…You're a miracle worker for me

You set my soul free like a ship sailing on the sea."

It was not just his soul that had been set free. It had been mine as well.

CHAPTER FIFTY-ONE

In between turkey leftovers and the commercial rush of Christmas, the furnace freaked out and then abruptly died, but not until it had eaten up $213.00 of a $300.00 tank of propane that was supposed to get me through the winter. So far in our limited tenure the house had suffered the loss of a hot water heater, a dishwasher, an air conditioner, a roof, one toilet seat, and a furnace. To their credit, the owners had replaced or repaired all in a survivable and timely fashion, but the message was clear. As much as I had counted on that house becoming my home, something inside said this was not the final space for us. Without the cushion of a healthy savings account, we realized that the wonderful disjointed home that had housed us in transition was one crisis after another in the waiting. Resigned, I decorated for Christmas and began to look for a much smaller home on the lake that might meet our needs without choking our enthusiasm.

Earlier in the year Spencer had told me something would happen on December 17th, and it did. On December 17th I received a call while I was at work. An ATF agent from Macon, Georgia had agreed to do some exploratory work on the case. After a brief conversation with the newly appointed agent, I was invited to give my entire presentation one more time, complete with updated information.

Earlier that year Spencer had given me another date of January 12th as significant. As always, when it was given, I had to parse between the inferences as it related to 1966 or to a more contemporary setting. Originally the agent asked for a meeting on the 9th, but complications with an interview for an ATF Forensics Lab job in Atlanta pushed it to the next available date on my calendar: January 12. Confirmation from the universe in hand that I was on the right track, I was ecstatic and spent much of my Christmas vacation reviewing notes and modernizing my dossier.

Shortly after New Year's and dressed for success, my husband and I made the trip to meet with the ATF once again. What took two hours the first go around took over four and a half the second. I felt sorry for the agent as his poor head must have been swimming from sensory overload. But I was so happy to have another audience that I promised to hold his hand every step of the way. As far as my interview for the lab position in Atlanta, I realized twenty seconds into the interview it not only wasn't what I wanted, it was not at all the way God intended for me to serve my divine purpose. Weeks later when a generic letter confirmed I didn't get the nod, I was superficially upset, but mostly relieved. A position in a lab would not have fed my soul the way writing and theatre did, nor would its reduced pay scale honor my new mortgage. The cosmos knew that. Spencer buffered the blow by telling me the cosmos had bigger and better things planned for me.

Information continued to stream its way in with more impressions of Jessica's body being burned in a fire that was being watched by two men, one of whom I believed to have been Grim, the other, a yet unknown. This one continued to evade me until I remembered something from Kaye's journal that dovetailed with something Spencer had seen in an earlier session.

Do you understand the woman who cans the yellowed fruit? She is in charge of the canning. She works in a canning factory of sorts. She saw something out the window.

This fit perfectly with another clue about a fight between Charley and Kaye a few years before 1966 that had involved some sort of pickled fruit. It had come through the day Jules was with us.

They show me a jar of something yellow. It was three years before, a fight, something thrown against a wall. A glass jar shattered. She bought these all the time; they were canned. Something to do with alcohol. It signaled the beginning of the end. They show me they are on the same page — that the marriage was over.

Remembering that, something else struck a chord with me. Charley was not a drinker, and that's why I didn't make the correlation right away. It wasn't easy, but after weeks of research I finally figured out the connection. During her line of questioning with Callenwald, Kaye had given it away. What had happened three years earlier that involved alcohol that would have had her hurling a jar of pickled peaches against her kitchen wall in anger over something that somehow included Charley?

What about this bootlegger's wife from over around Douglas that he was supposed to have been involved with?

Clearly, Charley was not an innocent man when it came to matters of the heart. The fact that Kaye spoke so blatantly about it to Callenwald after Charley's death left little doubt that there was trouble in paradise long before G arrived on the scene. Combine that scenario with another testimonial overheard from another source: *"I knew it wasn't suicide. Charley would never have committed suicide over a woman. He had had other girlfriends before."* If you threw that in the mix and added a healthy dose of Kaye's fermented anger, that would pretty much answer why there had been exploding jars of pickled peaches in the Covington kitchen. Everything seemed to fit. That's why the next two clues gave me shivers.

The man at the fire had a son who had some sort of problem with his leg. He had a brace or something that kept him from running fast. It used to frustrate his father. That man was there... there at the fire.

At last I was getting closer. They said Jessica had died in July. They also said there had been a huge fire in July, and Spencer had talked about somebody's foot being burned. There were two men who watched the fire. I believed the first was Grim. Now they described the second man as a man who had a son with a crippled leg. Later additions to the clue about the canning brought it all together.

Do you understand the woman who cans the yellowed fruit? She is in charge of the canning. She works in a canning factory of sorts. She saw something out the window. Everyone thinks she is too sweet to have known. She would not have talked; nobody ever questioned her. She knows something; she saw something out that window. Everyone knows the woman who cans the fruit, even Kaye. Find that woman!

If you put the clues together, there was indeed a connection between Kaye and this canning woman: the yellowed fruit that Kaye always bought. The yellowed fruit could now be identified as the jar of pickled peaches that Kaye had thrown against the wall while yelling at Charley about his affair with a bootlegger's wife, three years before G! Did the canning woman also know of the Covington household trials? This woman, who had seen something she was not supposed to? After several calls and a few more nights of research, I figured out the woman was married to a relative of Jeb Finch. The problem? There was the possibility of it being one of two men. The man the canning lady was married to was not the father of the boy with the crippled leg, but his uncle. This fact complicated things. When I questioned Spencer, she said they show the relationship as fatherly. Sometimes this can be either literal or figurative. Either way, both of these men would have been related to Finch. Further complication: he could have been an Einstein. Not the psychic's Einstein mind you, but another man named Albert. Why did everybody have to share the same freaking names all the time?

Specificity demanded that I parse the logistics to see if it could narrow the selection down to one. The canning factory was located in town, out by the high school. I was uncertain if it was actually the canning factory's window that was being referred to, so it took me a while to figure out where the bonfire could have been. I tried to triangulate between the known address of the factory, the address of Grim at the time, and the potential addresses of both men who could have fit the fatherly role for the boy with the crippled leg.

In the end, I surmised it didn't matter. No matter which window, this woman had seen something she was not supposed to. Somewhere around the 11th of July 1966, this woman had seen either her husband or another man related to Finch and Grim burning something in a huge fire she knew not to be garbage. Although I wanted to be able to say definitively which other male had been Grim's partner that day, sometimes getting close was the best I could do.

It was very much the same for a few other players in this case. Take, for instance, the elusive identity of LT from the very first session. Some days I was certain LT stood for one man, some days for another. It drove me to distraction. Each time I threw the dice, a new option would be presented with a potful of impressions that I had to wade through and analyze. No matter the detour, I always came back to my notebooks. Everything ever granted from research or Spencer was recorded there. My notebooks continued to hale as my English bible. Satisfied I had at least nailed down the significance of the fire, I refocused on my lack of progress with the LT connection.

From the very first session, Spencer had given me impressions about G's triad: Charley, the older LT energy, and the younger law enforcement. In order for everything else to gel, I needed to figure out which person fit best with the imprints. So I went back to the other sessions for help. Charley at one time had drawn a large circle around the county area, suggesting to Spencer that with the exception of the two high-ranking state officials, this was mostly a local scandal. So my need was to focus more on those within its measured boundaries.

Session clues suggested that my older man was senior to G by some twenty years, socially and economically elevated, fancied a lucky rabbit's foot, and possessed a gold medal for something that may have been related to another WWII reference, had a thing about cradle scythes, liked feathers in his hat, and in fact had been buried wearing his hat. Pairing that with the earliest reference of the judge's gavel from Charley's opening appearance in the first session, I held tight to recent discoveries and waited for further guidance.

CHAPTER FIFTY-TWO

In the days and weeks that followed, I did my best to explore every combination of those initials, but in the end could not find a perfect fit to all the information necessary. For me, the search had ended. Placing that disappointment behind me, I tried to refocus my attention on the fourth in flannel, in particular, the man who bore the initials "RL." Since my original pipe smoker had not solidified as the definitive fourth, I looked closer at the recent newcomer RL.

A few weeks later, Spencer called to tell me about an early morning visit from Roxanne. Lying in bed somewhere between slumber and sunrise, Spencer was suddenly pulled under the murky waters of Saddle Bag Lake by Roxanne. Lying on the bottom of the swampy floor, she pointed up towards the water's surface. It was dancing with multicolored lights and there was Grim, standing next to another man who smoked a cigar. He was tall, wore a camel-colored coat. The twirling lights of Grim's cruiser bounced off the flashy cufflinks and gold engraved watch he wore bearing the same initials. His image fluctuated in the rippled waters above Roxanne's watery grave. He had been identified as the man who flashed about his money with his monogrammed shirt sleeves, his arrogant swagger, and his associations with law enforcement. This was the man with the silver engraved lighter that had been in Charley's possession when he died and the lighter that Callenwald had nearly bitten Kaye's head off for. He was the man who smoked a cigar as easily as mint tobacco in a pipe and held the watch associated with Roxanne and the MOT from the very start.

But just like my candidate for G's older man, so many other citizens bore the same initials and similar backgrounds and associations that I became blind with speculation. Eventually I gave up quick-fix confirmations and told Charley he would have to plug the lingering holes of doubt himself. Desperate to find real traction, I returned to my notes and interviews, hoping against hope

448

that I had missed something that could help stiffen my resolve. With the blog in full-swing circulation, clues began to flood in.

Having previously placed other bait out on the blog about the purported railway bootlegging, I finally reeled in a clue from the oddest source of all. Winston Wahlberg, who had overheard folks talking, finally crawled out from the shadows long enough to educate me. In an email he made it clear that he had neither been involved or knew about such an activity back in 1966. A simple denial would have been enough, but he didn't stop there. Wahlberg continued to protest his innocence stating he knew nothing about the supposed moonshine run on rail cars that ran between the Valdosta/Clyattville area and Thomson, Georgia. (For those of you who are geographically challenged, Thomson, Georgia is located NW of the Clyattville/Valdosta area.)

Pairing Wahlberg's information with the longstanding impressions from Spencer about illegal hooch being run on the rails out of Valdosta to areas just NW on the short GA/FL RR spur, I wanted to immediately write back and thank him. Why? Up until that point I had not known the end game location of the infamous bootleg line — only that the hooch left Valdosta in a northwesterly direction to a station further up the GA/FL line. The irony was sweet. Here he was doing his best to cover his tracks. but without realizing it, he had just plugged the only hole left in the railroad scenario. Thanking him at that point seemed grossly obtuse, so I left my appreciation for his concerns on the table and then smiled like a Cheshire cat. Two days later my grin elongated when I learned that Thomson had also been the hometown stomping grounds of Damon Cummings — the Grim Reaper, who was rumored to have travelled between Valdosta and Thomson quite often in those days. Add that to an election associate of the governor, and the corroboration ratio was almost too convenient to be true.

Wahlberg stayed on the radar quite a bit that month as it came to light that he had also been a crime scene photographer in 1966. Information suggested he worked closely with Bookman Studios on a regular basis and that began to raise my other eyebrow.

(Remember: Winston Wahlberg was the one who made the threatening calls to Beau Colbert's son that night after my first set of interviews at the Historical Society, demanding that the original files and crime scene photos of Charley's body be turned over immediately to officials of the local Historical Society or back to the Sheriff's Department.) Though it is well documented that Wahlberg took crime scene photos mostly for the VPD and filmed both athletic and other social events for the locals, who's to say he didn't occasionally moonlight for others when it was necessary to "arrange and photograph things" those outside the law didn't need to see? Remember, the young boy witness said he never saw photos being taken while he and his friend were there. Also, none of the photos are shown taken during the rain, but both the witnesses and the National Weather records show that copious amounts of rain fell after 11:00 pm that night.

Again, you can see how perception is everything as information sometimes takes on a life of its own. The information about Thomson and the crime scene photography only added to the weight already upon the scales against both Wahlberg and Cummings being completely innocent of the railway shenanigans and potential involvement in the extensive cover up of Charley's murder.

Later in February, winter winds blew favorably again across my emotional landscape and brought forth another soul to energize my investigation and move justice forward. As stated, the blog has always been a blessing for me. It allows me to think out loud, to vent my frustrations and chum the waters with bait for more information. Near the end of that month, it did what fishing always does best: it brought me a fish.

That night I received a response to my fishing blog. The message simply read, "I may have info," and the person left a contact email to engage if interested. Thrilled, I responded to the unknown author, stating that I would be most discreet in all communications. I invited the person to call my cell. Several more cryptic emails flowed between us before my very clandestine counterpart felt comfortable enough to seriously consider the offer of cellular effacement. Days later I finally received a call.

When the phone rang, I recognized the area code and answered casually, assuming it was a regular contact. The voice on the other end, however, was soft, Southern, and foreign to my dossier. In measured cadence she asked if I was the author of a blog she'd found on the internet about a man named Charley Covington. I reached for my notebook, poised for information, and identified myself as the author. Once secure, she informed me that someone had told her about the blog. She then informed me she had spent the entire week reading it from start to current inductions over and over and was shocked at what I was implying.

I explained briefly I had been given permission by Charley's daughter to explore her father's death and that my findings had suggested homicide and conspiracy. She asked more questions, but refrained from identifying herself. Uncertain as to why she was being so inquisitive and how this timid dated debutante fit in to the picture, I finally asked if she felt comfortable telling me who she was and why she was so concerned.

Without bravado or barricade, she admitted that doing so would constitute one of the bravest acts she would ever perform in her life. Then without segue she simply broke through her fears. "TA? This is...how shall I put this more delicately?" and the air went silent.

"Yes?" I prompted.

Suddenly a more playful side broke through. "I'm trying to think exactly how you would name me in this darn blog of yours," she mulled out loud.

"I...I have no idea, as I still don't know who you are," I chuckled, hoping to keep the atmosphere between us light. "Could you at least tell me if you knew any of the alleged key players in the blog?" It was a bold move, but I wanted to honor her daring.

Silence ensued as I left the invitation there on the metaphorical table for her.

"Let me see if I can remember the nickname you used for a particular one of the four in flannel. There were many players in this conspiracy, but only four in the intimate boy's club she was referring to. Heart pounding, pen hovering, mouth dry, I waited to record her first name on the top of the page.

"I believe if I appeared in your blog, you would refer to me as... a very close…friend of Mr. Einstein."

Identity established, my pen dropped and so did my jaw. Eighteen hours earlier I had Facebook stalked this person, hoping to find a way of getting in touch with her. I had thrown out random bait to the cosmos, and now Charley was doing everything he could to reel in the rest of the ocean for me. "Then your first name would be..."

She dove in head first. "Please... let's not use our real names right now. I have no idea if this is being recorded. Just so you know up front, the email address used was not mine. This phone number is not mine and I do not wish to complicate matters further for any of these people, as they have already gone out of their way to help me find you." She paused, took a deep breath, and finished. "Let's just talk a bit and see if we have anything worth sharing with one another."

My heart was pounding, but I imagined far less more profoundly than hers if she had indeed been intimately involved at some point with my Mr. Einstein. "Ok," I said and wrote what I knew was her entire real name and the date at the top of my page and waited for further instructions.

She opened first and told me that way back in the day, she and Einstein had been high school sweethearts. Sometime after graduation, they had a falling out. She married someone else, moved away, and had a child. Decades later, she returned to Valdosta. Somehow the two met up again, but unlike the fairytale romance of their pheromone-filled teenage personas, romance did not carry them over the bridges of middle age. Soon the two were estranged again. With a somewhat watercolored version of their background, she lurched forward and began to paint a more realistic portrait of their current status.

"I have been trying to walk away from him for years. He's a sick man. A sex addict, I think you call them. He has all kinds of what I like to call 'Johnny Jump Up' pills to keep himself hard, and he collects all kinds of magazines, sex toys, and gadgets. It makes me sick, all the porn. Magazines, movies, pictures...you name it, he's got it. And now that I know he was capable of murder too," she blurted and it was then that I realized the impact of what I was doing with the blog.

Using hard evidence to help prove truth is one thing; using suppositions and conjectures without concrete evidence is quite another. Even though it's part of the discovery process to do so, I felt bad. If I was wrong about all this, I had just placed a heartless bias inside a woman's head I had no right to and I told her so.

"You needn't worry about that, little miss. You think I ended things because the man was a saint?" and she giggled as though we were teenage girls who had just shared a secret behind a bathroom stall. "I told you. I knew he was trouble long before you and your blog ever crossed my path." Absolved of an unassigned sin, I eased while she continued to engage.

"So why don't you tell me what you think really happened to Charley that night beyond what you try to hide in that blog of yours? And after that, just how involved you think your Mr. Einstein, as you call him, was involved?"

"Ok, but first..."

I reiterated that she need not share anything until she was ready and gave her a brief overview of what I suspected were the events of that night. With a gracious spirit she listened and made comments here and there about information she had gleaned from various entries, epiphanies about things she had suspected, and rumors she had heard. I reminded her she could simply give me whatever information she felt might be of help and I would do my best to vet it without compromising her further. I waited for her reply. When none came, I assumed that I had breached the bounds of propriety and her new found silence was her way of signaling that the conversation was over. Before the anticipated rejection, I tossed in my disclaimer.

"I understand this is a lot to take in, Miss...." and I caught myself. "Sometimes I have a hard time believing all this myself, but so many things have happened that I have no choice. And it's not just what Spencer and I have been able to piece together. With support from other evidence, like page 2 of the GBI's State Crime Lab Report that was removed because it showed a ballistics report that proved that there were two guns. And then there are six of the eight original crime scene photos we recovered from the Deputy's son, plus the witness statements about the two girls and other interviews I haven't told you about. There's just so much that doesn't add up right for me. It's impossible to deny he was murdered and..."

And she cut me off. "You say you feel you know who the shooter was?"

"Yes."

"Was it...Mr. Einstein?" she entered gingerly.

"No. It was somebody else."

"Where do you think they hid the second gun?"

I knew it took courage for her to reach out. I didn't want to insult her by being vague and obtuse. I told her that the Crime Lab Report confirmed two weapons and then after the impression of the gun exchange at Sam Daily's store that night between Gerri Baldwin, Logan Booker, and the red-headed go-to man I believed the alleged shooter, Hank Sloan, was told to take the gun, go home, keep his yap shut, and not talk to anybody until advised what to do next.

"Hank Sloan?"

"Yes...that's what I believe." I confessed. It took a couple of minutes for her to digest that bit of information. "I'll explain how I figured all that out later," I added, so as not to disrupt the flow.

"Ok," she managed. "And then what happened?"

"And then I believe he [Sloan] took that gun home and hid it somewhere on his mama's property that night. He was divorced at the time and staying with her. There were only two people who knew where he hid it: he and the other fourth in flannel he confided in. Spencer saw a back porch and a concrete round slab off to the right that I believed to be the description of a well cover. Later with more information, I was able to Google Earth Satellite the place and sure enough, her description was spot on."

"So you think it's still there?" she asked.

I was curious as to why it was so important for her to be certain of its whereabouts as her previous association, Einstein, had just been discounted, but speculated further.

"The infamous 'they' said there were only two who knew where the gun was hidden. Sloan's dead, so that leaves just one other person who would have known where he hid it."

"So, you think it's still there? In that well?"

"Well, let's just say that up until Hank died, I believe the gun was there. After that? I don't know, because I'm not really certain who the other person was who knew where it was hidden. Maybe they figured with Hank dead, nobody would ever go looking there anyway."

"Why?"

"Because at the time he lived about six miles from the murder site, just across the Georgia /Florida border near Cherryville Lake. Nobody would expect it to be hidden somewhere out of state."

"Cherryville Lake?" she repeated.

I replayed my answer over inside my head and didn't want to mislead her, so I added, "The home wasn't actually on Cherryville Lake, but near another town in the same area as Jenkins or Jasper, Florida. I can't remember right now which one; I'd have to check my files. The point is nobody would have looked out of state or even at a member of the law enforcement at the time. Remember, they first said it might be moonshiners and then a few days later settled on suicide."

"Was Sloan's house near a lake?" she asked.

"Uh, I don't know. I've never been there. I sent Clint to get photos one weekend, but he was up to his ass in Sloan mailboxes by the time he found the address. He got out to take a few photos and then got the hell out of Dodge because folks started asking too many questions. He never said anything about being near a lake, and the Google Earth satellite was only focused within a few hundred feet of the house to look for the well cover. But shit, it's in Florida and the border area there is full of a hundred stupid little lakes and ponds. I could pull the address up. I flagged it as a Favorite. It won't take but a minute. Do you want me to? I could email it to you."

She never made a plea one way or another.

The air between us became very heavy, and the humming of her raspy breath stopped. I listened for a second longer and heard nothing. There was a crackle kind of sound that popped in my ear and then again nothing. I thought maybe the line had gone dead, but I wasn't sure. "Are you there? Are you ok?" I asked, afraid I had somehow in my unbridled enthusiasm broken some unspoken code in our tentative agreement. "Hello?" The light on my cell face went out, and I wasn't sure if it was just a bad battery or if she had actually hung up on me.

"Shit! I lost the connection," I muttered under my breath and reached to hit REDIAL. "God dammit, I was this close," I whimpered into the air.

Suddenly I heard a thinned voice. "T.A.?" Amazed and embarrassed she was still on the line, I blurted out her first name. "Cecelia….I'm so sorry. I thought you had hung up."

As I apologized for the breech, she shushed me and then in hushed tones relayed "I think I know where the second gun is." My jaw locked and I remained silent. "I believe I was with him the night he got rid of the second gun." While the cellular connection was still intact, my brain was not so much. Dumbfounded, I still could not respond.

"Did you hear me?" she asked. "I think I know where your second weapon is." I tried to regulate my breathing. "T.A.? Did you hear me?"

I managed to signal my recognition while everything began to scramble in my head. Suddenly clues began to flood my brain about the shooter and the night of the gun exchange.

"Do you understand the small white house… The Wizard of Oz? *Do you understand the root cellar… at the front of the house… the circular concrete block…a well in the backyard… looking from the back porch…the tree line and the fence…lives with an older female energy… shut your yap…do not do or talk to anyone until I tell you…go to man… red headed."* I remembered asking Spencer way back in the beginning if the gun was still there. *"Is it, they say, is it? Who would take it? Who would care? Only the two knew where it was. Too much time has passed… too much time."*

What the hell did that mean? *"Too much time had passed, too much time?"* Too much time had passed for what? For people to care? For the gun to remain in the same place…down the well hole, buried in the backyard of the shooter Sloan? Hidden in the muddy boots of Mr. Einstein or tucked inside the torn hat of the State Trooper Damon? Too much time since it had been moved to somewhere else? Had someone moved the weapon from where Sloan had taken it to that night, thinking it would be too hot to keep it where he lived while things were being investigated? Or had Sloan given the .38 pistol to the "other person" as soon as the investigation had been closed to get it out of his hands? How was I supposed to know?

I heard Cecelia on the other end of the line talking about how much Einstein liked to fish, but my mind was still on intellectual jetlag. Was it possible the second person retrieved it from Sloan's homestead after the shooter's passing to keep subsequent Sloan family members from finding it and turning it in unaware of what it had been used for? Or had both the weapons used belonged to someone other than Charley, in which case knowing where one was still left me without the second weapon's location? The Crime Lab Report had clearly denoted two bullet fragments from two separate weapons. Had the .38 Colt Special they offered as Charley's suicide weapon not been fired at all? The possibilities were endless.

Two people knew about the location of the second weapon. The shooter and the man he confided in.

Could Einstein have been that second person and not the red-headed go-to man? And if so, when did he first retrieve the weapon from the shooter's well? Where had he kept it all those years and why? What prompted him to dump it again somewhere else?

"T.A.?" she whispered again. "I have to go soon."

"Ok," I panted. "But Charley was murdered in 1966. You said you came back to Valdosta about nine years after, so that would be about 1975. How could you have been with him when he got rid of the second gun if you didn't live there then?"

"Because it was way after 1966 when it happened — when he got rid of the gun."

"What?"

"What year did you say Sloan died?" she pleaded.

"I didn't...I didn't say. Why?"

Her breath began coming in short spurts. "Do you know?" I quickly did the math and gave her the timeline of when I thought it to be and heard her heavy sigh. "Oh no...no. Oh my God. I'm so sorry...how could I have known?"

"How could you have known what?" I implored, desperate to get her to commit to something intelligible.

"That it was the... I didn't know it could have been the same. Oh, my Lord," she gasped and began to hyperventilate. If left alone to wallow too long in her private epiphany, I knew she would place herself in a physical and an emotional vice and so tried to cut her off at the pass.

"It wasn't your fault. You couldn't have known. When was this? When you were with him and saw the gun? And do you know for sure it was 'the' gun?"

"Well, it was a gun. And it had to have been that gun...it just had to!" and somehow she sounded more like a small child than an older woman.

"But are you sure it was 'the' gun?" I badgered, wanting specifics.

"I... I don't know. I don't know anything for sure now. Let me think... let me think!" she admonished. "What has he done?" she hurled into the cosmos between us.

"Did you clearly see the gun? Can you testify to that?" I begged.

"He showed me the gun. He said he had used in something illegal... something that had been real bad. Said if the Feds ever found out about it..." and she stalled to catch her breath.

"Go on...please," I begged.

"It was in his hand that night on the boat." And her breath became ragged again. "He kept rolling it over in his hands. He got off on things like that, showing me bad things...telling me about the bad things he liked to do. He... he...he's sick you know? He's not right!" and she began to breathe heavy again.

"Ok...ok. I'm sorry. Just calm down and tell me what happened next. You saw the gun and then what?"

"I...I never knew about Charley back then. I wasn't here then, so I never knew. But I heard about it later, heard people talk about things. I knew Gerrilynn."

"How did you know Gerrilynn?"

"He...your Mr. Einstein...used to take me fishing to a little lake just the other side of the Georgia/Florida border. Sampson Lake, I think the name was. We used to go there quite a bit back then. Why, I was never quite certain. Like you said, there was a stupid fishing puddle every ten feet in that area, and there was no need to drive that far each time just to go fishing. But Albert liked that place for some reason. We always had to go with Gerrilynn and her second husband, Nolan. Oh shit! Please tell me he wasn't part of this, was he? He seemed like such a nice man," she commented.

"No...no, he wasn't, as far as I know. Go on, tell me about that night."

"Ok. I guess I'm just a bit jumpy. I keep hearing doors open and close," she said, held her breath for a minute, and then began again. "He was such a nice man, Gerrilyn's second husband. I never knew her first husband, but this explains a whole lot about her."

Curious, I broke my own rule and redirected the witness. "What makes you say that?"

"Something about her gave me the willies. Mostly her laugh. She cackled like a witch. It was most unattractive laugh, loud, obnoxious. Yes, cackling is the perfect word." Satisfied G now made an ideal match for the witch from Jules's childhood Halloween book, I redirected back to task.

"Sampson Lake, you say?"

"Yes, it was called Sampson Lake. We fished a lot back then, sometimes more out of habit than enjoyment. One evening he took me there. While our friends were out in their boat across the lake, he showed me a gun that he said he had kept as a souvenir. He was very cagey about from where and then simply stated that it was from a job or a raid he had been on several decades before. When I asked why he didn't just sell or pawn it, he told me he couldn't. The gun had numbers on it and like I said before... he told me if the Feds ever found out he had it, they would send him to prison for sure. He got off on showing and saying those kinds of things. He's a sick man...sick." And as an afterthought she added, "I'm sorry I didn't tell someone about this before. I'm sure there are probably other things I know; I just don't know that I know yet."

My heart began to race. Charley was killed forty-six years ago to date. If I added the years between Charley's murder and when the shooter died, then added the years that Einstein told his then wife he had kept it hidden in his possession as a souvenir, then subtracted all that from the year 2012, it fit exactly into the necessary timeline to be the weapon that was used to murder Charley on October 9, 1966.

"Do you remember where he threw it?" I pumped. "What section of the lake?"

"If I saw the lake again...probably. Oh, I hope so. It was so long ago. I swear I would have paid more attention to everything if I'd have known it would be so important so many years later."

"Just do your best to remember. Think about the shoreline and where you were that night in directional terms: N, S, E, W, NW, SW, etc. Then I can zoom in from there and look for any landmarks that might help you remember. I'll pull up Google Earth and take a look while I have you on the phone. Do you remember a road or a town that is nearby that would help me find a starting point?"

"Sampson is near Mauldin. Mauldin, Florida. Hurry… I think I hear someone."

Nervous, my fingers groped clumsily at the keys on the laptop like a teenage boy unhooking his first brassiere. "It might be easier if we looked at the same time. I can email you a satellite photo of the lake. If you can get to a computer, you can get me closer to where you think it was and then I can pass this information on to Spencer." I shoved the cell between my right shoulder and ear, so I could talk while manipulating the keys. As I waited for Google Earth to load, I recorded what she had told me in my notebook. "I can't believe this shit," I exhaled.

"*You* can't believe this shit? I just found out I slept with a murderer!"

"Right…. you win! You definitely win!" I chortled and smiled at the 8 x 10 at the corner of my desk. Google Earth expanded on the screen. As I waited for the little man and the push pins to appear, I thought I heard the sound of a door closing on the other end of the line. Suddenly my Southern fried angel addressed me in a completely different tone.

"No, I already get the weekend newspaper. Sorry, I won't be needing your services, but thank you very kindly for calling. Bye, bye now."

"But I..." I began and she lowered her voice.

"I have to go. Please... no emails and do not call this number back. Remember: no real names. Promise?" she whispered.

"I promise. You can just call me Delores. What do you want me to call you? Hello?" and suddenly it dawned on me I had no other way to find her. "Where do I send the email with photo of the lake? You said I couldn't use the one you contacted me on or this number, so where do I..."

And the line went dead.

CHAPTER FIFTY-THREE

No sooner had I sent the photo of the lake to Spencer than she returned it with a push pin intact with a small note that said she felt most drawn to the NW corner of the lake. Later that night I wandered through my emails and noted another stray correspondence from "chameleon" had made it into my INBOX. Silently, I prayed it was from the second mystery contact. Ecstatic and hopeful that I had not lost her confidence, I opened it first. True to her word, she had done some thinking and wrote to tell me she had remembered where on the lake Einstein had thrown the gun in.

Dear Delores,

Wanted to let you know that special fishing spot we both liked so much was at the NW end of the lake. Hope this helps! Will be in touch soon.

I Googled the lake, added a push pin of my own, and fired it off to Spencer. Once again she had nailed the location with little help from me. Armed with potential evidence, I sent the information on to the appropriate agents and prayed that they would find the time to check it out.

With spring well underway, my mind refocused on more immediate tasks like work. The theatre had been given a very limited budget to produce a small family production. Because it constituted a fairly flexible cast and a static set, I had chosen *Charlotte's Web*. Weeks of rehearsals filled my evenings and schoolwork the mornings. Hours ran into days, into weeks. I was grateful for the comfort of routine. The play went well. Life continued. So did schoolwork and the rigors of our move. What in winter's fancy had flirted among snowflakes as the little house of my dreams soon became the nightmare of a spring move in the rain. What we didn't get through the door, we donated to a nearby church. Exhausted on every level, I collapsed into a heap by the end of the month.

Between cardboard boxes, I did everything I could to keep every agent up the food chain up to speed, praying that they would take the cup from my hands and move the case forward. Continually stalled by obligations to more current cases, the agent from Atlanta seemed to slow in his progress. I worried that too many of those left behind would die before their audience could be met. I knew the agent was doing what he could, that wheels were turning that I could not see. So I prayed for patience and trust in the process. I will not lie. It was hard to be patient after so many years and so much work, but I was left no choice and so returned to what was left that I could help them with if called upon again. Patient herself, Jules checked in every so often. While fantastic things had happened here and there, I was disappointed to tell her I was more no closer to bringing the case to fruition than in the months before.

March rolled in and rolled on out with little to show for my efforts. April was soon proving to be little more than its twin when suddenly the winds of change blew new hope in my direction. On Good Friday something other than our dear Lord arose that defied logic and proved that the universe was not finished with me yet. After finishing with a grueling schedule of back-to-back shows and copious amounts of forensic homework, I arrived at home to something unexpected. Instead of uninterrupted hours of reading my textbooks while my husband grilled on the deck to the backdrop of beautiful ripples on the lake as planned, I arrived home only long enough to get out of my car to take the dogs out to pee and then return to my seat behind the wheel.

Now I do not begrudge my husband for not wanting to cook occasionally because in truth, it wasn't really that. I think the boy had cabin fever. Even though we have a lovely cabin, I got the hint. The man needed scenery other than what he had been staring at all day long. So, homework postponed and plans to become an intellectual slug waylaid, I made a deal. If I had to delay homework for a few hours and get back into a car after driving home for over an hour, it was going to be on my terms: Thai food.

Here's where this gets really interesting.

There is a delightful Thai restaurant on the square in, are you ready, the Norman Rockwell-esque town of Covington, Georgia! This charming Thai restaurant is one which I had been dying to go to for over a year. And since I had waited forever to go there as somebody else's choice or checkbook always superseded the desires of my own, I decided that would not be the case that night. If he was going to summarily cancel my date with a glass of wine and pleasant landscape, I was going to get what I wanted in the exchange. So, armed with obligatory guilt, I informed my husband that I would agree only if we went where I decided. Happy just to get out, he agreed without complaint, and I set my course for the restaurant of my craving.

On the way I eased in my annoyance. Once there, I ordered a very large White Zinfandel and perused the menu. Eventually he decided on the wonderful salmon with mango chutney special and I, my favorite: the Curried Masaman Shrimp. Because it was still early, we enjoyed a bit of privacy, but not for long. Soon one or two couples began to dot the tables along the windows, but none in our proximity.

The restaurant was not cheap, but because we seldom splurged I decided to just enjoy the ambience and the wine and skimp on pennies somewhere else later in the week. Appetizers done, we sat and chatted about recent clues in the case and the day's events. We watched with squinting eyes as a young couple made a beeline for a table in our area. Generally such a thing does not create a problem for me, but it felt like an intrusion on my lovely holiday as there were so many other tables both distant and open at the time. They presented as a typical nuclear family: two young, athletic parents, manicured and muscled, and two precocious youngsters full of dimples and the devil. The brown-headed boy and tow-headed girl, ages nine and six, respectively, squirmed inside their seats as their parents purveyed the menu. Why is that a matter of curiosity? You will see in a moment; just bear with me.

Five minutes into their residence, the tanned and toned soccer mom ordered white wine, the clean shaven father a beer, and the kids some sort of cola. As we ate, I publicly remarked at how cute the children were, but privately to my husband that I would never have thought to take our girls at such an age to such an expensive and exotic restaurant. After all, there was not a Chicken Mc Nugget, plate of Mac' N Cheese, or a French fry anywhere on the menu. Secretly I worried that our dinner might be spoiled by their eventual disappointment. My husband agreed. I decided we should drink more and eat faster. The waitress served our dinner and proceeded to their table. Riveted, I sat and listened for their cultured choices as the waitress stood with pen and pad in hand, ready to take their orders.

"Sorry, we're not ready. The children haven't decided yet."

"Haven't decided yet? Hell they can't even read it yet!" my husband chuckled under his breath.

The mother said it would be a few more minutes before they could order. Vindicated, I cackled to myself and smiled at my husband. Kids were kids, but I remained curious as to what this mother would be able to order that the two imps now bouncing back and forth between chairs would actually eat. In between my vindication and the next round of drinks, I overheard the little girl ask her mother a question which almost shot a shrimp straight from my mouth through the very large and very clean bay window on the opposite wall.

Ready?

Climbing back into her chair and holding the menu upside down, she raised her face to the ceiling. When her mamma asked if she knew what she wanted, she responded with this little McNugget of her own: "Who is the Grim Reaper, Mamma?"

Half choking on my curried bait, I croaked at my husband, "Maybe she should ask me that question instead," and his eyes glazed. I did my best to salvage the pink and white striped blob that had slid its way onto the tablecloth, still sporting a few of my tooth prints, and slid it back onto the rim of my bowl

A bit startled, her mother responded "Why do you ask?" The child remained constant and with eyes the size of dessert plates explained she had seen it on TV just that afternoon and wanted to know who he was. The mother gave a swift look of disapproval to her older sibling who seemed impervious to her glare.

"Well, I don't know what you were watching, but…" the mother began tentatively. "The Grim Reaper is the guy in the hooded cloak with the red eyes. You can't see his face usually, and he carries a big long stick with a long blade thing on the end." And she stared at the young male who was now emptying sugar packets all over the tablecloth. "He's the guy that shows up just before somebody dies. They call him the harbinger of death."

"What's a hair banger?" the little girl mangled.

The mother laughed and then completed her definition. "He's the man, er a … ghost/spirit thing that appears when somebody dies."

"Is he the man that kills them?" the little tot asked.

"No… he's just the ghost-like thing in a hood you see right *before* somebody dies. Did somebody in the TV show die?"

"Yes…" the child said, "A man died." The mother paused while the child slurped some more of her Coke. I in turn slurped more of my wine and snatched the shrimp from the rim of the bowl and shoved it in my mouth to keep from screaming. "Well…people die all the time. Maybe it was just his time," the mother stalled.

"Maybe it was just his time?" I wanted to yell. The waitress interrupted their remaining conversation to get their orders. Taken aback by the impromptu epilogue, I missed their orders. Obviously not the important issue here. Now I am not saying that all this didn't give me great pause, because even after everything I have been through, I still freak a bit when this stuff happens. I took the clue, though, made the mental note, but was uncertain as to how I was supposed to apply the information to my current understanding of the case.

Who was the Grim Reaper "hair banging" for and how long before it would happen? The question had to have been a sign; it was way too random not to have been. And what was it about that particular family unit that rang so familiar? A mother, a father, a girl aged six, a boy aged nine? Hmmm…can't guess? Charley, Kaye, Jules, and Martin!

As we finished our meal and paid the bill, I smiled at the couple and told them to have a wonderful meal. The youngest smiled through her puffed pixie cheeks as a small bit of shrimp climbed back up my throat and made me gag. Once outside of earshot, I commented to my husband that the Grim Reaper question was just a little too coincidental for my comfort level. Really…what are the odds that anyone would sit in a restaurant in Covington, Georgia and a child the same age as Jules and a boy the same age as her brother Martin ask about the Grim Reaper, who is the man alleged to have manipulated both their father's murder and the cover up of his untimely death? I'll tell you: about a gazillion to one and I can't even count that high.

Spooked, we left the restaurant (which by the way was excellent) and headed towards the Mustang in tandem disbelief. When we got to the stop walk, we paused and waited for the light in silence, still pondering the synchronicity in it all. Just as the light turned from red to green, a car went past us, and well… you know me. I immediately read the tag for a numerological sign, hoping that I had not lost my sanity as well as my shrimp. The tag read 1111. Good numbers to be sure, basically saying pay attention to what just happened.

Later that night I talked with Spencer about a few other things that had been flopping back and forth inside my brain like a half-dead mackerel. Charley had previously given me the TIC-TAC-TOE sign when asked about a newly appointed choice for the four in flannel. He gave the above sign with a strike through the diagonal, and I immediately found positive confirmation there. My first reaction was joy until I remembered TIC-TAC-TOE only gives you three in a row, not four. Befuddled, I completely spaced the entire Grim Reaper dinner debacle and forgot to bring it up. This is where you need to sit down...I'll wait. (PAUSE) Sitting? Comfy...cozy?

GOOD!

Among the many things that night that came through to Spencer was another image I had never heard her speak of before: black roses. Spencer told me that she had been presented with black roses only a few other times in her tenure as psychic, and they had always preceded someone's death. Shocked, I took a moment to process. Was I about to lose another critical witness like Marjorie? My heart sank.

Spencer took a moment herself and then continued. Black roses always meant one thing: a death premonition. She sensed it was one of the four in flannel.

They show me it is one of the key players...a male energy... possibly one of the four in flannel. They show me he is married. I can see several long black cars in a funeral procession...more black roses and what's this?" and you could hear her sniff into the end of her cell. "I smell...it's... something. What is that... sulfur?

I added stench of sulfur to the equation with black roses and came up with the very appropriate, but very unpopular answer: the smell of death, perhaps even the Grim Reaper himself in the same fashion and with the same olfactory presence as he had shared with Piper the year before. Suddenly, my stomach started to roll and the curried shrimp wasn't sitting so well.

"When? Who?" is all I could muster.

That I do not know. Only that it is one of your key players. Do not limit yourself to just the four in flannel. Others were definitely key players in this as well. All they present is that it is a male energy, older in age with a wedding ring, which signifies married. You can do the math from there. How many are left? Who is married? Who may already be near death or in a hospice situation? she added and I trolled through recent information.

Who was near death? Unfortunately, several of them, including Einstein's first wife, Bobbie Lee. Bobbie Lee had been the one person who tried to tell Kaye the truth about that night, but years of abuse and intimidation had left her emotionally mute. In one of the more recent sessions, impressions had come through concerning her health.

They present a cane. The cane is wooden and shiny. The numbers 2412...curlers... her features, waxy looking...sickly... they show me the name Jezebel, the biblical reference. Do you understand the Jezebel reference? They show me a room. It is very rustic... lots of wood. They are walking me through the house; she is ill, on oxygen. What is this?? They show me Einstein... putting tape across her mouth. I do not think this is real. I believe they mean this metaphorically. They show her struggling... she is screaming she wants to tell, but there is tape. He is keeping her from speaking. She will talk ... she will talk.

It made perfect sense. Einstein had kept her from telling Kaye the truth forty-five years earlier. It was a given he would do the same now if threatened. The numbers helped, but not enough. I still couldn't find her. Months had been spent in tracking her from a trailer in the woods in another county to a cancer treatment center to a relative in Louisiana and back again. And all for nothing it appeared. When I finally got the number to call her, she had little to say or little she felt she could afford to say. Perhaps the metaphorical tape was still intact. In her fragile state, I saw little need to beat her up. If Einstein had gotten to her first, she would never speak without protection from the feds, so I just informed her that Kaye had written of her in her journal. When she asked why, I told her that out of everyone involved that night, Kaye claimed that she had been the only one to tell Kaye that her husband had been involved with another woman.

The black roses may have meant death. While Bobbie Lee was not far from it, Spencer had clearly said a married male, so it couldn't have been her. As for the men left, there was only a handful that might have been a fit, although technically Mr. Einstein was still legally married to another woman. I rummaged through my remaining players. It could have been Grim, Einstein, the failing Waverleigh, my current tag for #4, the very much alive former state superior judge or even more insane, the former highest ranking officer of the State of Georgia who was still residing somewhere in the Atlanta area.

No matter who the black roses were meant for, the coincidence of all this happening without ethereal segue was beyond comprehension. You do the math. What are the odds such a combination would occur in a town named after my victim? A six-year-old girl discussing the Grim Reaper as a ghost who comes as the harbinger of death, followed by the image of black roses meant as a death premonition?

Now I may be going out on a huge limb here, but after three years of learning the shorthand of the dead, and I could be wrong, I thought somebody needed to confess and soon. Bolstered by Spencer's visions and reminded by my undulating and acid-churning innards, I told Spencer what had happened just hours before at the restaurant.

This time I think even she was amazed.

CHAPTER FIFTY-FOUR

The third weekend in April of 2012, Jules and Cole came down to see the new digs and share a day on the lake. It was much too cold to enjoy the water, but we took a cruise on the boat and enjoyed the view. In appreciation for bed and board, they surprised me with a tape that was recorded just a few weeks before Charley died. It was a tape made the day of Jules's sixth birthday party. Charley's voice was somewhere on it. I could scarcely breathe. For over three years I had heard his ethereal voice inside my head. The thought of listening to its earthly tone both fascinated and frightened me. After dinner that night, we gathered around the table. With wine in hand, I listened to Jules's brother as he narrated and described the juvenile festivities.

"This is Martin Covington, and I am recording this on...." Tedious as it may have been for others, I hung on every word and enjoyed the insight into the young genius' mind. Children played and prattled about in the background as the cruise director Martin gave a minute-by-minute report on what everyone was doing, good, bad, or annoying. Eager to hear Charley's voice, I gave little attention to other adults whose vocal patterns danced among the airwaves above my head at various intervals with mundane announcements of arrivals and departures. Kaye's voice broke through occasionally, and I was surprised by how low and rural it sounded.

Cole tried to warn me that Charley spoke only a handful of words on the tape. He merely walked into the party room and twenty seconds later out again after speaking only to the rambunctious Jules about her birthday presents, and that was all of him the recorder had picked up. Anxious, we sat about the table as each minute clicked us closer to the awaited sound. Thirty some odd minutes in, there was a commotion, and you could barely hear the entry of his voice above the din of the chaos over a game of musical chairs. His performance lasted less than a minute. Feeling cheated, I asked Cole to rewind the tape and play it again. The voice was hollowed and graveled, not at all the voice in my head. In some respect I wished I'd never heard it. In another, all I wanted to do was cry that that was all there was. He sounded unfamiliar and countrified, like an untrained field hand who'd wandered in among the gentry. I was taken aback. This was not the smoothed voice of compassion and reason I had imagined in my head; this was man who typified the stereotype of Southern status. We rewound the tape several times. Each time it played, I could not seam the man in my head together with the man on the recording.

Naturally, Jules heard what echoed from her past, and Cole seemed unaffected by the timbre of this man's voice as well. Perhaps it was my watered-down acquaintance with rural accents, but whatever it was, I was not prepared for what I had heard. Dowsed in metropolitan colloquialisms, I had grown a deaf ear to the rural inhabitants of my subject's world. In order not to appear ungrateful, I accepted my copy from Cole, smiled, gave gratitude for the precious family memento, and never played it again.

With the echo of Charley's voice banging inside my head, I tried to make peace between the man on the tape, the man on my desk, and the man who lay moldy and lacerated six feet under just four hours to the south of me. Had I painted him unfairly in my mind to fit my composition and not his situation? Had I made G more bitch than battered to make her easier to hate? Or made Jessica and Roxanne more innocent than they deserved? And what of the MOT? Had I asked less of these people in the other world than I had right to in this? What other attributes had I granted through osmosis that had no real bearing on their circumstance?

I tried to differentiate between what was real and what was realistically feasible about the victims in this case and worried that I had done the same with those in my day-to-day life. Had I projected onto others what I needed them to be more than what they really were and then punished them for not achieving some unwritten standard? But most important, had I served both my God and my sense of justice well enough to pen this story?

That night I went to bed with a troubled heart, worried that I might have let them all down in their greatest moment of need. With the tape of Charley's voice tucked safely within the top drawer of my desk, I kissed his 8 x 10 and slowly headed off to bed. Slumber did not come easy, but once attained I was mentally placed back inside my theatre with the set from *Charlotte's Web* oddly still intact. The barnyard motif with its bright reds, picket fences, and climbing greens remained untouched. I was terribly confused.

Had I not just cleared this set three days prior? Assuming I had dreamt my real life strike of the set, I began pulling props from the scene and down from the walls. Just as I ascended the ladder to gather Charlotte's prop egg sac, a group of people entered down the ramp and flooded onto the set.

Reality or dream, I felt bad because I knew either way the show had already closed. Oblivious to the disarray, the group began to form in a line as if waiting for admission. I advised them that the show had just closed the weekend before. They didn't seem to care. I worried that it was perhaps I who was mistaken and was prematurely destroying a set I was about to need. Curious, I checked my watch and the date proved me correct. The show indeed had closed the Sunday before, but there was something about this group that suddenly pulled me out of step. They were obviously not here to see the show. So what were they here to see?

There were four women, two men, and one small boy. When they came in, they looked around. After I informed them a second time that the show had already closed, they went to the front row of seats and sat awaiting my recognition. The odd thing was, everything around them was in full color, but the people and their immediate auras were that color of sepia that you sometimes see or create when you process old photos.

Intrigued, I crossed the room and went to the first woman. She had short hair and pearls on. It was an odd combination for contemporary purposes, but the hairdo gave her away, and I immediately recognized her as Kaye. She said hello and thanked me with a huge hug. Stunned, I smiled and turned to the next seat which held a man I did not recognize. He smiled and nodded his head. Puzzled as to his identity, I moved on. The next woman had long hair done up in a mock French twist, thick blue eye shadow, and painted lips. She smiled big like the singer Adele, batted a set of full black lashes. Suddenly I knew she was a slightly older version of the young, blonde debutante Roxanne. Shocked, I spun around and saw another young woman I deemed to be Jessica and ran to hug her too. When I pulled away and wiped a tear, I saw the last woman sitting eight chairs away, at the end of the row, waiting.

Stiff in the seat, she sat rigid and tight-lipped with a cold look on her face. Though I did not immediately put two and two together. I could not understand why she would not look me in the eyes. Emotional and muddled, I slowly moved down the line to stand in front of her. When I leaned to embrace her, she balked. When I asked why she seemed unwilling to look at me, her answer confused me.

"I cannot look you directly in the eyes; it would pierce my soul."

I had never heard such a thing before and did not understand what she meant. Immediately I feared the fault had been mine. Had I harmed this woman somehow? Had I done something to anger or alienate her? In a room filled with people I felt love coming from, why was she so cold to me? Who was she and why would she say something so odd when the others seemed so happy to see me?

It was then I realized the only person left untested in the equation was G. It took me a moment to process, and I stumbled away from her in silence and stared at the others. Struck by the assembly, suddenly all the chips fell into place. I realized who the entire group was. The other man I had not recognized from the front of the line must have been the MOT. If he was the MOT, then where was…

Suddenly I heard a child laugh and turned to see a young boy run from the hands of a man who stood silent on the other side of the room. He smiled. I smiled. The child I assumed to be one of the children Kaye and Charley had lost to miscarriage. Quietly I watched as the child ran about as playful as my own had been at that age. He was a young boy that would have captured my heart and my complete attention had it not been for my need to see someone else: the man who stood calmly in the distance watching him.

As the child squealed with delight and skipped off in another direction, I looked up and saw him. The man whom I have talked to and cried with for over three years. The man who had patiently waited forty-four years to save me so that I could return the favor and save him. The man who took the broken pieces of my life and glued them back together with the fragments of his own. A man you have come to know as Charley.

Grayed at the temples and minus a bit more hair, he walked slowly towards me. His eyes shown softer than the painted steely blue of his 8 x 10, and his voice, graveled like the snippet on my recording, remained true to his birth. No longer in black silhouette, no longer made of wispy smoke, this man was real. And he was Charley, my Charley: my guardian angel, my shepherd. He smiled again and told me I was beautiful. It was an odd compliment. Embarrassed, I brushed it aside, knowing I had gone to bed in worn pajamas and a ponytail. Nonetheless, he said it again and I knew it to be the compilation of his impressions of both my heart and soul. It made me cry.

He was there: a whole person just as I had prayed he might appear one day. Not a bust of a man or a postcard imprint of a personality: he was there in person, just the way I imagined he appeared to Spencer. Filled with gratitude and love, I ran to hug him and prayed that I would be able to feel something more than air beneath my fingers.

I tell you now, I hugged that man for everything I was worth and sobbed into shoulders that held up to the touch. He was real. Charley was real, and I knew in that instant that maybe the reason why I had not been able to finish the book and let justice follow its own course was that I had not been able to let go of something I had never held. He kissed me on the cheek. I held him tight as I cried like a child begging him not to go. He thanked me again, and I held tighter knowing that heaven would soon take him away. I whispered I loved him, that I had done everything I could to help, and that I never wanted to lose him, though I knew he couldn't stay.

Heaven is an amazing place and I held tight until I awoke with tears on my cheeks. The time? It was exactly 1:11 am. Even now as I write, tears stream… but for joy, not for sorrow.

Earlier that evening I had said a prayer that I wanted for us all to be able to move forward, that the case would come to fruition, that those living would confess and those that were dead would repent and find a new path for their evolution. With absolute sincerity I had prayed to be able to finish writing the story because I wanted to be able to release them all to where they needed to be. But I confessed that while I wanted Charley to be free, I did not wish to lose him. Openly I acknowledged that maybe that was why I could not commit to the ending. Later I would find out why it wasn't the only reason.

CHAPTER FIFTY-FIVE

Trying to distill the facts of this case into quantifiable hard evidence proved far more difficult than the distillation of its metaphorical moonshine. Still, I found that if I at least got most of the key players right, the rest of the information generally fell into line. Aside from more intimate personal information that remained absent on my #2 high ranking person of interest, I was forced to concentrate more on the local branding. Minus the one clue that asked *"Who later became a Lieutenant?"* all other impressions continued to point to more a local choice. Absent the above, I reviewed my notes for other confirmations and found another name that had been pointed out by one of Valdosta's citizens.

Written on the backside of an old envelope, the notation was dated 4/23/2010. Since I am often times in my car or away from my desk and home when information comes through, I generally grab the closest thing to record on and later add it to the files in the appropriate timeline. Apparently this had been stuffed inside the book, but not transcribed.

It began…

The mention of the State Trooper Cummings; they show me deceit; absolutely involved, not the trigger man, but involved. Manipulator. Two locations of energy: front tire, front of car… staged witnesses…

Because this was information I had already processed, I had apparently not read any further, but I should have opened the envelope up completely for the very next words were as follows:

When you mention the name Latham Tanner, they present a 'T' in wrought iron. The hat association…a hat… something about a hat...significant. Showing me wrought iron...hammering... a gate with a 'T' and again with the hat...

This man's first name began with an "L" and his last name with a "T." My heart skipped a beat. I continued to read as another name was written just below and beside it the notation:

Possibly a relation, NOT to Charley, but a brother or close relative to the other male energy. When you mention the name Jack Tanner, they present a general store association...something about a store...toothpaste, food items. He is standing behind the counter. They show me a 'J' and a reference to Oak Street. Check this relationship. They say use this as the identifier: they both had sex with the same female energy.

And then scrawled across the bottom almost illegibly:

...the female energy with the red fingernails.

Obviously I had been driving at the time. I read it again and held my breath. Had I just re-found my LT connection? Why had it taken so long for this to resurface? Grateful that I had another person I could now focus on, I hugged the envelope and placed it back in the notebook. Next I called Clint to try and get more confirmation on this man's background. Once that was done, I sent an email to my newfound friend Cecelia, asking her for much the same. Clint responded that Tanner would have to have been older, a fact which fit the demographic of my LT. The suggestion of a huge monogrammed wrought iron gate suggested social stature, big money, old money maybe. Eager to find another segue from the gavel image, I plowed ahead and closed my eyes. Clint promised to canvas some of the local geriatrics who might still remember those days, and Cecelia promised to search out elders in her association as well.

An hour later, Cecelia came through.

Old friend knew Latham's brother Jack, but her memory is a bit shaky. I will keep asking and see if we can get some answers. Oh, and I believe your Mr. Tanner had a big wrought iron 'T' gate at the end of his long drive. There is a road named after him: Tanner Road. Will do a little more digging for you to get more info on the rabbit's foot and the scar on the left hand thing, though everybody had a stinking rabbit's foot back then!

I appreciated the gesture, but it no longer mattered. The initials fit, the age fit, the socio-economics fit, and he had a thing about hats. Maybe he even owned one hat that he was buried in. Sure the gavel thing hadn't been obvious, but maybe there was something else in this man's history that might bear that impression out. The bottom line was I could spin it all forever and never really know if I was condemning the right man. I knew I would have to wait for other pieces of the puzzle to be confirmed, but for now at least I could breathe knowing I was leaving no stone unturned.

The next day I contacted Spencer to try and get other clues about the infamous hat of G's LT. She responded:

Again they show he had a thing for feathers...one feather in particular. It was brown and white. He put the feather in the band of his hat. This is G's LT.

My new LT had the wrought iron gate with the "T" in it, had a thing about hats, and had been specifically called out by spirit as having had sex with the same female energy as his brother. That was the one piece of information I could use to move in another direction and did. Had this "J" mentioned actually been for this man's brother or another moniker for our dark-haired vixen that'd once had ties to a home address on Oak Street?

If not for the mention of the fingernails, one could have parsed even that, but a female energy with long red fingernails meant but one thing. The only female energy that the spirit described with the red fingernails was the same female energy that had sex with countless other males, besides my LT and his brother. She was the same female energy that used those red fingernails in the throes of passion during sex. The same female energy that had stolen the P.O. Box keys from Charley's wallet. The same female energy that had been there the night Charley was murdered. The same female energy that dumped coffee grounds all over Kaye's kitchen as a "fu...you" message two weeks after my Charley had been murdered. There was no way you could doubt that the female energy mentioned as the identifier was the infamous Gerrilyn Baldwin.

Released, I threw my hands in the air, thanked the stars, and finally "let go and let God," knowing I could literally do no more to decipher the true identity of Gerri Baldwin's LT. As I tucked the paper back into the notebook, I made mental apologies for any man who held the same initials and prayed that one day all of Valdosta would forgive the uncertainty inherent to this process. With residual joy, I continued through the end of April and on into May of 2012.

CHAPTER FIFTY-SIX

In June, Charley came through with even more to help me tighten my timelines and close the circle. Off and on through the summer and early autumn, I kept pace with my job and tried to tie together loose ends within the book.

By the forty-sixth anniversary of Charley's anniversary on October 9, 2012, I had finally pieced together enough clues to identify our man standing at the water's edge over Roxanne's watery grave. Roxanne had described the mysterious Mr. R.L. as a tall, cigar-smoking man who was thick as thieves with Finch and Cabbot Jr. and had ties to all the other ingrates. My fourth in flannel bore the name of Robert Lang, a Buick car salesman with Goldwyn Motors. Lang had ties to the American Legion, to law enforcement, and to an apartment complex owned by Cabbot Jr. He was given an apartment of his own for "other duties as assigned." He was infamous for always being cold, wore a camel-colored coat, and thoroughly enjoyed the company of exotic cigars and young, pretty girls. As a bonus, he had a brother that worked on the slot machines for Finch. It was a match made in Hell.

Charley had once told me in order to figure out who the fourth in flannel was I should look in the car, Kaye's car: the Buick. With my discovery of Lang, it now made perfect sense. But there was more to help seal the deal than just his occupation. Our Mr. Lang was apparently a bit of a showman: wore gold cufflinks, monogrammed shirts, and a flashy gold watch with the initials "RL" engraved on it and a lighter too. He drove a huge, fancy car just like the one Jessica described when she was being held down in the back seat by several men. And just like the one that gave Jules and Martin a ride home from the local fair two years after their father had been murdered. Even more, this man was with Damon Cummings the day his car lights twirled in the early morning light when they dragged Roxanne's battered body from Saddle Bag Lakes.

By Thanksgiving of that year, I had been contacted by another person who did not want to identify herself. She found me through my blog. One of the first questions I asked was where she was from. The answer came back Tallahassee. Thus, I thought I had finally had received my letter of information from Tallahassee. Amazingly enough, this young woman helped me put the final touches on my confirmation of Lang. Frightened for her safety, she too talked about fear of reprisal by the KKK. Too young to have been one of the chosen, she gave me information about her mother. Apparently her mother was one of the many back in the mid 60's and early 70's used by the notorious gang for sexual pleasure. She told me her mother had been about Jessica's and Roxanne's age when she first met the younger Cabbot. Married, she carried on an affair with him, divorced her husband, and then eventually married someone else out of fear that alone she would be under Cabbot's thumb forever.

She even testified against Jeb Finch and Cabbot Jr. in their court trials just a few years after Charley's death. Frightened after her testimony, she had been placed under the watchful eyes of a U.S. Marshal from Southern Georgia. Guess who? Why none other than our infamous Mr. Muddy Boots, A/K/A Albert Fitzpatrick, who by then had climbed the law enforcement ladder to become a U.S. Marshal. This fact can be verified through the indictments 506F and 514F. He escorted her under a witness protection program out to Texas. A little bit like leaving the cat to watch the canary now, isn't it?

This woman told me her mother had claimed that during her time in Valdosta, she had been put up in a fancy apartment (Park Avenue Apartments), had been given money, and was used for sex. Most interesting of all? She was given a little red sports car to tool around in. Quite possibly this little red sports car was the one that had once been used by our fourth in flannel to deliver Jessica and Roxanne like pizza.

As the year moved close to its end, it was mind boggling how all the pieces began to float together. Images of a gold bugle in a velvet case, along with the image of WW II hats and being an accomplished pilot continued to point to the governor's involvement at some level in this case. In between other clues, specific impressions came through as well to help confirm the identity of the mysterious "Albert Einstein" as a definite candidate for the fourth in flannel that liked to torture and beat his victims. In addition to the constant portrait of the genius scientist Marjorie used to denote Einstein, Spencer was shown several odd metal objects in great detail. The day the clues about the canning lady and the bonfire came through, she was shown a set of brass knuckles and another similar set of brass knuckles attached to long curved blades — like those used for the character of Hugh Jackman in the mutant movie series *Wolverine*. They also showed her star-shaped blades, like those thrown by ninjas in those cheesy B-rated Kungfu movies. All in all the images seemed like an odd collection of weapons for your basic rural thug, but then it was not my job to decide what information was or was not relevant. All I could do was make the notations, try and corroborate their existence as evidence through a witness, and move on. Just as the moon in the autumn skies above, clues continued to wax and wane between feast or famine, each continuing to either cancel or confirm my suppositions.

Shortly after Thanksgiving, G came through to Spencer talking about a specific car: a Thunderbird. She kept yelling at Spencer something about a missing "T." Unfortunately, I was unable to discern whether this had to do with a name or the nameplate on the back of the car. Spencer felt it had to do more with the name of a person. Perhaps the MOT was really a man whose name or initials were MO. When Spencer pressed our ethereal mistress for more specifics, G spit and screamed at her, yelling again about the missing letter and the man who drove the silver car. During that same conversation, she also echoed a prediction by Charley. Each had said that the date of December 12th, 2013 would be significant.

In all the time since the late spring of 2012, I had kept the ATF agent in Atlanta updated with every suspicion and clue. The last thing he had told me was he would not go unless he could get them all at the same time. Intellectually, I understood, but with each day I feared I was losing viable information through witness attrition. Each time he neglected to respond to my updates, I bit my tongue and held my ire.

Rumor had it that every one of my remaining persons of interest was in compromised health. Only Cecelia seemed resilient enough to weather the storms. When 12/12/12 rolled across the calendar, I prepared myself for cosmic intervention. In the days leading up to the infamous date, I had had several locutions and more impressions. One impression that came through Spencer showed a check made out to me with a mountain logo in the upper lefthand corner of the check. They presented that the signature at the bottom would bear the last name of my LT energy, finally giving me the absolute confirmation I needed to close that part of the case for keeps.

In the first locution, they whispered in my ear *"The little guy will be the one to take them down."* Desperate as I was to understand what they meant, I could not decipher and became increasing distraught as the day wore thin into the night. Had I dreamed the words or misunderstood the translation? All day I sat on pins and needles, eyes alert, ears pricked, waiting for any sign from the heavens that warranted the heads up from both G and Charley about the significance of the date.

When the hands of the clock waved goodbye to midnight, I slumped into my pillow and cried. Tears stained the linen. Exhausted, I told the cosmos I was sorry I had not been smart enough to discern whatever had been sent. Somewhere just after 4:43 in the morning, I dreamt about a long dirt road that led to a tall cathedral-style set of rusted iron gates. The shape and desperation of their signature made me feel they were stationed at the entrance of a cemetery. As I began walking towards them, an angel appeared above and behind the top portion of the lefthand gate. Billowing with gauzy illumination, I watched the angel's wings stretch and undulate in the heavy air. It was an odd combination superimposed over the stark and barren winterscape which surrounded the gates. The road and the surrounding area held no light. Nothing luminous emitted from anywhere, save the wings of the creature.

With each step my feet felt heavier. The closer I got, the light of the creature began to dim and the once-flowing feathers of light began to tarnish. One by one, they began to curl and wither at the stem, each drifting away and becoming little more than dust as they fell. Curious, I stood before the gates and watched until all that was left was a disgusting skeletal representation of what it had once been. Uncertain of why I was being shown such, I stopped in my tracks. Annoyed that I had stalled in my approach, the creature, now void of light and gray with decay, flung itself at the gates. Four boney appendages clung with claws to the rusted bars, shaking and screeching at the top of its lungs to get free.

I should have been frightened, but it was more sad than horrific. I woke that morning and recorded the dream in a blog. Apologetic to my readers that I had nothing more to offer, I acknowledged my 12/12/12 apparition to be little more than late night tuna salad laced with a healthy dollop of hot Southern style chow-chow. Disappointed that my cosmic connection had been little more than earthly indigestion, I went off quietly to work and licked my wounds. I knew my readers had expected more because I had expected more. Two hours into my day, I spoke with Spencer about my disappointment and the dream. She asked me if I understood what it had meant.

"Of course," I said. "It meant I should never eat spicy foods that late at night before I go to bed," I chuckled.

"No, there is more," she offered.

"More than spicy tuna?" I asked, trying to redeem myself. I had been such an idiot, boasting in the blog for days that something important to the case would happen on the 12th. And then when nothing happened, I felt cheated and very much the fool. Charley had never let me down before. Since G had echoed his sentiments about the date's importance, I felt doubly insulted. Perhaps the universe thought I was smarter than I was.

"Do you not understand what you saw?" she asked.

"No, I really don't."

"First, did the being feel male or female?"

I thought it odd that she asked, but suddenly realized that without question the energy had felt female.

"Female...why?"

"What you saw is similar to what I am shown sometimes. Yours was not exactly the same, but there are enough similarities that I think I can help you understand." When I didn't respond immediately, she continued. "I think what you were being shown was the transition of a soul."

"What?"

"The transition of a soul. Someone who is trying to move on to the next level, someone who has been tied to his or her earthly experience, trapped by what the person has done and is now trying to change the karma and evolve beyond it."

I tried to take it all in and let her carry on.

"You said 'it' felt female. So what females are involved in this case that we have not witnessed in transition?" she asked.

I thought about Jessica and Roxanne and the session months earlier where Spencer was shown the shooter unable to cleanse his hands juxtaposed against the bodies of the two young females rising unstained through bloody waters and Georgia clay without taint or blemish.

"Who is left in the mix? Who is it that has suddenly decided to help with information and told you the 12th would be significant? Who told you about the missing 'T' and the silver car? What female has yet to transition?"

There was only one female left in the equation of Charley's murder: Gerrilyn Baldwin.

"So this was about her trying to move on?" I whispered.

"I do not wish to interpret, but perhaps it was her. She has tried to help bring closure to this case lately, don't you agree?" I a-hummed and let her continue. "Charley has forgiven her on the other side, but here…on this earthly plane… she still has much to answer for."

"But why first as angel, then as skeleton?" I asked, confused at the order of appearance.

"Her recent contrition has helped her understand what she has cost herself. Maybe there is unfinished business that keeps her tied to the earthly plane she is so desperate to escape. You said yourself that she threw herself at the gates and sounded like she was screaming to get free. Maybe there is something left undone, something she must complete before she can be totally freed."

"Maybe," I muttered. It wasn't just enough to say she was sorry. Like the rest of us, contrition must be followed by an act of forgiveness.

"Were you frightened at what you saw?"

While the figures had been graphically different, I tried to explain that my immediate response was more curious than cautious, more concerned than disconcerted. I knew I was asleep, yet I had known it was not a dream. We talked a bit longer, and even though the experience had been incredible, I still felt as though there had been something more tangible to the case I was supposed to receive.

Twenty minutes after I hung up with Spencer, my phone began to beep. One text, two texts. My phone continued to beep for twenty seconds as text after text came through. All were from Jules.

I know you don't think anything big happened on the 12th, but you're wrong. Earlier this week I tried to find my dad's guns and remembered they were with my uncle. Yesterday I was able to make a deal with him to get them back! Isn't that great? Now Charley's grandsons will have something of his! I'm going to get them sometime this...

The next few texts were about how she had navigated the deal and minor details regarding the impending transfer. The next few minutes were claimed by both happiness and disbelief. Yes, how wonderful that her boys would finally have a piece of their father's history. And wow, how unbelievable that she had never once over the course of the last four years ever told me she knew where the guns were. Somehow we had either never broached that or I had just made the assumption that they, along with all the other important evidence had simply been destroyed or lost. Anxious for her to understand there was so much more at stake than family heirlooms, I frantically texted back.

"What guns are they?"

"His .357 Magnum and the little .38 Colt Special. Why?"

My head was about to explode. She really didn't understand what she had. The .38 was the weapon law enforcement had claimed he had given to Mrs. Baldwin, the gun that was missing from Kaye's closet since the night of Charley's murder.

Knowing I had the original missing page 2 of the GBI Crime Lab Report from 1966 with the ballistics analysis of the two projectile fragments meant I had the evidence I needed to push this thing through! All I had to do was get the gun, get it to the ATF, and have a test fire done and the fragments sent off for analysis. One of two things would be proven: either the test fire bullet would match one of the fragments or neither of them. Either we had a match for one bullet and would know for certain that we were looking for only one gun, or neither would match and we would finally know we were searching for two. That of course was all predicated on whether or not any of the original projectile fragments were still available to match. Without original evidence, the best we could do was determine the number and directional spiral of the lands and grooves. At the very least we could compare the lands and grooves to page 2 of the original Crime Lab Report.

I thought about the shooter who took the gun to his home across the state border into Florida and dumped it down the well. Either the gun had been left there, providing the location for weapon #1, or it had been removed by Albert Fitzpatrick sometime after the shooter's death and flung into Sampson Lake some nine years after Charley's murder and the shooter's death in front of his almost estranged wife.

"When can you get them?" I texted back.

"I can get them this weekend," she responded.

My head was on fire. With equal fervor I wanted to scream two things: get them to me as soon as possible and how narcissistic of me to think that the spirit had ordained only one road could lead us back to Rome. Inside I apologized to Charley and humbly accepted that the angels had seen fit to give Jules a chance to participate in her father's vindication.

She promised to call me later.

CHAPTER FIFTY-SEVEN

As soon as I got back to my office, I ripped through the pages of Kaye's journal.

Sometime at home some of the officers asked me where that .38 pistol of his was, the one with the short barrel. I looked in our bedroom closet; it was not there. There was not a pistol of any kind at our house. Bill Hardy, Deputy Colbert, and Mr. Thornton stayed over in Millen after the funeral. They came to Charley's mother's house on Thursday. Mr. Hardy had all these guns and asked me to identify them. I knew all of them except the one that killed him. I told them that I had never seen that gun in all the twenty years we had been married. I told them I did not know the government had issued him one and that it was odd he had never mentioned it. I asked them where it had been all that time. They said they didn't know. They showed me his short barreled .38. I asked them where they found it, and Mr. Hardy told me that Mrs. Baldwin had had it. I asked him why and he just shook his head and said that Mrs. Baldwin had told him Charley had given it to her. I asked Mr. Hardy if that was the gun, the .38, that killed him. Deputy Colbert, I think it was, said 'No, Charlie gave it to her for protection.'

"I said 'protection from what?' He said she had been bothered by prowlers since her divorce and that Charlie had given it to her. I told them at the time that Charlie had better sense than to let a woman have a pistol of his. Deputy Colbert said, 'He loved her very much; he wanted to protect her.'

I remember asking Mr. Hardy if he knew of any love affair and he told me no, that if he had heard anything he would have talked to Charlie. He asked me why I had not told him about that before. I told Mr. Hardy that I did not know about it, that Bobbie Lee Fitzpatrick had told me that she was after my husband, but that Sal, Mr. Greenville, and Mr. Fitzpatrick had told me there was nothing to it. That day they started to try and put the fear of God in me about that woman. Mr. Hardy and Mr. Thornton told me not to say anything to anyone about that woman as the government sure frowned on scandals...

Deputy Colbert or Mr. Hardy asked me if Charlie had ever threatened to kill himself. I told him the only thing that he had ever said was about a month before this happened. He was reading the Moultrie newspaper and it said the police chief there had sat down in a rocker, put newspapers all around it, and shot himself. Charlie looked at me and said, 'They may find me shot sometime and it may look like suicide...but you be sure and have it investigated, because I don't have the nerve to shoot myself.'

It didn't matter to me why Charley would never have committed suicide. It was the fact that thirty days before his death he had felt he might be found shot to death one day under similar circumstances. I reread the entry in the journal over again, and it triggered a memory about something else I had read.

In her diatribe with Mr. Hardy, Charley's superior and head ATTD case investigator, Kaye had asked something else about this gun, something that should have been a red flag to everyone involved.

Her question is at the end of a series of questions she asked about Charley's clothes and the clothing that Baldwin claimed she had purchased for Charley on his birthday three weeks prior. The K will stand for Kaye and the B for Bill Hardy.

K: Where are all of these clothes that she gave him?

B: There were two shirts; they were at the office in a drawer. Sal took them home with him. He figured you did not want them.

K: Why in heaven's name would Sal want them?

B: He just took them. He said, "Mrs. Baldwin said she wanted them back and told me again to get the.38 pistol for her."

K: I told Mr. Hardy to tell her that I had better not hear anything more about that pistol. I asked him if it had been fired, and he said, "There was no reason to test it."

No reason to test it? I almost choked! That should have been the very first weapon tested and yet the lead ATTD investigating agent and immediate boss to Charley had flat out told Kaye there was no need to test a weapon allegedly given to the alleged mistress of a Federal Treasury Agent just before his death and not returned until after. What?

With Jules's 12/12/12 epiphany and both the .357 Magnum and the short barreled .38 Colt Detective Special, I felt I stood at the threshold of prosecutable discovery and evidence. Once Jules had the weapons in her possession, I negotiated an agreement with her for a second transfer to me upon the agent's request. She agreed. I immediately contacted the agent from Macon with my information. As he had not answered my emails in over six months, I decided it better to make a call. Twenty-four hours later he responded. His response left me filled with angst.

A few minutes into the conversation, he confessed he had done very little since the spring due to increasing workloads. Even though I could totally empathize, I was immensely disappointed. People were dying to testify and some people just plain dying. Thus far I had done everything in my power to keep from scaring away potential witnesses. With Herculean effort I had held my tongue and shipped all pertinent information up the pipeline, thinking I was fueling the fire. I had endured months of silence, so as not to compromise his alleged efforts. Now he had the audacity to tell me he had been doing nothing all along?

It was unconscionable to me that he had never bothered to call Cecelia, never heard her brave story about witnessing the dumping of a similar weapon by a man within the center spotlight of interest. Never concerned that her fear of discovery or its potential reprisal was real. Never done anything with the former Superior State Court Judge's confession about knowing Charley's death was not a suicide. Never a question about the evidence he claimed to have viewed seven years after Charley's death confirming that fact. Never explored any of the other testimonial evidence presented that supported the fact that Charley's death had been a homicide.

In the spirit of the season I continued to listen and acknowledged his trials, though I mentally perceived them to be mostly excuses. In his defense, he reminded me that everybody including the FBI had turned down the invitation to investigate and that he was the only one who had offered to help.

Grateful as I was, he needed to remember that by accepting the challenge he had also accepted the responsibility to diligently pursue it. I emphasized that his acceptance had granted false hope to everyone involved who had waited forty-six years for somebody in the law enforcement community to do the right thing. Further, I prompted that the two guns now in Jules's possession, along with aforementioned information could help provide his ticket to the Promised Land. The weapon in question had been in the possession of Charley's alleged mistress just before and then surrendered a week after Charley's death when presented to the widow in Millen for identification. And even though I felt certain there would be no remaining original fragment evidence to match a test fire to, the signature of its lands and grooves would have been of supreme interest to me. If requested, I could also easily direct him to the suspected locations of the alleged second weapon and the potential remains of both Jessica and Roxanne and the eternal resting place of the MOT. Everything was being handed to him on a silver platter. What more did he want? He asked for a week or two to get through the holidays and discuss the situation with his superior after the New Year holiday.

As I hung up the phone, I prayed that his conscience would nag him into action. I prayed that a Christmas at home surrounded by his lovely wife and smothered by the laughter and hugs of his children might be remind of the four decades of Christmas memories lost for Charley and his family.

In the end, however, a collective decision was made to suspend ATF activities until further prosecutable evidence could be garnered. In the briefest of emails I was offered the feeble band aid of thanks for my dedication and tireless efforts to help the Covington family. In my heart I wanted to be more gracious, but here was the same agency that had spearheaded and compromised this investigation forty-six years earlier repeating the same reticent history I was so desperately trying to undo. For me the counterfeit gratitude just wasn't enough and I felt betrayed.

Devastated, I wallowed in discontent for days. Beaten but not yet beat, my next and final call was to the District Attorney's office of Lowndes County. Desperate to be engaged, I left a rather lengthy voice mail explaining my needs. A week went by. In those seven days I saw the essence of my faith wax and wane, edited away half this book, and resigned myself to make peace with those things clearly no longer in my control. Convinced that God and Charley had decided the mere exercise of writing this book had been enough, I made the decision to try to finally let go and let God. To release control was the hardest thing I have ever done.

For four years I had been investigator, judge, and jury. Inside my head I had tried and condemned, capitulated and pardoned, a hundred different people for a thousand different reasons — none of which apparently mattered to anyone anymore, but me. My faith was shaken.

The following day I completed the second of what became a series of interviews for the next book about another district attorney who had been assassinated in Jackson County, Georgia in 1967. Just as I was saying goodbye to my guest, my cell phone began to beep. Not wanting to be rude, I let it go to voicemail. When I got into my car, I reviewed the number on my cell and my heart skipped a beat. At exactly 11:11 on January 18, 2013, I heard the most glorious words in the world: "This is the District Attorney for Lowndes County."

"Yes," they said. Finally someone else would listen and if the evidence presented warranted, the recently acquired .38 Colt Detective Special that ATTD agents had neglected to test for ballistics analysis forty-six years earlier could be tested at the closest ballistics test fire lab available: the lab affiliated with the City of Valdosta Police Department.

The irony was so sweet that I almost forgot to reply.

As I watched the other car pull back from my rear view mirror, I took a brief moment to look into mine. What I saw behind me was four years of living this case, 24/7, 365. No matter the personal cost, no matter the criticism or the inconvenience of ignorance, I had carried Charley at the forefront of both my head and my heart and done everything I possibly could to help alter his legacy and bring him justice. After four years of wading through what I suspected truly happened that night out on the Clyattville-Nankin Road, I thought I had finally come to the end of the line... the thin gray line that separated what I knew in my heart to be true and what I hoped could eventually be proven in a court of law.

Unfortunately, weeks of scheduling mishaps and miscommunications between Jules and me compromised not only my ability to be present when the weapons were finally delivered, but our friendship. At first I was terribly hurt that I had been denied the chance to participate in the drop, but eventually surmised it was the universe's way of allowing others to be part of the process. Amazingly, once ego had been pushed aside I also came to understand the nuance of one of the final locutions the angels had whispered in my ear: *"The little guy will be the one to help take them down."* For you see, the weapon(s) in question were actually delivered by Charley's only daughter and Charley's youngest grandson Cole, the little guy who was not quite so little any more.

In spite of my bruised ego, the poetic justice made me smile. Though I'd hoped the deliverance of the weapon(s) would become my golden ticket to the Promised Land, in time the opportunity became just another complicated delay. Having not been part of the party that couriered the weapons, my need for specific information had not been translated. The weapon(s) were tested and the obvious result of "no match" was eventually conveyed to me. Even though I was grateful to the VPD and The DA for having taken the time and resources to test them, I had already suspected the outcome even before it was announced.

Of course there could be no match. Both IBIS (Integrated Ballistics Identification Systems) and NBIN (National Integrated Ballistics Information Network) databases had been created decades after the Covington murder took place and God knows how many years after I'm certain the evidentiary bullet fragments were either destroyed or lost to further delay the path of justice. But that wasn't even the point.

What I had actually been hoping for was information concerning the specific combinations of striations depicted within the projectile's lands and grooves. I wanted to see if they matched either of those stated in the original page 2 of the Crime Lab Report from 1966; either the 3 lands or grooves with a lefthand twist, or the 6 lands and groves with a lefthand twist. As I was not immediate family, I could not receive information directly through the VPD. That information needed to come to me through Jules. The request was submitted on more than one occasion and when silence was all that was returned, I laid down my pen.

Not since the first few chapters of the original manuscript begun in the summer of 2009 had I ever felt so obstructed. Stagnated by injured ego and remorse for having spent so much of my life for what now felt like nothing, I walked away from the book and returned all my attention to school and work. In between finals, I prayed that the universe would move things forward for me. But again, nothing. It seemed as though everyone's monumental efforts had been for naught and that just like Moses, I could stand at the border of the Promised Land, but never cross into it.

For the next few weeks I stared at the 8 x 10 on my desk begging for guidance, but he remained as silent as his daughter. Angry and confused at the abrupt turn of events, I internally threatened to burn all 436 pages of the book along with everything else Jules had intended to burn herself four years earlier. But I could not.

In the oddest presentation of dichotomies, the universe continued to send mixed signals. Messages from Spencer reminded me that I must continue to trust the process. Final messages from Jules stated that she and her brother did not believe in psychics and suggested the psychic participation in the case had potentially discouraged law enforcement from furthering their investigations. The rationalization for such was "If psychics were real, there would be no cold cases left because they would all be solved."

I was flogged.

What had happened to the woman who three years earlier had sat across the table from me in Atlanta hoping to find a connection to her father? What had happened to the woman who had conversed with a fleshless entity through Spencer about "bats in her school," red dresses from her mother," "white unicorns," and "flipping mattresses" when she gets frustrated? Where had that woman gone?

Though I disagreed with the rationale presented, it was not my place to try and convert anyone to believing that we can communicate with those who have crossed over, not even Charley's children. To be fair, she said she appreciated my work and that the book might be better suited as fiction and that was pretty much that. But that wasn't pretty much that for me. Labeling it fiction denied the reality of everything I had experienced; including the connection with my parents. I could not bring myself to expressively ransom my authenticity for want of someone else's secular comforts.

Torn between being true to myself and relinquishing authorship to what Jules now seemed to be latently dictating, I called Spencer for advice. Calmly she asked me to consider the possibility that maybe the universe had never intended the book to be published, only for me as a way to positively process my grief over the loss of my parents. I was shocked. Why would God have led me on such an incredible adventure if not for it to be shared? Why would Charley have introduced the other victims to me, if not to help their families find them and lay them to rest? What good was it to know you would not be forgotten by those you loved, even if only by a silly childhood pet if nobody ever heard about it?

Trapped within my own considerations, I reflected upon this incredible journey and saw myself standing between two different worlds: one where faith and trust had guided and expanded my understanding of God and my place in the universe, and the other where the words faith and trust would eventually become little more than Sunday morning rhetoric and Monday morning quarterbacking.

Spencer breached the elongated silence and asked, "How different would your life have been without the introduction of Charley?"

It didn't take long to appreciate that difference, for I was now standing in the exact same place I had been four years earlier: paralyzed by confusion and alone.

"Now, think about what could happen with the publication of this book."

Other than the litigious nightmare its contents might pose, I suddenly thought about many people I knew who had lost someone they loved and could be saved from such a place of despair if they only knew that it was possible to reconnect. Then I took that number and times it by 10; that number by 20, and so on. Publishing the book became a matter of faith.

Regenerated, I toyed with the ending of this book a hundred more times before settling on something I thought everybody could live with. But in the end, trying to select words and meanings to make everybody comfortable with what I had experienced began to sound like the same lies told forty-seven years before. Ending the book prematurely with just the delivery of the guns and no follow-up left others who had placed themselves in danger out in the cold did nothing to change the wording on Charley's death certificate or dispel my angst over the fact that Jules and I now seemed to be on separate paths.

While the truth about that night may be a lot of things, including uncomfortable for those of you who read this and disagree with my findings – I had to finally accept that it would never be the same for any of us. Charley and the others would always see that night through their eyes as victims. Grim and the four in flannel would see it through their eyes as an absolute necessity to maintain their positions of power and profit. Jules and her brother would see it through the eyes of children left without a father or proper explanation for their loss. In the end this book needed to be seen through my eyes, the eyes of an investigative author who has been both transfixed and transformed by this experience.

My only additional need was to find a way more permanent and public to protect, honor, and thank everyone else who had boldly come forward to help me discern the reasons why Charley Covington was murdered. Publishing the book seemed the only way to accomplish that. So after much deliberation, I decided to break my silence and go public with these findings.

CHAPTER FIFTY-EIGHT

With the book under final editing and a post review underway by my attorney, I began to concentrate on the selection for the cover art. Several printed options presented as marketable, but none had the impact I wanted, so I gave myself over to spirit and decided to let them take the lead.

What did I want the cover to make people feel?

I thought about the night Charley was murdered and was able to find several black and white haunting images of rural back roads that resembled those near the river that separated Brooks and Lowndes counties where his body had been found. Anxious, I sent them to my husband and asked him to Photoshop several cover options for me. He complied, but they were all too dark to deal with. Frustrated, I went to bed that night and said a prayer for further guidance. Later the next day I was perusing the manuscript when I stumbled upon the awkward dream sequence after my father's death. I thought about my childhood friend and instinctually knew exactly what to do. Determined that I was on the right path, I searched the internet again and discovered the perfect image that visually expounded upon my desired theme.

Desperate for an additional nod from the cosmos, I called Spencer and because she was driving her car I carefully described each detail about the image I had chosen. She audibly winced and for the first time, I was able to ask her to "trust my process." She laughed, but told me she felt the image I was describing might be too morbid for the message I intended. I agreed that on its own she might be right, but asked that she reserve judgment until she saw it against a striking black background, with the title embossed above it in tones of silver and gray. When she got home and saw the mockup, she concurred. The broken image of my childhood pet, curled in eternal repose, was not only a reminder of my initial innocence about the thin gray veil between life and death, but also a way to bring this story full circle The image now fully relays the significance of the opening to this story:

At the age of six Jules lost her beloved father, Federal Treasury Agent Charles Gordon Covington. In that same year at the age of eight, I lost my beloved pet rat Squeaky. I know the comparison doesn't seem quite fair. Still, none of us ever gets to choose how we first experience death. Odd as it may seem, if Charley Covington hadn't lost his life in the middle of the Clyattville-Nankin Road that rainy night in 1966, he could never have come back to save mine forty-four years later. I know this to be true because in the summer of 2009, I began to write his story and several chapters in I stopped.

As a professional writer I have learned that if a story refuses to write itself, there are but two reasons why. Either a story is not yet ready to be told, or a story is not yet ready to be heard. In the case of Charles Gordon Covington, both reasons appeared to ring true. So I put down my pen and waited for further instructions from the cosmos as to what to do next...

Only this time it was seven days, not seven months later that the cosmos saw fit to answer me again.

The first locution that came through once the cover art was set was *"Someone is talking to someone,"* and indeed they were. The next bit of information came from the image itself. Remember , both G and Charley had signaled the date of 12/12/12 as significant, and indeed it had been important for reasons other than Jules finding out about the whereabouts of her father's guns. The date in question was registered as the date the cover art image had first been produced.

Freed from the shackles of ego and the necessity to claim some sort of victory over histrionic evil, I finally understood that the real goal of this adventure was to help Charley and the others release themselves from their earthly trials, provide whatever information could be found to the proper authorities, and for me to experience the healing of my heart and garner the remembrances of those I had loved and lost. What the authorities do with this information now will be up to them.

I thank Jules for the introduction to her father and all those who had been brave enough to step to the plate with information, prayerful that they will continue to find a way to remain safe and comfortable with their collective decision to share until this case is resolved. Also, I pray that one day law enforcement will come to realize that the evidence that brought the ATF to re-open the case in the first place has never changed. Any information received from Spencer has not altered it; it has merely supported it.

As I closed my electronic file on this case, my phone jangled gently in the background. Tired, I took a sip from my cup, looked at the number, and grinned.

A familiar Southern drawl oozed into my ear, "So what are you doing this bright and early morning?"

"I'm just finishing my first cup of coffee. Why?"

"I'm just finishing my third."

I looked at the clock to my right. It was not even 8:00 am. "My, you're quite the early bird yourself today. What gives?"

"I propose a toast!"

"Ok," I answered and help up my coffee cup to join in. "What are we toasting?"

"To justice! I just received a call from…"

An hour later, I stared into the bottom of my coffee cup and sighed. Like I always say… *"Maxwell House coffee! Good to the last confession!"*

After almost forty-seven years, a murder that law enforcement had once tried to convince us had been committed over two people drinking a simple cup of coffee was perhaps finally on its way to being a murder solved by law enforcement and another two people drinking coffee.

The End...?

CHAPTER FIFTY-NINE

So here is my personal disclaimer.

Without absolute knowledge of having been there that night and minus the direct confession by one of the remaining four in flannel still alive, or further supportive testimony and evidentiary disclosures that may eventually come to provide clear and irrefutable proof that Federal Treasury Agent Charles Gordon Covington was brutally murdered by members within the collective law enforcement community at the time and the further compromise of his legacy by the cover up collectively instituted and maintained for over forty-seven years by his fraternal brethren, and the man referred to as the MOT and the two young females allegedly also sacrificed at their hands, this is as close as I believe the world will ever get to the truth of what happened to Charley that distant and rainy night of October 9, 1966.

I believe this discourse to be a realistic representation of what Charley and the three other victims might have lived through and died for because of the impending fear of complete disclosure as to their identities and lascivious activities. I also believe that I have served Charley and his family as well as any individual ever could, in and/or outside of the legal justice system. I can have no regrets for the years spent on this case and the lessons learned, no matter the final outcome.

As far as working with various members of the psychic community, there can be no greater respect for the value of your incredible gifts. As to my dearest friend and mentor Spencer, she had been right. Shortly after the final visitation, she had promised I would know exactly when and how to finish this book, to let go and let God. The time has finally arrived. With the opportunity for further discovery, I am at peace with this journey. It is now for God and the rest of the world to decide what is just and proper.

Have I answered all the questions or plugged every hole in this forty-seven- year-old case? No. But then did you or Charley, or even God ever expect that I actually could? In the last forty-nine months, I have given numerous speeches about this case, written over 565+ blogs, made a dozen formal reports, spoken with hundreds of people, and received and/or applied over two thousand different psychic impressions, testimonial clues, anecdotal evidence, and intuitions to bring this case to layman's fruition. The fact that I can walk away and leave a measly handful or so on the table yet untethered for future law enforcement agencies to divine is a small miracle in itself. For me, this case will never be over until all the victims have been metaphorically raised from the dead, exonerated from shame, and Charley's death certificate changed from *Suicide* to *Homicide*. Even now as I write this ending, I have emails waiting to be answered, impressions yet to ponder, and new clues yet to be deciphered... all which will be forwarded to the appropriate authorities.

For those who remain guilty of this crime and still walk the streets of Valdosta, Georgia without consequence? Well, as much as I would like to think that the wheels of justice will continue to turn outside my limited purview and beyond my restricted scope, I may one day find that the end game for all involved was never meant to be the same. It could be that this book was only meant to provide a vehicle for those who were hurt by this travesty to exorcise their demons in tandem as they experienced the exorcism of my own. Or maybe for those of you who are still alive to see through the thin veil of this charade and recognize the players and to know that their honor is false and that their legacy a sham. Or maybe, it is only meant as mirror for our fragile human need to place blame, cultivate closure, and find peace with those things we cannot control.

Regardless, if only one other person comes to know the truth of what happened that night, then justice has been served. If only one husband stops in his tracks to sit and share a cup of coffee with his wife to remember why he fell in love with her in the first place, if only one more parent stays the course to read a child another goodnight book, or lingers in gratitude to tuck another child into bed, if only one more person comes to know the power that compassion and empathy can bring to the life of a victim of crime, or the faith it takes to look at the stars and know that their loved ones are really looking back — it has been worth the journey.

Is it important that the guilty parties' names be called among the scrolls of those who walk the long and lonely concrete halls of a distant prison? Maybe. Maybe not. That concern can no longer be my driving force, for that is now neither my quest to pursue nor my decision to make. Ultimately, whether it be here upon this earthly plane or somewhere else upon another, justice will prevail and a higher authority will stand in judgment and grant those involved opportunity for trial, contrition, and restitution. What I have been asked to do, I have done. Whatever the outcome, I am now at peace with my part in this story.

So four years and 96 days after Jules first uttered the words "Let me tell you a story about my daddy," I have finally been able to respond with one of my own.

For Charley

EPILOGUE

In May of 2010, after 18 months of research and investigation, author T. A. Powell presented a formal report plus peripherals on the Charles Gordon Covington case to SAC agents from the Federal Bureau of Investigation (FBI), Alcohol, Tobacco, Firearms and Explosives (ATF), and the Georgia Bureau of Investigation (GBI). One month later GBI agents from the Middle District of Georgia were on the ground in Valdosta questioning those on the author's list and following up on her three-year investigation. Six months later, ATF jumped into the fray, assigning a Special Agent out of Macon, Georgia to do an exploratory foray into the case. The author made yet another presentation to bring the ATF agent up to speed on her continuing investigation.

In January of 2012 a member of the Communications Department of ATF, under the guidance of the Assistant Director Agent Gant and the National Archivist for ATTD/ATF Barbara Osteika, made contact to make certain files were brought current and that the name of Charles Gordon Covington would appear not only on the Wall of Fallen Agents located in Washington, D.C. but also be listed in the Alcohol, Tobacco, Firearms National Archives as "Killed In The Line of Duty."

On June 6, 2012 while standing inside a Federal Express/Kinko's store in Athens, Georgia talking to an employee named Brenda, I received a call from Special Agent Janice Kemp from ATF in Washington, D.C. She and ATF National Archivist Barbara Osteika had just been informed that ATF was officially reopening the investigation into the murder of my dear friend and shepherd, Charles Gordon Covington, based on information provided through my research.

On January 11, 2013 the ATF office in Macon, Georgia suspended the brief investigation due to lack of resources and available man hours, with the caveat that the case could be reopened in the event further prosecutable evidence could be brought to light. Days later I made a call to the Lowndes County District attorney's office in a final attempt to move this case forward.

On January 18, 2013 at 11:11 am, I received a return call from the Lowndes County District Attorney's office. They would take an appointment to discuss Charley's case. If evidence and witness information warranted, the .38 Colt Detective Special that ATTD and law enforcement had claimed Charley took his life with back in 1966 would finally be tested. The designated lab for ballistics analysis would be the Valdosta Police Department Test Lab.

On Friday March 15, 2013, the weapon in question was transported to the office of the District Attorney of Lowndes County, Georgia and then to the office of Chief of Police in Valdosta, Georgia to be processed for the ballistics testing.

The Thin Gray Line is the first in a series of True Crime Investigative Memoir novels by T. A. Powell. The next novel in this series, *The Dead Line*, carries on the author's introduction to the Dixie Mafia through the eyes of Hospice Chaplain G. Richard Hoard, who tells how at fourteen he watched the body of his father, Floyd G. Hoard, Jackson County [Georgia] District Attorney, twitch and smolder inside the twisted steel of his family's sedan in the front yard of his Jackson County childhood home. The District Attorney's body was used to send a message to all those who would challenge the rag-tag band of murderers and thieves hell bent on following the template of their Sicilian counterpart. Impaled by a steering wheel to the bloody upholstery of the back seat, Hoard received the message: fear of the law no longer held any power over the redneck lords of the back roads of the North Georgia Piedmont region. The District Attorney for Jackson County, Floyd Hoard was murdered on August 7, 1967, exactly ten months and two days after the brutal slaying of Federal Treasury Agent Charles G. Covington.

In this sequel, author T. A. Powell drags the reader by the ankles through the horrific assassination of Jackson County District

Attorney Floyd Hoard and into the muddied water of Georgia history as she swims her way through the dark and nefarious underworld of what locals nicknamed the "Cornbread Mafia." Along with another talented psychic/medium detective named Dane Meyers, T. A. Powell digs deep to breathe new life into the bedside confessions of convicted serial killer, Billy Sunday Birt, as taken by an undercover snitch inside the Reidsville Prison over thirty years ago. Juxtaposed against the ethereal pleas from the victims as they begged for mercy, Powell paints a disturbing and graphic caricature of the murderer as he tells an unknown snitch about who, about why, and about how he executed each victim for moonshine, for money, for revenge, or for grins. One by one…all in a line…*The Dead Line.*

Look for *The Dead Line: Confessions of a Dixie Mafia Assassin,* by T. A. Powell to be published late 2014.

Series:

The Thin Gray Line

The Dead Line: Confessions of a Dixie Mafia Assassin

The Formosan Homewrecker

The Joshua Treaty

"What is the statute of limitations for murder in the state of Georgia? Ironically, it is the exact same amount of time the victims in a case will remain dead: an eternity. With that much time, anyone should be able to discover the truth."

T.A. Powell

Special Thanks To

The Source

My husband

My children

Spencer Reynolds (The Psychic/Medium Detective)

My parents, Carol and Vern

Charles Gordon Covington (My shepherd)

The other victims: Rox, Jessica, the MOT, and Bugman McFallon

The Covington Family

Charles H. and M. L. Weems

Members of the Lowndes County Sheriff's Department

Members of Alcohol, Tobacco, Firearms & Explosives (ATF&E/ATTD)

Members of Georgia Bureau of Investigation (GBI)

Members of Federal Bureau of Investigation (FBI)

Members of Lowndes Historical Society (especially Erin Blanton and Donald Davis)

L. and D. Rutledge (Retired Gwinnett County Sheriff's Department/Atlanta Police Department)

S. P. Rounds, Attorney at Law

Muzette (Psychic/Medium)

Sarah V. Bell, Ph.D., Editor (Doctors of English)

Scott Edwards (Book Formatting and Book Trailer)

Members of the Valdosta Police Department

The Lowndes District Attorney's Office

The Witch of Hissing Hill, by Mary Calhoun, illustrated by Janet McCaffey; William Morrow & Company (HarperCollins Publishers), New York: 1964

Angel Numbers 101, by Doreen Virtue; Hay House, Inc. (www.hayhouse.com), New York: 2008

Field of Dreams, Universal, 1989

Paula and Delores (Dear Friends)

And a heartfelt thanks to the hundreds of citizens of Lowndes County, Georgia and the many active and/or retired law enforcement agents/officers who helped with this investigation, who wished not to be publicly recognized in this publication beyond their contributions and efforts.

Made in the USA
Lexington, KY
08 July 2013